A Psychohistory
of Zionism

A PSYCHOHISTORY
OF ZIONISM

Jay Y. Gonen

MASON/CHARTER

NEW YORK 1975

Library of Congress Cataloging in Publication Data

Gonen, Jay Y   1934–
  A psychohistory of Zionism.

  Bibliography: p.
  Includes index.
  1. Zionism—History. 2. Jews—Psychology. 3. National characteristics, Israeli. I. Title.
DS149.G5493   956.94'001   74-32355
ISBN 0-88405-098-X

To my children
Julie and David

Contents

Introductory Note

In this book I should like to share with my readers a method that may be new for them. What I shall do is apply psychoanalytic models, which are more traditionally used in clinical practice with individual persons, to the Jewish people as a group. Freud's idea, as I interpret it, was that cultural developments of peoples can bear some similarities to the developmental histories of individuals. He also suggested that the factors which combine to determine the emergence of repressed wishes in peoples sometimes parallel those which decide the timing of such expressions in single persons. I decided to follow this construct because of my feeling that the use of psychoanalytic models would immensely facilitate for me the task of organizing data. I also expected it to enhance my sensitivity to the many meanings that can be embedded in each single piece of information. Thus, my choice of methodology was based not on a discovery of a new cornerstone on which the validity of the Freudian orientation could be founded, but on a feeling of hope—hope that this approach would prove fruitful and that the richness of the results would justify the initial decision. Throughout the book I have tried to accentuate the psychological aspects of historical developments, which is the task of psychohistory. Nevertheless, I wish to state my conviction that psychohistory is a complement to history, not a substitute for it.

I am indebted to several persons who contributed to this work. George Awad, M.D., shared with me his reactions to the material on the "Arab problem." This information affected the final shaping of that chapter. James Gumina, Ph.D., provided valuable assistance in the early phase of the work. The final editing by Miriam Hurewitz greatly enhanced the quality of the manuscript. Barry Nathan deserves special thanks for bringing the publisher and me together. Sidney Rubin, M.D., helped me with the application of psychoanalytic models to historical events. His contribution thus relates to the heart of psycho-history. Most of all, I am thankful to my wife, Susan Duvé, M.D., for giving me ideas, for editing the book more than once, and for providing me with emotional support.

Jay Y. Gonen
Rochester, New York
October, 1974

1.

The Timeless Love for Zion

ZION, WON'T YOU ASK ABOUT THE
WELL-BEING OF THY PRISONERS?

—Judah Halevi

Zionism is a movement of the Jewish people which set for itself the goal of rebuilding a home for the Jews in Eretz Yisrael (The Land of Israel). This rebuilding was to bring about a national and spiritual revival of the Jews both as individuals and as a people. From its beginning, Zionism has been a mixture of different orientations. The common theme running throughout its development was the caring for the city of Zion, Jerusalem, which served as a focal expression of passion for the land of Israel and the fate of the Jews. However, this unifying theme sometimes obscured the underlying diversity of the movement. Perhaps the most contradictory Zionist aspirations were on the one hand to become "a light of the nations" (Isaiah 49:6) and on the other hand wishing "that we also may be like all the nations" (I Samuel 8:20).

Most of all, the Zionist movement was characterized by its focus on a rapid transition from inferiority to overcompensation.

Jewish history was perceived as beleaguered by inferiorities, defects, and fatal flaws. The flaws were there for anyone to see—anyone, that is, who was willing to look rather than just pray to the Lord and wait another two thousand years of exile until such time as the Lord sees fit to redeem Israel. The defects were many. The Jewish people were scattered, stateless, persecuted, passive, demoralized, assimilated, segregated, and sunk in an abnormal economic existence. They lacked a common language and were plagued by dark psychologies: by masochism, by love of suffering, and by rationalizing some kind of a divine mission to explain their vulnerable existence and miserable way of life.

Zionism was going to change all that. To the scattered it offered an ingathering; to the stateless, a state; to the helpless, mastery; to the passive, activity. Put more blatantly, to the inferior Jews it promised a new generation of freedom which eventually culminated in the sabra "superman."

One way for a movement to be strong enough to "change history" is to draw upon primitive and most potent sources of psychic energy. In the case of Zionism, the major source of strength has been the age-old Jewish love for Zion. Throughout the ages this love has been so intense that it can be regarded as a timeless factor in Jewish history. Indeed, as has been pointed out by the noted Israeli historian Jacob Talmon, the quality of timelessness that characterizes Jewish history is anchored in the traditional Jewish idea of redemption. Indeed, an orientation toward future redemption sets up a fixed goal which does not wither with the passage of time. Transient events come and go and are subject to the effect of time. This is not the case with a highly cathected hope for the future or a heavily emotionally invested aspiration for a redemption that is yet to come. A redemption which serves as the historical culmination of generations of trials and tribulations and which gives meaning to them all is timeless. Similar thoughts were expressed by the Israeli journalist and writer Eliezer Livneh in his discussion of the implications of the Holocaust to the Israeli sense of destiny. He asserted that the Jewish notion of time fuses the past, present and future. This traditional notion includes the classical talmudic concept of the remote future as including a horrendous dualism. When redemption takes place and the glory of the past is being restored, two major events will happen concurrently. One is the "ingathering of the exiles" and the return to Zion; the other is *hevlai mashiah,* which means premessianic cataclysms.

The Hebrew word *hevlai,* which literally means "pangs" or "throes of birth," is attached to various other words to denote the suffering and tribulations that are the price of any major initiation. A person can experience birth pangs, pangs of acquiring a new language, pangs of death, pangs of creation, pangs of love, or pangs of living, as well as pangs of redemption. Other common expressions in which *hevlai* stands for suffering include labor pains, the sufferings of hell, human sufferings, and lastly the premessianic cataclysms that will befall mankind during *hevlai mashiah.* Thus, no birth, growth, death, or afterdeath or rebirth can evolve without a bitter toll of "pangs." Any major initiation, whether in the past or the future, carries with it its pangs. From this view of time there is undoubtedly a fusion of time periods; each always has major pangs to bear for initiation and growth. Therefore, all times are alike. The final initiation flowing into redemption at the end of time is no exception: it also will involve pangs of redemption and messianic cataclysms. Redemption and the Messiah are the sweetest, most blissful, most wonderful, glorious, joyful, and absolutely most desired objects one could ever wish for. It would be unrealistic to expect an initiation into the utmost of everlasting joy without first going through untold pangs. As a matter of fact, for this kind of ultimate wish fulfillment the pangs to endure may well be the most cataclysmic of all.

The scholar Julius Greenstone once pointed out that the various talmudic references to this painful period prior to the advent of the Messiah contain predictions of social and political explosions. Drunkenness and immorality will proliferate, respect for parents will be abandoned, family ties will be loosened, the law will not be studied, anarchy will prevail, "and the house of public convention will become a house of harlots." What these talmudic revelations add up to is sin. The social and political order will turn into chaos, law and tradition will be toppled, sexual indulgence will be rampant, and the sanctity of the family will be destroyed. This sin and chaos can be viewed in a traditional way as the price of suffering which precedes the great messianic holy joy. Sin, however, can also be viewed as the enticing sweetness that results from the tasting of forbidden fruits. In this case sin, like virtue, becomes its own reward. From such talmudic hints as these, Jewish mysticism developed complicated antinomistic concepts that revolved around the central idea of the holiness of sin. This idea was brilliantly explored by Gershom Scholem, the acknowledged authority on Jewish mysticism. He demonstrated that this antinomistic conception was intimately connected to messianic yearnings. To this one may add that, in a psychoanalytic perspective, both the sinful and the sacred refer to the forbidden and tabooed. Incest is, of course, such a tabooed sin and can be accomplished only by violating the sanctity of the family. Psychological speculations are therefore possible concerning the future messianic era which follows on the heels of the premessianic sufferings. Could it possibly be that the desired messianic bliss represents the undisturbed joy of sin—the sweetness of forbidden acts? Is the license for this uninterrupted joy obtained by paying the appropriate "pangs" of punishment in advance during the premessianic tribulations? Were the tribulations intended to be postmessianic, the way a punishment follows a crime, and were they shifted to the premessianic period in an attempt to disguise the forbidden nature of messianic joys? We shall return to these questions later.

Whatever the meanings of messianic sufferings and joys, one need not await the arrival of the Messiah to acquire further confirmation of the concept of fused time, which always revolves around the dualism of initiation and pangs. Indeed, if we go back to Livneh, we discover that he maintained that the contiguity of the Zionist renascence and the Nazi Holocaust in the twentieth century provided horrifying validity to the traditional Jewish notion of time fusion.

Whence this quality of timelessness in Jewish history? How could the Jews for nearly two thousand years cry year after year on the ninth day of the month of Av as if they had lost their Temple in Jerusalem only yesterday? Apparently it is this very timelessness of the history of the Jews that has prevented time from eroding them and dumping them into the wastebasket of history. At this point some of the basic insights of the great originator of psychoanalytic theory, Sigmund Freud, are critical. In many of his writings, more specifically, in *The Unconscious*, he taught modern men that there is a potent realm of the human psyche that is indeed characterized by timelessness: the unconscious. Within this realm, logical order and rules of formal logic are nonexistent. The compulsive chronology of clock time, the ordering of events along an endless series of befores and afters, is utterly disregarded. In the unconscious, anything can be juxtaposed with anything else, and what determines these links is not logical order but rather appetite and the special logic of emotions. Most important here are the strength of a wish, the symbolic meaning of an image, and the amount of psychic energy cathected on the image. What counts in the unconscious is an emotional investment, not considerations of formal logic. By virtue of the activities of this psychic realm, emotions are reflected through wishes onto the hallucinatory images of the desired objects and considerations of time and place do not stand in the way of appetite. What is more, contradictory or mutually exclusive ideas can exist side by side, and since they do not negate one another, are able to coexist forever.

The timelessness of the unconscious manifests itself as a disregard for chronological or logical contradictions, a procedure which characterizes primary process kinds of thinking. We all know how in our daily conscious life we frequently encounter the bitter truth that we cannot have our cake and eat it too. Not so in the unconscious; there are no negatives and no nonexistence. One wish coupled with another contradictory wish adds up to a singularly stronger wish. The primitive mental images that occur in the unconscious are all positive and add to each other. Thus, a person might respond to a felt need for oral gratification by the wish to eat a cake, and therefore derive hallucinatory gratification from primitive visual images of it. Moments later he might once more wish to eat it but would not be hindered by the concept of its being gone. All that happens is that the wish to eat the cake becomes even more charged with drive energy.

Visual mental images of the desired object and the hallucinatory gratifications that accompany them exist, of course, for all sorts of "cakes." Jewish history, culminating in Zionism, demonstrates how a cake baked across the ocean and two or even three thousand years ago can be enjoyed here and not there, now and not then; and, what is more, one can have it and eat it and have it, on and on, ad infinitum. Hallucinatory gratifications kept the wish alive and focused, gaining in strength until the Jews were able to opt for the real Zion instead of having to be content with the dream of Zion as their only form of wish fulfillment.

It seems highly probable that the long history of the Jewish predeliction for ignoring major considerations of realpolitik represents a case of an impingement of the unconscious which desires a cake that is not readily available but whose image is vividly alive. Strong appetites lead to wishful thinking which clearly disregards reality. A similar impingement of the unconscious in daily life is manifested by the Jewish ability to experience major but remote historical events as "only yesterday" or even as present sources of joy or distress. If we can imagine for a minute the land of Israel as a large, luscious cake that whets the appetite the same way the "glory" of the historic homeland propelled Chaim Weizmann, the leader of Practical Zionism, then we have to admire the ability of the Jewish people to smack their lips for centuries as if they were indeed standing in front of the cake rather than being separated from it by distances of oceans and generations of time. Zion is a mystical and spiritual image, not a raw instinct. Nevertheless, the lofty ideals of Judaism had to be cathected or invested with raw emotional energy derived from the enormous storehouse of energies within the id in order to survive and become timeless. It is from this depth of raw emotional appetite, this blend of instinct and mysticism, that Zionism derived the chutzpah to claim Israel from the world's nations many generations after its loss. The Zionists did so as if reclaiming Israel were a simple, natural thing to accomplish and as if they were not facing overwhelming odds but were merely one step away.

Among the Jewish people, love of one and only one God, love of justice, love of the Bible, and love of fellow Jews reached beyond consciousness. These great symbols of advanced spirituality fused with primitive images from the unconscious, such as hunger for nourishment or love of warm contact, to produce an unparalleled emotional investment of a people in their cherished ideas. Raw impulses by themselves do not evoke conceptual admiration. On the other hand, spiritual ideals, while important, may be discarded. But a fusion of primitive images with great ideas can have a lasting effect. Because of this fusion, the Jewish people had an inexhaustible store of energy with which to support their dedication to imperative ideals.

In order to explore what is at the bottom of such a fusion of instincts with ideals, we must focus on the timeless love of Zion by the sons of Israel. In order to understand this love, it is necessary to alternate between Freud and the Bible.

In the earliest phases of personality development, all infants desire to be in full possession of their mothers. Warm contact, milk, rocking, soothing sounds, all come from the sweet and blissful source that little babies wish to secure for themselves forever. Yet sole possession of the mother is seldom possible. This becomes increasingly clearer to growing children, and therefore in the course of their development they have to learn to transfer some aspects of the love toward the mother to the love of other men and women. This development may be fraught with frustration and rage, especially for boys, when it takes place in a culture that places strong emphasis on paternal authority. Judaism is such a culture.

The strict paternal qualities of the Jewish religion are well recognized in the Bible. The God of Israel, the all-powerful father in heaven, can be merciful and forgiving. However, the Bible warns that God is also El Kana, meaning a jealous and angry God. With infallible memory, El Kana remembers to exact vengeance, even on the great-grandchildren of those who offended him. His harshness, coupled with his love, ensured obedience and instilled in his Jewish children remarkably strong superegos. The superego or conscience is that psychic structure which makes a person feel loved and virtuous when he abides by the parental commands, but guilty and threatened with harsh punishment when he transgresses the rules. For helpless infants, even the threat of withdrawal of parental love is harsh punishment because it is a threat to survival. Active forms of retaliation by mighty adults are perceived as intolerable threats by small babies. An angry adult can easily snuff out the life of an infant with one swift movement; babies cannot really afford to incur the rage of adults. Similarly, the children of Israel could not afford to provoke the wrath of their father in heaven.

The biblical image of God is the collective projection by the Israelites of the image of the loving but jealous and vengeful father in their ancient culture. Perhaps it was the overwhelming love which was also expressed by the angry father that led the children to such an emotional investment in the paternal authority. For good or bad, Jews acquired the cultural inheritance of a rigid image of male dominance; the result was a cultural bias favoring masculinity. For generations Jewish men blessed the Lord for not making them women. Women, on the other hand, meekly blessed him for creating them in accordance with his will. This sexist thanksgiving in Jewish prayer is still practiced; it runs deep in Jewish culture and manifests itself in both subtle and not so subtle ways. That the male is what counts is made poetically clear in a verse from the proverbs of Solomon: "A wise son maketh a glad father; But a foolish son is the grief of his mother" (Proverbs 10: 1).

There must have been a price to pay for instilling such long-lasting paternal dominance. Psychoanalytic principles of personality development suggest that, at the time, the harsh image of an avenging father resulted in massive repression of hostility and jealousy which the competing sons must have felt toward him. This repression fostered such overt love and obedience both to actual fathers on earth and to El Kana in heaven that it ensured an incomparable loyalty. By the same token it ensured group loyalty and the unique survival of the loyal Jews during centuries of immense trials and tribulations. The psychoanalyst Theodor Reik suspected that for generations Jews unconsciously welcomed punishments to mitigate guilt feelings over unconscious hatred for their God-Father. He believed that in the unconscious this hate remained as alive and as intense as in the ancient times in which God's representatives were murdered. In other words, underneath the love and the everlasting devotion to God lurks a hostility so strong that the Jews are still unable to take a look at it, for fear of opening a "Pandora's box." The Jewish superego thus remained strong and unyielding.

Before Reik, Freud suggested that what might be found in the box, so to speak, is the murder of Moses by the Israelites. This murder reiterated the old and prehistorical heritage of countless murders of primal fathers in primitive hordes of men. To my mind, the alleged murder of Moses cannot be adequately supported by the biblical sources. Any allusions to such an act in the book of Hosea seem to at best be farfetched. However, in the history of a culture a murderous rage is as important as an actual murder. By asserting after Freud that this emotion played a prominent role in Jewish history, we are on solid ground. It not only makes sense psychologically, but it is indicated in many biblical stories. On frequent occasions the children of Israel "have had it" with their father in heaven and with their leaders on earth, not the least of whom was Moses. Time and again this anger had to be tamed and rebellions smothered. Time and again God inflicted vengeance on his sons to restore obedience. The psychological results of such a course of development are especially pertinent to superego formation.

The essence of the Jewish superego was respect for one's own father and total obedience to the Lord. This obedience was observed even when the Lord requested Abraham to sacrifice his only son, Isaac. The solidity of their superego is what turned the Jews into remarkable people who were destined to become a great cultural force, a civilizing influence on humanity, but also unhappy people. The Jews suffered not only from persecutions from without but also from an internal yoke of oppression. Psychoanalytic theories can provide us with additional insights concerning the unique history of the Jews.

From the assumption that during the formative years of Judaism oedipal conflicts played a key role, it seems to follow that the possessive sexual love toward the mother had to be controlled and repressed. The Jews accomplished this by setting up the cultural image of a harsh and authoritative father. Therefore, the mother had to be renounced by the growing sons if retaliation by the mighty father was to be avoided. In two of his three articles under the title *Contributions to the Psychology of Love,* Freud delineated the neurotic forms of men's love for women that are likely to develop under such conditions of paternal dominance. He observed that in normal development love represents a successful, or at least a workable, union between two currents of feelings: tenderness and sensuality. Both feelings manifest themselves in infancy and surge up during adolescence. Although a unity between the two is the adaptive goal for the adult person, disunity can often result for various reasons. One obvious reason is a case where a strong, tender, as well as sensual love toward the mother is blocked by inner fears of retaliation from a jealous and mighty father. This situation results in massive repression which, however, is not omnipresent. Only the sensual element of the love for the mother is repressed, while she continues to be the object of tender and affectionate love. Thus, a split in loving takes place whereby affection and sensuality cannot be expressed together. From now on tenderness is reserved for the mother and for women like her, while sensuality is directed toward prostitutes or other loathsome women. Such women can be degraded by base sex with no guilt or anxiety on the part of the intruding male. Although such a man views sensuality as demeaning to pure or good women, he sees no such desecration being incurred by cheap women, whom he holds in low esteem. These women deserve what they get—forever sensuality but never tenderness. Tenderness simply cannot be expressed toward bed partners. To do so is to run the risk of becoming aware that the number-one object for tenderness—one's own mother—was also once, or even still is, desired as the original and most wanted bed partner.

The split of love into disunited feelings of tenderness versus sensuality and the polarization of love objects into "mother" and "prostitute" results in specific neurotic forms of love. These forms relate both to the nature of the love objects and to the peculiar ways of loving. Concerning the loved object, a neurotic need develops for "an injured third party." In order to qualify as a love object, the woman must already belong to someone else, but not necessarily a husband. This third party symbolically stands for one's own father, to whom one's mother belongs. Another neurotic need that develops in relation to the love object is that the loved woman must be a prostitute or at least promiscuous. This "love for a harlot" is what allows for the expression of sensuality. One may say that sex with such a woman is "kosher" because she is not the least like one's mother, with whom it would be a desecration to have sex.

In regard to peculiar ways of loving, Freud mentioned the compulsive quality involved in the high overrating, but also frequent replacement, of sexually available women. A neurotic person may continually replace women who are generous with their sexual availability; yet, as he goes through this series of replacements of loved women, he overvalues each one. While each woman lasts, she is not viewed as "easy come, easy go," even though this is what the frequent replacements seem to imply. On the contrary, each woman is loved with sincerity and intensity to the point of an obsessive, compulsive absorption. Freud hypothesized that the reason for this placing of the highest value on women who come cheaply is that what appears in consciousness as two contraries is usually, in the unconscious, a united whole. If each cheap women is unconsciously also the opposite—that is, the beloved mother—then each cheap woman has to be overrated. She is also bound to be replaced time after time because all of these women remain as inadequate substitutes for the real, but unattainable, mother.

Another neurotic form of love is an overwhelming desire to rescue the beloved. It consists of an unrealistic belief on the part of the neurotic lover that his beloved is in dire need of being saved from moral degradation and needs him to keep her on the path of virtue. The rescue fantasy can relate to other forms of lifesaving as well. In his clinical work, Freud was able to trace such rescue fantasies back to an early wish to possess the mother. The logic behind this conclusion is as follows: To rescue a person means in effect either to save a life or to give a life. Originally the mother gave the son his life by giving birth to him. In return, he wishes to rescue her or to give her a life; this he can do by giving her a baby. By fathering her baby he could, in a magical sort of way, replace his father's role and become the life giver to his mother and even the father of himself.

Although Freud's contention is very revealing of the nature of early infantile development, it does involve very complicated issues. In order not to be drawn into theoretical speculations about this matter, therefore, we might use a different illustration. Common fantasies which people entertain, especially during adolescence, refer to the equation of rescuing with giving life and impregnating. A young man with a crush on a lovely girl engages in rescue daydreams, in which he saves his trembling beauty from the claws of a stalking tiger in the nick of time, and bare-handed, or pulls her to shore and breathes life into her water-filled lungs. Her tender, heart-touching "Oh thank you, thank you" is all he wants—but it is not all he wants. He saved her life, and in return she will be grateful forever and will be his forever. While the overt tale holds within it a future promise, the symbolism involved in this language of fantasy relates to an already accomplished fact. As he rescued her from the water, and/or as he breathed life into her, he has already impregnated her. The fantasy of rescuing and saving life is in essence a fantasy of giving life by loving and impregnating. This equation of rescue with sexual union is of paramount importance for understanding the long-held Jewish dream of rescuing Zion.

Freud asserted that under the simultaneous pressure of desires for the mother and wishes to inflict revenge on the father, certain fantasies develop, fantasies of the mother's infidelity, which could relieve the simultaneous pressure. The infidelity holds a dual promise: it hurts father and also signals mother's sexual availability. If ancient Jewish culture was as we understand it to have been, then fantasies of the mother's infidelity should be present. If God is a harsh father whom the children of Israel resented at some level, and if Zion is God's bride and the collective mother image of the Israelites, then psychoanalytic notions concerning neurotic forms of love indicate that Zion is bound to be portrayed not only as a mother but also as a prostitute.

The Jewish prophets delivered many exhortations to Zion for her betrayal of God. In these condemnations, Zion is portrayed as God's bride, who, upon discovery of the material and pleasurable rewards of prostitution, turned her back on the Lord her husband. In the case of the prophet Ezekiel, the detailed descriptions of Zion's sexual indulgence betray the temptation that lies behind the prolonged exhortations. Time and again Zion's unabashed sexual exploits are recounted: "Yet she multiplied her harlotries, remembering the days of her youth, wherein she had played the harlot in the land of Egypt. And she doted upon concubinage with them, whose flesh is as the flesh of asses, and whose issue is like the issue of horses" (Ezekiel 23: 19–20).

The jealous fantasies over the magnitude of the phallic prowess of the Egyptians (or other persons) is an old sentiment in the history of peoples. Some white Americans perceive the sexuality of black men as Ezekiel perceived the potency of the Egyptians. As for the Jews, they sometimes felt that the uncircumcised Gentiles had a greater ability to satisfy women. This idea preoccupied Jews and in the twelfth century Moses Maimonides discussed it in *The Guide of the Perplexed*. His major thesis was that circumcision is a means of reducing the strength of the sexual drive. Thus, the price of circumcision was obviously high. As an old Jewish saying goes, a woman who has had sexual intercourse with an uncircumcised man finds it difficult to break away from him. It is not hard to imagine the nature of the repressed feelings that underly this fantasy. Because of their covenant with God, because of their obedience to him, the sons of Israel end up with shorter penises. Having yielded to circumcision, they will never be endowed with the same phallic prowess as the Gentiles, and will never have as good and big a penis as their mighty father. Thus, they have to be careful that Jewish women do not learn that Gentiles are more satisfying and they have to continue to love the God-Father whom they also unconsciously hate.

Ezekiel's obsessive enumerations of Zion's prostitutional acts reveal an underlying fascination with sexual indulgence. Nevertheless, as the person whose life role was to function as the living superego of his people, he could preoccupy himself with the subject only through negation. Through the use of incessant condemnations he could at least dwell on the subject and carry out a detour around the repressive forces. In his struggle to ward off strong temptations for incest and sexual promiscuity, he created the detailed descriptions which illustrate the point that literature which appeals to "prurient interests" can have "redeeming social value." Ezekiel may also have secretly gloated over the Lord's tarnished reputation, in view of the fact that Zion, his bride, was running around shamelessly and even stooping so low as to engage in public harlotry. By reproaching Zion with great zeal, he could also needle the Lord who was, to use Freud's language, "an injured third party."

There are numerous biblical references to the prostitution of Zion or Jerusalem. Two passages are of particular importance for understanding the connection between Zion, the mother turned prostitute, and Zionism, the rescue operation of Zion by the sons of Israel. The first passage is from Ezekiel. Chapter 16 reveals how the Lord God rescued Jerusalem: "And as for thy nativity, in the day thou wast born thy navel was not cut, neither wast thou washed in water for cleansing; thou wast not salted at all, nor swaddled at all. . . . And when I passed by thee, and saw thee wallowing in thy blood, I said unto thee: In thy blood, live; yea, I said unto thee: in thy blood, live." From our knowledge of the dynamic meaning of rescuing or of giving life we could predict what would happen. The little infant Jerusalem whose life God saved was destined to become his mate. Indeed, later in the chapter Ezekiel describes how God revisited the naked Jerusalem who by now had developed breasts and (pubic) hair. He found her eligible for love and wedded her. Jerusalem, however, was not content with the luxurious clothes and food which the Lord showered upon her. "Thou hast built unto thee an eminent place, and hast thee a lofty place in every street. Thou hast built thy lofty place at every head of the way, and hast made thy beauty an abomination, and hast opened thy feet to every one that passed by, and multiplied thy harlotries. Thou hast also played the harlot with the Egyptians, thy neighbors, great of flesh; and hast multiplied thy harlotry, to provoke me." In short, the wife and mother turned into a prostitute.

Ezekiel accused the stray wife and mother of being more than a prostitute: "Moreover thou hast taken thy sons and thy daughters, whom thou hast borne unto Me, and these hast thou sacrificed unto them to be devoured. Were thy harlotries a small matter, that thou hast slain My children, and delivered them up, in setting them apart unto them?" In the context of an exhortation against idolatry, a warning is in order to sons as well as daughters: both can be sacrificed to other gods. However, in the context of an exhortation against adultery, the danger is only to sons. From a psychoanalytic outlook, danger does loom ahead for the sons when the mother offers herself to any passer-by. From their vantage point it may seem, during flickering moments when repressed impulses break through, that if the mother is free for all, then the family should come first and the sons should top the list of lovers. Such thoughts, whether acted out or not, involve anticipatory fears of retaliation. The angry and injured father represents mortal danger to the sons. In his rage he could kill them. The threat of death or castration because of oedipal impulses is an experience that has been lived and relived countless times in human history. In the Greek myth Oedipus blamed himself, but in our biblical narrative Ezekiel laid the blame at the doorstep of Jerusalem. His standpoint was something like "If only mother were not a prostitute!" However, regardless of where the blame lies, the sons could hardly avoid heeding the warning implied in his narrative and becoming fully aware that if the mother starts prostituting they had better watch out for their lives.

After the descriptions of Jerusalem's harlotry and betrayal of the Lord her husband, one would expect God to leave her with disgust and abandon her for good. At least for a while it seems as if this is the case when Ezekiel lashes at Jerusalem with added exhortations, beginning with the angry cry "Wherefore, O harlot, hear the word of the Lord!" But as he exhausts his supply of angry words the Lord finally and magnanimously forgives her and renews their covenant. Yet the ambivalence in his forgiveness surfaces when he promises her that his very act of forgiveness will exacerbate her shame: "that thou mayest remember, and be confounded, and never open thy mouth any more, because of thy shame; when I have forgiven thee all that thou hast done, saith the Lord God." Like a neurotic lover, God continues to place high value on a woman who has already proven worthless. Time and time again he has to rescue her and save her life or save her from moral degradation. In doing so, he behaves like a son who is still looking for mother in a cheap woman, and he overrates her. Somehow God's promiscuous mate is always worth saving. Thus, Ezekiel's narrative contains unconsciously fused images of father and sons, that is, the God of Israel and the sons of Israel.

Another biblical passage that illuminates the meaning of the rescue of Zion is by the second Isaiah, who was a contemporary of Ezekiel and who also prophesied during the Babylonian exile. This passage alludes to the hidden hopes of the sons to share in the prerogatives of the father (a feat which may be hard to accomplish without patricide). Like Ezekiel's narrative, it is characterized by fused images of the father and the sons. Addressed to Zion or Jerusalem, it runs as follows (Isaiah 62: 4–5):

> Thou shalt no more be termed Foresaken,
> Neither shall thy land any more be termed Desolate;
> But you shall be called, My light is in her,
> And thy land, Espoused;
> For the Lord lighteth in thee,
> And thy land shall be espoused.
> For as a young man espouseth a virgin,
> So shall thy sons espouse thee;
> And as the bridegroom rejoiceth over a bride,
> So shall thy God rejoice over thee.

This cheerful promise to both mother and sons foretold the second Zionade—the ingathering of the Babylonian exiles back in Zion. It was delivered by the emissary of a benevolent father. His surprising generosity in allowing his sons to husband his wife can only be explained as a result of a fusion of images whereby the rivalry between father and sons is masked and the longings of both are promised fulfillment. But the sons should be leery of the benevolence of El Kana. Possessing the mother is always a mortal sin for which sons can be sacrificed, and it does not matter who promotes the sacrifice, the father in Genesis or the mother in Ezekiel. A sacrifice it is, and in Judaism the final authority always rests with the father.

The promise of a happy repossession of the motherland continued to keep Jewish hopes alive during centuries of exile and finally led to the third Zionade, which was implemented by modern Zionism. The returning Zionist sons were enflamed by a sacred zeal to fertilize Zion. *Hafrahat hashmamot* or "making the desolate land bloom" was a major aspiration and a central slogan in the entire settlement effort. The Israeli journalist and author Amos Elon drew attention to the interesting phenomenon in that the early Zionist settlers described their return to Zion not only in usual terms such as "homecoming" or "rebuilding" but also in stranger terms such as return to the "womb" of history or return to Zion the "betrothed." This led him to conclude that a "libidinous link with the soil" was taking place and that the old liturgical references to a mystical "betrothal" between Israel and the promised land was being given new personal and political meaning. Elon reported a statement by the old-guard Zionist leader Meir Yaari to his pioneer followers, in which he proclaimed that the land they tilled was their bride. Yaari compared the *halutzim* to a bridegroom who abandons himself in his bride's bosom or to the motherly womb of sanctifying earth.

From a psychological and historical standpoint, such a frame of mind is meaningful and full of connotations. It implies that once again mother Zion was being fertilized and impregnated by the ascending sons who came to her rescue. Since they found her desolate, they husbanded her and made her bloom again. And mother Zion, after being made love to by her "homecoming" sons, gave birth to new life. Thus, the children replaced their father, husbanded their mother, and fathered themselves. They therefore experienced a Zionist "rebirth" in which they played the new and masterful role of the potent life giver. Through the mediation of mother earth or the "desolate" land of Israel, they were able to fuse the role of the Lord and master with that of newborn babes. In this fusion they tapped the energy source of an early infantile omnipotence which can do magic. It can have a great impact on reality if the discharge of the old-new energies is harnessed by the ego. (The father of Zionism, Theodor Herzl, captured this same timeless quality by calling his second book *Old-New Land.*)

Indeed, this intricate balance was accomplished. The "newborn babes" simultaneously served as masterful adults who symbolically played "father." On the one hand, they were able to beget new life because they were reborn; on the other, they were reborn because they could display new mastery and could now beget. They thus concurrently played father and sons in relation to their motherland, with each role sustaining the other or simply being the other. These hidden meanings of the Zionist settlement efforts have their roots in the repressed aspects of the developmental course of the Jews. The *halutzim* or pioneers gave a disguised and condensed expression to these impulses by singing a popular song that went: "We came to the land to build and be rebuilt." In a condensed psychoanalytic translation the song would run: "We came to the motherland to beget and be reborn." Neither of the two can be achieved without mother. Father, however, could be replaced.

The Zionist endeavor was a magnificent obsession containing the idea that the sons of Israel ought to return and rescue their mother Zion. In the twelfth century, Judah Halevi remained obedient to his Lord and only pleaded with despair: "Zion, won't you ask about the well-being of thy prisoners?" In the nineteenth and twentieth centuries the Zionists turned the tables; instead of a plea they served notice. They were in a sense saying: "Zion, we ask about thy well-being" and they came to her not to die like Halevi but to live and work and to experience a "rebirth." They did this in flagrant violation of both the heavenly father's will and the will of their parents.

Indeed, many Eastern European parents from the founding generation of Zionists objected to their children's decision to move to Palestine. In terms of the traditional Jewish home, the children's disregard of parental objection meant mostly breaking the authority of the father. Amos Elon reported that many pioneers carried with them memories of violent scenes at home. As strife in the home increased, many young Zionists came to rely on the local Zionist club as a second home or a substitute family. Their decision to go to Israel was implemented in spite of rabbinic condemnations as well. Thus, commitment to Zionism frequently meant that the yoke of the father was broken in both personal and religious terms.

A minority of religious Jews adopted the Zionist stance of immediate effort as the only way to restore the Jewish state. Rabbi Hirsch Kalischer of Thorn was such an early prominent example. Later, the Mizrahi movement was willing to weave itself into Zionism. However, the majority of religious Jews stuck to the traditional orientation of waiting for the Messiah to be sent by God. For the few Zionists in Western Europe an even more discouraging attitude presented itself in the ranks of Reform Jews. The latter felt that active measures for rescuing Zion should be abandoned. Instead, they believed in the meaningfulness of Jewish dispersion as a vehicle for implementing a godly design. This was a basic tenet of Orthodox Judaism as well, but among Reform Jews it reached self-effacing proportions. In his book on Zionism, Richard Gottheil reported that German Reformists, rather than regarding dispersion as a punishment, viewed it as a blessing. It was designed to spread the worship of the true God everywhere. Hence, in the history of humanity the Jewish loss of Palestine signified progress. This belief led the Frankfort Rabbinical Conference of 1845 to vote the remarkable resolution that "All petitions for the return to the land of our fathers, and for the restoration of the Jewish state, should be eliminated from the prayers."

To impatient young Zionists in any European country, it made little difference which Jews were not willing to pray for the restoration of the Jewish state and which Jews were willing to pray for it fervently for another two thousand years. There was something exasperating in this everlasting obedience to the Almighty. This readiness to pray forever seemed like dodging active efforts for self-mastery; the convenient attitude of putting the burden on the Lord appeared bankrupt. Thus the secular zealots or Zionist pioneers broke away from paternal authorities, both mundane and heavenly. Faith in the Almighty and obedience to his will were cast to the winds. The rabbis could use faith as proof of the feasibility of the redemption of Zion only when God willed it. The Zionists had their own actions to prove differently. They therefore brushed aside the religious commands to delay and pray. The implication of these brazen acts by Zionists was not lost on Orthodox Jews. They suspected that many Zionists intended not only to rescue Zion but also to send the Lord to kingdom come.

Because of the ungodly flavor of Zionism, Orthodox rabbinic Judaism managed with difficulty to coexist in an uneasy armistice with it. However, after the establishment of Israel, it seemed foolish in the eyes of the Orthodox parties to let the fate of the state be decided by the secular heretics. These parties therefore became active participants in the state's politics. Soon a political status quo developed which became subject to constant tugging and pulling, occasional explosions, and continuous strain. Chances are that if it were not for the need of unity in the face of Arab threats, as well as deep fears on the part of the secular leadership of the consequences of a final break between Jewish religion and Israeli nationality, a big explosion and final settling of accounts would have taken place by now.

Orthodox Israelis regard the Zionist achievement as a "miracle" caused by the benevolent intervention of the Almighty Father in heaven. To them, the creation of the State of Israel is an irreversible execution of the divine will of the Lord. But the religious persons are painfully aware of the fact that most of the Zionist pioneers pushed God to the sidelines and took matters in their own hands. They know that the implication of all this for Judaism is bound to be far-reaching. It is not for naught that in a famous short story ("The Sermon") the novelist Hayim Hazaz let the hero flatly state that Zionism and Judaism are not merely different but in all likelihood contradictory and that Zionism starts where Judaism collapsed, where the nation's strength gave way to exhaustion. Quite understandably the religious Israelis intensified their battle over the future shape of the Israeli state. Since they remained loyal to their father in heaven it is their natural duty to try to rescue the state from its original rescuers; it is now their turn to save the Land of Israel from secular moral degradation. One may therefore conclude that, as usual, the dialectic forces in Jewish history keep swinging. It is legitimate in such instances to look for the underlying unity or meeting ground of the opposing forces. In this particular case it is a fair assumption that both those who wish to obey father and those who wish to depose and replace him want, in effect, to be like him.

Zionism was characterized not only by great expectations but also by a grave sense of foreboding and an eleventh-hour psychology. The survival of the Jewish people seemed to be at stake and Zionism was perceived as the last chance in the very last hour. Historical developments such as pogroms and expulsions contributed heavily,to this deep feeling of an impending danger, but so did the underlying wishes to stand up like men. These wishes included more than conscious desires to be good Jewish nationalists; they also contained more primitive and repressed urges to replace the father and to taste forbidden fruits against his will. These urges carried with them a component of threat. Because of the prohibited explorations of the maternal territory, something terrible could happen. Just as in biblical times, the sons of Israel could once more be sacrificed as a retaliation by the enraged father. As history continued to unfold, something terrible indeed happened, the horror of the Nazi Holocaust. Historically speaking, the Third Zionade did not cause either the rise of German Nazism or the mass extermination of a full third of the entire Jewish population. Psychologically, however, a causal link might be formed between these two momentous and fatal events. Happenings of this magnitude, such as a Zionade or the destruction of the Temple, are expected to occur only once every few hundred years. That two such events took place together is bound to leave its mark on the unconscious heritage of the Jewish people; each is an unforgettable event which joins the body of the most influential Jewish lore and leaves an impact on countless future generations.

In this body of sacred lore, the third return to Zion joins the first two Zionades from Egypt and Babylon while Hitler takes his place with Amalek and Haman.

Indeed, the impact of Zionism and of the Holocaust on the Jewish heritage of cultural prototypes could become a joint impact. Such a joint impact could fit neatly into the traditional Jewish perception of time, which includes the dualism between redemption and *hevlai mashiah*, as pointed out by Eliezer Livneh. He, however, viewed the possible link between Zionism and the Holocaust within the framework of Jewish traditional thought. A psychological perspective on this joint impact reveals something more specific about the nature of this link. Although no one can predict with certainty the emotional makeup of future generations of Jews, the psychoanalytic identification of what are "timeless" issues enables us to state a likely probability. The present and future generations of Jews could develop a certain perception of these two extraordinary events, even if this perception does not reach full awareness. They might draw a conclusion which links the two: *For infringing on father's territory one can be castrated or killed, and in return for Zionism one gets a Holocaust.*

Timeless issues in the history of a culture are rooted in traumatizing infantile experiences. These issues survive because of the eternal imbalance between wish and wish fulfillment that is a prerequisite of civilization. This imbalance imposes repressions and delivers the infantile wishes into the realm of the timeless unconscious. The more primitive or uncivilized the infantile wish, the more it evokes threats, punishments, and subsequent renunciations. Similarly, the greater the renunciation of primitive gratifications, the greater the discontent with civilization. The treasure house of all these repressed, festering discontents is the unconscious. The thwarted but timeless wishes can be partly gratified in dreams. In *The Interpretation of Dreams*, Freud proposed that dreams are wish fulfillments. The wishes that are partly fulfilled in dreams are largely "immortal infantile wishes" and usually are associated with infantile traumas. These wishes remain timeless because they are unconscious. As Freud put it, "It is indeed an outstanding peculiarity of the unconscious processes that they are indestructible." It is intriguing to note that this has also been the image of the Jews—indestructible. The American historian Max Dimont even named one of his books *The Indestructible Jews.* This Jewish image of timelessness or indestructibility played an unfortunate role in provoking anti-Semitism. Dimont centered mostly on the "civilization" aspects of the image of Jewish indestructibility and neglected somewhat the "discontent" side of it. He saw the Jews as an eternal civilizing force on humanity; many Jews did indeed play this role because of the extraordinary restraining strength of their superego. But the restraining forces have been applied to everlasting, yet tabooed, infantile impulses. Both the primitive impulses and the restraining forces are largely unconscious. Thus the Jews were doubly "indestructible" because they erected an unyielding superego to keep the lid on immortal infantile urges. This timeless play of forces and counterforces again takes place in the unconscious, that special realm of the human psyche where nothing is ever lost.

Timeless issues that occasionally break through also involve a

question of timing. From time to time, taboo wishes manage to penetrate the barrier of repressive forces and secure for themselves partial
fulfillment through personal or cultural expressions. In the life of individuals the wish fulfillment can take the form of a dream. In the life
of a people, the fulfillment takes the form of cultural changes or new
political developments. Various factors combine to determine the
timing of the expression of timeless wishes. Three factors contribute
most to this determination: the current strength of the repressing
forces, the pressure exerted by the repressed impulses, and the presence
of recent events, which produce associations and impressions that are
related to the repressed wishes and therefore add force to them. Freud
suggested that this combination of determining factors operates very
similarly in the lives of both individuals and nations.

All three factors entered into play with the rise of Zionism. First,
the persistence of anti-Semitism and persecution, even in a modern
world of reason, enlightenment, and social justice, added insight to
insult and intensified the rage toward the heavenly father and the
determination to violate his will. Second, the restraining counterforces
were weakening. The European crisis of faith affected Jews too, in the
West earlier than in the East, and weakened somewhat the hitherto
unshakable Jewish superego. This development was most troublesome
to Ahad Ha'am, the leader of Cultural Zionism. His obsession with the
unique Jewish sense of morality can be viewed as an attempt to uphold
the Jewish superego as it was losing its religious footing. For trying to
find secular or even simpleminded biological substitutes for religious
faith, he was perceived by many with incredulity. For instance, the
Israeli literary critic Baruch Kurzweil criticized Ahad Ha'am's doctrine
that retains the Jewish people as a chosen emissary on earth while doing
away with the God who did the choosing. Ahad Ha'am makes more
sense, however, if viewed as a leader who tried to maintain a special
kind of continuity—the continuity of an unshakable Jewish superego.
In this respect, he did not break away from the past and was able to
preach against such breaks with a clean conscience. From a psychoanalytic vantage point, his efforts did not seem doomed to failure. For
adults, the discrediting of parental authorities does not have to result
in the toppling of the superego; the parents who instilled it in the first

place can go, but the superego can stay. Similarly, God could be dead but a keen Jewish sense of morality could stay alive. These issues are not yet settled. They are still alive in Israel, and become especially subject to controversy because of the Arab question, which arouses so many complicated issues of morality, justice, and fairness.

The third factor relates to the rise of nationalism. As many European peoples were trying to grab their fair share of fatherlands and motherlands, the awareness of these dramatic developments sank deeply into Jewish souls, there to become associated with archaic dreams of the redemption of Zion and to reawaken the old rescue fantasies. In combination, these three basic factors resulted in a new balance of forces which allowed for greater investment in actual rescue operations. A wealth of newly released energies could now be available for intense efforts to recreate the Jewish state. Now the timing was right.

2.

The Psychological Price

IT IS HARD TO BE A JEW!

—A Jewish saying

The exiled Jews had found it increasingly difficult to maintain peace of mind, since their split identity forced them to be next to nothing politically, yet spiritually the greatest. True, they took pride in the great contributions by Judaism and Jews to humanity, and at home they could safely absorb themselves in the worlds of spirituality created by previous generations of Jews. But sooner or later they would have to venture outside of their homes, walk the streets of the Gentiles, and feel second-class, unwanted, and vulnerable. Hence, a Jewish genius at home, with voluminous treasures of mind, became on the street a luckless and inept schlemiel, unable to achieve security and equality with his non-Jewish neighbors. This coexistence of spiritual pride with political shame could only be achieved at the price of some schizophrenic-like qualities, and the increasing signs of strain indicated that the time of coexistence between spiritual pride and political shame was nearing its end.

The psychological toll exacted from the Jews can easily be detected in literature. For example, it can be found in the late nineteenth-century writings of Sholom Aleichem, "the Jewish Mark Twain," a superb humorist with a great love for his people. In his story "The Town of the Little People," he described the people of Kasrilevka, who were especially proud of their old cemetery. Not only were great scholars and pious and famous people of old buried there, as well as the victims of the massacres of the cossack Chmielnicki, but the cemetery was the only piece of land in which the Jews were masters. It was the only place where the grass and trees and fresh air belonged to them, and therefore the only place where they could breathe freely. This particular sketch stamps a terrible judgment on Jewish life.

It takes a superb comedian to tell people with a smile that conditions are funny—so morbidly funny, in fact, that something has to be done lest death in life become their lot.

The judgment implicit in this story by Sholom Aleichem closely resembles the psychological descriptions by the British psychiatrist R. D. Laing of psychotic persons who have trouble delineating and defining a sense of self. Laing discussed the developing split within peoples' psyche as they continue to experience difficulties in interacting with others. He provided many phenomenological descriptions of how people relegate their dealings with the outside world to a false self-system. This false self-system, a type of phony mask, talks with people and may even display consistent attitudes and values toward others without really having a genuine feeling or commitment to these values and attitudes. But the false self accepts them anyway. Where the true commitments allegedly lie, and where the real attitudes and genuine sense of values are supposed to be, is the true self. This true self is shut inside and protected completely from the outer world by the false self, which copes with the outside environment. Although the protected, hidden true self is supposedly safe and free, somehow this phenomenon strikingly corresponds to the mythological freedom of the graveyard.

As Laing has put it, the whole inner world of the shut-up self comes to be increasingly more impoverished, and consequently the person may eventually feel that he, i.e., his own true inner self, is merely a vacuum. This is not surprising, since without action or interaction, and when everything is correspondingly delegated to a false self which does the job, the true self can easily become a nullity. A person may still console himself with the realization that he does have a true self, even that he is lucky to have an inner, secret self that nobody else knows about. In truth, however, when the time comes to fall back and rely on the hidden self, all that he experiences is a vacuum.

Similarly, breathing freely in a graveyard is but a mirage, and cannot serve as a substitute for true freedom. This is the lesson that Sholom Aleichem was trying to impress upon his readers. A miserable Jew living in a shtetl, or small Jewish village, who in his dealings with the external world cannot walk erect anywhere until he retreats to his little corner of freedom, the graveyard, suffers from a divided self. Not only does he lack freedom outside the graveyard, but also within it. Sholom Aleichem implied this by taking care to point out that this corner of freedom, this precious graveyard, also included the dead from the massacres of Chmielnicki's time. The destruction of the Jews is apparent both outside and inside the graveyard. Freedom is not divisible, nor is a sense of self. A divided self is a destroyed self. The rise of Zionism can be seen as a reaction to the need to heal this division and do away with the split in Jewish souls.

The heroes of Sholom Aleichem's stories are frequently luckless schlemiels. In discussing the schlemiel in Jewish literature, including Sholom Aleichem's works, the literary critic Ruth Wisse pictures the schlemiel as a challenge to the accepted notion of heroism. The schlemiel questioned not only the feasibility but also the desirability of heroism. Within this ability to subdue his urge to be a hero, Wisse detected a quality of strength. The schlemiel could indeed display remarkable endurance. But it was obvious that he was perceived by many Jews with disdain rather than admiration. Together with the schnorrer, or beggar, the schlemiel served as one of the more notorious examples of the Jewish negative ego-ideal. A negative ego-ideal was defined by the American psychoanalysts Stanley Kaplan and Roy Whitman as "the introjected negative standards of the parents and of the culture," and whoever fulfills these negative standards is bound to experience great shame. To many Jews who suffered from a divided self, the schlemiel represented a false outer self that should have been discarded. They looked forward to the day when their true inner selves would rebel and come to the fore. While the schlemiel questioned the value of heroism (Wisse), the inner selves of many Jews craved for overt acts of heroism, and therefore longed to be like the fighting Maccabees of old. Very perceptively, Wisse pointed out that the schlemiel was in some way inverting the famous Theodor Herzl dictum by turning it into "If you will it, it is a dream." Thus, one side of the divided Jewish self accepted the chronic lucklessness of the schlemiel as fate, which permitted the realization of Jewish hopes only in Jewish dreams. But the other side of the same self responded with alacrity to Herzl's call, "If you will it, it is no dream," and in the process freed itself from the shackles of schlemieldom.

In addition to the storyteller Sholom Aleichem, others also stressed the point that things could not continue as they had, and that the price Jews were paying was very high indeed. The noted scholar and

writer Hannah Arendt in her discussion of anti-Semitism summed up
the situation incisively. She indicated that modern anti-Semitism, in
interaction with Jewish assimilation and secularization, corresponded
to the erosion of the old religious and spiritual values of Judaism. Just
at the time when Jews were threatened by physical extinction from
without, they were also threatened by dissolution from within. Arendt
also suggested that the long history of a people without a country,
language, or government had resulted in a lack of Jewish political ability
and judgment—a harsh statement, but one which is nevertheless cor-
roborated by Zionism. The early Zionist decision to form a political
movement is testimony to the diagnosis of political "malady," just as
the history of the Zionist movement provides testimony to the success
of the political "cure."

Perhaps the most shattering experiences in terms of identity and
dignity were felt by the assimilated Jews in nineteenth-century Europe.
Arendt poignantly described the situation. The Western European Jew
had the option of either remaining a pariah and thereby being more
or less excluded from society, or of becoming a parvenu who conforms
to general European society but nevertheless retains his Jewishness in
some mysterious way. Therefore, an enlightened Jew could not choose
to be Jewish or pariah and still remain an enlightened man of society,
but if he rejected the role of pariah to become a parvenu, he then found
out that he was still regarded as a Jew and an outcast. Thus an enlightened Jew could not retain his identity either as a Jew or as a man of
society, and consequently floated in a twilight world where the social
and psychological tolls were immense.

Other important psychological effects that beset the Jews were the
hypervigilance of the haunted, the alert scanning of the insecure, and
the continuous suspiciousness of the vulnerable. It is with a sense of
tragedy that one reads the French philosopher Jean-Paul Sartre's descriptions of how, after the Second World War, many French Jews
found it advisable to underplay their role in the resistance to Nazi
occupation. They felt that if they underscored their role by being vocal,
it might evoke some negative feelings or even reprisals toward Jews.
This suspicion serves as but a single illustration of the many instances
where Jews had reason to wonder about the implications for them of

new events and developments. This anxiety about the possible negative implications from a variety of events concerning the fate of the Jews has resulted in a pervasive tendency to view most things through "Jewish glasses." It is an attempt to make sure that any underlying connection between an issue and the Jewish problem is exposed. The compulsion to unearth such a connection, even when it is apparent to the Jews themselves that the specific issue has little, if any, relation to the Jewish problem, betrays a basic sense of insecurity.

Particularly in terms of a sense of peace with one's own identity and basic sense of security, one is reminded here of the writings of the famous American psychoanalyst Karen Horney. She underscored the importance of the concept of basic anxiety, which she described as a pervasive condition of some children whereby they feel helpless, abandoned, isolated, and thrown into a hostile and dangerous world. Horney maintained that some children develop this condition when their early environment is flooded with disagreement, broken promises, overprotection, isolation from other children, hostility, discrimination, injustice, and a variety of similar destructive intrusions which might also be traumatic. As a people among the nations of the world, the children of Israel were similarly thrown into a traumatic, hostile, discriminatory, and unpredictably dangerous environment. Obviously, this analogy between threatened children and the threatened Jews is far from perfect; some similarities and differences between the two situations will be discussed later in the chapter. It is likely, however, that historical conditions did breed among the Jews a kind of "basic anxiety," a dread that any event could have an important bearing on Jewish fate. This dread produced a defensive reaction. It seems that the function of the compulsion to discover a linkage between any specific issue and the fate of the Jews is to transform an unknown danger into a known one. For a known danger is less frightening, and also provides at least a minimal reassurance in terms of escape potential.

As a result, any event that makes the news, whether local or international, is discussed in terms of the question, "Is it good for the Jews?" Israeli schoolchildren sometimes become tired of studying world history by having to assess almost every development in terms of its impact on, or meaning for, the Jews. This chronic view of human

affairs through "Jewish glasses" has become a joke, and has even acquired the name of "The elephant and the Jewish problem." One
version of the joke runs as follows: A public competition was announced
concerning the writing of a book about the elephant, and a Frenchman,
a German, and a Jew became competitors. After a month, the Frenchman returned carrying a small book of artistic illustrations entitled
"The Love Life of the Elephant." A year later the German came back
with a three-volume work summarizing extensive scientific research
under the title, "The Functional and Structural Physiology of the
Elephant." Three years later the Jew appeared with a ten-volume
masterpiece entitled "The Elephant and the Jewish Problem." The
funny but nevertheless serious implication is: Why not? If one thinks
long enough about any subject, one could discover a link between it and
the Jewish problem. The self-laughter evoked by this joke may be
wholesome, but the underlying anxiety it betrays is no laughing matter.

So notorious is the obsession with the "Jewish problem," that on
one occasion a humorous panel discussion of the topic "Women,
Money, and the Jewish Problem" was included in the popular Israeli
radio program, *Three in One Boat* (Ha'ezrahi and Shim'oni). As it was
explained to the audience, some people suffer from fixed ideas, that is,
obsessions with single topics. In such cases, no matter what topic is
raised, it always reminds them of women, money, or the Jewish problem. The task for one of the panel members was to respond to various
statements as if he were a person who was obsessed with the fixed idea
of the "Jewish problem." In other words, whatever "elephant" was
presented to him, his task was to find its inevitable link with the Jewish
problem. For example, when a hypothetical bus driver announced that
there was no more room on the bus, the panelist said that this is how
it always was and always will be, because the only room for Jews is in
Israel. This reaction, however, is not an unfounded paranoia or obsessive suspiciousness devoid of any basis in reality.

In fact, the idea that there is no room for the Jews has haunted
them throughout their tragic history. Expulsions and persecutions became the daily fare of Jewish life, and also found their way into Jewish
humor. The Israelis Uri Sela and Shraga Har-Gil, in their book on
political humor, included jokes which express essentially similar senti-

ments. One joke asks: What is the evidence that Adam and Eve were Jewish? The answer: The fact that they received an eviction order. Another joke recounts that on the eve of Hitler's taking over Austria, a Jew enters a travel agency in Vienna for consultation about his travel plans. The agent hands him a globe and instructs him to search for a destination. The Jew looks the globe over carefully, turns it around a few times, and finally says with a typical Jewish sigh, "Mr. Agent, do you have another globe?" With this kind of reality it is relatively easy to develop obsessions with fixed ideas. However, by the time the Jewish problem serves as an *idée fixe* for a humorous radio program, it appears that Israelis may already be in the process of ridding themselves of their "Jewish glasses." Their self-mockery suggests that they have made inroads toward gaining some distance from the problem, but nevertheless it still exists.

There is a sad irony in the fact that a Palestinian colleague and friend of mine told me the same "elephant" joke, except that this time it was "The Elephant and the Palestinian Problem." He was surprised to hear that I had known this same story as a Jewish joke since my childhood. It is certainly true that political jokes can cross national and geographic boundaries, as Sela and Har-Gil have pointed out. As a matter of fact, my friend thought that the transformation of the elephant joke only enhanced the idea that now the Palestinians have become "the Jews of the world." When I asked him about the meaning of his remark, he responded by saying that nowadays the Palestinians are obsessed with their problem and have developed a paranoid outlook which sees any world event as somehow related to the Palestinian problem.

It is interesting to compare "the elephant and the Jewish problem" joke with another one which concerns anti-Semites rather than Jews. The American author Nathan Ausubel, in the introduction to his book on Jewish humor, reported a well-known joke about the anti-Semite and the Jew. "The Jews are to blame for everything," said the anti-Semite. "Definitely," replied the Jew, "the Jews and the bicycle riders." "Why the bicycle riders?" asked the anti-Semite. "Why the Jews?" retorted the Jew. What the Jew is telling the anti-Semite is that the bicycle riders will do as well as the Jews, because the need for a scapegoat comes from within the hostile anti-Semite himself. Therefore, any target for hate would be at least as legitimate as the Jews—just as any subject of fear, including the elephant, could serve as the source of danger to the worried Jews.

At this point it might be helpful to review what Horney saw as potential reactions to feelings of insecurity, anxiety, and living with a sense of looming danger that might strike unpredictably. Some of these basic reactions include the development of hostility as an emotional outlet, the growth of competitive motivation and a desire to win, and the turning of aggression inward through self-derogation. It seems that the psychological development of a child living with a family that provides him with an uncertain environment resembles the development of certain psychological traits among Jews who were cast among hostile nations and exposed to uncertain environments. Hostility, a wish for vengeance, and a competitive drive to win developed in both instances, but were nevertheless coupled with submissiveness, feelings of inferiority, and self-depreciatory attitudes. A child who suffers from basic insecurity frequently hates and blames himself. Similarly, Jewish self-hatred became a distressing problem for the Jews.

The analogy between children reared in conditions of insecurity and the children of Israel leading insecure lives among many nations may seem farfetched, and is of course incomplete. However, there are similarities between both the distressing conditions and the negative consequences in both cases. The Israeli psychoanalyst Abraham Weinberg seems to have been aware of this analogy, although he was careful to draw a distinction between the morbid feelings of basic insecurity and the more common feelings of uncertainty. This effort was particularly important to ensure against a wholesale application of Horney's concept of basic insecurity to Jewish history, and his caution is commendable as long as one recognizes the fact that there is an analogy here. One basic difference, however, is the ability of the Jews to fall back on their own kind for group support, a most important resource for health and survival which is not readily available to small children. Living in a dangerous and uncertain environment seems to be the major similarity between Jews and children.

Weinberg also discussed the prevalence among Jews of what the

American sociologist Everett Stonequist has termed "marginal men," that is, men who live between at least two antagonistic cultures but do not fully belong to either. In this regard, Weinberg suggested a connection between the prevalence of marginal personalities among Jews and the incidence of mental illness. We may recall that Arendt spoke of the heavy emotional toll which the Jews paid by living in a twilight zone. In view of this cumbersome price, it is not surprising that Weinberg also wondered about the possible connection between historical conditions of marginality in the Diaspora and the development of such traits as Jewish self-hatred and self-pride. This takes us full circle back to Horney, who regarded both the compensating drives to win and the self-derogatory feelings of inferiority as stemming from earlier feelings of basic anxiety and insecurity. It seems, therefore, that the insecure and marginal conditions of the Jewish people have left their mark on many individual Jews, especially since such conditions can easily threaten and oppress both children and adults. Nevertheless, it is wise to bear in mind that these feelings of uncertainty did not blossom into the morbidity of basic insecurity and anxiety for all Jews.

The hypervigilance and suspiciousness of the Jews was a response to a cruel reality, and is something that even Israelis cannot rid themselves of, as long as they are cast as a lonely nation among hostile neighbors. The Holocaust, an atrocity which defies imagination, fortified the haunted outlook and suspicious alertness of the Jewish people for generations to come. Mistrust of non-Jews was inevitable, and many examples of this can be found in the literature. At one point, when the Zionist leader Chaim Weizmann was repeatedly frustrated in his political efforts, he remarked that the real opponents of Zionism can never be placated because their objection to the Jews is the fact that Jews exist. One cannot really blame Weizmann and most other Jews for being so suspicious. Oversuspiciousness in this case would constitute no more than the commonsense logic of "playing it safe." If Jews sound paranoid at times, then it is because all too frequently in the past their worst suspicions turned out to be realities rather than dreams.

The dangers which constantly threatened Jews from the outside prompted a closing of the ranks on the inside. Therefore, the marvelous phenomenon of *Kol Yisrael haverim* (All Israel are brethren) has evolved, bringing with it an intense feeling of belonging which has saved the Jewish people from extinction (Weinberg). Jews are rightly proud of this noble sentiment, but at the time we are speaking of, closing of the ranks in the face of adversity was no longer good enough. All in all, the psychological toll exacted from the Jews throughout their long history was heavy. Their political ability lay dormant, their religious and spiritual identity had undergone a process of erosion, and their literature and folklore included the message that it was a time for change through self-help. Something had to be done to uproot adversity in the first place. Zionism rose to the task.

3.

The Coming of Political Zionism

IF YOU WILL IT, IT IS NO DREAM.

CALL ME DONKEY, JACKASS OR
ANYTHING ELSE YOU LIKE, BUT
OBEY AND FOLLOW ME.

—Theodor Herzl

In 1881, after the assassination of Tsar Alexander II, pogroms and massacres of Jews spread throughout Russia. As a result, the Russian Jewish physician Leo Pinsker became so disenchanted with the assimilation and emancipation movements that a year later he published his revolutionary pamphlet *Auto-Emancipation*. Because of the pogroms many Jews were emigrating to the United States and elsewhere, while many others, according to the historian of Zionism Israel Cohen, were exchanging their faith in assimilation and enlightenment *(haskalah)* for the Jewish national idea. Thus, a "Zionist" movement called Hibbat Tziyon (Love of Zion) was formed prior to the official establishment of a Zionist organization. About twenty-five students from the University of Kharkov, an active Jewish center for national aspirations, spread out over Russia, proselytizing and recruiting about five hundred Jewish followers who were eager to emigrate to Palestine in order to rebuild it. They called their movement Bilu, after the initial letters of the words of Isaiah 2, 5: "O house of Jacob, come ye, and let us walk." In 1882 their first settlement was founded near Jaffa and was named Rishon Letziyon (First of Zion). The Hibbat Tziyon movement spread throughout Eastern and Western Europe and even reached America. It also established a few settlements in Israel, which had rough going because of small numbers and relatively minimal financial support. Although the Hibbat Tziyon established a bridgehead for Zionism in Palestine, the rebuilding of Zion on a larger scale had to wait until the Zionist Organization entered the picture to offer new hope to the by then somewhat discouraged early settlers.

At this time the writer Ahad Ha'am ("One of the People") published his famous first article in Hebrew under the title "This Is Not the Way." The article, which caused a sensation, criticized the Hovevei Tziyon (Lovers of Zion) for adopting the wrong methods of establishing a Jewish national rebirth in Palestine. Ahad Ha'am believed that Palestine was not suited for mass migration, and that the land of Israel should instead be used for the cultivation of the Jewish spirit. In order to implement his idea of bringing about a national spiritual revival, he formed the Benei Mosheh (Sons of Moses) movement, which many Lovers of Zion joined. These were the roots of an ideological rift that would eventually cause great strains in the Zionist movement. The Hovevei Tziyon movement contributed to the spirit of the age by fostering great expectations for national revival without as yet mobilizing a mass national movement among the Jews. In spite of the many failures of the Hovevei Tziyon movement, its tangible achievement for Jewish history was that of founding agricultural settlements in Eretz Yisrael (Land of Israel), which prepared the ground for the launching of the mass movement.

In 1896 Theodor Herzl's book *Der Judenstaat (The Jewish State)*, was published in Vienna and was immediately translated into English and French. It made a huge impact on many Jews and brought fame to the author. Indeed, only a year later Herzl opened the First Zionist Congress in Basel, Switzerland, and almost overnight the Jewish people had their king before they had their country. Herzl, a journalist and playwright, began to write his momentous book in 1895, shortly after being shaken to the marrow by the Dreyfus Affair in France. Although it was not his first encounter with anti-Semitism, it was the most impressive. To Herzl, as to many fellow Jews, it was not only a question of an injustice done to one individual, a Jewish captain named Alfred Dreyfus, but also a question of the magnitude of the conspiracy against him and the wide popularity of anti-Jewish sentiments in various social strata in France, one of the most liberal countries in the world. Indeed, for many Frenchmen the choice between injustice to the Jews or a blemish to the honor of the French army was quite clear.

All this finally convinced Herzl that anti-Semitism would never go away, and that the only solution to the problem would have to be a radical and political one. Understandably, the Dreyfus Affair was of paramount concern to all Jews who had any access to world news; the interest in the trial on the part of the common shtetl Jews comes across clearly in Sholom Aleichem's story "Dreyfus in Kasrilevka." Now

Herzl's concern suddenly placed him on common ground with the Jews of the shtetl. The sight of wild mobs chanting anti-Semitic slogans evoked in him a dramatic return from assimilation to national Judaism. Herzl was never the same man after that, and for the rest of his life he was obsessed with compulsive work toward one, and only one, goal —the national renascence of his people. Since he came from a family which seems to have had a genetic vulnerability and predisposition to both physical and emotional ailments (Stern), this high obsession and tireless effort quickly consumed him, and ultimately resulted in his death at the early age of forty-four. Within his short life, however, Herzl managed to earn an immortal place in the annals of perhaps the most peculiar people in the history of man.

Herzl considered the main idea of his pamphlet, the restoration of the Jewish state, as an "ancient one." He was not aware of the fact that his ideas had been expounded by the grandfathers of Zionism, but nevertheless he knew that they were not new. In this connection, Cohen has pointed out that political Zionism owed much to the fact that its founder was ignorant of his predecessors. Perhaps Herzl's ignorance of previous struggles and failures contributed to a sense of optimism and dedication which was needed for the success of the movement. Cohen also states that, unlike Pinsker, Herzl had worked out in elaborate detail a plan for the settlement of the Jews in a country of their own; on the other hand, like Pinsker, he did not commit himself to a particular territory. This lack of geographical commitment eventually resulted in a resounding explosion during the Sixth Zionist Congress, as we shall see later.

The old, yet new, idea of the Jewish state spread like wildfire among the Jews. What contributed to Herzl's success, where his predecessors had failed, were his practical efforts to establish an executive body that could implement Zionist ideas. These efforts resulted in the First Zionist Congress in Basel, Switzerland, which met from August 27 to August 29, 1897. A total of 204 Jewish delegates from various parts of the world attended, and constituted the parliament of the Jewish people before they even had their country. The majestic Herzl, with his impressive, bearded countenance, was most compulsive in executing the ceremonial formalities of the ongoing assembly, down to the last detail, with the most delicate nuances. His previous experience as a reporter and observer of political discussions in national assemblies now came in handy. What is more, with an intuitive genius, Herzl perceived that questions of form were at least as important as those of content. This compulsive execution in a majestic fashion of the ceremonial and formal aspects of the gatherings is what gave the First Zionist Congress a state-like aura, and sharply differentiated it from other community gatherings which the Jews had had many times in their history.

A product of the First Zionist Congress was the Basel Program, which called for the creation of a home in Palestine for the Jewish people by means of: (1) Jewish settlement in Palestine; (2) establishing a federation of all Jewry to help toward this goal; (3) strengthening national sentiments among the Jews; and (4) working with world governments to secure their consent to this program. Hence, the Zionist movement was launched by its father, and it was with pride and prophetic vision that on September 3, 1897, Herzl wrote the famous note in his diary (Lowenthal): "At Basel I founded the Jewish State."

Herzl initiated a brand of Zionism that later came to be known as Political Zionism, which was characterized by what can be termed a "charter psychology." This constituted the belief that negotiation with the major powers of the world, such as the British Government, the Kaiser of Germany, or the Sultan of Turkey, could result in one or more powers' initiating a charter to allot a territory for the colonization of the Jews. This territory would hopefully be in Palestine but might be in some other place. While Herzl carried on this political activity, it received little backing from the Jewish Yishuv (Settlement) in Palestine, whose growth was rather meager. The Yishuv consisted mainly of the First Aliyah (immigration wave) of the Lovers of Zion, which had resulted in about eighteen old and new Jewish settlements. In 1904 the Second Aliyah started, lasting until the First World War. This aliyah, though never large in numbers (35,000-40,000, most of whom either emigrated or were expelled from Palestine) left a lasting impact on the Yishuv because of its ideological zeal and convictions. For example, members of this aliyah developed the kibbutz (collective village) movement. As matters stood then, however, Herzl, who died in 1904, could not rely much on strength from "below," from the rank and file of the small Jewish settlement in Palestine. He had to rely on Sultans, Kaisers, and world governments, to work from above—hence Political Zionism.

Political Zionism, that is, high-level negotiations with world powers, was needed not only because of the weakness of the Jewish settlement in Palestine, but also because it was a psychological necessity. Herzl said to Jews everywhere that if they willed it, it would not be a dream; but to keep the will going it was necessary to provide the Jewish people with at least a foretaste of the realization of the magnificent dream. The sight of a "Jewish king" dealing with the mightiest of world leaders, when the nation he was supposedly representing existed merely in the form of an IOU allegedly given to him by the Jewish people, was incentive enough to create a strong drive in the people to honor and fulfill that IOU. Herzl was operating on credit. He showed that he was aware of it when on September 3, 1897, he wrote in his diary that the essence of the Jewish state lay in "the will of the people for a State." Yet his entire Zionist scheme might have ended in another bubble burst, and Herzl might have turned out just another impractical Jewish dreamer. That Herzl's dream did not end that way was partly due to the fact that Political Zionism presented to the Jewish people not another old type of pleader or interceder, but a king.

Thus Herzl's major impact on the Jewish people was his ability to become a "king"—a prominent symbol of their dormant aspirations for nationality. As they learned of Herzl, the nations of the world and the Gentile political leaders may not have been overly impressed by his bargaining and lobbying style; for them there was nothing new in this phenomenon. For the Jews, on the other hand, it was new, exciting, revolutionary. So great was Herzl's impact on the Jewish people that his legend grew and his reputation sometimes preceded him. For instance, on January 23, 1904, he had an audience with the Italian king. In his diary, Herzl indicated that the topic of messianism entered their discussion, the king wondering whether messianic hopes were still alive among the Jews. Herzl explained to the king that the Zionist movement had a purely national character and added, to the king's amusement, that he deliberately avoided using a white horse or ass during his visit to Palestine so that nobody would embarrass him by confusing him with the Messiah.

One scholar of Zionism, Alex Bein, has suggested that it was the

Jewish people who transmuted Herzl into a king and Messiah, and that the picture they drew of him lay beyond the truth since it represented the longing of the masses. Indeed, in a pamphlet entitled "Theodor Herzl," the British Zionist Paul Goodman (Cohen) described him as a king in the making who stood taller than his people, much as King Saul once did. Similarly, in his introduction to Herzl's diary notes on the First Zionist Congress, Marvin Lowenthal quoted Herzl's British associate, Israel Zangwill, who wrote that he was very impressed with Herzl's majestic oriental figure, which reminded him of Assyrian kings such as Tiglath-pileser. It is interesting to note that when he finally stood up, Herzl did not appear as tall as Zangwill had expected him to be. We can see here the effect of symbolism, which makes a legend grow taller than the actual man.

It is also interesting that it was the Assyrian king Tiglath-pileser III who, in 736 B.C., decreased the borders of the northern kingdom of Israel after the Israeli king Pekah, son of Remaliah, joined in a rebellion against Assyria. Indeed, Tiglath-pileser is one of three Assyrian kings—the other two being Shalmaneser V and Sargon II—who stand out in Jewish history as being closely associated with the loss of the Kingdom of Israel. Why Zangwill associated Herzl with Tiglath-pileser rather than with some nineteenth-century monarch is intriguing. What may have been in operation is the psychological mechanism of identification with the aggressor. The famed psychoanalyst Anna Freud once explained that this mode of identification appears in children during the early stages of superego development. By identifying with the aggressor and introjecting his qualities, the child converts himself from a fearful subject into the hitherto dreaded figure. This way he masters anxiety and attains feelings of pleasurable security. Similarly, the small child (and later the adult) manages to bring about a psychological switch from a passive to an active role, and no longer dreads being the victim of aggression.

Perhaps Zangwill felt that it was time for a new breed of fighting Jews to "do unto others" for a change. He was also probably overwhelmed by a certain quality of "immediacy" in the Jewish past which was consistently impinging on the present. Whatever it was, there was something in Herzl's appearance and conduct which stirred up very deep and very strong feelings among Jews.

To a large degree also, Herzl's impact was due to a quality of chutzpah, or unmitigated gall, which became an integral part of Zionism and was subsequently elevated almost to an art form by native-born Israelis, or sabras. It took a measure of boldness and a daring mentality for Herzl to negotiate spontaneously with world leaders. He regarded his dream as an imminent reality, not because he was an unrealistic schlemiel but rather because of the pressing need he felt to realize a dream. So compelling was this need that he and his fellow Jews had no choice but to make it a reality. In such a reckoning, "no choice" is as good as reality, and is not a "perhaps" or "maybe" but an inescapable "must." Here we see the early Zionist roots of the famous Israeli "no-choice" psychology, which is saturated with a sense of historical inevitability and in turn begets chutzpah, that is, bold actions which seem so much against the odds that they impress people with their sheer impertinence. As for Herzl, his treating of his dream as reality and his stylish negotiations with world leaders constituted a primary example of chutzpah.

Herzl's chutzpah, coupled with the dedication which comes with total ideological conviction, enhanced the impressive appearance of this nineteenth-century "King of the Jews," and left a lasting impact on many people. For instance, in his introduction to Herzl's diaries, Lowenthal reported that in Dr. Martin Buber's memory, Herzl had a countenance that was lit with the glance of the Messiah. Indeed, his facial countenance was imposing, especially his long black beard. Sela and Har-Gil even report that there is a joke about it, in which a European Gentile leader meets Nordau, Herzl's colleague, and expresses his fears that the whole of Zionism depends on the impressive black beard of Dr. Herzl. And, should he ever shave it off, Zionism would lose its strength. Nordau, with a smile, answers: "Perhaps so, but the next day the beard will start growing again." Here, the skeptic non-Jew voices the opinion that Zionism covers up its weakness with much ceremonial ado. He also expresses the fear that the Jews might become strong like a modern Samson whose strength is tied to his hair. Nordau's reply implies that the strength of Zionism is not a passing phenomenon and cannot be brushed aside as mere ceremonial maneuverings.

Indeed, Herzl's impact on many Jews can truly be termed "electrifying," in the sense of the sudden freeing and mobilization of hitherto bound energies. There are some indications that even Sigmund Freud did not escape this impact, and was so impressed that he even seems to have dreamed of Herzl's majestic appearance. This is the opinion of the psychohistorian Peter Loewenberg, who postulated that Freud, who offered redemption through insight rather than political action, could not espouse Zionism. He may therefore have repressed his latent attraction to Zionism as well as his possible envy of Herzl. Nevertheless, his fascination with the idea of political redemption for the Jews, i.e., Zionism, could not be censored in his dreams. Be that as it may, there is no question that Herzl's credo as well as his style of delivering it evoked in his Jewish listeners in all walks of life the response of "it rings a bell."

In the first chapter of his book on Herzl, Bein reports a dream by the twelve-year-old Herzl. In his dream, Herzl was visited by "The King-Messiah" who took him on a flight to a cloud where Moses dwelt. The Messiah told Moses that it was for this child that he had prayed. To young Theodor the Messiah issued an order to go and declare to the Jews that the Messiah would come soon and perform great wonders for his people and for the whole world. This command is not unlike the one Moses himself once received from the Lord: "Come now therefore and I will send thee unto Pharaoh, that thou mayest bring forth My people the children of Israel out of Egypt" (Exodus 3:10). In the epilogue to his book, Bein indicates that the Jewish masses had transmuted Herzl into a king and a Messiah who was to lead them into the Land of Promise. Thus, the dream of the boy Theodor became true. Little wonder, then, that his motto "If you will it, it is no dream" was as much a reality for him personally as it eventually became for his people. His dream was to do something on a grand scale. The plight of his people convinced him that something drastic needed to be done. Yet this conviction was shared by many other Jews who nevertheless did not aspire to become the King-Messiah. He, however, chose to lead the people in this fashion. Why and how did he do it?

Loewenberg has provided some answers. The reasons consisted of a series of adverse emotional reactions stretching from childhood to adulthood. Throughout his life Herzl's tender, affectionate feelings remained closely attached to his mother and sister. As a result, the normal development of detachment from significant figures in child-hood did not reach completion. While sensual feelings were detached from mother and sister, affectionate feelings were not sufficiently de-tached and continued to predominate in his life. In other words, in the course of Herzl's life a split developed between the tender current of feelings and the erotic current. If this assumption is correct, it is highly likely that the father of Zionism himself craved to possess the Jewish people and even mother Zion in an unconscious attempt to play "fa-ther" or his mother's husband. Thus, the founder of Zionism could have shared the same unconscious drives which energized many a Zionist and which were discussed in the first chapter.

An additional outcome of Herzl's emotional split between the tender and erotic currents of feelings is also stressed by Loewenberg. This was the strengthening of homosexual tendencies. Since neither tender nor sexual women could satisfy all of his emotional needs while women who combined the two were either avoided or misperceived, others than women had to be sought for gratification. Usually this means men, but in the case of a person who aspires to leadership the source of gratification becomes more diffuse. Since the desired gratifica-tion is adoration by the masses, the coveted source of blissful feelings is the people as a whole.

Add to these emotional difficulties of Herzl the tribulations and sense of flaw which he endured at the age of twenty because of venereal disease and the anxiety which he suffered over a penile discharge, and the need for megalomaniac fantasies as a compensation is likely to arise. For these reasons, Herzl was first a gambler before he switched to political gambling. Gambling could compensate and even rectify. The gambler who hits it big and lays his hands on the jackpot feels like a daring risk-taker who could have gotten killed but who instead got away with "murder" and grabbed the big prize. In such glorious moments he rides on top of the world (or, one could say, on top of mother). As Loewenberg asserted after Freud, winning could stand for orgasm and killing the father while losing could mean castration or being killed. It's a "do or die" psychology, which is why the compulsion to gamble usually includes the compulsion to gamble with big stakes, perhaps bigger than a person can afford. The stakes were truly high for Herzl. He was compelled to step into the world's political arena, there to become a second Moses or a most notorious flop.

This analysis of the reasons why he chose to lead places Herzl in the same corner where many Zionist rebels were caught, with a repressed yet surging urge to settle scores with actual fathers and with a father image. The urge could remain alive yet dormant were it not for anti-Semitism. The external reality that called upon Jews to resist oppressors could provide Herzl with acceptable channels for expression of the internal and unconscious urges to overcome a paternal despot. Therefore these rich psychoanalytic speculations about the "reasons why" become plausible. The Herzl depicted by Loewenberg probably suffered from a split between his tender and sensual emotions. In all likelihood he needed grandiose actions in order to compensate for his feelings of inferiority and in order to symbolically act out on his oedipal urges. When, as happened frequently, grand actions failed to materialize and his action was blocked, he compensated in fantasy. Sometimes he was able, with a few strokes of a pen, to switch from defeat in reality to victory and even a manic grandeur in fantasy. For instance, after failing to enlist Baron de Hirsch to his cause, Herzl wrote him a letter on June 3, 1895, in which he said: "You cut me short with your polite derision. I am still likely to be disconcerted in conversation. I still lack the aplomb which will come with time and which I shall need in order to break down opposition, shatter indifference, console distress, inspire a craven, demoralized people, and traffic with the masters of the earth" (Lowenthal). Here is the almost instant transformation from dejection to a mood of triumph that takes place sometimes in manic states when the ego and the ego-ideal fuse together, as described by Freud in his book on group psychology.

The reasons why Herzl needed to become a great man do not explain, however, how he succeeded in becoming a charismatic leader. Here, two major ideas of Loewenberg merit attention. They deal with what happened to Herzl as he strove for leadership and with the manner in which he went about achieving it. The first is that his object relations centered primarily on ideas rather than on persons. A more "normal" individual, who loves other persons and who likes people in general, could not withstand ridicule or contempt as well. But a person like Herzl, who loves his ideas most, can tolerate large amounts of abuse and scorn without abandoning his cause. In the eyes of such a person, the frequent tribulations that he endures reaffirm the fallibility of other people rather than of his ultimate orientation. He who loves his ideas and his cause is often comforted by them the way an obedient, devoted child is comforted by his parents. For Herzl, ideas became as real and more loved than people. In a way, ideas can be more reliable than people and investments in ideas are bound to yield handsome returns. This happened with Herzl. His love for the Zionist idea reinforced his personal need to be a savior and thus rebounded to become love of himself. There is no mystery in this. After all, did he not deserve to be loved for becoming the grand rescuer of his people? Thus, love of Zionism (the Zionism that made him a Messiah) and love of self were mutually reinforcing. That is why he was able to invest so much energy in the cause to the point of being driven to his deathbed. That is why he could put such faith in the strength of the will and could clearly envision the Jewish state as already embedded in the will of the people. That is also why he could display such tenacity and persistence in the face of overwhelming odds, to the point of seeming at times naive.

What happened to Herzl is what also happened a long time ago to the biblical prophets. In them, too, libidinal investments in external objects were withdrawn in favor of inner feelings and ideas. Using psychoanalytic terms, the American psychoanalyst Jacob Arlow described what happened to the prophets as a regression from love to incorporation, from object relation to identification, from object libido to narcissism. This is like saying that the prophets' love of their great ideas was at bottom love of self. It could only be accomplished by falling back on primitive self-centeredness. Undoubtedly this is a regressive mode of living which can bring with it both greatness and trouble. It brought both to the Jewish prophets but it undeniably served them well. It was therefore an important observation of Loewenberg's that Herzl too trod in this path of narcissistic regression.

There is another outcome to a leader's overwhelming identification with certain ideals. In discussing group psychology, Freud once indicated that leading ideas can substitute themselves for leaders while leaders may take the functions of guiding ideas or of the ego-ideal (which Freud later renamed "superego"). This is possible because, as Freud emphasized in *On Narcissism*, the ego-ideal has a social side in addition to an individual side. The ego-ideal is common to members of a family, a class, or a nation and is therefore of great importance for understanding group psychology. As the above-mentioned substitution takes place, it results in a fusion between ideas, erected as ideals during the formation of conscience, and contemporary leaders. Just as these ideas once received an embodiment through the parents, they are now embodied by the leaders who become bigger than life. The leaders now stand for more than their individual selves and are able to command the people, who under their leadership become united like brothers and sisters. This is so because the people adhere to a common set of ideals which receive a common embodiment in the person of the leader.

The legendary Herzl was obviously such a leader. He became the ego-ideal of the Jewish people. Yet the people shared their ideals all along and not every leader could take the place of the great ideas or vice versa. The people must have sensed something in Herzl which let them complete the process. What they could hardly help sensing was the obsessive and unyielding dedication to the idea of the Jewish state. With body and soul Herzl believed in the feasibility of the idea. It must have come across so loud and clear that for a time messianism and the Messiah became one. The "King of the Jews" in the person of Herzl became a classical example of leading ideas and a leading person being interchangeable because both fulfilled the same role—that of the ego-ideal.

The second point made by Loewenberg concerning how Herzl achieved leadership is that he was able to bring the theater into politics, to make politics a drama. We have already mentioned how important ceremonial features were for Herzl. If a Jewish congress were made to look like a parliament of an independent nation, then it could become one. A well-staged drama can start on a make-believe basis but in the process evolve into the real thing. If the audience lives through it and experiences genuine emotions, then it leaves an affective and cognitive impact which lasts beyond the drama. Herzl not only sensed this; he even had the necessary talent for satisfying it. As a narcissistic person he frequently served as his own audience, and his private appreciation for his own performance probably sustained him like mother's milk. Becoming caught up in his own play, he realized that what was true for himself was also true for others. If a drama is played convincingly enough to give people a taste of the real thing, they may no longer be content without it. He also realized that in order for drama to motivate a whole people it must use a language whose meaning is shared by the people and whose impact on them is peculiarly powerful. In other words, an actor on a national stage must be aware of the potent effects of symbols and be ready to use them.

Herzl's awareness of the power of symbolism and the special role that leaders play in relation to it was emphasized by Joseph Adler. As illustration, he quoted a famous passage from Herzl's letter of June 3, 1895, to Baron de Hirsch: "And then you would have asked in mockery, 'A flag, what is that? A stick with a cloth rag?' No, a flag, sir, is more than that. With a flag you can lead men where you will—even into the Promised Land. Men live and die for a flag; it is indeed the only thing for which they are willing to die in masses, provided one educates them to it" (Lowenthal). All in all, there seems to have been a burning desire in Herzl to become a kingly educator of the masses, and he had the insight to act in a dramatic and symbolic fashion.

We know something about the underlying motives that pushed Herzl to greatness and the manner in which he tried to evolve his charismatic leadership. Yet we can learn more about Herzl and about the Zionist movement if we focus our attention on his own formulation of the nature of his leadership. Herzl explicated his conception of leadership in *The Jewish State*. It was anchored in the Roman legal concept of the *negotiorum gestio*. Roman law asserted that if a person is for some reason unable to negotiate his affairs and thus protect his property, an agent or *gestor* will direct his affairs until such time as he is able to conduct his affairs. Thus, for a while the *gestor* enjoys joint ownership with the people although the consent of the numerous joint owners is at best a matter of conjecture. This point troubled Herzl. Democratic representation was dear to his heart in spite of his personal authoritarian style.

Indeed, there was an issue of representation. The Jewish people were like a principal who needed an agent to direct his affairs. As Herzl put it, they were "prevented by the Diaspora from conducting their political affairs themselves." They were in a pre-state condition in which representation usually is a sticky legal issue in the affairs of peoples. Herzl could not accept Rousseau's notion of a social contract as the legal or logical basis for representation. Prior to the framing of a constitution and to the forming of state institutions, there cannot be much of a contract when one party to the contract—the people—is in disarray. The more likely logical and legal alternative is for the spontaneous leadership of a *gestor* to occur. His intention is to work for the good of the people and he is ultimately answerable to them. Yet the people's consent is only conjectured, and that included the consent of the dispersed Jewish people. Safeguards are therefore needed to insure that the *gestor* will serve the people's interests, not his own. In pre-state conditions such safeguards are as close to securing a consent as can be and are also as legal as can be in view of the prevailing conditions of lack of unity and the absence of a constitution. In emotional language, Herzl declared the necessity for safeguards in his book *The Jewish State:* "This gestor cannot, of course, be a single individual. Such a one would either make himself ridiculous, or—seeing that he would appear to be working for his own interests—contemptible. The *gestor* of the Jews must therefore be a body corporate."

Yet we know that members of the Inner Actions Committee were frequently enraged at Herzl's autocratic conduct and single-handed decisions as well as negotiations with world leaders. And we also know that he wrote on June 7, 1895, in his diary: "In the State there is only a *negotiorum gestio.* Thus, I conduct the affairs of the Jews without their mandate, but I become responsible to them for what I do (Lowenthal)." His language is clear. It says "I conduct," not "we conduct." In light of this clear language, the above quotation from *The Jewish State* betrays a suspicious emotional adamancy. Herzl's intense expression probably stemmed from underlying attitudes that were truly characteristic of him. His inner feelings could be restated as follows: The *gestor* is most likely to be a single sturdy individual who does not fear ridicule and whose motives are above reproach, whose life is dedicated to serving the interests of the Jewish people, and whose only self-interest or reward is the satisfaction inherent in leadership as such. With this frame of reference, one could genuinely aspire to be not only the greatest but also democratic. Chances are that Herzl wished to be both.

In discussing Herzl's views on leadership, Adler concluded that the central feature of these views is the core conviction that the burden of history rests on the shoulders of an elite group of leaders. What distinguishes these few leaders is their ability to express the inarticulate aspirations of the masses and to show the way to the realization of these yearnings. Deep in his heart Herzl probably believed in the primacy of one leader, king or messiah. That one leader was himself by virtue of the symbolism and legend which he wore as a mantle and which made him bigger than life. However, whether the *gestor* is first and foremost Herzl himself, as comes across in his diaries, or whether it is "the Society of Jews," as he suggested in *The Jewish State*, the fact still remains that his conception of leadership was elitist. It included some form of substitution of the people by the leader or leaders who stand in their place. As Adler pointed out, Herzl gave his conviction an original expression by turning a legal concept *(negotiorum gestio)* into a political concept. Nevertheless, the conviction that a minority could exercise the right to act as a trustee for the majority of people was embedded in the tradition of European revolutionary movements of the last three centuries. It is therefore interesting to compare Herzl's concepts with similar notions with which Russian Communists struggled in the beginning of this century.

The historian Isaac Deutscher has indicated that as the Russian exiles headed by Lenin contemplated revolution they espoused a doctrine which Leon Trotsky termed "substitution." He referred to the conception of the party's acting as a locum tenens for the proletariat, that is, temporarily holding the place of the proletariat. To Trotsky's mind, the process of substitution was dangerous. First the party would substitute itself for the proletariat, then the party organization would substitute itself for the party, and eventually not only would the central committee substitute itself for the party organization, but a single dictator would substitute himself for the central committee. In view of Trotsky's subsequent tragic fate, Deutscher concludes that Trotsky should have heeded the warning of his own prophetic utterance.

Yet in 1921 and 1922, Trotsky embraced the notion of the party's serving as locum tenens for the working class. A combination of events placed the party in the unenviable position of representing a would-be proletariat which the party itself would yet have to create. These events included a successful revolution but a war-ravaged country. The class of urban workers disappeared as the workers were driven by hunger to the countryside. Thus, the Soviets which gave the Communists their original mandate also disappeared, and the new postwar Soviets were not the deed of the proletariat, but the creatures of the Bolshevik Party itself. Therefore, they could not really deliver to the party a mandate from the working class. As Deutscher put it, the party members discovered to their great chagrin that a *force majeure*, a social catastrophe had turned them into usurpers but they were nevertheless unwilling to see themselves as such. The reluctance to be regarded as "usurpers" is understandable and so is the similarity between Trotsky's and Herzl's concerns.

Call the state of disarray of a people social catastrophe or Diaspora; justify the need for a nondemocratic representative as *force majeure* or as "higher obligations authorize him to act" (in Herzl's language); call the new but temporary form of representation locum tenens or *negotiorum gestio*—whichever name one chooses, one still has to call it a particular form of revolution. An elite group takes it upon itself to exercise some form of "substitution" and to stand in place of a class or a nation which it has still to forge. Presumably, once this new creation is accomplished, "substitution" will be dropped so that the newly united and organized people can represent themselves on their own. The "substitution" is therefore meant to be only temporary. It usually, though, becomes permanent. Deutscher explained why in the French Revolution it was the army which finally substituted itself for the people and did not relinquish control. He also discussed why in the Bolshevik Revolution the well-organized party was able to hold its ground and to effect a lasting substitution. Nevertheless, an initial belief in the temporary nature of the usurpation is a genuine revolutionary phenomenon. But there is always the danger of a temporary, substitute representation's becoming a permanent dictatorship.

Herzl realized this danger, as Trotsky initially did, and that is why he insisted in *The Jewish State* that the *gestor* should not be a single individual but the Society of Jews. True, Herzl had his personal megalomania of becoming the kingly representative of his scattered people, the grand necromancer who would single-handedly alter its fate. But his aspirations were tempered by the realization that his solo act on the international stage should be succeeded by a broader and more representative body. If his true successor were indeed to be the Society of Jews (his initial term for the Zionist Organization), then his solo act was bound to remain a unique marvel. Such an outcome must have looked appealing to a person of Herzl's ambition. Of even greater importance, such a succession would serve as a safeguard against usurpation by a string of single leaders. Herzl's notion of a Zionist salvation did not include the mockery of the subjugated Jews trading Gentile dictators for Jewish ones. Thus, his concerns were in effect the classical concerns of leaders who stand in the midst of an early crest of a revolution. Yet in comparison to Trotsky's, his fears seem somewhat more dramatic as well as less realistic. The Jews were in effect subjugated by others rather than in any concrete danger of being ruled by a Jewish dictator. In accentuating the democratic safeguards of the Zionist revolution, Herzl seems to have reacted to a danger that emanated from inside, from his own grandiose aspiration to become an incomparable modern leader of the Jews.

Many years later, somewhat similar worries preoccupied modern Israel's first premier, David Ben Gurion. In 1941 he said: "Perhaps sometimes dictatorship is necessary, especially during a big historical crisis. But there is always a danger in it because it is in the nature of dictatorship that it loves to perpetuate itself even when it turns into a destructive and harmful force." Ben Gurion was talking about democracy and dictatorship in countries other than Israel, and emphasized that a Zionist policy which relies on the Jewish masses could only be implemented in democratic countries. But he probably had in mind dangers to Jewish democracy as well. In those days, as the Jewish community in Palestine was clandestinely arming itself, the moral and democratic use of weapons became a central issue. Known as *to'har haneshek* (purity of weapons), it implied that weapons should be used only for self-defense against the Arabs and the British. According to the Israeli scholar and left-wing politician Meir Pa'il, this concern over the moral use of arms persisted even after the Six Day War. Also implicit, however, was a concern over a corrupt use of weapons by Jews against other Jews. This fear was inspired by right-wing Zionism, which created its separate underground military organization, the Irgun Zvai Leumi. However, it was the major underground organization, Haganah, which became the main offender. Thus early in 1945 members of the Irgun were hunted by special units of Haganah, imprisoned, and some delivered to the British authorities. Thus, because the Irgun refused to accept "national authority," its members were given a taste of what such an "authority" could mean.

The two related issues of the purity of weapons and national authority flared up again less than a month after the State of Israel was established. In spite of the cease-fire declared by the United Nations, and in direct violation of the commands of the Israeli government, the Irgun was bringing a shipload of arms to Israel's shores. The name of the ship was *Altalena* (a literary pseudonym of the late militant Zionist leader Vladimir Jabotinsky). At Ben Gurion's orders the ship was finally sunk by cannon fire off the shore of Tel-Aviv. Ben Gurion later praised the cannon and called it "the holy cannon." In these first days in the life of the new state the issue of national authority was much clearer than during the earlier time of the "hunting season" on Irgunists. Ben Gurion felt morally in the right and to him the cannon was "holy" probably because he thought that it was used for sacred goals in the best tradition of the purity of weapons. The goals were to prevent Jewish dictatorship by means of a right-wing takeover as well as to nip in the bud any possibility of civil war. Ever since the mysterious murder of the Zionist "foreign minister" Chaim Arlosoroff in 1933, allegedly by right-wing Revisionists, there had been fears of Jewish fascism. As for fears of civil war, they stemmed from the traumatic chronicles of the self-destructive divisiveness that obliterated the Jewish resistance against the Romans. Ben Gurion was determined to prevent a repetition of that historic catastrophe.

All in all, it seems that the issue of the purity of arms included an implicit concern with the possibility of Jews using weapons on other Jews. At bottom it was an issue of national authority. A somewhat similar issue in Communist China led to the famous dictate, "The party controls the gun." In Israel, the danger was not of Bonapartism or of the army's overriding the revolution. A multiparty system was taken for granted. The issue was of recognizing the "national authority" of a democratic majority coalition. That national authority had to be accepted, had to "control the gun." Ben Gurion stood by this principle and did not shy away from a showdown. As things stood at the time, the dangers of Jewish dictatorship were hardly imminent but neither were they unheard of.

In fact, one of the greatest achievements of the Zionist revolution has been its democratic character. Zionism therefore compares favorably with other national or social revolutions. There was no cause for any Zionist Trotsky in 1904 to share the concerns of the real Trotsky. There was no good reason to fear that first the local Zionist branch organizations would substitute themselves for the local Jews, then the delegates to the Zionist Congress would substitute themselves for the local membership, and eventually not only the Inner Actions Committee would substitute itself for the Zionist organization but a dictatorial president would substitute for the Inner Actions Committee. Jews were used to tyrannical political rule by others. On the other hand, self-rule was meaningful only in terms of community organization. There, the authority of the learned man, the *shtadlan* or court Jew, and the local rich reigned for many generations. But these authorities were losing ground. There was a political vacuum and there were yearnings for national political organization, but what patterns to follow was anybody's idea. Gentile institutions could be emulated, biblical hints of the old ways of independence could be sought, but above all Jews had to fall back on voluntarism. Operating in so many states and under political domains which were not their own, the Zionist revolution was unable to create a central organization which would effectively control the local branches. Such a potent central Jewish power might fit the fantasies of anti-Semites, but it was not political reality. Voluntarism was the key approach and its role became even more accentuated during the era of "the state on the way." No one person could control the scattered branches of the Zionist organization, not to mention the scattered Jews.

Dispersion therefore worked for democracy. So did the import of

European ideals about the rights of man which were added to the old biblical heritage of antislavery, both individual and collective. Therefore, when the Jews finally united in Israel and achieved political independence, equality of representation was preserved. Yet, although Zionism has been one of the few revolutions that did not betray its democratic ideals, its democratic character is now in some danger. Should Israel be tempted to annex territories against the will of their Arab inhabitants and without giving them full rights and citizenship, the democratic character of the state may be lost after all. It is possible to learn a lesson from history even though historical analogies are incomplete. Deutscher provided perceptive descriptions of how the Bolshevik Party killed free debate within its own ranks once it decided to forbid such free interchange in a multiparty system. Much agony and self-doubt on the part of sincere Bolsheviks were involved in the decision to curtail the freedom of others, a decision which inevitably resulted in loss of self freedom. Deutscher's illustrations constitute a lesson to remember. The present requirements of survival and security put an understandable strain on Israeli democracy, and additional strain may be imposed by motives that transcend the security requirements. Appetite for new territories is one such motive. Should such appetites lead to the permanent occupation of Arab populations denied political rights, it would inevitably affect Jewish rights. Denying political rights to Arabs not because of security but because of chauvinism would be a decisive step toward tyranny for Jews as well.

Thus while the potential for Jewish tyranny imposed on Jews is not a close danger, it is nevertheless within the realm of possibility. Should it be out of the question to give freedom to Arabs, the authorities would be hard pressed to give Jews a free hand in launching a political campaign to allow Arabs full political rights. It could happen in the future that as intra-Jewish debate and factionalism are slowly suppressed, a chain of "substitutions" would take place and at the end of the chain a permanent dictator could emerge. This probably will not happen, but if it should, then Herzl's worry will acquire peculiar pertinence. Once again a single *gestor* will appear on the stage. He will not be a pre-state *gestor* like Herzl, who wrote in reference to his scattered people: "I conduct the affairs of the Jews without their mandate, but

I become responsible to them for what I do." Rather he will be the State of Israel *gestor*, who proclaims to the gathered and united people that he has a supreme mandate. If it comes to that, the rationale invoked for the divine "substitution" is likely to include "security."

All in all, Herzl's conception of leadership yields two important conclusions. The first is that contrary to the current fashionable New Left accusations that Zionism is counterrevolutionary and reactionary, Zionism has been an authentic revolutionary movement. Its founding father underwent the classical soul-searching that typifies leaders of revolutions in early stages. The second is that out of his own megalomania, Herzl developed an acute sensitivity to the danger of a single leader's turning a temporary trusteeship into a permanent dictatorship. As his gaze turned inward into idiosyncratic personal features, Herzl saw something of great importance—the dangerous temptations that face revolutionary leaders who temporarily stand in for their people. There is reason to hope that this one intuitive apprehension of his, unlike many others, will not prove prophetic.

4.

Cultural Zionism

NOT BY MIGHT, NOR BY POWER,
BUT BY MY SPIRIT, SAITH THE
LORD OF HOSTS.

—Zechariah 4:6

While Political Zionism was making tremendous inroads into the hearts of Jews, it encountered resistance from Cultural Zionism, whose major spokesman was Ahad Ha'am. His real name was Asher Zvi Ginzberg, but he preferred to publish his Hebrew essays under the Hebrew pseudonym Ahad Ha'am, which means "one of the people." Born in Russia, he received both Jewish and general education, and became fluent in a number of languages, especially Hebrew. Ahad Ha'am published his first article in 1889, and from then until his death in 1927 in Tel-Aviv he was admired for his success in harnessing the newly revived Hebrew language in the service of the modern essay. He became famous for his devotion to the idea of a Jewish spiritual revival in the land of Zion, but his love for Zion dictated to him a different course of action from that of Political Zionism.

Ahad Ha'am's disappointment with Political Zionism, particularly after attending the First Zionist Congress, was summed up by the translator of his work into English, Leon Simon. Simon stated that to Ahad Ha'am the Zionists, just like the Sadducees before them, were trying to save the body but not the soul of the Jewish people. A similar though more elaborate point of view was held by the Israeli philosopher Nathan Rotenstreich, who suggested that Ahad Ha'am's main contribution to future generations was his insistence that there must be a link between the problem of physical existence of the Jewish nation and the question of the revival of the Jewish spirit. To Ahad Ha'am, a revival of the Jewish nation meant more than building up a huge concentration of Jews; the essence of nationality was cultural and spiritual uniqueness. The physical problems of Jews as individuals or as an assorted collective could be solved by political means, but the problem of consciousness of historical continuity, which he regarded as indispensable to an authentic sense of national identity, could be solved only by attending to spiritual and cultural rejuvenation. Both material and spiritual problems should therefore be given attention, especially since they are linked together. Rotenstreich was not particularly impressed with the solution that Ahad Ha'am suggested—a small cultural center in Israel—but was nevertheless highly appreciative of Ahad Ha'am's perceptive analysis of the problem that was facing those who took it upon themselves to promote a Jewish national revival.

Like Herzl, Ahad Ha'am evolved his own conception of leadership, which was elaborated in the two articles "Priest and Prophet" and "Moses." His notions of leadership were anchored in his understanding of society. He believed that both in society and in "the microcosm of the human soul" a play of forces is always in action. The outcome of this play of both volitional and unconscious forces is a "compromise" which yields interindividual and intraindividual harmony. This harmony, however, is a temporary balance of forces which masks the stormy clashes that preceded it. In the cultural and social history of the people of Israel, the prophets were the habitual disruptors of equilibrium. They tossed bold new ideas at their people and turned each idea into a "primal force" which triggers changes and effects a radical shift in course. The prophets were leaders with a massive impact who needed a fanatic personality and even a bruising style to help them reach their goal. That is why the prophet has always been a one-sided man who is interested in purely universal and uncompromised ideas. In a way, he has always been a narrowminded extremist, obsessed with what ought to be rather than what can be. Using psychoanalytic language, one could paraphrase Ahad Ha'am and say that the prophet had an uncompromising superego whose noble but extreme demands could not be met in full by ordinary people.

In contrast to the prophets, Ahad Ha'am posited the priests. The priests had a more mundane personality and their subscription to prophetic ideals was tempered by pragmatic considerations. The prophetic demands for universal and absolute justice, which Ahad Ha'am regarded as expressions of the unique Hebrew national spirit, had to compromise with the mundane play of forces that always makes people run. Therefore, after the prophet jolted the people with the primal force of a new idea, the priest would come and help to ease the process of building the inevitable bridge between the pure ideal of the prophet and the muddled reality of the common people. In psychoanalytic terms, the priestly personality can be characterized by the predominance of a reality-oriented but not very imaginative ego. The priest is like the modern garden-variety dull politician. He has his full share of what might nowadays be called "American pragmatism," and like so many politicians before and after him he is clever and manipulative but not a great statesman or a leader of people. The Israeli Prime Minister Levi Eshkol was such a person. He was known for his advocacy of compromises, and unlike the ancient prophets he was not a "one-sided man." It is possible to imagine him as an ancient Hebrew priest. His kind of leadership failed miserably during the tense days preceding the Six Day War. On the other hand, Moshe Dayan, the people's choice as Minister of Defense during that time of crisis, fared better. His leadership lifted up the sunken national spirit. It would not be easy to imagine Dayan or his mentor Ben Gurion, or the latest Israeli hero Arik Sharon, as priests in the style of Ahad Ha'am. In fact, it would be difficult to imagine them in any role within Ahad Ha'am's framework. The leader of Cultural Zionism was selective in his choice of historical precedents for leadership. The ancient kings and chiefs of staff were omitted because their leadership style could only foster the aspirations of the Political Zionists. Yet what the Cultural Zionists wanted—"the preparation of the hearts"—called for prophetic teachings tamed by priestly realism.

Ahad Ha'am's most cherished example of Jewish leadership is the greatest prophet of all time—Moses. In his article "Moses," he made it perfectly clear that the subject of his adulation was not the Moses of the scholars, not the Moses of those who seek historical or archeological truth and in the process become absorbed with less than significant details. It was the Moses of the Passover Haggadah, the archetype of Hebrew prophecy. Ahad Ha'am saw a similarity between the days of Moses and the dawn of the Zionist era. In both periods, a major transformation in the life of a people was sorely needed. A shift from slavery to freedom and the forging of the national bond had to take place. In the past this situation called for not just any leader, but the greatest prophet ever. It is not unlikely that Ahad Ha'am hoped to

become, if only in a small measure, a new prophet or even a modern
Moses. The perceptive Bialik honored him thus in 1903 in the poem
"To Ahad Ha'am." There Bialik described the Jewish people as being
suspended in an inbetween time, a twilight time of end and beginning,
destruction and construction, old age and youth. In their perplexity,
the people called for a prophet of truth to show them the way. And
there he lighted up like a star—Ahad Ha'am the teacher—and the
people saw their way out of the mist. This image of a star showing the
way is reminiscent of the pillar of fire that lighted the way for Moses
and the Israelites during the night (Exodus 13:21–22).

The hallmark of the prophet, according to Ahad Ha'am, is his
being a man of truth, yet an incorrigible extremist. He does not bow
to the world, but neither does the world bow to him. In order to exert
an influence, therefore, the prophetic demands must go through intermediary human channels. Thus, Ahad Ha'am clearly adhered to the
notion that an effective prophetic leadership must contain a priestly
touch. In forging his own style of leadership, he was influenced by this
conviction. Ahad Ha'am was also impressed by the fact that Moses
found it necessary to train a whole new generation for the life of
freedom. Moses must have recognized that to opt for an immediate
switch from the old to the altogether new is to embrace fantasy. A
prolonged period of "preparation of the hearts" is needed for the
psychological and spiritual adjustment. This was true for Moses and his
people in the past and is also true for Ahad Ha'am and his people in
the present. Thus, Ahad Ha'am faced with gravity what he considered
to be the great challenge of his time. The people of Israel were about
to undergo one of those fateful transformations from the old to the
new. To guide them through such a journey was among the greatest
of tasks that could befall a leader. It called for a leadership that would
tilt toward the side of prophetic truth and extremism but that would
incorporate the mundane, pragmatic talents of the priestly type. This
new leadership, or leader, would need the patience of Moses for a task
that was bound to last more than one generation. One may add that
the chosen leader, who has a rendezvous with fate, would also need no
less than Solomon's wisdom. This conception of the needed type of
leadership, as outlined in "Priest and Prophet" and "Moses," was a big

order, and as we learn from other articles by Ahad Ha'am, he ended by doing something quite different.

The great Moses, the subject of Ahad Ha'am's admiration, was not merely the Cultural Zionist of his era. He risked his life for social justice and even killed for it. He laid down the law and became the standard bearer of morality for his people. More, he organized his enslaved and disunited people and prepared them for mass migration. He fought political battles and managed to secure a half-hearted consent from Pharaoh for the Exodus from Egypt. After the Exodus, he led the Hebrew people in wanderings and in battles. During that period, other leaders helped the people to implement his ideas. They included not only Aaron the priest but also Joshua, the commander of the fighting forces. Thus, Moses' accomplishments were both spiritual and political. In contrast, Ahad Ha'am's vision was never as broad. He aspired to build a small cultural center in Israel. By necessity, therefore, he evolved a style of leadership that suited this particular aim rather than the broader goal of sweeping revolution. Since his leadership was tailored to his vision of his people, it helps to discuss his understanding of his people's plight.

Ahad Ha'am's diagnosis of the Jewish national malady was schematic and redundant. It involved a dualism of two extreme orientations kept apart in an unhealthy state. The required remedy was to fuse them in a creative synthesis. In "Flesh and Spirit," the pathological breach is between the material and the spiritual, or body and soul. There was, however, an encouraging precedent in Judaism for bridging the gap. The Hebrew word for soul, *nefesh*, refers to the unity of both the body and the soul during the lifetime of each individual. In "Past and Future," Ahad Ha'am warned of a developing schism between the two. His proposed synthesis of these contradictory time orientations yielded the conclusion that "the path of the national Ego" was largely shaped in the past yet awaits its completion in the future. Similarly, in "Two Domains" the developing pathological break is between the old and the new. In "Positive and Negative," the contradiction is between traditional systems of thought and new orientations which, in reaction to the old ones, totally negate them. The outcome, which resembles what is known in psychiatry as "negative identity," can be a final separation between the old and the new. This tragic divorce between old and new systems of thoughts leads to a corresponding separation between the adherents of each system. New negative sects are formed whose members zealously segregate themselves from the body of people from which they sprang, the way the Karaites did in the eighth century.

The frequent warnings in Ahad Ha'am's writings against the dangers of a wide breach between two extreme orientations show his obsessive concern with the dangers of Zionism. He feared that should Political Zionism prevail, one extreme orientation would triumph and the people be doomed to an abnormal, one-sided life-style, in which the flesh would dominate the spirit, the profane would rule over the sacred, the means would rule over the ends, the future would expropriate the past, and the new would eradicate the old. Thus the triumph of a Political Zionism that neglected the task of spiritual revival could bring about a new "negative sect," which would follow the precedent of the Karaites by separating permanently from traditional Jewry.

The remedy for preventing this irreparable cultural split, as prescribed by Ahad Ha'am in his "Two Domains," bears on his concept of the leadership role. It is "men of wisdom and foresight" who can detect the contradiction between the old and the new before the old is fully destroyed, and who therefore have the opportunity to fight this process while there is still time, that is, while the people are still bound by ties of affection to each of the opposing cultural forces. One duty of such men of wisdom is to understand exactly how the people can serve two contradictory orientations—which is like serving two masters who are at war with each other.

The answer that Ahad Ha'am, himself a man of wisdom and foresight, provided to this mystery was that the people remained unaware of the contradiction because they used what we now call the defense mechanism of isolation. As he put it, conflicting ideas about the past and present were being kept by a mental barrier in separate compartments. "Isolation" is the psychiatric term for a process in which people manage to avoid a conflict either between content and affect or between opposing mixtures of desires and attitudes by keeping them apart in separate or "logic-tight" mental compartments. It frequently involves a convenient scheduling of repression. When one attitude is expressed the contradictory standpoint is repressed, and vice

versa. This clean-cut separation enables persons to maintain contradictory wishes and/or ideas without acknowledging their logical incompat-
ibility, and even to behave inconsistently without being aware of it.
Because the Jewish people resorted to this defense, they were blind to
the danger that Political Zionism could cost them the tragic price of
a new negative sect. They clamored for a bright future that would bring
about the revival of the glorious past, but did not see that their actions
were accelerating their flight into a future that would be divorced from
the past.

Thus Ahad Ha'am, the schematic diagnostician of a fatal split,
also managed to pinpoint the defensive maneuver that prevented the
multitudes from realizing the duality in their culture. He believed that
one of the two extremes would triumph soon. In the face of such
danger, the duty of men of foresight is clear. They must become
therapists to their nation, must expose defenses so as to neutralize them
and to bring the inherent contradiction into the people's consciousness.
Armed with this new awareness, the people could then make an in-
formed choice. At such times, people are more likely to elect to retain
their ties of affection to both old and new, spirit and flesh. What is
more, they could opt for a creative synthesis of these polarities along
the established Jewish tradition of *nefesh*, which encompasses both
body and soul.

Throughout his lifetime Ahad Ha'am wrote and taught his ideas
with the hope of changing the psychological condition first of a small
cadre of elite people and second of the multitudes of Jewry. He diag-
nosed the dangerous cultural contradiction, unraveled the defense of
isolation that was keeping them unaware of this contradiction, and, as
an alternative to the pathological development of a new negative sect,
he offered the old Jewish promise of a healthy synthesis of dualities. In
reiterating his ideas during a lifetime of teaching, Ahad Ha'am was
neither a prophet nor a priest. What he tried to become was no less
than the therapist of his people, but what he ended up being was
merely a preacher. His Hebrew was admired by all; his ideas were
admired by some but followed by very few. This paucity of tangible
results casts him in the image of a somewhat more glorified version of
the Jewish *melamed*, or teacher.

For someone who adopted the style of a *melamed*, it was an

achievement to avoid the image of a *luftmensch,* or impractical dreamer, and to become an admired national figure. It was a limited achievement nevertheless. Although Ahad Ha'am obviously believed that he offered a synthesis of the old and the new, in reality his ideas smacked too much of the old. Preaching morality as the essence of Jewish nationalism must have looked to some Jews like prescribing sugar to a diabetic. While he was willing to add a drop of the political to his spiritual remedy, they were willing to add only a dash of the spiritual to their political one. That created some room for him in the Zionist movement, but not enough to mobilize the masses the way his admired Moses had. Ahad Ha'am's disdain for the political and for political leadership ruled out his becoming an effective modern version of either priest or prophet, not to mention king or commander. So he preached. Later, his preaching was preached in turn to Israeli school-children amid yawns of boredom. The issues he raised were valid in spite of his rigid schematizations. But his prescriptions were of questionable priority. Other things seemed more urgent. As for his leadership style, it was largely ineffective. A glorified version of the *melamed* was not the mode of leadership that the masses wanted or the times called for.

In spite of Ahad Ha'am's great reputation as a writer and the apparently high esteem in which he was held by many Jews, he did not have a large following. Thus the poet Bialik, in his poem "To Ahad Ha'am," exclaimed that the "teacher" did not have a large following. "Your hosts are not large, teacher." As has been pointed out by the American sociologist Ben Halpern, Cultural Zionism's central idea of consolidating the Diaspora around a spiritual nucleus in Israel appealed only to a minority of intellectuals who suffered from the undermining of tradition. Most other Jews sensed that the times called for the alternate orientation—the political one. To this day, ardent Old Guard Israeli Zionists like Yitzhak Korn object strongly to contemporary cultural definitions of Zionism, such as a willingness to help and receive inspiration from Israel while living in the Diaspora. In disagreeing with the nonpolitical and nonnational nature of this definition, Korn calls it "Pseudo Ahad Ha'amism."

Herzl and Ahad Ha'am, the two early Zionist leaders who worked

out their own conception of leadership, were very different in tempera-
ment, in their analysis of the Jewish problem, and in their understanding of the tasks of leadership. Herzl was somewhat manic and hectic;
he was alarmed by the problem of the Jews, and as a remedy he
subscribed to a fast revolution. Ahad Ha'am was of a more even temper-
ament; to him the major problem was not of the Jews but of Judaism,
and the healing effects were to be achieved by slow evolution. Ahad
Ha'am dreamed of being both priest and prophet, tried to be a national
therapist, and ended up merely being a respected teacher. In contrast,
Herzl dreamed of being the king-Messiah, tried to become one, and
succeeded. Ahad Ha'am's failure and Herzl's enormous success are
rooted in the different responsivity of the masses. In retrospect it is
clear that, like Herzl, the majority of them also gave priority to the
problem of the Jews over that of Judaism. Like him, they felt an acute
need for a quick revolution and craved for a kingly leader rather than
for one more teacher, no matter how good he was. Herzl read them
correctly. He had to. For an ambitious megalomaniac it was indispensable to sense accurately what the people were feeling. Without such
knowledge, dreams of messianic grandeur could easily turn into dust.
It was the greatness of the charismatic Herzl that he did not let this
happen.

5.

The Uganda Affair

IF I FORGET THEE, O JERUSALEM,
LET MY RIGHT HAND FORGET HER
CUNNING.

—Psalms 137:5

The biggest crisis that beset Zionism during its early years was one that later became known as the Uganda Affair. The events leading to the crisis began in 1903, when a series of pogroms swept Russian cities and villages, the most memorable occurring in Kishinev during Easter, when forty-seven Jews were killed and about six hundred others were wounded. The Kishinev pogrom left a lasting impact on Jews. Because of these massacres, intense preoccupation with questions of Jewish resistance and Jewish anger and shame arose to provide a foretaste of similar reactions following the Nazi Holocaust.

The reactions evoked among Jews were expressed with a piercing voice by the great modern Hebrew poet Hayim Nahman Bialik. In 1903 he wrote "On the Massacre," which gave vent to his feeling of impotent rage. He could find no appropriate vengeance for the spilled blood of little children, and he rejected as grotesque the idea that justice might appear, but only after the Jews were obliterated. He felt strongly that if there was justice at all, the time for it was now. He called upon the heavens to pray to God on his behalf, since he could no longer find God or pray to Him. In this poem, Bialik was mainly settling accounts with God. He settled his account with the Jews in his 1904 poem "In the City of the Slaughter." With fury, he lashed at husbands, grooms, and brothers who, from their hiding places, watched silently as Jewish women were first raped, then slaughtered by Gentiles. The sons of sons of the Maccabees fled like rats and died like dogs wherever they were found. On the next day those who escaped death went out begging and displaying their wounds to evoke pity and charity. The incensed Bialik called on the beggars to go to the graveyard and dig up the bones of their ancestors so as to use them as merchandise in the marketplaces.

In regard to this poem, the critic Mary Bateson has stated that it was necessary to confront the situation of the Jews' being passive while the Gentiles were violent and unjustly successful. Bialik succeeded in raising the consciousness of Jews concerning their passivity. As Bateson put it, his lines were quoted all over Jewry, so that Kishinev brought him not only personal crisis but also a sudden rise to fame. Some of his lines became very famous, especially those in which he eerily juxtaposed the slaughter of humans with the undisrupted beauty of spring. In the language of the 1970s, his raging messages can be expressed in terms of "Where was the Jewish Defense League?"

Bialik's poetry gave voice to a shock that was shared by most Jews. Herzl was so horrified by the news of the pogroms in Russia that he developed a deep sense of urgency concerning the need for an immediate solution to the problem of the Jews. This prompted him to support the ill-fated East Africa Scheme, which was better known among Zionists as the Uganda Plan. The territory under consideration, really part of Kenya, was mistakenly regarded as Uganda. The tentative offer by the British Government for Jews to colonize in the East Africa Protectorate, under British control but with some measure of autonomy, reached Herzl when he was already disappointed by the failure of his many efforts to secure a charter and a place of colonization. The last of these, a plan for colonization in El Arish in the Sinai, had gotten nowhere. The shocking impact of the Kishinev pogrom in 1903 made him decide that the Sixth Zionist Congress, which was to take place in August of that same year in Basel, should consider this offer. He therefore suggested at the congress that an investigating commission be sent out to explore the territory in question. Even this tentative approach, which did not call for an adoption of a colonization plan but only for the sending of a commission of inquiry, was enough to create a huge storm.

The significant issues involved in the Uganda Affair were already symbolized by the physical setting of the Sixth Zionist Congress. As Chaim Weizmann told it, the map of Palestine that had hung on the wall behind the president's chair was replaced by a map of the Uganda Protectorate. This symbolic action filled Weizmann with a sense of foreboding, which, in view of the subsequent developments in the congress, was fully justified. At first, however, there was a sense of exhilaration. The fact that the British Government made an official offer to the representatives of the Jewish people was to him, and others, like a reestablishment of the identity and legal personality of the Jewish people. Nevertheless, the initial enthusiasm died fast. By the time the first session of the congress was over, a young woman had run up to the platform to tear down the Uganda map. These external physical maneuvers were symbolic of very significant and highly charged emotional issues.

The resolution to send an investigating committee to explore the colonization possibilities in East Africa was passed 295 to 178, with 98 delegates abstaining. But so heated were the emotions concerning this issue that after the resolution passed, in spite of the stiff objection by most of the Russian delegation, the same woman who had earlier torn down the map shouted in French, "Mr. President, you are a traitor!" Following the passage of the resolution, the dissidents, including most of the Russian delegation, assembled separately and sat down on the floor in the traditional ritual mourning of the ninth day of the month of Av, the day of the destruction of the Temple.

As a consequence of the stormy congress, Russian Zionists who were adamantly opposed to the Uganda Plan convened in Kharkov in October 1903, less than a year before Herzl's death in 1904, and passed a resolution which challenged the Zionist leadership. The delegates who had formerly voted against the Uganda Plan called themselves "Zion Zionists." At Kharkov, a decision was made to demand that Herzl once and for all foresake all territorial plans for the Jews except those in Palestine and Syria. This was presented to Herzl in the form of an ultimatum, and in 1904 he had to exercise delicate diplomacy to avoid an open breach in the Zionist movement.

The Sixth Zionist Congress was the last that Herzl attended. He died on July 3, 1904, and the Seventh Zionist Congress in Basel was presided over by his colleague Max Nordau. After hearing the report of the investigating commission, which found the territory in question unsuitable for colonization, the congress rejected the East Africa Scheme on July 27, 1905. The commission members may have been eager to seize upon technical difficulties as a means of disposing of a plan that became a threat to the continued existence of the Zionist

Movement. In contrast, Zionists often flatly rejected opinions that judged Palestine to be mostly uninhabitable or to be able to absorb only limited numbers of immigrants. In Eretz Yisrael, the prophetic passion of conviction put the "experts" to shame.

The commission's rejection, however, was not the end of it. The tragic Sixth Congress, as well as the Kharkov meeting and the final rejection of the East Africa Scheme by the Seventh Congress, produced a reaction, mainly among English Zionists, of working for an immediate territorial solution even if it was outside Zion and outside the Zionist movement. This effort was led by the British Zionist leader and man of letters Israel Zangwill, who formed the Jewish Territorial Organization, the members of which became known as Territorialists. The goals of this organization were to solve the immediate pressing Jewish need for finding land suitable for colonization, whether in East Africa or other territories. It did not meet with much success; after the Balfour Declaration of November 2, 1917, when it seemed that Zionism at last had reasonable chances for a successful completion of its program in Palestine, Zangwill rejoined the Zionist movement, and the Jewish Territorial Organization was officially dissolved in 1925.

The polarization of the Zionist Movement into Zion Zionists and Territorialists suggests that the ill-fated Sixth Congress did not explode over trivia. Jewish history had reached a crucial crossroad that offered a tragic choice: giving up Israel or giving up a temporary asylum for the persecuted Jews. The historian and writer Barbara Tuchman has described Herzl's painful moral struggles in trying to convince himself as well as the members of the action committee, which convened before the congress itself, that they were justified in promoting a plan that "was not Zionism" and was not consonant with the original program of the First Congress. Max Nordau, Herzl's Hungarian colleague, tried to reconcile the contradiction between only Zion versus any territory at all by introducing the concept of *Nachtasyl*, meaning a night's stay or a temporary asylum. It was impressive that even the delegates from Kishinev, perhaps representing the Jews who needed a *Nachtasyl* most, were adamantly opposed to the Uganda Plan. To explain the nature of this stiff resistance, Tuchman refers to the influence of Ahad Ha'am's idea that Palestine is the only source of spiritual strength that can recreate a sense of nationhood among the Jews.

In defense of Herzl, the researcher Oscar Rabinowicz claimed that neither Herzl nor his British associate, Leopold Greenberg, ever considered dropping Zion from the Zionist program. However, his documentation about the East Africa Scheme, and his own conclusions, indicate that both Herzl and Greenberg may have been swayed by two basic principles of Zionism—statehood and nationhood—and were considering bypassing, or at least postponing, Zion as an immediate practical goal.

Not long ago the scholar Robert Weisbord raised the unanswered question: What would have happened to the Jewish settlement in Palestine if an additional Jewish settlement had taken root elsewhere? He especially wondered whether an additional territorial solution would have saved the Jews from the Nazi Holocaust. After all, Herzl was prompted to espouse territorialism after the Kishinev pogrom because of his intense concern for the fate of the Jews and a sense of foreboding about the future. This is a question which cannot be ignored after the Holocaust. Weisbord also indicates that in the late 1930s even such a militant Zionist leader as Vladimir Jabotinsky was already speculating on whether the establishment of such an extra refuge would have given the Jews a refuge from Nazi persecution at the same time that Palestine's doors were locked by the British. More recently, Dr. Herzl Rosenblum in his regular column in the Israeli newspaper *Yediot Aharonot* expressed his feeling that Herzl was prophetic in his insistent recommendation to establish a "night refuge" for the Jews, even outside the Land of Israel if need be. Rosenblum concluded that it would have been better to have a few million Jews in Uganda now, than to mourn the deaths of millions of slaughtered Jews who do not even have graves to bear their names. Thus, "Uganda" still gives Israelis and other Jews something to think about.

The Uganda Affair bears the signs of an identity crisis. Herzl underwent inner struggles; Nordau unsuccessfully attempted to sweeten the bitter medicine by introducing the concept of a temporary asylum or a night stay; and some Zionist delegates simply regarded the plan as treason. The defection threats by the Zion Zionists, the splitting off of the Territorialists, the preoccupations with the Uganda issue lasting to the present day, suggest that deep psychological conflicts were taking place. To further understand these conflicts we must investigate the concept of identity itself.

It is to the noted psychoanalyst and psychohistorian Erik Erikson that we owe a good share of our knowledge concerning the development and formation of identity, as well as the dangers of identity crisis and identity diffusion. "Identity" refers to the overall integration as well as the consistent internal organization of the many separate identifications, attitudes, and learned roles a person assumes. It includes an awareness of the continuity of self over time, as well as the continuity of the ego's intricate synthesizing and integrating methods which give rise to a sense of self sameness over time. It also includes a sense of uniqueness and sense of belonging to a group. Feelings of belonging to a group (religious, ethnic, national) and of being unique are important and must be sustained. Here Erikson followed in the footsteps of Freud, who asserted that the oldest human psychology is group psychology and that because other people are always so obviously involved in the mental life of each person, individual psychology is at the very same time social psychology.

One of the most important functions of a sense of identity is to provide a sense of self-esteem. If self-esteem is absent, a person experiences strong urges to disrupt the sense of sameness over time and to refrain from identifying himself with the despised person he has been in the past; a person he does not want to be. Thus, without a reasonable measure of self-esteem, a basic sense of identity is subject to disruption.

Sometimes when the mutual reciprocal interaction between ego functioning and social organization is disrupted, the outcome can be a sense of negative identity. Negative identity was described by Erikson as an identity perversely based on identifications, attitudes, and learned roles, which at the time were presented to the person as most undesirable but also most real. In other words, these are all the acts and attitudes which authority figures abhorred, but of which they never said that they were ineffective and impotent.

The tragedy of a negative identity is that it does not evolve through constructive building and integration of a body of new rules and behavior norms, but instead develops as a protest and negation of a set of established rules, paired with a search for the opposite rules. There is no happiness in the road leading from an almost automatic protest against the regulations of authority figures to an equally automatic, rebellious adoption of conduct that is the opposite of the rules and makes a mockery of them. This rigid adoption of behavior norms is a fruitless way of searching for authentic individuality.

The significant relationship between negative identity and the positive and negative ego-ideals was brought out in two articles by the psychoanalysts Roy Whitman and Stanley Kaplan. They defined the negative ego-ideal as the introjected negative standards of the parents and the culture. If a person finds himself engaged in a behavior that meets these standards, the resultant feeling is that of shame; he may perceive himself as a jerk, slob, klutz, schnorrer, sad sack, or schlemiel. The disappointment can be of various degrees, starting with shame, continuing through chagrin and humiliation, and ending with utterly intolerable mortification—at which stage a person may wish he were dead. The shame also gives rise to rage that can be directed either against the people who put the person in such an unenviable position or against the self. The positive ego-ideal consists of internalized positive standards of the parents and the culture. These are the things to look up to, emulate, and reach toward. If an individual engages in a behavior that reaches the standards with which he identifies, then the resultant feeling will be not disappointment or shame, but rather satisfaction, pride, and even an exhilarating sense of triumph.

Whitman and Kaplan underscored the notion that negative identity is ego-syntonic; that is, it is congruent with at least some of the general orientations of the person's ego even if it is not congruent with society at large. On the other hand, the negative ego-ideal is ego-alien, or totally unacceptable to the ego. The fact that negative identity is ego-syntonic (although it involves some self-negation) does not imply that it can provide the deep satisfaction and great pride that a positive ego-ideal can give a person who is at peace with all parts of himself and his surroundings. Whitman and Kaplan also emphasize that *negative identity can sometimes represent a compromise between a wish to avoid a negative ego-ideal's behavior and an inability to reach that of a positive ego-ideal.* In other words, when proud actions are utterly impossible

and shameful behavior is completely unacceptable, a middle road is a
rebellion against the status quo that takes the course of negative identity. It may not be desirable but it is acceptable; and while not being
shameful, it is very real. However, the price is undercutting one's own
roots by overzealously rejecting all the authorities that played a meaningful role in one's past.

An identity crisis is what befell the Zionists during the Uganda
Affair. Torn between an unattainable positive ego-ideal and an unacceptable negative ego-ideal, they sought a temporary refuge, a "night's
stay," in negative identity. This solution was finally rejected by those
who either did not want it in the first place or did not believe that
Nordau's solution would remain temporary. Their intuition told them
that nothing could become so permanent as temporary measures taken
under pressure.

The origins of the negative ego-ideal were clearly to be found in
the shameful Galut (Exile), with its related dispersion, persecutions,
expulsions, pogroms, homelessness, and helplessness. The positive ego-
ideal was also a well-defined notion for Jews, made up of Israel, Zion,
nationhood, homeland, independence, country, and normality and
health. After all that had happened, including Kishinev, Galut or
negative ego-ideal was utterly unacceptable. Unfortunately, Eretz Yisrael and a healthy Jewish nationhood were not readily attainable in
1903. Therefore, some Jews, like Israel Zangwill and also Herzl and
Nordau, were proposing a negative-identity solution in the form of
Uganda—at least as a temporary compromise. The Uganda Plan was
not what the positive ego-ideal dictated; it was not the ancestral land,
the beloved Zion, which unfortunately seemed unattainable. But it
implied no more Galut, no more accidental dispersion, but rather an
"ingathering" by design.

The historian Max Dimont once drew a distinction between Exile
(Galut) and Diaspora: Exile occurs by accident or misfortune, whereas
Diaspora is an extension and relocation by choice of a people. Using
these terms, one can define the Uganda Plan as an attempt to replace
the shameful, abnormal, no longer acceptable Exile with a Diaspora.
Uganda meant territorial congregation, political autonomy, and a more
normal life, even though not under ideal circumstances. Not particu-

larly acceptable or desirable, it was at least not a pipe dream. The British government had officially offered it—an act that made it seem real indeed.

Now we see why emotions raged so intensely during the Sixth Zionist Congress. An old, yet young nation, one might say an ageless nation, was going through an identity crisis. And a cruel choice had to be made. The Jewish people could flee from the negative ego-ideal of exile by trying to dash straight for a positive ego-ideal—the ancestral Zion—which seemed unattainable to many of them. But they could also flee from the negative ego-ideal into the embrace of a negative identity—a Diaspora, a state anywhere on earth, inhabited by a nation like all the other nations—which seemed attainable and real.

At the time, the passing of the Uganda resolution was seen by many as an obliteration of Jewish identity and the end of all hopes. But Herzl and Nordau were later swayed by the feelings of Russian Jewry and the subsequent Kharkov meeting. As for Territorialism, it never met with much success; Zangwill eventually reembraced Zionism. And so it came to pass that during the Uganda Affair, when the Jews took a desperate flight from the unacceptable negative ego-ideal of an abominable exile, they decided after much soul searching not to seek the possible—the course of negative identity through Uganda—but instead to seek the nearly impossible and unattainable—the shining positive ego-ideal of Zion and the land of Israel.

6.

Practical vs. Militant Zionism

ZIONISM WAS AT THE CROSS-
ROADS; IT WOULD EITHER LEARN
PATIENCE AND ENDURANCE, AND
THE HARD LESSON OF ORGANIC
GROWTH, OR IT WOULD DISINTE-
GRATE INTO FUTILITY.

—Chaim Weizmann

TIME IS A FATAL FACTOR IN ZION-
ISM. WE DO NOT HAVE MUCH
TIME.

—David Ben Gurion

A series of disappointing historical developments contributed to the replacement of Political Zionism with Practical Zionism. As it turned out, the German Kaiser, the Turkish Sultan, and the Russian Government were not very responsive to Herzl's suggestions. Similarly, the British Government developed cold feet after first displaying some initial interest in a colonization plan in El Arish in the Sinai Desert, and then later in Uganda. Political Zionism fulfilled its function of recreating a legend and creating a representative organizing body for the Jewish people, but investing energy in political activities at the higher echelons without much practical work in Palestine itself seemed to have reached a point of diminishing returns. What is more, the creator of Political Zionism was dead, and the storm over the Uganda Plan had naturally led most Zionists to focus their attention on the colonization of Palestine itself. It was now time for work from below rather than above, and for a slow and organic development of strength to create a strong Jewish settlement in Palestine which would provide adequate backing for Zionist aspirations. This orientation has become known in Zionism as Practical Zionism. Indeed, the colonization work of the Second Aliyah, or immigration wave, was taking place without waiting for a "charter." Outside Palestine, at the leadership level, the Jews were now having presidents rather than a king. The most famous of them, Chaim Weizmann, was a staunch supporter of Practical Zionism.

While carrying on political activities, Weizmann invested a lot of energy in developing executing bodies which would take care of the practical problems of the settlement work in Palestine. The organic growth of the Yishuv, or Jewish settlement, in Palestine (Weizmann preferred the term "organic" to "practical") later gave him more political muscle. This, coupled with his supreme talent as a lobbyist, eventually resulted in the famous Balfour Declaration. As a lobbyist, Weizmann had his full share of disappointments, but he also had his successes. His ability to convince others was to a large degree due to his skill in presenting himself not as a lobbyist for narrow interests, but rather as a person able to demonstrate his cause in terms of history, humanity, and fate. His efforts bore fruition on that day in November 1917 when Lord Balfour issued a declaration in the form of a letter to Lord Rothschild stating that His Majesty's Government was viewing with favor the establishment of a national home for the Jewish people in Palestine. The declaration also included the statement that nothing shall be done to prejudice the civil and religious rights of non-Jewish communities in Palestine.

The historian George Kirk has shown that, in effect, the British government here made two largely incompatible promises to two peoples without adequately consulting one of the parties involved, the Palestinian Arabs. The diplomatically worded declaration lent itself easily to mutually exclusive interpretations. Jews could interpret the idea of a national home to mean a predominantly Jewish state in the whole of Palestine, whereas Arabs could cling to the broad definition of "civil and religious rights of non-Jewish communities in Palestine," a definition that would include national rights. England could not possibly fulfill the promises which each side read or wanted to read in this famous declaration. It is fair to say, however, that the declaration held more promise for the Jews than the Arabs, particularly since it was the result of more effective lobbying by the former and insufficient British consultation with the latter.

So important was the Balfour Declaration in Jewish history that it immediately catapulted Weizmann into a position of unrivaled leadership. The British Zionist Paul Goodman likened it to the famous decree of the Persian King Cyrus in 538 B.C., calling upon the Jews to return to Zion from the Babylonian Exile. The combination of the electrifying news of the Balfour Declaration and the uprooting and suffering caused by the First World War prompted many Jews to seek their salvation in Palestine once again. Thus, the Third Aliyah, which numbered about 35,000, began shortly after the war, and together with the Fourth, which brought another 67,000 Jews to Palestine between

1924 and 1928 (mostly from Poland), swelled the ranks of the Yishuv as well as its sense of purpose. The Fifth Aliyah, which started in 1929 and terminated with the outbreak of the Second World War, consisted mostly of German Jews who were escaping the rise of Nazism in Germany. The arrival of approximately 200,000 immigrants doubled the Jewish population in Palestine. While the Fifth Aliyah was not characterized by the prominence of Zionist or socialist ideology, it infused into the Jewish settlement in Palestine such desirable characteristics as industry, punctuality, quality of work, and good manners. Although these German Jews were frequently the butt of jokes by their fellow Jews, they contributed markedly to the final quality of the Yishuv, which combined a sense of industry with an ideological zeal to produce a thriving urban society.

The growing Jewish settlement put a premium on developing autonomous and voluntary organizations to institute self-help in every area of life, from education to distribution of water supplies. This policy resulted in a new psychology, which is the crowning achievement of Practical Zionism—the psychology of *hamedinah shebaderekh* (the state on the way). This psychology was characterized by a high sense of purpose, deep dedication, and voluntarism. Without compulsion, and out of voluntary ideological conviction, the Jews formed numerous self-help bodies that would be ready when the day came to take over all functions of the government, large and small. These functions included, among other things, military power. Therefore, when Practical or Organic Zionism was beginning to bear fruit, including the fruitful psychology of "the state on the way," it already included the seeds for the next stage, which, although based on the achievements of Practical Zionism, would adopt new styles and a new psychology. Thus the creation of underground military organizations, the largest of which was Haganah (Defense), produced a change in the psychological and political mood. The local Zionist leadership in Palestine was now bound to assume a more militant posture in the struggle with the British toward the establishment of a Jewish state. It should be remembered that from the start the switch from Political to Practical Zionism —that is, from "charter" politics to "organic" building up of the land —represented a switch in methods rather than goals. Once the practical work was beginning to bear fruit, a shift to the more militant and maximalist demands of the original Political Zionists was bound to evolve.

Weizmann and other leaders of Practical Zionism worked outside Palestine helping to strengthen the Yishuv. On the other hand, the local Zionist leadership could better assess the strength of the Jewish settlement and wished to use it to influence the outside, especially in regard to the fate of Jews abroad. Thus, the leadership of the Yishuv and the leadership abroad viewed things from different angles and with different degrees of militancy. This generated tension, as well as a conviction among the members of the Yishuv that the outsiders, the Diaspora leaders, could not view things realistically.

The psychology of the "state on the way" was initially a result of the efforts of Practical Zionism, which advocated patience, slow pace, and organic growth. Nevertheless, it was inevitable for the builders of the state to espouse a more militant orientation as the moment to convert the state on the way to an established state drew nearer. Ben Halpern has indicated that as early as 1932 the Labor Zionist leader Chaim Arlosoroff (whose subsequent assassination enabled Ben Gurion to assume the role of the most prominent Israeli leader) concluded that Zionist national goals could no longer be achieved by gradual "evolutionary" or "organic" means. It was clear to Arlosoroff that sooner or later the people would have to risk their strength in order to bring about a new political situation. Halpern has also pointed out, and rightly so, that after the British White Paper of 1939, which severely curtailed Jewish immigration, the gradual buildup policy of Practical Zionism ran into a dead end. From then on, spurts of growth could take place only through illegal means—which meant militant means in the service of active opposition to the British authorities. Hence, Militant Zionism came into being.

The logic of the change is quite clear. The Jewish Yishuv in Palestine was increasingly growing, and became more and more a living and breathing "state on the way." The more ready the Yishuv was to assume all the functions of state and government when the historical hour arrived, the stronger was the swing away from Practical Zionism toward Militant Zionism. This trend was reinforced by the rise of

Nazism and a growing conviction that a refuge for European Jews in the land of Israel was mandatory for survival. The growth of the actual power of the Yishuv convinced some of the more militant of its members that it was time to aspire for maximalist goals and to work toward them with leaps and bounds rather than in the gradual fashion of Practical Zionism. In his autobiography, Weizmann indicated his objection to Herzl's Political Zionism because he did not believe that things could be done in such a hurry. This basic belief was the reason for the establishment of a new trend in Zionism toward an organic or practical orientation. However, in the 1930s and especially in the 1940s, the Zionist leaders of the Yishuv strongly objected to Weizmann because he seemed to be too slow and moderate for them. They felt that things should be accelerated, particularly in regard to demanding and effecting Israeli independence.

Thus, the practical men of action in Palestine who were doing the job on the spot went beyond Practical Zionism. They swung back to a sort of Political Zionism, which though less impractical than the original Herzlian one, bypassed or overtook the slow Weizmannian one. However, as things stood at the time, active resistance to the British during the Second World War was beset with a moral dilemma. To the degree that Britain was fighting the abominable Nazis, it was the ally of the Jews, but to the degree that it tried to curb the growth of the Yishuv in Palestine, as with the issuance of the notorious White Paper restricting Jewish immigration in 1939, it was the enemy. It was in reference to this dilemma that David Ben Gurion laid down his famous guideline on September 12, 1939. "We should help the British in their war as if there were no White Paper," he said, "and we should fight the White Paper as if there were no war." Thus, with the wisdom of a seer he summed up the growing sentiments of Militant Zionism during the 1930s, and thereby outlined the future policy for the 1940s.

The growth of militancy within the Zionist movement was not uniform. A switch toward maximalist goals did not imply the extreme of militancy as a means or the whole of Palestine on both sides of the Jordan River as a goal on the part of everybody. During the 1930s there was a fast-growing trend toward a more militant stance among the majority. There was also a minority which adopted a clearly militant course. The party that aspired to the maximalist goals of creating a Jewish state on both sides of the River Jordan as soon as possible and by any means possible was the militant Revisionist Party formed by Vladimir Jabotinsky. It made its first official appearance at the Zionist Congress of 1925, when its members adopted the name Revisionists because they demanded a revision of the Zionist policy of organic growth so as to espouse the original Herzlian goals of speedy work toward the establishment of a Jewish state. Eventually they developed their own separate underground National Military Organization (Irgun) which adopted the symbol of a map of Eretz Yisrael stretching on both sides of the Jordan River. In front of the map was a hand holding a gun with a printed slogan saying *Rak kakh* (Only this way). This symbol was self-explanatory: it laid claim to maximal goals through most militant means. Years later the Revisionists became active in political life in the State of Israel, and continued to follow a maximalist position. Therefore, it is no surprise that from their ranks came many of the members of the Greater Israel Movement which was formed after the Six Day War of June 1967. In the history of Zionism the appearance of the Revisionist Party was like the arrival of a flock of swallows bearing tidings of the coming of the summer of Militant Zionism. The mainstream of the Zionist movement soon followed suit, although more moderately than right-wing Revisionists. The new and more militant course was adopted by the Yishuv leaders in disagreement with Weizmann, and it led to the successful conversion of "the state on the way" into a real state.

Weizmann regarded the new trend with regret and never wavered in his steadfast and consistent opposition to active armed resistance on the part of the Yishuv against the British authorities. Here he differed in his opinions from Ben Gurion and many of the local leaders of the Yishuv, not to mention the superactivist Revisionists. The breach was a pronounced one. The leaders of the Yishuv believed that it was time to let the guns speak, and that voicing their opinions in this way would impress the British the most. Weizmann, on the other hand, was thinking about world public opinion. After the manner of a *shtadlan* —something which Weizmann did not want to look like—he took the position that in order to cultivate a good public opinion, which would be responsive to the pleas of the Jews, one had to avoid provocations. Hence, Weizmann's consistent opposition to militancy and his protestation that he had never believed that the Messiah would arrive accompanied by the sound of high explosives.

Ben Gurion, who saw things differently, locked horns with Weizmann over the issue of assuming a militant posture toward the British. Writing about these matters in retrospect many years later, Ben Gurion perceived that Weizmann's genius lay in his role as interpreter to the non-Jewish world. The political tragedy of Weizmann's life came when Britain reneged on its original intention to aid the Jews in building a national home for themselves. Weizmann was hurt and disappointed, but his deep faith in the British people colored his vision and prevented him from seeing that the days of Practical or Organic Zionism were over, and active resistance against the British was the order of the day. Such a shift involved a tragedy to the person who, more than anyone else, merited the name of Mr. Practical Zionism. However, as Ben Gurion noted with relief, the story of Weizmann's life did not end in tragedy: history rewarded him with the first presidency of the State of Israel.

With the growth of the "state on the way," the need arose for a new type of leadership: a leadership of the local Yishuv rather than of Jews in the Diaspora, of a wielder of power rather than a figurehead, of a premier rather than a president. Out of the few local leaders who served as potential candidates, this role was eventually filled by David Ben Gurion. His symbolic ascendancy to the premiership can be dated to the Extraordinary Conference of American Zionists which took place in May 1942 in the Biltmore Hotel in New York City. This was, in effect, an international conference which resembled a Zionist Congress, and which resulted in the so-called Biltmore Program. In the history of Zionism, the Biltmore Conference served as the major forum where the more militant stance, which had been growing since the late twenties, received official endorsement. This is where the younger Ben Gurion rather than the aging Weizmann obtained a grip on the reins of leadership and tossed out the challenge of moving from the stage of a "state on the way" to the stage of actually having a state. That meant adopting a more militant attitude, a willingness to negotiate with the British at the point of a gun if need be—something which Weizmann was unwilling to accept. It meant calling Britain to task, to make good on its promise of the Balfour Declaration, and, if necessary, force it to keep its word. It also meant political negotiations abroad, intense colonization of Palestine by legal and "illegal" means (illegal in the eyes of the British), and the building of a nucleus of an army for a possible final test of wills. It also meant, which was not foreseen at the time, that when the gratifying moment arrived where the "state on the way" became an actual state, as finally happened in 1948, the psychology of voluntarism would sadly collapse. With the change of structure, a change of psychology was inevitable.

After the establishment of the State of Israel in 1948, a sudden switch took place from the psychology of the "state on the way" to a mentality of officialdom. This was especially characteristic of the leadership on an intermediary level. Overnight many of the functions of the Jewish self-help had become governmental functions. Local economic and voluntary organizations had to transfer their functions to the local and state governments. Activities were no longer financed by voluntary contributions but by state and local taxes. Leaders rushed from their party posts, labor union posts, and Jewish Agency posts to occupy governmental posts. Being sent on missions abroad and having the use of official vehicles became important to the political functionaries. Living in extravagance at the expense of the state, while recommending austerity to the people, became the style of some of them. This phenomenon of leaders preaching to the public what they do not practice themselves was relatively new in Israel and therefore created public resentment. All this was both sad and inevitable. The psychology of a state cannot be the psychology of a state on the way. Voluntarism and ideology were bound to be deemphasized while pragmatism was bound to be accentuated. Eventually the new pragmatism of younger leaders such as Shimon Peres or Moshe Dayan was given the derogatory term *bitzu'ism* (meaning "implementism" or "executism") by the resentful Old Guard who valued ideology more. Nevertheless, new modes of dedication to ideals had to be found, modes which would better fit a developing technological society and independent state.

Militant Zionism, tempered by a realization that a Jewish state in

Palestine would be based on a partition plan as a result of compromise with Arab claims, succeeded in realizing the Zionist dream. It proved that Herzl was right all along. The state, which existed in the will of the Jewish people for a state, finally came into being. It was Ben Gurion's greatest historical moment when on May 14, 1948, he issued the State of Israel Proclamation of Independence in Tel-Aviv. In the name of a "natural and historic right" he declared the establishment of a Jewish State in Palestine to be called Medinat Yisrael (the State of Israel). Years later he described the core of his feeling at that historic moment as a sense of relief over the fact that at last Jews were responsible for their own destiny. The pride in Jewish hearts all over the world, the Israeli dancing in the streets, the grim determination of the members of the "state on the way" just turned into an actual state to defend it against Arab foes, are all well known. So are the subsequent Israeli victories that Ben Gurion later attributed in Herzlian fashion to the superior will and determination of the Israelis. The glory of that moment, on the fifth day of Iyar 5708 in the Jewish calendar, is hard to describe. It reverberated with the echos of generations of Jewish history. After that day, the image of the Jew in his own eyes and the eyes of others could never be the same.

7.

The Revival of Hebrew

DABER IVRIT—ATAH BE'ERETZ
YISRAEL!
(SPEAK HEBREW—YOU'RE IN THE
LAND OF ISRAEL!)

—A common Israeli
exclamation

The revolutionary changes in Jewish self-image launched by Zionism, which continue to evolve to this day, operated in several spheres. Territorial congregation in Zion, the ancestral Eretz Yisrael, was, as we have seen, of crucial importance. Yet equally crucial to the revision were two other closely related developments. The first is the revival of the Hebrew language; the second is the raising, in the ancestral land, of a new Hebrew-speaking generation that had never tasted Galut.

The revival of Hebrew as a modern functioning language with adequate coverage for the many facets of contemporary life has been one of the most symbolic and successful acts of the Zionist renascence. This revival proved to be a means as well as an end. It should be noted that this was not a case of reviving a "dead" language, as is sometimes assumed. As Chaim Rabin has reminded us, throughout the centuries Hebrew remained alive as a written language. Indeed, the practice of speaking one language but writing another was, until recent times, a prevalent one. Not until the rise of nationalism in Europe did the idea come to the fore that people should also write the language they speak, rather than relying on some international lingua franca for commerce, diplomacy, and science. As Rabin points out, Hebrew was not simply a dead language that was revived. What did happen was that Hebrew was extended from a written language used for religious and scholarly purposes into a spoken language applicable to daily activities. Thus it became a national language. What is more, because the Hebrew language carries with it a heritage of thousands of years of Jewish history, introducing it as a spoken language in daily life provided a needed sense of historical continuity that has proved to be beneficial for both the literature and the people.

The revival of Hebrew assumes particular importance because knowledge of the language carries with it an awareness of a long history.

First there is the biblical language, the oldest layer, which offers access to the magnificent biblical writings in the original. Then there is the talmudic Hebrew, more refined and versatile and very eloquent. Later comes the Hebrew in which philosophical treaties were written in the Middle Ages; this Hebrew is the language of science and logic. Also from the Middle Ages comes the beautiful poetry, which, following the tradition of the Hebrew religious poems prior to the Roman exile, expanded to cover secular topics. During the Haskalah period toward the end of the eighteenth century, when Hebrew began to be revived as a modern literary language, elements of all these layers of the language were reintroduced. The new novels and poems added a modern layer to the old heritage—with the emphasis on eloquence. This extreme dedication to eloquence led the American writer Robert Alter to talk about an inner contradiction in the Haskalah literature. The Haskalah writers assumed that the Hebrew language, if used with eloquence, is uniquely suited to express the eternal qualities of human nature. In fact, however, the intoxication with the esthetics of the Hebrew language deterred the Haskalah writers from honest self-confrontation and from attending in a more concrete way to the details and complexity of life. Some of the Old Guard Zionists in Israel still display this intoxication with eloquence. Their number, however, is dwindling; the younger sabras do not follow in their footsteps, but choose more mundane forms of expression.

In Palestine, as Hebrew became more and more a spoken language, it was enriched by the language of daily life, the colloquialisms of the newspaper, the radio, the documentary. By now, the ever-expanding needs of a living language in the twentieth century have resulted in the incorporation of all the various layers of Hebrew so as to cover every area of life, from poetry to science. Thus, by reviving Hebrew, the Jewish people provided themselves not merely with a contemporary symbol of a national identity but also with a rich heritage of literature concerning various walks of life dating back about four millennia. This is something that Yiddish, the spoken language of European Jews, could not do. Yiddish could not provide such a rich and ancient heritage, nor could it make the Bible in the original readily available to the Jewish people. This availability alone was like a shot in the arm for Jewish national identity.

It is important to reflect on the fact that the national implications of the Hebrew revival were clear to most Jews who were familiar with the Bible. Chapter 11 of the Book of Genesis relates how the whole earth had one language until God confused the language of the people and scattered them all over the earth because of their attempt to build a tower in Babel with its top in the heavens. This story caught the imagination of many people throughout the ages. In the first century A.D. it was treated by Philo in his *On the Confusion of Tongues.* In the fourth century it preoccupied St. Augustine in his *The City of God.* It is interesting to note that Augustine even attended to the question of what was the original language spoken before the confusion took place. He suggested that it was Hebrew, named after Eber, the great-grandson of Shem, Noah's son. However, prior to the confusion of tongues, Hebrew had no special name: being the only existing language, it needed none. In the eleventh century, Rashi, Rabbi Shlomoh Yitzhaki, the most famous commentator of the Bible and Talmud, also suggested that the original unified language prior to the confusion was Hebrew. Jews were familiar with the story of the Tower of Babel since all Jewish boys studied the Torah, including the Book of Genesis.

For Jews this story stood not only as an example of sin and punishment but also as an example of the idea that the dispersion is a natural result of the lack of a unified language. The confusion of tongues scattered the people all over the earth—just like the scattered Jews. But the diagnosis also implies a cure: *If a confusion of tongues can cause dispersion, a unified language can bring about an ingathering.* This of course is the heart of the idea of a Jewish national revival. The lesson of the story of the Tower of Babel, that there is a definite link between the fate of a language and the fate of a people, was not lost on Jews. Some of the Orthodox rejection of the Hebrew revival can be understood in this light. Sensing the ideas of national revival, which were looming behind the wishes for a revival of Hebrew, Orthodox Judaism may have objected to it as another form of *dhikat hakets*, or pushing to bring about the end. That meant another form of messianism, another heretical impatience that manifests itself through the unwillingness to wait for the Almighty to redeem the Jews, when and only when He so wills.

The modern revival of the Hebrew language began in the work of the Haskalah (Enlightenment) movement in Eastern Europe during the last quarter of the eighteenth century. In commenting about the Hebrew literature of that era, as well as of earlier times, the Israeli literary critic and author Simon Halkin drew attention to the fact that a unique feature of Hebrew literature was its interest in the Jew as a universal Jew. It was less interested in the particular Jew belonging to this or that country or culture. In other words, Hebrew literature, unlike Jewish literature in other languages, insisted that the Jew retain what Halkin termed his "historic Jewish identity." This insistence referred mostly to the less preserved aspects of this historic identity, namely to Jewish nationalism. Toward the end of the eighteenth century, if the national meaning of this heightened dedication to Hebrew was not yet fully crystallized, the secular revolt and the wish to flee the confinement of Orthodox Judaism was very apparent. Naturally, Orthodox Judaism did not take kindly to the extension of the sacred language *(leshon hakodesh)* from religious practices to secular use. The objections that were voiced made it clear that the revival of Hebrew as a spoken language represented a definite shift from a religious emphasis toward an emphasis on national, secular identity. In describing David Ben Gurion's life, the author Robert St. John pointed out that when Avigdor Green insisted that his son David Green (later Ben Gurion) study Hebrew and speak it fluently and as proficiently as Russian, it was considered a sacrilege by the holy men of Plonsk, who held that Hebrew was meant for religious services alone.

Nevertheless, it would be a mistake to regard the Hebrew revival of the Haskalah period as motivated only by antireligious sentiments. In discussing the Haskalah movement in nineteenth-century Eastern Europe, Dimont made two important points. One is that the choice of Hebrew as the language of the Haskalah writing was not coincidental; its intention was to escape the assimilation which took hold of the Jews in Western Europe whenever they wrote in the local national languages. The second point related to the particular form and content of the Hebrew writings: the choice of the historical novel as the preferred form, and the concentration on such elements as romantic lovers, brave warriors, and men of action. In Dimont's opinion, these writings were intended to destroy the image of the Jews in their own eyes as ghetto dwellers, as well as to imply that by political action rather than passively waiting for the Messiah the Jews could effect a change of their image.

Dimont's thesis pinpoints the aim of this literature as a radical revision of image. Weizmann had already commented that only the revival of Hebrew could lead to the shaking off of the mental and moral servitudes of the Jews in the Diaspora as well as a revival of the Hebrew spirit of old. Indeed, the choice of the historical novel as an artistic form involved a discontent with the present state of affairs, a turning toward the more remote but also more glorious past in order to find an identification and linkage with a proud Jewish history. It represented an attempt to overcome the anxiety and discontent that stemmed from feelings of historical discontinuity, servitude, and shame. In 1954, when the historical novel *A King of Flesh and Blood*, by Moshe Shamir, was published in Israel, the literary critic Kurzweil discussed this sense of cultural discontent and its accompanying 2,000-year jump into the history of the past in search of a sense of continuity. Kurzweil demonstrated gleefully how the book's attempts to impose present-day ideologies of progressive socialism on remote Jewish history resulted in artistic and ideational poverty, whereas in the parts of the book where this artificial imposition did not take place, the breathtaking wealth of Jewish history came to life with artistic authenticity. What the critic seemed to be implying was that even the most political, nonreligious members of the younger Israeli generation had discovered a need for a sense of historical continuity. This sense can come about only through an authentic return to the past, that is, a return not only to the remote past but also to the recent one, and not only to secular history but to religious history as well. Just as it is impossible to extract religion from Jewish history and still have Jewish history, it is impossible to rule out religion from contemporary Israeli life and still enjoy a secure sense of historical continuity—as will be expressed later in this book.

In view of the phenomenal growth of Hebrew, it is not surprising to read Ben Gurion's report (Ben Gurion and Pearlman) of how impressed the Irish nationalist leader Eamon de Valera was with the "miraculous" revival of Hebrew. He had reason to be impressed: the Jews did succeed in reviving their ancient language. In return, Hebrew combined with the homeland to give the Jews an authentic sense of nationhood, a rich historical heritage, and a proud self-image.

8.

The "Cute and Thorny" Sabras

DON'T JUST LOOK AT THE JAR BUT
AT WHAT'S INSIDE IT.

—Talmud, Avot

The ardent Zionists who dedicated their lives to effect a revolutionary change in the self-image and physical conditions of the Jews managed to accomplish all this through three major changes: country, language, and a new generation of freedom. The territorial battle resulted in Zion Zionism, the resettling and reclaiming of the original fatherland, the Land of Israel. The battle of the languages resulted in the ascendancy of Hebrew. These two revolutionary gains made it possible to achieve the third major goal: that of raising a free young generation, a generation that had never tasted Galut or persecution, and that would grow in Israel and speak Hebrew. The parents were not familiar with being brought up under such conditions and therefore could not foresee how it would turn out. This attempt to raise a new kind of Jew resulted in the marvelous first generation of sabras (native-born Israelis).

Of the origin of the nickname "sabra," the French writer Georges Friedmann tells us that immediately after the First World War, children of European immigrants, who therefore came from a cultured environment, did better in the Herzlia secondary school in Tel-Aviv than did the young native-born Palestinian Jews. To compensate for their feelings of inferiority, the young native Israelis would challenge the star pupils to peel a prickly pear (a thorny cactus fruit). It takes a proficiency that comes only with practice to be able to uncover the sweet, juicy insides of the prickly pear without getting numerous tiny thorns stuck in one's fingers. This may have been one of the original expressions of the sabra attitude, which Friedmann termed "action without ideology." Smooth peeling of a prickly pear is what counted, not smart cultural talk or good grades in secondary school. Because the native-born excelled in peeling sabras, they became known as "sabras."

One of the more obvious characteristics of sabras is their chutzpah. Chutzpah has many meanings, such as impertinence, gall, being fresh but smart, direct and charming, naive yet clever, and last but not least, bold and daring. The quality of chutzpah comes across clearly in many of the jokes about young sabras, such as those collected by A. Gad and A. Cohen. In one example, some children are arguing over their parents' great deeds during the War of Independence. One of them says: "My mother didn't participate in that war, but she sure makes war at home every day." Another story portrays a little kibbutz girl walking with her mother. Upon meeting a fellow member, she shouts at him "Ass!" "You'd better ask forgiveness right away," says her mother, "or I'll not speak to you." The girl then walks up to the kibbutz member and says "I'm sorry, ass." In another, an employee in a factory invites his boss to dinner at his home. At the dinner table the employee's son asks, "Mother, is that ass meat?" The mother responds, "Why do you think of something like that?" Her son replies, "Because this morning Daddy said that he was going to bring an ass home for dinner."

Teachers are often the butt of these jokes. For example, Teacher: "There is so much noise in the class that I can't hear my own voice." Pupil: "Never mind, Sir, you're not missing much." Or, Teacher: "I can't understand how one person can make so many mistakes in one small composition." Pupil: "Teacher, it was not one person, my Daddy helped me." Another story has two children listening to a lecture. One of them falls asleep and begins to snore. The lecturer addresses the other child and asks him to wake up his friend. The child answers: "You put her to sleep; you wake her up!"

These jokes illustrate the theme "Our sabras are cute and thorny," which used to be the title of many jokes and cartoons about Israeli children in newspapers and magazines. Thus a joke appeared under this title in *Ha'olam Hazeh* as recently as October 1971: "Mom, how did I come into this world?" "The stork brought you." "So it's true what the neighbors say about Daddy's being impotent?" A typical feature of such jokes is that they accept the infliction of damage by children on grownups as long as it is done cleverly and has the piercing directness of youthful innocence. Adults are expected to accept with resignation, even with delight, the thwarting of social plans, the hurt feelings, and the loss of self-esteem. The adorable impertinence of the youngsters brings such joy to the grownups that it more than compensates for the suffering inflicted by the stings of chutzpah. Indeed, the behavior of young Israelis, as manifested by these jokes, is characterized by a high degree of chutzpah or gall; it is direct, blatant, unruly, clever, humorous, and indicates a certain lack of sensitivity to social requirements. Thus the jokes reflect an insensitivity to the final nuances of social demands coupled with the perception on the part of the sabras that their parents want them to violate many of the family rules and social mores.

This disregard for rules, regulations, social norms, and good manners is summed up in the term *letsaftsef,* which means to whistle away or pooh-pooh. Sabras manifest their chutzpah by brazenly pooh-poohing away many things with *tsiftsuf ehad gadol* (one big whistle)—or so it seems if one pays attention to the "thorny" exterior only. This brazen attitude comes in very handy when important things are at stake and the hearty interior of sabras is touched. Then they stand up for home, country, and ideals. Their selfless and courageous behavior on such occasions contradicts the impression that they dismiss most things with one big whistle; rather it indicates that when it is really necessary, they do not find it hard to pooh-pooh away their habitual *tsiftsuf.* As we may recall, native-born Israelis are named sabras after the cactus fruit, which is covered with spines on the outside but sweet on the inside. Hence the theme "Our sabras are cute and thorny" in jokes and cartoons. The behavior of sabras as illustrated by these jokes is "thorny" indeed, but the implicit reaction of the parents is "Aren't they cute?"

Interestingly enough, this is not habitually supposed to be the attitude of parents. Outside Israel the reaction of "Aren't they cute?" is permissible for grandparents, who do not have to worry about discipline and can concentrate more on spoiling the children. For them it is quite legitimate to derive joy from the grandchildren, even though the joy stems from behavior on the part of the children that is antisocial. However, if parents rather than grandparents encourage the children's "thorny" acts, then it raises the possibility—among clinicians, at least—that the parents are engaging in acting-out behavior. In the United States, for instance, if parents encourage their children to tell authority to go to hell, then mental-health practicioners might interpret this as acting-out on the part of the parents—as well as the parents' vicariously living the actions of the children by encouraging them, consciously or unconsciously, to carry out hidden impulses and wishes which reside in them rather than their children. In Israel, such behavior must be viewed differently. For one thing, it is the cultural norm: Israeli parents who encourage their children to be thorny, by letting them know that in being so they are also being cute, are no different from most other Israeli parents. They may indeed vicariously enjoy the realization of their own suppressed or repressed impulses, but they are not merely yielding to individual temptation. What they are doing is actively carrying on the implicit or latent dictates of the Israeli culture as a whole.

It seems to be a cultural norm for Israeli parents, many of whom were born outside Israel, to be fascinated by the direct but frequently tactless attitude of the sabra who speaks his or her mind regardless of whether it is polite or not to do so. Subtle encouragement is given to the young for behaving in ways that are impertinent and at times result in a lack of adequate social sensitivity. Because of this, many young Israelis run into social difficulties when they go abroad. Sometimes older Israelis are bothered by this lack of sensitivity as displayed by young, and even not so young, Israelis while abroad. Thus, every so often articles or letters to the editors appear in newspapers in which people complain about the behavior of Israelis abroad. If they make too much noise at quiet beach resorts, or use worthless Israeli coins to buy things from vending machines, or spoil antiquities or archeological sites by inscribing names or messages on them, and especially if any of these matters appear in the foreign press or result in complaints to the local Israeli embassy or consulate, then of course the Israelis are bothered by it. But in the meantime, at home, the subtle education to be thorny and to disregard rules continues.

A culture that encourages disregard for accepted rules and norms can be expected to consist of disgruntled adults. However, Israelis, especially Old Guard Zionists, are very proud of the achievements of Zionism. Therefore, it would be a mistake to interpret their encouragement of unruly behavior as a subtle attempt to roll back the history of Zionism simply because of discontent with the results. On the contrary, it is an attempt to insure a continuity of the Zionist success as well as the Zionist style of doing things. Elon has already detected the peculiar attitudes of members of the older generation who in their youth, sometimes their teens, executed a Zionist rebellion against ferocious parental objections, but who now rule Israel with tight reins and expect the young to obey. Well, they do and they don't. They want obedience in the sense that they want the young people to carry on the Zionist renascence to which the Old Guard dedicated their lives. But they also want to see an impertinent disregard of rules, an attitude that will continue the rebellious style of the older generation.

This older generation once faced a world in which the rules were that the Jews were not a nation, but a dispersed and even cursed people, and that a Jewish state was *verboten*. Any sane person could see that it just was not possible for the Jews to have their own state. Thus Weizmann's famous comment that to be a Zionist, it is not necessary to be mad, but it helps. Yet the early Zionists went against the rules, against overwhelming odds, and professed that where a Jewish state once had been, a Jewish state again would be. It is important to emphasize the notion that going against the rules also meant going against the odds; this has been the essential feature of Zionism all along. It takes chutzpah to go against overwhelming odds with what may look like cocky self-assuredness, but which nevertheless masks fears and trepidations. When Militant Zionism clashed with the mighty British Empire, Zionists continued to feel that, as usual, they were fighting against overwhelming odds. These trepidations rose to new heights in 1947 and 1948 when the Yishuv faced the prospect of fighting the numerically superior Arabs. The creation of the State of Israel did not change these feelings. Although facing an ocean of Arabs, the Israelis were able to change the odds through a combination of strength of will and technological advance. They continue to feel, however, that only by supreme effort and dedication can they manage to turn successes against the odds into a routine.

Given this history, it is not surprising that the lack of respect for rules on the part of the young is sanctioned by the total culture, especially because it expresses the historical conviction that it was exactly this kind of disregard for both rules and odds which enabled the Zionists to remake Jewish history. Thus certain aspects of child-rearing practices in Israel foster the passing-on of the parents' rebellious and antiestablishment attitudes. Under the "establishment," rules set up by both Gentiles and Jews inhibited normal life. Zionism began as a

rebellion against these rules, against the status quo, against the authorities—both Gentile and traditional Jewish. Zionism called for changing
the rules and for establishing a new condition for the Jews, no matter
how much against the odds it seemed. It certainly appeared to be
against the odds since the Zionists were repeatedly told so; fortunately
they had the rare talent of knowing when not to listen. Thus in Herzl's
diaries we learn that immediately after the publication of his book *The
Jewish State,* acquaintances would stop him on the street and inquire
whether it was a joke or meant to be serious. In Weizmann's autobiography a quotation appears from Lord Bertie, who, after visiting Palestine in 1924–1925, wrote that the thought of making it a Jewish
national home seemed just as fantastic as it had always been. To the
Zionists, however, this idea seemed quite possible.

This flavor of Zionism, that the impossible is possible, is still a
living force in the hearts and minds of many Israeli parents. It continues to call for direct, even blatant behavior, and for a straightforward
rebellion against the established authority even if it seems against the
odds. For this reason, generous dashes of chutzpah in their young is,
in the eyes of Israeli parents, not merely "thorny" and much more than
"cute"; it is a hope and salvation as well as a radical change of image
shifting from shame toward pride. In view of this emotional and psychological inheritance within old and young Zionists, it is not surprising that some features of child-rearing in Israel express deep-seated
wishes to change the rules of the game—the game being Jewish history.

In discussing the chutzpah of the sabras, the Israeli writers Herbert Russcol and Margalit Banai characterized it as a national vice that
began as a pioneer virtue. Bold attitudes were needed by the early
pioneers who intended to turn Palestine into a laboratory for daring
social experiments. In fact, the main virtue of chutzpah seems to be
its survival value. In recent newspaper article entitled "Only By Chutzpah," the journalist Mila Ohel claimed that a small, weak nation
cannot exist except through chutzpah. Looking back at the history of
resettling Israel, one observes chutzpah in action. The historical declaration of independence of the State of Israel was also chutzpah, as is
its winning wars against the larger and more numerous Arab nations.
In the post-Six Day War period, when the future seems dark and

uncertain and Israel is dependent on other nations, it will take chutz-pah to save it from the Arabs, the Soviet Union, and the United States. For chutzpah has always helped the Jews in the past and will continue to do so in the future.

Besides chutzpah, there are other characteristics of the sabra that relate to Jewish history, including Zionism. While Israeli children study Jewish history up to the Roman Exile with some degree of enthusiasm, they are quite reluctant to study the history of the Jews during their almost 2,000 years of exile. Most sabras prefer the remote to the recent (excluding modern Israel, of course), Israel to the Galut, the Bible to the Talmud, and nationality to religion. Their historical view of their own heritage leads directly from an independent nation nearly 2,000 years ago to an independent nation now. The years that are skipped and rejected are considered abnormal, shameful, and bor-ing, as well as more or less irrelevant to the present national identity. Thus, although Russcol and Banai have described the sabra as being thoroughly bored with Jewish history since the fall of Jerusalem, it may be closer to describe his reaction as one of irritation and rejection of negative ego-ideals.

There are historical roots for these preferences. For instance, there is no question that the majority of sabras possess a great love for the Bible. The Israeli journalist and maverick politician Uri Avneri has made the comment that strangers are unable to comprehend how lively the Bible is in the eyes of people who studied in Israeli schools. To them, the Bible is closely related to present politics in Israel, much more so than the Constitution of the United States is linked to Ameri-can politicians or the Communist Manifesto to the leaders of the Soviet Union. Avneri believes that the only reasonable analogy is, perhaps, the influence of Chairman Mao's thoughts on current politics in Commu-nist China. For most sabras the appreciation of the Bible, much more so than the Talmud, stems not from religious sentiments, but from nationalistic ones that they have inherited from deep sources in Jewish history, such as the Sadducees and Karaites, as well as from their parents.

The shift of emphasis from the Talmud to the Bible among Zionists, and even more so among Israelis, except for the minority of the very Orthodox, is a meaningful one. It is no coincidence that Weizmann described himself in his early days of studying in the cheder, or Hebrew school, as not relishing the talmudic teachings but as adoring the teachings of the Prophets. The sabras have followed Weizmann, the Karaites, the Sadducees, and the generations of Jews that adored the Bible. Indeed, Russcol and Banai characterized the sabras' love of the Bible as having little to do with religion, but rather being a love for the archetype in the Jungian sense. However, the archetype in this case is not universal to all man, but refers to collective images within the cultural history of the Jews. These omnipresent and ageless images, these inner pictures and unconscious representations, stand first and foremost for national ascendancy.

Love for the Bible as an expression of commitment to national ascendancy is fine with the sabras, but has not been approved by everybody. Ahad Ha'am, in his article "The Spiritual Revival," expressed his objection to the new Zionist trend of regarding only the Scriptures, which were mainly produced in Israel while the Jews were leading a normal life, as the true Hebrew culture. Ahad Ha'am objected to this conception as being overnationalistic. While agreeing that there is a difference between biblical literature and the Talmud, he regarded both as an expression of the essence of Jewish nationalism. In his mind, this essence was a particular genius for morality and an unyielding propensity to apply it to daily life. The Prophets with their extreme insistence on morality, and the talmudists with their equally extreme insistence on the details of practicing this morality in everyday living —both are products of the Jewish national spirit. Ahad Ha'am's rejection of the one-sided preference for the Bible stemmed from his own conception of the meaning of Jewish nationalism. Nevertheless, he was able to recognize that in preferring scriptures and dismissing nonscriptural literature, Zionists were reacting to their own conceptions, false as they might be, in his opinion, of what constitutes a return to a normal national life.

Another characteristic of the sabra is a mistrust of ideologies, "isms," eloquent expressions, and lofty ideals, in preference to pragmatism. This characteristic of the sabra was not foretold by the parent generation, which was very ideologically minded. This is why the Old

Guard Zionists are upset with the *bitzu'ism* (implementism) of the sabra Moshe Dayan. Dayan, in turn, had his own point of view. Friedmann cited a speech by Dayan which depicted the old socialist ideals defended by the Old Guard Zionist leaders as having nothing to do with the kind of people who now live in Israel. Friedmann concluded that to Dayan, ideology is a luxury that developing countries cannot afford. In this instance, Dayan was indeed a spokesman for the sabra generation.

Occasionally sabras have become aware that, because of their own reaction to their ideologically minded parents, they may have disregarded ideology too much. For example, the American social scientist Melford Spiro once indicated that kibbutz youths, who were on the whole disinterested in ideology, routinely accepted the "party line" and displayed no deep understanding of politics. One young kibbutz member who expressed this idea added that this was the reason why he devoted little time or interest to the Arab question, even though he disagreed with the party line on this issue. It seems that too much party line and overexposure to "correct" ideologies has resulted in an ideological indifference on the part of the younger generation, at a time when fresh thinking is needed. Sooner or later, this ideological indifference was bound to be transformed into an ideological revolt. After the Six Day War, ideological questioning on the part of young kibbutzniks was highly intensified. Basic assumptions of Zionism and the kibbutz movement were now legitimate topics for questioning and revision.

Because ideology was preached with great eloquence to the youth, distrust of ideology led to the distrust of eloquence. Spiro described how young Israeli kibbutz children felt about their parents' being overconcerned with ideology. He detected overtones of hostility in their attitude that expressed itself in the derogatory expression *le'hafits Tziyonut* (to spread or preach Zionism). Spiro indicated that this expression, which the young applied to the old, essentially meant "forget your platitudes." One of the most eloquent platitudes of them all is the idea of the Jews being the Chosen People, an idea which runs deep in the Jewish consciousness. Weizmann in 1966 expressed his deep conviction that God has always chosen small countries to convey His messages to humanity. He believed that if the Jewish qualities of neighborliness, love, and devotion found in many Jewish communities would merge, and the efforts to implement them could be combined in one state, then civilization would be enriched by a great example. On the other hand, Israel's Foreign Minister Abba Eban commented in 1968 that young Israelis tend to react with embarrassment to the utopian idea of Israel as a special people. He believed that their dominant tendency is toward normality and being like other nations. However, Eban also believed that in the hour of danger, just before the Six Day War of June 1967, there was a shift toward the old visionary views of Israel as a special nation with a chosen destiny.

It seems that the mixture of ideas embedded in Zionism has resulted at times in two generations, each choosing what it wants, and arguing over their conflicting aspirations. The older generation, which is closer to Jewish heritage and religion, has clung to the idea of being "a light to the nations" and a "chosen nation," while most of the younger generation has relinquished any religious mission or any other sense of uniqueness in favor of the desire "to be like all nations." In short, the younger generation had its bellyful of Jewish uniqueness, which essentially meant to them an abnormal and peculiar history, and wished instead for normalization. Frequently, when Prime Minister Ben Gurion in his speeches supported the idea of a "chosen nation," the younger members of the audience dismissed it with the idiom "to talk Zionism." "To talk Zionism" as well as "spread Zionism" or "preach Zionism" are phrases which mean talking eloquently but impractically. Thus, relying on pragmatism and a wish for normality, which they derived from Zionism, the younger generation rejected other aspects of Zionism such as a sense of historical and religious global mission, and eloquent visionary conceptions of Jewish life in Israel. There is an irony in the idea that by relying on pragmatism, which they derived from Zionism, young Israelis dismissed such "impractical" ideas as being "Zionism." As a result, "stop talking Zionism" became a popular phrase for rejecting any eloquent but impractical idea.

The dismissal of certain parts of Zionism as eloquent impracticalities, as lots of boring "yakity-yak" that adds up to nothing, became known as *Tziyonut bemerkha'ot*, or Zionism in quotation marks, i.e.,

"Zionism." With the ideological interest in Zionism on the rise ever since the Six Day War, lately it has become increasingly necessary to specify on occasion that the discussion is this time about *Tziyonut bli merkha'ot*, i.e., Zionism without quotation marks. This signals a serious intent, a wish for a meaningful discussion about real things, and assures the readers or participants that they will not be subjected to the old lofty "yakity-yak" of "Zionism."

Evidently the parent generation was surprised—not always pleasantly—by some of the unexpected results of rearing a first generation of Jews "born free," so to speak. Before the State of Israel was established, the surprise was at the sight of masculine, sunburned daredevils. In *Thieves in the Night*, the novelist Arthur Koestler described the young sabras as perceived by their parents; they seemed like "Hebrew Tarzans." They were not cosmopolitan like their parents, not knowledgeable about world literature and European history, but they knew how to cultivate the land, and feared neither Arab nor devil. In short, they had ceased to be Jews; they had become Hebrew peasants. This perhaps represented a step backward in terms of culture and sophistication, but certainly a great leap forward in terms of ability to survive and have a proud masculine image—hence Tarzan. As for the idea of ceasing to be a Jew and becoming a Hebrew, we shall return to this subject in Chapter 17. For now, unquestionably the sabras are markedly different from the parent generation. In delineating some of the differences between sabras and their parents, Russcol and Banai emphasized that, unlike their parents, the sabras distrust all "isms" or ideologies, and feel surprisingly little hatred toward the Arabs.

After the State of Israel was established, and throughout the 1950s, the parent generation was unpleasantly surprised by what they termed "the espresso generation" or "the youth of gold." These phrases allude to the young generation's preference for sitting in cafes drinking espresso coffee or seeking entertainment or self-indulgence, which are characteristics of the spoiled rich, in preference to ideological preoccupations and implementation of pioneer virtues. In fact, however, it was only the nature of the pioneering challenges in the State of Israel which was changing, not the ability of the young generation to be equal to the task. Some of the elders' complaints simmered down after the 1956

Sinai campaign, where sabras displayed devotion and heroism, but the virtues of sabras only received full recognition from their elders after the June 1967 war. In the few years preceding this war, disappointment with the young generation was still high. The older generation, which expected the sabra writers to glorify Zionist achievements, instead encountered literary productions that depicted these achievements negatively and expressed disillusionment with "Zionism." Alter regarded this negative image as an inevitable result of the implementation of the Zionist idea of "normalcy," which was bound to be disenchanting. After the Six Day War, however, things changed. Young Israelis no longer displayed disinterest in or apathy toward Zionism, although they strongly questioned its present course, and showed a willingness to attack sacred cows.

There are growing examples from literature (Shapira) and from conversations with sabras which indicate that the older sabra characteristic of daredevil blatancy is receiving an infusion of the sensitivity, introspection, empathy, and ideological-mindedness that typified the mentality of the Galut—with fruitful results. By now it is clear that the younger Israelis are better able than their elders to empathize with the Arabs and their predicament. Thus, the sabras have begun to display not only their thorny exterior to Israel's neighbors but also their soft interior. Ever since the Six Day War, these notorious sabras, who used to be known as "Jewish Goys," begin to look more and more like Jewish Jews. The image of sabras as Jewish Goys had been an image of negative identity. The way from the negative ego-ideal of the passive and oversensitive Jews toward the positive ego-ideal of self-masterful Jews, who opt for both action and ideology, included a temporary detour through negative identity. The Jewish Goy, who out-chutzpahed the chutzpah of ordinary Goys, was not very desirable from a traditional Jewish point of view, but nevertheless was certainly real. Now the sweet, soft Jewish insides of the sabra are coming to the fore, but not at the expense of the thorny outside. The result, to paraphrase Friedman, is action with ideology: a new breed of Jew who may yet work out the baffling questions of the negation of Jewish tradition and the crisis of historical continuity.

9.

Schnorrer and Luftmensch

IF YOU DON'T WANT "TO
STRETCH THE LEG" (GO BANK-
RUPT), THEN "STRETCH THE
HAND" (GO BEGGING)!

—A Hebrew joke

The Zionist reaction to the course of Jewish history was truly revolutionary. The changes that Zionism hoped to accomplish were radical and transcended concern over the physical welfare of the Jews. This is the mark of revolutionary movements. They do not merely attempt to implement a change of conditions, but aim to forge a new breed of men who think and feel differently from their forebears. Zionism, too, aspired to a far-reaching metamorphosis; from its inception, a psychological transformation and a change of mentality from shameful bondage to proud self-mastery was a sine qua non. In this striving toward a new psychological makeup, the newly emerging Jews found two related concepts particularly abhorrent. These were the schnorrer and the luftmensch, or the beggar and the pipe dreamer. Both were the result of a restrictive environment that did not treat Jews fairly, thus pushing them to the extremes of unsatisfactory breadwinning. While Zionism's major battles against these two images were won, the war is not over, even in the Israel of the 1970s.

Sholom Aleichem's story "The Town of the Little People" points to the fact that poverty imposed the role of the schnorrer on the Jew. A schnorrer is a beggar, a pauper, a pleader, a person who degrades himself and forfeits his pride for the sake of a handout. He is insistent in trying to receive charity, but it usually eludes him: his many efforts frequently result in downright failure. What is more important is that being a schnorrer involves an acute sense of shame. Even an occasional success in soliciting a handout involves the price of humiliation. A schnorrer, after all, is someone who has to goad and cajole others into giving him charity and sustaining him because of his previous failures. Whatever the result, all he manages to do is experience a further loss of pride. Thus the schnorrer courts failure and adds insult to injury.

The notion of insult added to injury, which runs deep in Jewish culture, was described by the poet Bialik in his 1904 poem "In the City of the Slaughter." Lashing out at his people for their behavior during and after the pogroms and for exposing their injuries in public the way peddlers exhibit their merchandise, he raged that as they have schnorred in the past so shall they schnorr in the future. Bialik wanted his people to actively defend themselves against massacres rather than to beg for pity afterward. In thus exhorting his people to rid themselves of such negative characteristics as schnorring, he implied that they were capable of doing this, and much more.

Bialik's writing clearly identifies schnorring as one of the standards of the Jewish negative ego-ideal. The negative ego-ideal consists of the introjected negative standards of the parents and of the culture (Kaplan and Whitman). If a person finds himself behaving in a manner that meets these standards, he experiences feelings of shame, humiliation, and mortification. The shame also gives rise to rage, which can be directed both against the persons who put an individual in such an unenviable position and against the self.

In this connection, it can be pointed out that Freud, in his classical work *Jokes and Their Relation to the Unconscious,* used a series of schnorrer jokes to illustrate tendentious jokes, or that class of jokes which direct a rebellious criticism either toward the self or toward a group or nation to which the self belongs. In Jewish culture, jokes about schnorrers serve as a good example of humorous self-criticism by means of tendentious jokes. Naturally, the schnorrer does not like to perceive himself as such, and engages in psychological maneuvers that reverse the situation and make him either the giver, or at least not the receiver, of charity. This is well illustrated by one of the jokes reported by Freud. One schnorrer, upon hearing from another that the baron was in a bad mood that day and was giving no more than one florin to each beggar, decided to go and see the baron just the same. His reasoning was as follows: Why should I give the baron a florin; does the baron give me anything? Thus the schnorrer was going to see the baron, not for the purpose of schnorring, but in order to avoid giving the baron a florin that he did not deserve. With this kind of rationale, the basic decision became whether to give or not to give a florin to the baron rather than to beg or not to beg for one. Whitman and Kaplan regarded Freud's book on jokes as a storehouse of illustrations depicting standards of the negative ego-ideal, even though Freud did not use this term. They pointed out that one way to cope with the humiliation that arises from reaching the standards of the negative ego-ideal is the use of wit. That is what the schnorrer did in the joke above.

Israelis have mixed feelings about schnorring. At one level, it is considered clever and smart to feed the richer Jews in the United States with eloquent propaganda, which local Israelis do not take seriously and which results in the movement of cash from America to Israel. From this point of view, what does it matter if as far as American Jews are concerned every Israeli farmer who ploughs the land of Israel is bearded and religious and every woman in the Israeli army is a good-looking girl with an Uzi submachine gun? The important thing is to provide emotional gratification in return for financial aid. A joke on this theme was presented in the Israeli motion picture *Salah!*, in which the simpleminded hero revolts against the practice of changing the names of American donors on plaques in a reforested area, depending on which American Jewish donor is visiting at the time. A similar episode appears in James Michener's novel *The Source*, except that in this instance the American Jew is aware of the deceit and plays along with it in order not to embarrass his hosts. I recall hearing another joke in Israel during the late 1950s which reveals self-awareness of the uneasiness that stems from schnorring behavior. A European tourist is being taken on a tour of Tel-Aviv by an Israeli host. They pass by the Hall of Culture, an impressive edifice with a sign indicating that it is named after Mann. "Oh" says the tourist, "is that the famous writer Thomas Mann?" "No" is the reply, "it is Frederick Mann." When the tourist asks, "What did he write?" he receives the reply, "A check."

One way of counteracting this sense of shame was to regard Jewish contributions from abroad as "Jewish taxes." The underlying assumption was that there is a scattered Jewish nation, in which the Israeli group is bearing the heaviest burden. Paying a "fair share" to bear this burden is every Jew's obligation. From this viewpoint, while Israelis are being taxed with both money and blood, the rich American Jews are lucky to get away with only blood money. At any rate, the concept of a Jewish tax, including as it does a notion of fairness as well as national obligation, avoids the shame of begging. Similarly, one could hear in Israel such statements as, "It is because of us that American Jews can walk around erect and proud for having their Israel, just as the Italian Americans have Italy or the Irish, Ireland." Such remarks represent an attempt at a rectification of a shameful image through a redefinition that does not involve the concept of taxation, but of fair trade. In this trade, if there is any imbalance at all, it is the American Jew who should say "Thank you." After all, is he not "buying" from the Israelis a rare commodity that no one else on earth could sell him? The reversal of roles in this conception is worth noting. Just as Freud's beggar reversed his problem from that of receiving charity to that of giving charity to the baron, so do Israelis reverse roles through their use of the concept of fair trade. The American Jews are not donating money, for which Israelis might feel shameful; on the contrary, the Israelis are donating pride. This "charity" is already given by the Israelis to the American Jews, and cannot really be withheld. But the American Jews have the option of buying it rather than receiving it free of charge, for which they should be grateful.

Another concept at work here is that of "insurance" or "investment." Jewish history has taught that a safe refuge today is not necessarily a safe one tomorrow. The United States has its share of anti-Semitism, paranoia, and hysteria in its politics; its fascistic potential cannot be discounted. American Jews may feel basically that "it can't happen here," but Israelis know that German Jewry once felt the same way, and they suspect that American Jews are just as aware of it as they are. Therefore, in case the unimaginable happens and the United States becomes a dictatorship and starts persecuting Jews, isn't it good to know that there is a sanctuary in the State of Israel? One feels more secure knowing that if the worst came to the worst there would be a place to go. So American Jewry pays the premium on the policy and receives the insurance. The Americans hope they will never have to cash in their "insurance," but they consider it a sound investment. As is the case with transactions, no party need be psychologically indebted to the other and there is no question of schnorring for charity.

These redefinitions only partially alleviate the uneasiness that accompanies a humiliating role. As a young Israeli I used to hear people discussing the United Jewish Appeal (UJA) in terms of "all that schnorr in the United States." Later, when I read the poetry of Bialik, I was astonished to find him using what I had thought was a modern term. It took more than one encounter with his poetry for me to begin to sense the historical depth of the entire preoccupation with the idea of schnorring, something against which I seemed to be well defended. I can also recall reading with anger some articles in the newspaper *Ha'aretz* during the mid 1950s, especially by Eliezer Livneh, who assaulted the schnorring foundations of the Israeli economy. My own impression is that jokes about and allusions to schnorring were generally always mentioned with a sense of discomfort in Israel. With all the Israelis' self-congratulation for their own cleverness in soliciting financial aid from abroad, they could not be immune to the sense of shame they felt. This sense of shame relates to an underlying strong conviction that the time has arrived for the Jew to stand on his own two feet, plead no more for charity, stop schnorring, and especially stop converting his own needs, or even his semi-fulfilled dreams, into merchandise.

This feeling prevails even if the schnorring is only practised among Jews, i.e., by Israelis on American Jews. Bialik's admonitions to the Jews did not fall on deaf ears. Even today, although there may be objective justification for it, Israelis feel uncomfortable and somewhat ashamed about playing the UJA game whereby they export "Zionist renascence" in exchange for hard currency. These feelings receded somewhat after the Six Day War and may further diminish because of the Yom Kippur War. By spilling their blood and providing the world with the living reincarnation of the fighting Jews of old, the ancient Maccabees, the Israelis have more than compensated for the shame involved in being the recipient of donations. It is very likely, however, that if economic self-sufficiency, rather than fighting against hostile neighbors, should come to be first on the agenda, there will be a resurgence of the feeling of shame over playing the role of the eternal schnorrer.

At this point it is important to emphasize that the need not to be a schnorrer is a deep-rooted psychological heritage of Jews in general, rather than Israelis in particular. American Jews are motivated by similar feelings in relation to American society at large. Thus, one can frequently hear American Jews say such things as "There are almost no

Jews on welfare" or "We take care of our own." Many of the feelings that enter into such pronouncements are of a positive nature and relate to the pride that comes with reaching the positive standards of one's culture. Such remarks indicate that *Kol Yisrael haverim* (All Jews are brethren) not only in word but in deed. Yet they also express feelings of "no more": no more discrimination, no more second-class citizenship, and so on. The pride in the negligible number of Jews on welfare rolls is not merely a pride in the intelligence or economic success of Jews; it is a deep historical sigh of relief over the fact that schnorring, the condensed symbol of the impact of slavery on Jews, is at long last disappearing from Jewish life.

Another facet of the negative ego-ideal that Jews wish to rid themselves of is that of the luftmensch. The luftmensch (man of air) and *luftgescheften* (air business or pipedreams) are familiar concepts in Jewish culture that were brought to Israel from Eastern Europe. The scholar Nathan Ausubel dedicated the first chapter of his book on Jewish humor to the familiar figure of the luftmensch. He emphasized that the economic conditions and restrictions in ghetto life inevitably created the man who would constantly engage in fruitless money-making schemes when in reality the cards were already stacked against him. Sholom Aleichem's work vividly illustrates the end result of the ceaseless efforts of his hero, Menachem Mendel of Yehupetz, who is probably the most famous luftmensch in Jewish culture. Menachem Mendel's brain is constantly fantasizing tremendous financial trans-actions, stocks, bonds, millions of rubles, and quick new ways for making big money. Although he always ends up losing his shirt, he never stops dreaming of great fortunes that are won and lost, and maintains his hope that by his compulsive moving on from one failed scheme to another he will eventually be rewarded by a great success that will enrich him for life. Inevitably the endless dreams of the luftmensch result in thin air. The title of one of Sholom Aleichem's Menachem Mendel stories, "The Bubble Bursts," represents the sum total of the ceaseless efforts of the luckless luftmensch. In discussing Menachem Mendel, the critic Maurice Samuel pointed out that the predominance of *luftmenschen* among Jews, especially in Russia, was the result of complex psychological and economic interactions. He added that similar restrictive conditions can produce Menachem Mendels among other peoples, but that Jews had more than their share. He concluded that while Menachem Mendel cannot be regarded as a fool, he definitely is sick and is "the apotheosis of Jewish rootlessness." Unquestionably, being forced into becoming a luftmensch, who has to engage in *luftgescheften* for a living, evoked a sense of shame which rankled deeply in many Jews.

This self-image of being *luftmenschen* stuck with the Jews, and they became desperately eager to get rid of it. It still sticks, however, and they are still trying to get rid of it. At one point in his autobiography, Chaim Weizmann indicated that during a difficult period in his life, when his political activities were frustrated and his laboratory and books were neglected, he began to feel that he was in danger of degenerating into a luftmensch. Not surprisingly, however, a leader with such stamina as Weizmann managed to escape this danger. Nowadays, one can hear Israeli students in high schools or in the universities referring to the humanities as *luft* or air studies. If you choose the sciences, then you're all right; if you choose the humanities, you may still be all right, but you are entitled to joke about it defensively and say that you are a luftmensch or that you study *luftgescheften.*

The literary personality of Menachem Mendel, which is the epitome of the luftmensch, has left a deep impact on Jews. Thus the Israeli Old Guard Zionist Rachel Feigenberg-Eamri stated that this literary figure reveals the enormous danger for Jews from the classical Jewish heritage of the Galut. Menachem Mendel, the unrealistic dreamer, represents the psychological inheritance of the Galut as well as the danger of transplanting this mentality into life in Israel. In essence, what Israelis regard as Galut mentality is the psychological attitude of seeing oneself as the victim of one's fate rather than its master, and the passive acceptance of the condition of exile, social discrimination, economic restriction, and mental and physical persecution. Feigenberg-Eamri would like Israelis to remain alert to this danger. The implication of her writing is that the Jews have the potential to remain eternal wanderers and dreamers of dreams, embroiled in fantastic and groundless transactions all over the globe, persisting in living that way no matter what goes on in the world. Should this trend assume the upper hand and prevail among Israelis, then the Jewish homeland will merely transform itself into another Exile. Feigenberg-Eamri's writing indicates not so much a realistic danger, as the lingering effects of an accumulated sense of shame that the Jews have not fully shaken off. The image of Menachem Mendel as the luftmensch has sunk deeply into the minds of Jews. Israelis do not act like "men of air" today, but they may still have a need to make sure that the image has indeed changed.

A recent example of the Israeli preoccupation with the image of the *luftmensch* involves the Israeli Air Force. In 1970 there appeared in the Israeli newspaper *Yediot Aharonot* an article by a former member of the underground Fighters for Israel's Freedom and now a journalist, Yisrael Eldad, entitled "The Air Force Against Menachem Mendel." In the article, Eldad put forth the idea that a redemption of the image of Menachem Mendel, the luftmensch who loves to engage in *luftgescheften,* has taken place in Israel. In order to erase this ancient shame, the Israeli Jews have based their life in their ancestral land not on thin air, but on real things. Thus in contrast to the thin-air transactions of their parents, the Israeli Jews have established the air force of the sons: "Our Air Force redeems us for our *luftgescheften.*" A further thought expressed in the article is that even though the sons of sons of Menachem Mendel of Yehupetz are the best pilots in the world and anything but *luftmenschen,* somehow the Menachem Mendel contamination has caught up with some Israeli youth, who engage in the kind of *luftgescheften* that has proven itself bankrupt. Like Feigenberg-Eamri, Eldad in his article sounds the alarm over the fact that Israel still has many Menachem Mendels, even if they now go by Hebrew names.

The vigilant attitude which calls for awareness of the fact that behind Hebrew names may hide the same old Jews characterizes the Canaanite movement, which will be discussed in Chapter 17. The Canaanites have traveled the route of negative identity to its bitter end, and consequently engage in almost automatic rebellious adoption of ways of conduct that contradict the Jewish past. To them there is not, and has never been, a Jewish nation, but there is, and always has been, a Hebrew nation, which in the course of time became afflicted with the disease of Judaism. This disease consists of the corrupting misconception that a nation can exist, not on the basis of its own language and its own country, but on the basis of religion. One can conclude from Eldad's article that the fear of Galut mentality can be found not only among Canaanites but also in many other quarters, including those of hard-liners who nowadays support the Greater Israel movement. Eldad attributed Galut mentality to those Israelis who advocated negotiating with Nasser and Arafat. Seeing the danger of Galut mentality lingering on in Israel, he asked: "Has Tel-Aviv become like Yehupetz?"

There is something both tragic and comic in this obsessive fear of the danger of Galut mentality lingering on and spoiling the success of the Zionist achievements. In spite of the extensive revision of Jewish self-image as brought about by the creation of the State of Israel, there is still compelling need to contrast the old *luftgescheften* with the new form of air transactions, the air force, so as to ensure the survival of the new Israeli self-image. Unlike the old pipe dreams and preoccupations of the *luftmenschen*, the new Israeli Air Force is real and solid and does not evaporate into thin air. It has to be ready to tackle other air forces and missile complexes. This is a deadly game in which human lives, and possibly even the fate of the Israeli nation, are at stake. However, it is somewhat pathetic to think that the Israeli Air Force, which, pilot for pilot, is probably the best in the world, has to use its American-made Phantoms not only against Russian MIGs but also against phantoms that keep emerging from the past. Menachem Mendel rides again, and Tel-Aviv needs to be protected, not only against attacks from Cairo but also from Yehupetz. From this emotional outlook, what good would it do to successfully tackle the "cowardly" Arabs, the "sly" Russians, and the "corrupt" Americans, if that would only ensure the survival of an Israel whose citizens are mostly Menachem Mendels with Hebrew names? Luckily, the alert Israeli Air Force can shield Israelis from all enemies, including the Jewish phantoms from the past. On Air Force Day, the aerial demonstrations are reported in Israeli newspapers under such headings as *Mashak Haknafayim Shel "Yahadut Hashririm"* (The Rustle of the Wings of "Muscular Judaism"). There could not be a clearer definition of the difference between the old and the new. There is no thin-air quality to the rustle of wings of Israeli airplanes, a rustle that could even escalate into a sonic boom. Muscular Judaism keeps Menachem Mendel at bay.

Yet overreliance on the new type of *luftgescheften*, the best air force in the world, represents an overreaction to the old Jewish image of luftmensch on the part of those Israelis who have not yet freed themselves of this image. The force of steel is indispensable when finally needed, but willingness to negotiate even with hated Arab leaders, such as Yasir Arafat, is not weakness. Being scorched with a sense of shame over the old image of the luftmensch should not lead to a misapplication of the new *luftgescheften* of steel. Such a misapplication carries with it the danger that everything will turn into thin air, that the whole Middle East will become a burst bubble, and that the Phantom jets will turn into real phantoms.

10.

Jewish Self-Image and Perception of Gentiles

BEWARE OF THE GOYIM, HIS
ELDERS TOLD JACOB,
. . . THEY ARE GOYIM,
FOES OF THE FAITH,
BEINGS OF DARKNESS,
DRUNKARDS AND BULLIES,
SWIFT WITH THE FIST OR THE
BLUDGEON,
MANY IN SPECIES, BUT ALL
ENGENDERED OF GOD FOR OUR
SINS,
AND MANY AND STRANGE THEIR
IDOLATRIES,
BUT THE WORST OF THE GOYIM
ARE THE
CREATURES CALLED
CHRISTIANS.

—Israel Zangwill

One form of the Zionist rebellion against tradition took the form of turning away from books and studies in favor of engaging in physical work, even with bare hands if need be. For too long in Jewish history only working with the head had been regarded as fruitful, while working with the hands had been considered shameful, degrading, or at least of secondary importance.

The roots of this tradition may lie in the old biblical phrase: "The voice is the voice of Jacob, but the hands are the hands of Esau" (Genesis 27:22). As we may recall, Jacob the tent dweller, who used his head, outsmarted Esau the skilled hunter, who used his hands, and cheated Esau out of his inheritance, Isaac's blessing. The blessing was the birthright of Esau by virtue of his being the first-born child. In Jewish tradition, Jacob came to symbolize the Jews and Esau the Gentiles. Thus, an image of contrasting roles was formed whereby the Jews were supposed to use their heads and the Gentiles their muscles. Jacob's voice and Esau's hands are therefore well-understood and condensed Jewish symbols for role distinctions between Jew and Gentile.

These role distinctions received expression in a folk song called "Jacob and Esau" by the poet Bialik. In this song, while Jacob spends his time praising the Lord and devoting himself to his family, Esau spends his time drinking and beating his wife. Thus, the superior Jew uses his head in a variety of worthwhile pursuits, both divine and mundane, while the inferior Gentile uses his hands in degrading activities. When I was a small boy in Haifa my father taught me a Yiddish folk song which expressed sentiments similar to those voiced by Bialik. The song can be translated from Yiddish as follows:

> Oy, Oy, Oy,
> A drunkard is a Goy.

Drunk he is,
Drink he wants,
A drunkard is a Goy.

My mother did not take kindly to the song; she believed that it fostered
wrong attitudes and that Jews should not be singing like that about
Gentiles, and she tried to discourage my father, my brother, and me
from singing it. However, she did not succeed. My brother and I used
to wink at each other with a tacit understanding. We felt that Mother
could be right as far as the letter of the law is concerned, but she was
interpreting it too strictly. Of course, no one pretended it was exemplary behavior, but it could do no harm for us every so often to laugh
at the thought of drunken Goys.

The perception of the Gentile and the Jew as menial and cerebral,
respectively, finds an analogous expression in another of Bialik's poems,
"On the Threshold of the House of Study." In the poem, a devoted
student of the Talmud asserts that he has not taught his arm to hit with
a fist, nor did he exhaust himself in drinking and prostitution. His
pursuits were of a different nature. His booty was that of righteousness
and his hunt was one of justice. This means that, if Jacob the tent
dweller is in any respect a skillful hunter, then his hunt and booty are
both justice. The allusion to Esau the hunter, and thereby to the
biblical story of Jacob and Esau, is clear. Also clear is Bialik's verdict:
Unlike the Goy who exhausts himself in wine, women, and the use of
his fists, the Jewish hero uses his head in dedication to God and justice.
The modern Hebrew poet was not merely speaking for himself. As on
many other issues, he was expressing the attitude of his people: "The
voice is the voice of Jacob, but the hands are the hands of Esau."

There are historical roots for this polarization of images between
Jacob and Esau, or between Jews and Gentiles. Dimont postulated that
the life of the Jews in either the city ghetto or the rural shtetl (village)
accentuated the psychological gap between Jews and Gentiles. In his
opinion, it was impossible for Jewish children not to sense early in life
the difference between their values and those of the neighboring Gentile children playing barefoot in the streets and barnyards. To Jewish
children, intellectual, scholarly, and spiritual pursuits became identified

as Jewish values, whereas sensual, gross, and menial preoccupations became identified as Gentile. Dimont therefore maintained that no matter how much contempt Gentiles had for Jews, they in turn were viewed by Jews with even greater contempt.

This whole issue is fraught with dialectics. Throughout their history, the Jews, or People of the Book, entertained feelings of superiority over the Gentiles who did not foster the popular tradition of learning as the Jews did. It therefore became a prevalent notion among Jews that they are supposed to use their heads while the Gentiles do the dirty work. Theodor Herzl was intuitively aware of both the Jewish conviction of superiority and their underlying feelings of inferiority and humiliation. In Barbara Tuchman's opinion, Herzl's personality reached out to a deep underlying conviction of superiority in Jewry, a conviction hidden beneath centuries of humiliation. One may add that he was also aware of the other side of the coin. With great insight, Herzl remarked in his diary of July 22, 1895, under the title, "Item on National Psychology," that the Jews being a despised people are hungry for *koved* (honor), and therefore by catering to it, one could lead them.

In relation to underlying feelings of Jewish inferiority, it is important to underscore the fact that with sufficient feelings of superiority and pride, people are able to put up with other feelings of inferiority and humiliation. They can tolerate a mixed score as long as there is sufficient compensation, not to mention overcompensation, for the feelings of inadequacy. Toward the end of the nineteenth century, however, doubts started to creep in as to who was faring better. Gentiles seemed to have geographic roots, some autonomy, and national identity; in short, they had something to fall back on for a measure of security and self-respect. What is more, they seemed to flourish in both material and spiritual cultures, and had great institutions of learning. On the other hand, the Jews, with all the use of their heads, did not have their own country as most other nations did. When it came to using their hands they were largely schlemiels, frequently due to their being barred from professions that required physical work. This verdict, by the way, reflects what was a prevalent notion and a general feeling in the minds of many Jews; it is not a statement of fact concerning the specific products of Jewish tailors, peasants, and other Jews who used their hands. At any rate, the time came when the superior Jews were feeling inferior and were once more grasping for a sense of superiority. They did this in a compensatory fashion by turning their liability into an asset.

The famous psychoanalyst Alfred Adler discussed the psychology of compensation and overcompensation which stems from initial feelings of inferiority. (See Adler and also Ansbacher and Ansbacher). A pertinent example is the Greek orator Demosthenes, who as a child used to stutter, and therefore practiced speaking with pebbles in his mouth and became a great orator. Adler related such striving for compensation to an inherent drive for power which most people share. He also stressed the fact that feelings of inferiority are taken as a sign of weakness by others and therefore evoke shame. For this reason, there is a complementary tendency to conceal feelings of inferiority. What this all adds up to is that a drive to compensate, or even overcompensate, stems from a sense of shame as well as from a positive impulse toward mastery and competence.

Adler suggested that there is an implicit distinction between direct and indirect compensation, that is, between compensating directly in the area where the defect lies or in another area. For example, a case of indirect compensation would be a person with a very slight limp who vigorously strives to become a master violinist. If the same person worked diligently at becoming a superb long-distance runner, he would be engaging in direct compensation. Adler also distinguished between compensation and overcompensation, the former meaning to bring the individual to an optimal level of competence and the latter meaning that the individual must excel in some area in order to feel adequate. It stands to reason that the latter case includes a strong component of shame as a motivating force. It also stands to reason that direct compensation in the defective area rather than indirect compensation in another area is motivated by a stronger component of shame.

The Jews felt "defective" for being exiled, persecuted, leading an abnormal economic life, and for not engaging in physical work to the extent that many people of other nations did. Now they were going to compensate for it, and the form this compensation took, using Adler's concept, was that of direct overcompensation. A. D. Gordon, who ennobled the ethic of working, was a spearhead of the movement from defect to excellence in the Jewish use of hands in physical work. He aimed at changing the score from what used to be a liability into an asset. In the process, he "judaized" physical labor by turning it into something much nobler and more moral than it used to be considered even by Gentiles who adopted the Protestant ethic.

Gordon was a Utopian socialist, but first and foremost an ardent Zionist, who at the age of forty-seven left his family in Russia and emigrated to Palestine. There he preached a "religion of labor" which Arthur Hertzberg, the writer on Zionism, has attributed to the influence of the Russian novelist Leo Tolstoy. Gordon alerted his fellow Zionists to the fact that the Jews had developed an attitude of looking down on manual labor. He warned that ignoring this great deficiency, or treating it with self-deception, would no longer do. Having attached such spiritual importance to manual and physical labor, done naturally and out of love, Gordon could not but oppose Ahad Ha'am's idea of creating a revived national culture in Israel. Lofty spiritual culture, not organically tied to physical labor on the national soil, was nothing to Gordon but a perpetuation of the old Jewish mistake of relegating manual work to the Gentiles. Thus, he vehemently opposed the established tradition that when it comes to physical labor, as he put it (Hertzberg), "Let Ivan, or John, or Mustafa do the work" while the Jews busy themselves producing a spiritual and cultural center. To paraphrase Gordon, it was time for Jacob to stop using Esau's hands and use his own for a change, or else a grave historical deficiency would perpetuate itself. The way Gordon made up for this deficiency was that of compulsive and direct overcompensation. Fostering normal work attitudes was not enough: labor had to be a "religion."

Although Gordon was aware that only a select few would be able to literally follow in his footsteps, his call for a religion of labor stirred the hearts of many of his fellow Jews. He became a well-known figure in the Yishuv because of his ability in late middle age to work hard physically in spite of his frail stature. Indeed, Gordon somehow made crude physical work seem like fine art. Those who followed his ideals created a youth movement after him, named Gordonia, and he remained a symbol of national rebirth through the sanctity of work, as well as an example of idealism at its best. The esteem in which he was held comes across in the writings of others. For instance, the Old Guard Zionist Mordechai Snir with loving admiration described Gordon dancing with such ecstasy that it reminds the reader of Hassidic practice, and supports the notion that in his own way Gordon was a mystic. The elevation of physical work to the status of religion, even though not in a traditional sense, and the tying of this idea to such concepts as natural, organic, national soil, land, revival and redemption, indicate that to Gordon the "religion of work" in its fullest meaning was the laying of the foundation for a holistic Jewish national revival.

Gordon's achievements and deep impact on his generation serve as a good example of how a striving for superiority can pass beyond mere compensation for inferiority feelings to the production of positive achievements. This again is in line with Adler's contentions. Adler stressed the point that the outcome of overcompensation can be positive: it can produce a genius, and may lead to the mastery of the environment, which he regarded as one of the major goals of human beings. He further believed that organ inferiority, or for that matter any basic defect, can have far-reaching individual and historical implications. For example, both Moses and Demosthenes had speech defects. Demosthenes, as we know, engaged in direct overcompensation to become the greatest Greek orator, while Moses, letting his brother Aaron speak for him, engaged in indirect overcompensation by becoming a great leader of men instead. As Adler has pointed out, organ inferiority, or an equivalent psychological feeling of some basic defect, can create wonders far more important than the compensating relief that they provide.

By analogy, one may say that the Jews living in exile had a basic sense of defect: they had no country or state, unlike other nations. Without implying that this was the only impelling power, it stands to reason that this feeling of inferiority, this sense of abnormality, contributed its share in driving the Jews toward achievement and overcompensation which, in turn, enriched humanity. History abounds with Jews of great achievement who were probably regarded by others, as well as by themselves, as having done wonders not only by being Jewish, but also in spite of it. The dialectics of inferiority and superiority, with pride masking shame but never quite obliterating it, have accompanied Jews for generations as a mingled blessing and curse.

There are other aspects of inferiority and compensation which are worth noting. Adler emphasized that feelings of inferiority can result in feeling unmanly, and that striving for superiority is a means of compensating for these unmanly feelings. He therefore termed this striving "masculine protest." There are many connotations to feeling womanly and feminine and to feeling manly and masculine; frequently they are stereotypes that do injustice to women. However, in terms of use of language, Adler pointed out that masculine and feminine were often metaphors for strength and weakness. One may add that they were also metaphors for activity and passivity. The drive for superiority involves a psychological transformation from passivity to activity, and can be true in the life of an individual or in the life of a people. One of the irreducible principles of the Zionist credo was the effecting of this very switch from passivity to activity. Even after the Six Day War, when Israelis were not expected to worry about their activity image, one could still hear severe warnings to Israelis, as, for example, by the late leader Yitzhak Tabenkin, not to slide back from activity to passivity and once again become helpless like in the bad old days.

Although Zionism represented a shift from passivity to activity in Jewish history, there has never been a clear-cut case of active Zionists battling it out with passive non-Zionists. Shifts of emphasis and debates involving this issue occurred within the ranks of Zionism itself; the issue was very much alive during the early controversy between Political and Cultural Zionism. Theodor Herzl, the father of Zionism and leader of Political Zionism, opted for statehood. He hoped to accomplish it by means of political negotiations with world leaders and by persuading one or more of the great powers to issue a charter which would grant Eretz Yisrael to the Jews. On the other hand, Ahad Ha'am, the spokesman for Cultural Zionism, saw spiritual renascence and "preparation of the hearts" as the all-important goal of Jewish revival. He hoped to accomplish this by establishing a small but vigorous Jewish cultural center in Palestine which would influence the quality of Jewish life everywhere. When Ahad Ha'am lost the battle to Herzl, it was a victory of sorts for those who were oriented toward activity.

However, later on, Practical Zionism shifted the emphasis from political work outside Palestine to practical efforts within Palestine itself. The goal was to enhance the "organic" growth of the Yishuv in Palestine. At that time, the Herzlian brand of Zionism, of seeking a charter and chasing after world leaders, seemed passive and perhaps even quixotic. Therefore, the ascent of Practical Zionism represented another victory for activity. Practical Zionism was definitely dissatisfied with the traditional Jewish attitude of waiting for a change for the better, this time in the form of a charter.

Eventually, the "activism" of Practical Zionism in turn seemed far from sufficient in the eyes of the Revisionists. The Revisionists chose this name because they demanded both a revision of the Zionist policy of organic growth and the adoption of the original Herzlian goal of bringing about a Jewish state speedily. They were not even satisfied with the achievement of Practical Zionism, which had brought about the realization of a major goal of the earlier Political Zionism. Oddly enough, the crowning achievement of Practical Zionism's greatest leader, Chaim Weizmann, was the old sought-after charter of Political Zionism, in the form of the Balfour Declaration. But to the Revisionists and others, this achievement merely represented a Gentile pronouncement, whereas the fate of the Zionist dream should depend on Jewish deeds.

Bearing this history in mind, as well as *the psychological equations of passivity with dependence on Gentile pronouncements and activity with reliance on Jewish deeds,* it is not surprising that a perceptive leader such as Ben Gurion gave strong expression to the feeling that Jewish self-action rather than Gentile pronouncements is what counts. He was, however, keen on drawing a line, and did not allow such strong psychological needs to color his perception of the realities of power politics. Thus after the Sinai campaign of 1956, Ben Gurion said that Israel is a small nation which would nevertheless not bow its head even to the mightiest of nations when justice is not on the side of those nations. These were strong words, and they injected pride. Ben Gurion also promised not to withdraw from Sinai, and reaffirmed that Israel's fate would be determined not by what the Gentiles say but by what the Jews do. This was a modern, large-scale version of the older objections to the "charter" politics of Political Zionism and to the traditional

Jewish style of pleading with the all-powerful Gentiles.

The emphasis on the idea that Jewish fate depends on Jewish action, and not on Gentile pronouncements, left a deep impact on the people. Thus, one Israeli veteran of the June 1967 war expressed the opinion that some of the Israeli military retaliations before the war were motivated by this idea (See Shapira). He related this kind of thinking to a feeling of inferiority, of deep insult, which Jews had experienced for generations. To him, the Holocaust was the sharpest expression of this insult. The soldier was correct, and so was Ben Gurion. Well aware of the psychological makeup of his people, Ben Gurion understood their craving to revise their demeaning passive image of the past and transform it into a proud image of activity. With skillful leadership, he managed to convey the impression that Israel resorts to as much self-action as is humanly possible, and that after that, if things still do not go its way, it is not a matter of ineffectiveness or passivity, but simply that no country operates in a vacuum or can have everything its own way. Subsequently, when he gave the withdrawal order from Sinai, after pledging not to withdraw, Ben Gurion was not resented by most Israelis or castigated for not keeping his promise. His message was understood all along. It was the greatness of Ben Gurion that he could both attend to the psychological needs of his people and at the same time help them accept the limitations of power politics.

It is not easy, however, to accept the hard facts of realpolitik, especially when strong emotional needs to believe in the infallibility of self-initiated action get in the way. Unfortunately, the long and tragic Jewish history of great achievements together with helplessness, humiliation, and shame has fostered in some Jews an irresistible need to believe in complete mastery over one's fate. It is as though coexistence with a compromised sense of mastery were tantamount to existential treason, to sinking low in the abyss of unauthenticity, to living with unbearable shame. The tragedy of it all is that whenever a particular need to believe becomes so irresistible, then reality becomes resistible. The result is misjudgment. It is an irony of fate that in falling into this pit some Israelis resemble to a degree the Arabs, whose notorious ability to resist reality they so deplore. Such was the fate of the late leader Yitzhak Tabenkin.

Tabenkin objected to Ben Gurion's willingness to withdraw from occupied territories, and referred back to the old arguments in Zionism over the source of strength, that is, whether it stems from diplomatic activities or practical work in Israel. Siding with the latter, he preferred retaining the occupied territories. To him, diplomatic activity was the old, passive way of waiting to see what the Gentiles say, whereas creating facts in Israel by Jewish settlement in the occupied territories was equivalent to what the Jews do, i.e., active mastery over one's own fate. Thus he was turning Ben Gurion's ideology against him, except that Ben Gurion's intention of creating facts by Jewish action was never meant to be accepted literally and with no qualifications at all. This is what most Israelis understood in 1956, but what Tabenkin failed to understand from 1967 to 1971. Indeed, Tabenkin's arguments reflected the old psychological needs of the Israelis, to which Zionism had attended through the change of image from shameful passivity to proud activity. However, when the need to reaffirm this image clouds an objective vision of power relationships, myth is confused with reality and the results can be destructive. Ben Gurion's approach, while injecting the Israelis with pride, allowed them to accept setbacks without being scorched by an intolerable sense of shame. The danger in Tabenkin's approach is that it could create in those who accept it a sense of shame, degradation, and humiliation, coupled with crippling feelings of mortification and self-hate, should events force a withdrawal from occupied territories.

Let us not lose track of the deep historical and emotional feelings which drive those Jews who share Tabenkin's outlook. The Bible said that the voice is Jacob's and the hands are Esau's. We have seen how neatly Bialik summed up what to expect from each—a learned Jew and a drunken Goy. But the Jews, who for too long confined themselves to Jacob's talking and praying role, felt passive and inferior and began to doubt their superiority. Meanwhile, the Gentiles used their hands actively, although not always in humane pursuits, and the deeds of some of them culminated in the infamous Holocaust. Now the Jews know what the Gentiles can do, so perhaps it is time to reverse roles and show the Gentiles what Jews can do. And now we know that they can even have "the best air force in the world." Listening to the Gentiles instead of relying on Jewish action is "Galut mentality," and represents to many Israelis perverted Jewish wishes to continue their dependence on Gentiles and endow Galut or exile an equal status with Israel.

In 1970 the President of the World Jewish Congress, Dr. Nahum Goldmann, was at the center of a heated controversy involving two matters. The first was his plan to go to Cairo as a private citizen, but with the knowledge of the Israeli Government, in order to meet with President Gamal Abdel Nasser. The second was his article "The Future of Israel," which appeared in *Foreign Affairs,* in which he suggested that Israel's existence should be guaranteed not only by its own political and military strength but also by the people of the world, including the Arabs. At that time he was subjected to many attacks, sometimes vicious, in the Israeli newspapers, where his personality, doctrine, or both were derogated. In one such attack, in *Yediot Aharonot* of April 10, 1970, the Israeli reporter Yeshayahu Ben-Porat underscored Goldmann's "demonstrative scorn for 'what the Jews do' and manifest admiration for 'what the Gentiles say'." This is the ultimate in character assassination in Israel. So strong are the feelings on this score that if one accepts the "fact" that Goldmann scorns what Jews do and admires what Gentiles say, then one may well wish him a speedy one-way trip to Cairo.

The results of these strong needs for feelings of self-mastery are conflicted perceptions. Reality has a claim on perception, and its claim is that Gentile talk, and certainly Gentile action, can be of crucial importance. On the other hand, the emotional need for a feeling of self-mastery, as well as the desire to turn the tables on the Gentiles, also have a claim on perception, the claim that Gentile talk is pale in comparison to Jewish action. These conflicting motives resulted in a perception of the Gentiles which the dean of law at Tel-Aviv University, Amnon Rubinstein, has termed "schizophrenic." In two articles, one in *The New York Times Magazine* and the other in the Israeli newspaper *Ha'aretz,* he elaborated on the Israeli "schizophrenic" attitude toward Gentiles whereby one moment Israelis feel like an immovable world superpower and the next moment they dread an impending American pressure which they do not believe they could withstand. Rubinstein warned that this kind of a schizophrenic perception may result in a very dangerous blindness. Indeed, such a split perception is not conducive to wise realpolitiking.

The schizophrenic coexistence of superstrength and mortal weakness in Israeli perceptions and actions can be illustrated by examining the Israeli policy of deep penetration bombing raids over Egypt in January 1970. During that period, while Israeli planes roamed the Egyptian skies with impunity, many Israelis were afraid to initiate any peace gesture lest it be construed as a sign of "weakness." Arab history has ill prepared the Arabs to wage war. Jewish history, with its intricate dialectics of superiority and inferiority, seems to have equally ill prepared the Israelis for "waging" peace. The official Israeli line concerning the bombings was that they were militarily necessary but were also needed to counteract Egyptian propaganda. The second argument seemed credible, while the first did not. Nasser's war of attrition had already backfired, and the Egyptian positions along the Suez Canal lay in ruins without the need for deep penetration bombings. As for Egyptian propaganda, it was argued that the Egyptian people would not be able to believe the victory stories broadcast over Cairo radio when they could see and hear the Israeli jets and bombings going on undeterred. The unofficial reason for Israeli bombings was a wish to topple Nasser, hoping that the leaders who followed him would then assume a more conciliatory attitude toward Israel.

By cornering Nasser the Goy and putting him in a situation where he faced a constant humiliation, which was intolerable, Israelis brought about his desperate attempts to extricate himself from this corner, which could be dangerous for Israel. Nasser had a talent for turning defeat into victory, at least in the eyes of his own people, and he only had one source to turn to for redress—the Russians. The end results of the deep penetration raids, therefore, were disastrous. The Russians moved in with both pilots and missiles, and escalated their intervention in the Middle East. The Israeli newspapers were full of articles of concern about the Russian intervention and future intentions. The Israeli leaders were caught by surprise. They had not predicted this sharp escalation of Russian intervention, and they found it necessary to engage in a propaganda of rationalizations that most sophisticated Israelis did not believe. The main points the government was trying to emphasize were, first, that increased Russian intervention had been predicted, and, second, that this Russian escalation was bound to happen anyway and had nothing to do with the deep penetration bombing raids. It was obvious, however, that the deep penetration policy had turned into a blunder, and the raids were stopped, while Defense Minister Dayan, through various public statements, sent signals to the Russians stating that where the Israel Air Force now draws the line is over the Canal.

The whole affair was a glaring case of ignoring the ABCs of power politics, which involved never putting Nasser in such an untenable position that he had nobody to turn to but the Russians. As for the Russians, the basic expectation should have been that after the tremendous investments in money, arms, and economic aid to Egypt since 1955, and with their big stake in the entire Middle East, they were not going to withdraw simply because of the Israeli Air Force. One must entertain the possibility that the blindness about the bombing policy and the inability to foresee its consequences was brought about by a raw emotional desire for the satisfaction of feeling like a superpower. It feels good to know that Jews appear strong to non-Jews. This feeling, however, does not make the Russians turn tail and run. Confusing emotional satisfaction with political expediency is a sin for which the leadership in many countries would be toppled. This is not the case in Israel because the general public shares with its leaders a most intense concern, not merely with physical survival, but also with the survival of a new image of the Jew.

These are difficult emotional issues that should be viewed from a broad time perspective. Driven by shame and a sense of inferiority, the Jews felt the need to compensate and even overcompensate. By now they have already experienced massive doses of pride. The need to compensate, however, led to a switch from passivity to activity in both thoughts and deeds. This switch was successfully accomplished, and the passive image has largely been rectified. On the whole, Jews are no longer regarded by themselves or others as passive weaklings who sit on their behinds and wait for fate to overtake or overrun them. In turn, however, the switch toward activity is dangerous when it carries with it the psychological equation of activity with fast Jewish action while the Gentiles only talk. If a corollary of Jewish action were to be *a projection of past Jewish inaction on contemporary Gentiles,* the results of such a misperception could be fatal. Since the Gentiles after all do not sit on *their* behinds waiting helplessly to see what the Jews will do next, it becomes increasingly apparent how right Ben Gurion was all along by insisting that Israel should always have at least one world power to rely on. Chances are that when the dust clears and things simmer down in the Middle East, the Israelis will be less conflicted and somewhat more realistic in their attitudes toward the Goyim.

11.

The Holocaust

AND HAMAN SAID UNTO KING
AHASUERUS: "THERE IS A CER-
TAIN PEOPLE SCATTERED ABROAD
AND DISPERSED AMONG THE PEO-
PLES IN ALL THE PROVINCES OF
THY KINGDOM; AND THEIR LAWS
ARE DIVERSE FROM THOSE OF EV-
ERY PEOPLE; NEITHER KEEP THEY
THE KING'S LAWS; THEREFORE IT
PROFITETH NOT THE KING TO
SUFFER THEM. IF IT PLEASE THE
KING, LET IT BE WRITTEN THAT
THEY BE DESTROYED. . . .

—Esther 3, 8–9

NOBODY TOLD US HOW IT COULD
HAPPEN, NO ONE EXPLAINED IT
TO US!

—A sabra friend

The shock and trauma of the Nazi Holocaust further complicated the Jewish attitudes toward Gentiles and deepened the feelings of suspicion and rage. What is more, although the Arab problem antedates the Holocaust it would be impossible to understand the present Israeli stance toward the Arabs without taking full account of the Holocaust. How almost six million Jews were exterminated and how contemporary Jews "live" with this reality is a story which is still unfolding and which may never be described in its entirety. So traumatic was the impact of the Holocaust on the Jewish people, and so self-evident it seemed to them that only a political solution in the form of an independent Jewish state in Eretz Yisrael would protect the Jews from future holocausts, that Ben Gurion included the Holocaust as a justification for a Jewish state in the Israeli Declaration of Independence.

In effect, the Holocaust was the culmination of a long history of Jewish afflictions. The list of afflictions suffered by the Jews throughout their tragic history at the hands of Gentiles is extensive and beyond the scope of this book. Raul Hilberg, who conducted extensive studies of the Holocaust, noted that Gentile official policies toward Jews since the fourth century A.D. fell into three major categories: conversion, expulsion, and annihilation. All three involved an untold amount of physical coercion, loss of adherents to the faith, loss of lives, and wanderings and migrations. All three left a dire impact on the psychological makeup of the persecuted Jews and fostered emotional traits that characterize minority and oppressed people. Two of these major traits, a basic sense of insecurity and feelings of paranoia, have already been discussed in Chapter 2. Both were anchored in reality and were by no means based on figments of Jewish imagination. Other historical reactions and psychological traits also evolved. These included the tendency to collaborate with the aggressors and to assume a submissive attitude toward them. These historical reactions constituted an adaptive response to the first two afflictions of conversion and expulsion. However, regarding the third affliction of annihilation, the traditional Jewish responses were only partly effective in coping with instances of pogroms and massacres. When it finally came to wholesale genocide in the twentieth century, the traditional responses were completely inadequate. They became maladaptive in the face of annihilation that grew with the aid of modern technology to become planned, conscious mass extermination. In this instance, the application of old and tried responses to afflictions yielded tragic results and added corpses to the ovens.

It is exasperating to read Hilberg's analysis of how the effectiveness of the destruction depended not only on its Nazi perpetrators but also on their Jewish victims. The beleaguered Jews responded to the Nazi threat to their lives in traditional ways. One characteristic way was that of attempts at alleviation. This included petitions, ransom fees, and protection payments, usually starting with petitions and moving to buying protection with money if need be. Another way was that of anticipatory compliance. This referred to the belief on the part of the would-be victims that if the Jews themselves were allowed to select the victims from among themselves, then perhaps the total number of victims would be reduced, or perhaps the young would be saved, and maybe the afflictions in general would assume a somewhat lesser magnitude. Next came the reaction of evasion of flight. Often Jews evaded flight while there was still time to escape the Germans. This particular reaction developed because of their history in which frequently there was nowhere to take flight to, except from one hostile region to another. When alleviation attempts as well as flight attempts failed or were missed, the next reaction pattern was usually that of inactivity and paralysis. Here Hilberg referred to such horror-striking scenes as the victims' gazing into the open graves, mute, unresisting, unable to take flight or to jump in.

These reaction patterns to danger and affliction had been instilled in the Jews for many centuries, for they represented a way to minimize losses and increase the numbers of survivors—at least until the twentieth century. But in the face of genocide, the old and tried patterns only made things worse. In Eastern Europe many Jews could have fled towns which were about to be taken by the German army. They did not. Hilberg explains it by saying that people do not flee their homes unless they are well aware of the nature of the coming danger. It is tragic that the Jews were not aware of the magnitude of the Nazi danger because of certain psychological blocks. One of these blocks was the historical notion that nothing good comes from Russia while many good things come from Germany. Weizmann described this pro-German bias during the First World War when it was impossible for him to convince many of his Zionist colleagues that Germany was not going to win. Hilberg's descriptions are shocking. The sight of Jewish leaders welcoming the arriving German units with letters and petitions instead of departing with the retreating Russian army borders on the grotesque —even if one takes into account that the Germans themselves did everything in their power to hide the true nature of their "final solution." Nevertheless, even if the Jews deluded themselves that they were being sent to work camps, still it seems macabre in retrospect that the Jews threw their lives away by greeting the German army when the Germans had already prepared their total destruction. Later, in front of the gas chambers, the Jews would be striken with paralysis because again, as Hilberg put it, over hundreds of years they had "unlearned" the art of revolt.

Hilberg's analysis is perceptive and painful. It is especially painful since he depicted the Jewish reactions as the result not of cowardice but of long conditioning throughout sixteen centuries. It is easy to document instances of Jewish resistance (see "Jewish Resistance During the Holocaust"). However, as Elon aptly put it, in a corner of the mind many Israelis know that there was less resistance than would appear from the voluminous speeches delivered on the subject. Hilberg's analysis provides some understanding of the vehement reaction on the part of sabras when they ask the agonizing question: "Why didn't the Jews fight?" After all, Israelis are well aware of the instances of armed resistance to the Nazis and they do not think that the Jews were simply cowards. Sick perhaps, but not cowards. Otherwise, Israelis would have their simple answer and would have no need to ask the question. Apparently, a sense of bitterness over the kind of sickness that an unfair history imposed on the Jews has something to do with the asking of this question.

In analyzing the role the victims played in their own destruction, Hilberg emphasized the fact that Jewish history taught the Jews that resistance in the face of an overwhelming force could only result in disaster. This tradition led to the attempt to tame the Germans as one would attempt to tame a wild beast, that is, by avoiding provocation. This time, however, such a course proved to be disastrous. If in the past this way alleviated Jewish afflictions to various degrees, it was utterly unadaptive in the face of a conscious policy of genocide supported by modern technology. Thus the Jewish victims were caught in the strait-jacket of their history. This judgment, painful as it is, is rooted in reality. It is exactly because so many Jews agreed with this verdict, that they reacted with a passionate cry of "Never again!" Not never again Jewish casualties, but never again *Jewish victims who avoid resistance.*

In Hebrew, the same emotions were expressed by the phrase *Asur shehasho'ah tahazor* ("It is forbidden for the Holocaust to return"). This intense sentiment serves as a driving power for many activities. Under the impelling force of the "never again" feeling the State of Israel calculates its political maneuvers toward the Arabs and world powers, and the American Jews render financial and moral support to Israel. "Never again" is not specific to the Jewish Defense League, whose members are acutely driven by a sentiment that they share with the majority of Jews. (This fact alone casts doubt on the wisdom of the rigid attitude displayed toward the JDL by more established Jewish organizations in the United States.)

The wide impact of the trauma of the Holocaust and the pervasiveness of the "never again" feeling were revealed in 1971 when the American Secretary of State, William P. Rogers, visited Israel. As reported by Peter Grose in *The New York Times*, when Rogers arrived in Jerusalem he was taken to Yad Vashem, the memorial to Jewish victims of the Holocaust. By this stop in Rogers' tour the Israeli authorities were signalling the emotional basis for, as Grose put it, "their rigidity and suspicion toward people around them." In other words, they were telling Rogers that whatever his elaborate plans were, "never again" comes first.

The "never again" vow is a reaction to Jewish passivity. Bialik, in his poem "In the City of the Slaughter," described how a mother would be raped in front of her daughters by seven Gentiles and the daughter in front of her mother, again by seven Gentiles, all this before, during, and after the slaughter. He therefore asked with derision where the husbands, grooms, and brothers were. The answer was: they were hidden under a bed, behind a barrel, peeping and watching how holy bodies of Jewish women were squirming under the flesh of donkeys of men. The Jewish men did nothing. When the slaughter was over, they came out of their hiding places, blessed the Lord for saving them, and everything went back to normal. With anger and scorn Bialik described "the sons of sons of the Maccabees" who ran like rats and died like dogs.

Putting it differently, yesterday's heroic Jews are today's yellow cowards. Why? What has history done to them since they were Maccabees? Why did they not fight? This piercing question, which continued to traumatize the Jews, reached new heights during the trial in Jerusalem in 1961 of Adolf Eichmann. Thus, Friedmann reported hearing sabras exclaim with exasperation that they could not understand why Jews allowed themselves to be led like sheep to the slaughter. In Elie Wiesel's novel *A Beggar In Jerusalem*, a young sabra proclaims that all the grand talk about humanity's conscience was invented by persecuted Jews as an alibi for not fighting. In this regard, Tabenkin asked whether passivity saved the Jews from death during the Holocaust, while Feigenberg-Eamri expressed the opinion that those Jews who rebelled in the ghettos against the Nazis saved the honor of the Jewish people—thus implicitly recognizing that there was an issue of honor that needed to be saved.

Unquestionably the need to revise the Jewish image concerning the Holocaust is very strong. Friedmann took note of the fact that in the teaching of "Jewish consciousness" in Israeli secondary schools during the 1960s, the Holocaust was less frequently described to children as such in order to avoid the suggestion of a wholesale slaughter of passive victims. Therefore, the Yad Vashem monument was now presented to the children as a memorial to martyrs and heroes. This trend was further accentuated in the 1970s. In 1972 the national memorial day to the Holocaust and heroism was celebrated in numerous public gatherings. On the days preceding the celebration, the newspapers were full of advertisements describing the gatherings as memorials to "the Holocaust and heroism" or to "the Holocaust and rebellion."

The issue of the role of the Jews in their own destruction is of course a most sensitive one. Although Hilberg's explanation made sense, the fact that he did so with regard to the dead did not make it any easier on the living. Tuchman, in her introduction to Gideon Hausner's book on the Eichmann trial, in which he served as the prosecuter, indicated that this question was fully clarified by Hausner's book for anyone who wishes to understand rather than to judge. Emotionally, she expressed resentment toward those who too easily assume that the Jews were responsible for their own slaughter. This criticism may have been directed at the views of the well-known political scientist Hannah Arendt, who also wrote a book on the Eichmann trial. It should be borne in mind, however, that Arendt blamed only the Jewish leadership, not the whole people. As for Hilberg, he did not come even remotely close to equating the responsibility of victim and aggressor. In fact, when Tuchman went on to summon for the defense of the Jewish character two thousand years of living as an oppressed minority, she was in effect adopting Hilberg's viewpoint.

Tuchman did acknowledge some cooperation on the part of Jews as they were faced with the point of a gun. In contrast, however, she pointed the Warsaw Ghetto revolt as an example of different conduct and compared it to the valiant Jewish fighting against the ancient Romans. In addition, she underscored the fact that the relatives of people who were exterminated in concentration camps fought valiantly in Israel. As a matter of fact, survivors themselves bearing green numbers on their hands defended Israel with valor. Lastly, she indicated that lack of resistance in the Nazi concentration camps was not unique to Jews. The issue still remains: Why was the question "Why did the Jews not fight?" so bluntly asked in Israel? Incidents of Jewish resistance to the Nazis are, after all, well known to both Jews and Gentiles. For example, William Shirer's *The Rise and Fall of the Third Reich*, which enjoyed an enormous worldwide circulation, contained a detailed description of the heroic Jewish revolt in the Warsaw Ghetto. Yet this knowledge did not prevent the asking of the question.

The French writer Jean-François Steiner tried to answer in his book on the successful Jewish revolt in Treblinka. In the preface, Steiner contended though that the sabras who asked the question at the time of the Eichmann trial failed to understand that heroism is not inherent in human nature. Heroism depends on circumstances in which a few cowards may determine the nature of the whole group. He also expressed the hope that his description of the successful rebellion in Treblinka would demonstrate that the initial helplessness on the part of Jews was sometimes overcome. Here we have to be careful not to muddle the issue.

For one thing, it is important to separate the overt content of the question from the latent message that accompanies it. The overt question is why did the Jews not fight in concentration camps, to which the answer is that sometimes they did and on many other occasions they did not, at which times they had with them many non-Jews who behaved the same. Another reply to this overt question is that a full answer to the question can only come from detailed inquiries into conditions in concentration camps and their debilitating psychological impact on people in general, not just on Jews. However, such inquiries would not provide an explanation as to why Israelis and Jews so persistently ask this question in the first place. In discussing the same question, Dimont dismissed the various psychological and sociological speculations on why the Jews did not fight as unrealistic and as betraying the inner anxieties of the writers rather than illuminating the peculiar situations in which most Jews were caught. In his opinion, the Jews, like so many non-Jews in the world, were for a long time unaware of the "final solution" plan which was kept secret by the Nazis. By the time most Jews belatedly learned the truth, they could only proceed in their death march as did the American soldiers at Bataan in similar circumstances. All this may be correct, except that Americans are not obsessed with the question of why the Americans did not fight. For each Bataan, Americans have their many Bastognes and they are not caught up in an image which they need to change.

Again, many Russians died in concentration camps and without a Warsaw Revolt, but we do not hear about the Russians asking why the Russians did not fight. This is specific to the Jews. True, no people on earth were so decimated by the Nazi horror as the Jewish people. Nevertheless, it seems that the obsessional preoccupation with the behavior of the slaughtered Jews, and whether they died as heroes and fighters, stems from historically accumulated feelings concerning a negative image. These feelings constitute a heavy inheritance, a historical burden which other nations do not share. This brings us to the latent message. "Why did the Jews not fight?" is not really a call for an objective inquiry into the impact of the Nazi concentration camps on their inmates. Rather, it is a desperate pledge that no longer will Jews, by plan or by default, be cast in a passive role. It is an affirmation of the fact that Jews have had enough of what they perceive as a history of Jewish passivity, that they believe that this degraded Jewish trait should have been terminated long before the Second World War, and that the atrocious events of the Holocaust are the final reminders that after nearly two thousand years of Jewish passivity this trait will no longer be prominent in the Jewish psychological makeup. Activity and self-mastery are from now on the name of the game. The incomprehensibility with which young native-born Israelis view the victims of the Holocaust is an expression of a credo: "After more than eighteen centuries of helplessness and humiliation we have acquired a proud identity and a new active disposition in our ancestral land. We can no longer imagine how Jews could live and think differently."

The questioning on the part of young Israelis represents a disclaiming of a negative ego-ideal and a public espousal of a positive ego-ideal of self-assertion. It also warns potential Amaleks, Philistines, Hamans, and Hitlers what to expect from the new breed of Jews. Tuchman's and Steiner's apologetic arguments have therefore missed the point. No matter how one explains the impact of concentration camps on their inmates or equates the behavior of Jewish and non-Jewish victims, one still fails to answer a question that was never meant to be answered. The question should really end with an exclamation point, not a question mark. It is an act of self-distancing from the negative ego-ideal role of being passive victims, and a declaration of intent. The message is: "From now on we are going to fight and you'd better believe it!" In other words, it is an exclamation of "never again," and needs no answer. It refers to the contemporary psychology of the living, not to the etiology of the emotional makeup of the exterminated Jews.

This defiant declaration of intent has sometimes been oddly expressed. During the 1950s, after Israel had absorbed many immigrants from Europe as well as from the Middle East and North Africa, some of the pale-skinned immigrants from Europe were taunted by being called *sabon* (soap). The allusion was to the German manufacture of soap out of the corpses of exterminated Jews. In the Israeli army, soldiers who did not speak Hebrew well, who seemed uncertain or fumbling, and whose white skin indicated a European ancestry and therefore former persecution by the Nazis, were laughingly called *sabon*. The immediate reference was to the person's status as green, unsure of himself, and therefore unable to adequately stand up for his rights. The remote and more ominous reference was to a kind of a passive person who cannot fend for himself and who would allow himself to be turned into soap. On one occasion, after a sailor who was a guest in a wedding party broke down and cried when so taunted, the Israeli navy took disciplinary action. The friend who told me this story was extremely embarrassed. She admitted to having called other people *sabon*, and was flooded with feelings of remorse. "We did it, but we did not really mean it" she kept saying. "Really when people were calling other people *sabon* it was just a phrase and they did not think about the Holocaust."

Yet the conscious meaning of teasing someone about being a rookie masked the more malignant, unconscious meaning of disdain for passive weaklings who would not resist aggression. Nor is this latter meaning altogether out of awareness. Otherwise, dark-skinned orientals would also have qualified as *sabon*. The cruelty of this practice can reach awareness at the sight of a sailor who breaks down and cries. Similarly, my friend was overcome with a sense of shame when questioned about it. Yet this is not cruelty, but a defensive maneuver characterized by self-reference. The true address is not the other but the self. By taunting others for being *sabon*, one declares publicly "I am not *sabon*." This means that the military was indeed the most appropriate forum in which to issue this cry.

The *sabon* story also suggests that to some extent the experience of the Holocaust was being repressed and that therefore feelings about it were expressed indirectly. Indeed, Eliezer Livneh characterized the first Israeli reaction to the Holocaust as that of "amnesia," and dated the recovery from this amnesia to the 1955 trial of Rudolf Kasztner, the former vice-president of the Zionist Organization in Budapest, who was accused of collaboration with the Nazis. Kasztner was convicted in 1955 and subsequently murdered in 1957 before his conviction was reversed by the Israeli Supreme Court. On the whole, no new thinking concerning the Holocaust emerged from this trial, which occupied front-page headlines for months. But the Israeli public's armor of amnesia was definitely cracked, and the ground was prepared for a more serious soul-searching under the impact of the Eichmann trial of 1961.

However, prior to the late 1950s the initial traumatic impact of the Holocaust on Israeli Jews evoked a variety of avoidance reactions. In this connection Hayim Shetzker maintained in an Israeli newspaper article that there has never been a rational, conceptual inspection of its impact on Israeli life and consciousness. Israeli society dealt with the Holocaust in four ways: demonization of the perpetrators, which freed Israelis from the task of seeking explanations within the nature of man; a wounded national pride, which ignored logical arguments; repression of the whole experience; and an attempt to overcome the same repression through public rituals and memorial days. In effect, these are four forms of what Livneh has termed amnesia. Shetzker asserted that as a result of these inadequate ways of coping with so painful an experience, the study of the Holocaust in Israel lags behind that of other countries, and that the Eichmann trial started a process of breaking through the repression but did not offer fresh solutions.

Until the Eichmann trial in 1961 the tendency to circumvent the recent shameful events was widespread. It included the public at large, the school system, the survivors who were ashamed to seek psychiatric help because of the negative attitude of the public, and Israeli psychiatrists who had blind spots concerning the psychopathologic effects of the Holocaust (See Zellermayer). The Eichmann trial broke the amnesia and resulted in a public rehashing of sentiments that previously had been given a more muffled expression.

To understand the meaning of the trial, we should refer to the testimony of one of the leaders of the Warsaw Ghetto Revolt, Zivia Lubetkin Zuckerman. She testified that the captive Jews simply could not imagine that the Nazi aim was not merely to humiliate and suppress but to literally kill a whole people. This tragic, costly disbelief is no longer held. Now Jews are ready to believe anything. Quite understandably, they frequently expect the worst whether from the Arabs or the United Nations and the deep suspicion engraved in their minds may not be eradicated for generations. One of the major aims of the Eichmann trial was to convert the unbelievable into the believable, to anchor the nightmarish story of the Holocaust in concrete, recorded, and thus believable history. Settling the score with one obedient bureaucrat turned into human monster hardly justified an immense trial, nor was it the reason for the tremendous emotional investment in the trial on the part of Jews and non-Jews alike. On the other hand, "historizing" the Holocaust through the medium of one representative example, one concrete and typical Nazi, was the ultimate and all-important aim of the trial. The trial was intended to make the Holocaust believable. It has become the most apparent source for Jews who wish to document their understandable reasons for feeling haunted. With the unbelievable made believable and well documented, they can now both feel and say: "We are not paranoid, only suspicious, and for good reason; we are not victims of delusions but rather realists who distrust this insane world which every so often erupts in explosive hatred of Jews."

Not everyone sees it this way, however. In her report on the trial, Hannah Arendt emphasized the failure of the Jerusalem court when judged from the viewpoint that the purpose of a trial is to render justice and nothing else. However, most Jews felt that it was really too late to render justice. They felt as Bialik did after the Kishinev pogroms when in 1903 he wrote in "On The Massacre" that if justice could not appear right away, if only after his death justice would appear, then he would rather see its throne tumbled forever. For the devastated Jewish people it was too late for justice and too early for puristic legalism, Arendt style. Eichmann's guilt could be proven in the usual tradition of court procedures, but there were additional and equally important goals, which were no secret. Most people understood that much more was involved in the trial than merely determining the past guilt and future punishment of an individual named Eichmann. The idea was to demonstrate in a believable fashion, to people everywhere, humankind's capacity for evil, "banal" or otherwise, and the tragic role that Jews came to play in it. My own reaction is: More power to the Israelis for having followed Bialik's notions and not Arendt's. What is more, as an active psychodramatist I agree with Hausner's refusal to turn the trial into a psychodrama as suggested by the American psychodramatist J. L. Moreno. By insisting on retaining the nature of the trial as a court case, Hausner displayed more conscientious effort to stick to due process of law than Arendt gave him credit for. As things stood in the post-Holocaust era, no matter what the Israeli authorities did, the Eichmann trial would have ended up as more than just a court case. It is fruitless to blame the Israelis for the fact that a tragic history gave this trial broad meanings and implications that transcend the boundaries of any court on earth.

The renewed interest in the holocaust following the Eichmann trial led to existential encounters in Hebrew literature about the meaning of it all. In his review of some of this literature, Alter detected more problems in terms of Jewish identity for Israelis than for American Jews. For the new Israeli Zionist vision of Jewish identity, which includes military self-assertion, is in effect inadequate as a retribution to the Nazis. If carried to its end, it would only result in some kind of a maniacal nightmare. Thus, the Holocaust casts doubts on some Zionist answers as an ultimate orientation for Jews. In a similar review of such literature, the Israeli professor of Hebrew literature Gershon Shaked uncovered a grim feeling that something fundamental has been destroyed, something that is embedded in such basic images as father, mother, God, faith, and hope. He may have sensed the timeless unconscious issues that were discussed in Chapter 1.

We have already suggested that in the Jewish collective unconscious an ominous conclusion was being formed—that for infringing on father's territory one can be castrated or killed and that in return for Zionism one gets a Holocaust. Those who sense this conclusion can be expected to feel that something shattering has happened to basic images. In many ways, the Holocaust does serve as irrefutable evidence for the validity of the Zionist solution to the Jewish problem—the need for the Jews to revive their ancestral Jewish state. However, Alter and Shaked clearly indicate that because of the Holocaust the Zionist credo, which was presented as a self-explanatory given and as a self-evident must, no longer enjoys its privileged status. Not surprisingly, these reviews do not reveal an abundance of cheap solutions. They do reveal the beginnings of a long, agonizing search for meaning in the recent earth-shattering happenings in Jewish history, among which Shaked has rightly included the crisis of faith, the Zionist movement, the birth of the State of Israel and its wars, and, of course, the Holocaust.

This reawakened interest in the Holocaust because of the Eichmann trial renewed the agonizing preoccupation with the issue of the lack of adequate Jewish resistance to the Nazis. Hilberg's monumental work, which the historian Oscar Handlin described neatly as an excellent work except for the idea that the Jews have lost the art of resistance, influenced Arendt to the point of harshly condemning the Jewish leadership. If it were not for their almost psychological need to cooperate with the Nazis, she claimed, many Jews would have been saved. Although Europe was trampled under Nazi boots, if the largely unarmed Jews had actively fought the Germans the whole Nazi machinery would have come to a grinding halt. This notion, as well as her tendency to minimize Eichmann's anti-Semitism and conscious responsibility for his actions, led the editor of *Commentary*, Norman Podhoretz, to characterize Arendt's book as "a study in the perversity of brilliance." Similarly, Feigenberg-Eamri described it as a sly, malicious piece of writing that does injustice to Arendt's own suffocated people, who were unable to defend themselves against fully armed and mechanized troops. With vehemence she expressed her opinion that Hannah Arendt had trampled the dignity of her slaughtered people.

Arendt's book impresses me as very biased. Hitler is the sole plotter of the "final solution," Eichmann considers the implementation of this "solution" as "a job" and serves as the embodiment of the "banality of evil," while the Jewish leadership represents, at least to Jews, "the darkest chapter of the whole dark story." Repeatedly voiced is the argument that the Jewish leaders, by agreeing to collaborate with the Nazi policy of setting up special categories of Jews to be spared, have tacitly acknowledged the Nazi right to exterminate the Jews. Thus, Arendt's view of what Hilberg described as "anticipatory compliance" learned by Jews through hundreds of years of persecution represents the heights of an unempathetic condemnation of persons caught in a living nightmare. In praising the Jewish people as a whole but singling out the Jewish leadership as the real culprit, she picked on those who were cornered most. Her harsh judgmental stance toward leaders who were caught in unimaginable circumstances is one I cannot go along with.

Yet many of Arendt's descriptions of Jewish forced collaboration with the Nazis seem correct, and support in detail Hilberg's contention that the Jews were caught in the straitjacket of their history. They also support Arendt's own contentions elsewhere concerning the Jewish loss of political ability. However, her interpretations need refuting, as one story by a former inmate of the Kovno ghetto shows. In a conference held in Jerusalem on manifestations of Jewish resistance, Leib Garfunkel described what happened when the Germans delivered 5,000 white certificates to be distributed only among laborers and skilled workers. Someone suggested burning all these certificates, which in effect consisted of 5,000 tickets to life. But the people—and Garfunkel emphasized that these were the common people and not the leaders—objected adamantly to this idea, in simple terms. They saw only two choices. One was to buy time for 5,000 people. The other was fighting the Germans empty-handed, which meant collective suicide. The people, not the leadership, preferred collaboration. How could anyone, including Hannah Arendt, pass judgment on leaders who were caught in such a nightmare?

One possible answer is that together with other Jews, Arendt shares a revulsion toward the *shtadlonim*, the old-style pleading leaders who interceded with Gentiles on behalf of the Jews. This revulsion is particularly strong in Israel, where the *shtadlonim* are associated with everything passive in centuries of Jewish history, including the Holocaust. In a newspaper article entitled "The Shtadlonim," the journalist Nathan Baron referred to this old style of leadership as a pitiful phenomenon and condemned the community leaders of ghetto Jews for rejecting the efforts of Jewish youth to fight for their lives. Those who feel like Arendt or Baron are reluctant to face the very plausible fact that the Jewish leaders were tailored to their people and that the leaders changed only after the people changed and craved for new styles of leadership. Both leaders and people were the product of the same reality and had a mutual impact on each other. It is therefore unfair to focus the blame only on the leaders, if blame one must.

Hausner, who was well aware of Arendt's criticism of the Jewish leadership, found it necessary to clarify one point with regard to members of the Jewish Councils in the ghettos. Their type of leadership was that of a shtadlan, or interceder with the authorities. For their errand of mercy, the council members frequently paid with their lives. They were summarily executed when they refused to comply with orders, when they were caught with Underground contact men, or when other Jews tried to kill German guards. In comparing the role of the member of the Jewish Council in a ghetto with the well-known historical leadership role of the shtadlan, Hausner said of the latter that underneath his outer clothing the shtadlan used to wear the traditional Jewish grave clothes, for he might not come back alive from his mission. Hausner's analogy suggests that Jewish leaders in the ghetto followed a long tradition of leadership that was established during a long exile. Therefore, to blame the Jewish ghetto leaders is to conveniently brush aside historical perspective.

We have focused on the feelings of Jews about themselves, the dead and the living. Equally important is the issue of Jewish feelings toward Gentiles after the Holocaust. Stanley Meron regarded the two major failures related to the terrible destruction wrought by the Nazis on the Jews as, first, the lack of resistance on the part of the world community to this destruction, and, second, the lack of resistance on the part of the Jews toward their persecutors. The inaction on the part of the Great Powers with regard to the fate of the Jews was described in Hausner's book, leading Barbara Tuchman to say in her introduction that its descriptions of what the world did not do is sufficient reason why the Jews cannot forget. In this connection the researcher of the Holocaust Nora Levin underscored the fact that the Allies not only refused to take any concrete actions to stop the destruction of the Jews, but even refused to acknowledge that the Jews as such had been selected for destruction. Levin arrived at the conclusion that the Allies had written the Jews off as wartime casualties. Reading the descriptions of the "attempts" made by the Allies to do something about the Jews (See Levin and also Morse),—stories replete with red tape, and a bureaucratic machinery that behaved as if it had all the time in the world while in reality mass murder was being relentlessly executed— is enough to make any man a pessimist, and any Jew a paranoid. These bitter experiences have resulted in what Levin termed a new breed of Jews in Israel who are tough, realistic, and militant. One may also add to the list cynical and antiideological. The Israelis "know the score"; they have no illusions about this world.

The Six Day War of June 1967, which can be called the holocaust that did not happen, catapulted into consciousness the need for an exploration of the meaning of the Holocaust. Prior to this war the Arab barrage of boastful promises to drive the Jews into the sea evoked in Israelis and in Jews around the world a déja vu feeling. Once again the axe was raised against the ageless, badly scarred Jewish tree. Oddly enough, the start of it all was not ominous. Nasser paraded his forces in Cairo on their way to the Sinai Desert to fight Israel. It seemed like propaganda for internal use only, since who would glaringly reveal his preparations to the enemy if his intent were serious? Prime Minister Levi Eshkol was subsequently criticized for his tardiness in recognizing the seriousness of the threat and his belated mobilization of the Israeli reserve units. Meanwhile, Nasser scored diplomatic successes and seemed strong, clever, and a leader of stature. Many Israelis began to wish that the Old Man (Ben Gurion) was still at the helm. But Ben Gurion was indeed old. He had, however, a protege and potential heir, Moshe Dayan. In response to public pressure, therefore, and in spite of Golda Meir's resistance, Eshkol had to accept Dayan as defense minister. The Israeli army's command was not fearful of the military confrontation should it become inevitable. They trusted in victory. So did the American intelligence community. Israelis, however, were gripped by fear.

The fear now turned into rage and an urge to fight so as to relieve the tension of waiting. Eshkol and Eban, rightly or wrongly, seemed to be waiting too long and pleading too much with President Johnson to do something about the Egyptian blockade of the Straits of Tiran. Once again Jews were sitting idly by and waiting for the all-powerful word of the Gentiles. At least, this is the way it looked to the public. One need not have been a prophet, therefore, to forecast that it would not be long before Israelis would stop listening to what Gentiles say and show them instead what Jews can do. Once Dayan announced that Israelis did not want American soldiers to do the fighting for them, the die was cast. It was time for the new breed of Jews to demonstrate on their own how they handle holocaustal threats.

I can recall the enormous upheaval that gripped American Jewry as they identified with the fate of their Israeli brethren and became acutely aware of the threat of a new holocaust. So genuine and so manifest were these feelings that they contributed to a feeling in Israel of greater closeness to Diaspora Jewry than ever before. As for the feelings in Israel just before the Six Day War, they were aptly summarized by Abba Eban in his speech before the United Nations General Assembly, part of which he quoted in his book *My People:* "On the fateful morning of June 5 our country's choice was plain. The choice was to live or perish; to defend the national existence or to forfeit it for all times."

The great Israeli victory in the Six Day War averted another holocaust. Right after the war one could hear voices in Israel saying such things as: "If only the six million could see us now!" What they meant for the six million murdered Jews to see was how well Jews fought and how well they kept their vow of "Never again!" What the Israelis were really saying was, to paraphrase Hilberg, "Haven't we snapped out of the straitjacket of our history?"

The Six Day War shattered the amnesia concerning the Holocaust and deepened the search for the meanings of this cataclysm. Kibbutzim veterans of the war expressed awareness of a meaningful link between the two events (See Shapira). The preoccupation with the issue of Jewish resistance to the Nazis also intensified. An article appeared in *The New York Times* on research done in Israel concerning the Holocaust, with the title "Israeli Historian Denies Jews Yielded to the Nazis 'Like Sheep' " (Shenker). The article described an interview with Yehuda Bauer, Head of the Department of Holocaust Studies at the Hebrew University in Jerusalem, who stated that in 1967 the will of many Israelis to fight was rooted in a determination not to cooperate in their own destruction the way they believed the European Jews did. While Bauer disagreed with the verdict that the Jews went to the slaughter like sheep, he had to acknowledge the impact of this impression on young Israelis who failed to appreciate the obstacles to resistance which the European Jews faced. What Bauer seems to have suggested is that this issue of not fighting is more relevant to present living Jews than to those slaughtered in the early 1940s, and that there is a relationship between this issue and the prevailing mood in Israel before and after the Six Day War.

The new mood of a more penetrating search for meaning has already yielded a few daring ideas. Eliezer Livneh gave bold public expression to the conclusions of his own agonizing self-scrutiny. The largest and strongest Jewish group, American Jewry, did just about nothing and refrained from exercising pressure on President Roosevelt. The self-conscious group of Zionist Jews in Palestine did attempt rescue operations, but committed the deadly mistake of giving priority to Jewish immigration to Palestine over the more pressing goal of rescuing Jews everywhere and by any means possible. Livneh may have been too harsh with the Jewish Yishuv, whose power to influence events in Europe during the Second World War was minimal. But the questions of principle and priority that he raises do not lend themselves to easy answers.

After the Six Day War, when I became actively interested in Zionism and Jewish history, I had to discard my own amnesia about the Holocaust and to do what earlier in life I had considered undesirable, that is, "reading too much about it." Now as I read the literature, especially Hilberg's book, it came to me as a shocking revelation that, short of advances in technology, there was nothing new in the story of the Nazi annihilation of the Jews. History was merely repeating itself. The various ways of persecuting Jews and destroying their bodies, souls, or both, were not new. The basic philosophical rationalizations for treating Jews this way were not new either. Nor was the Jewish reaction of avoiding resistance and trying to avert the danger by the use of petitions and compliance. The Jewish view of flight as something futile and the final compliance and paralysis when the inevitable became clear were also part of the tradition of unlearning the art of resistance. The fact that as usual, Jews were selected for the most monstrous treatment, is something for the Jews specifically to worry about. However, that it has all happened before, that human nature seems in this infamous chapter in history to be as it has always been, that the only thing that has changed is the growth of technology and means of mass destruction, should give humanity at large something to worry about. In a world not bent on its own destruction, the cry of "Never again!" should remain not just a Jewish cry but the vow of humanity as a whole.

Reading the literature on the Holocaust was a very painful experience. Sorting out my reactions was no less painful. An initial "gut" reaction of mine was the fervent wish that all this had never happened. Ludicrous as it may sound, this wish sprang not foremost out of a humanistic concern for the millions of murdered victims, but from the need to remove a huge stain from my history and the history of my people. It is like a sign of Cain, a stigma, an irrefutable evidence of inadequacy. In the twelfth century the famed poet and philosopher Judah Halevi instilled in the Jewish people the notion that the irrefutable historical evidence for the chosenness of the people of Israel by a living God was His revealing himself to His people in public. In the Holocaust the exact opposite took place. The people of Israel were murdered on an assembly line. The Christian contention that Israel is a cursed people was given tangible evidence by the murderous acts of many Christians, while other members of the religion of love watched silently and left active rescue attempts to a minority of their faith. By the criterion of Halevi, this public mass murder was irrefutable public proof that God is malicious, dead, or at best retired. We Jews were murdered as individuals and castrated as a people for the whole world to see. Something is deadly wrong with us, I thought, although with the world too, and it will take us generations to find adequate recompense.

I also became convinced that the preoccupation with the issue of not fighting is a living reality for living Jews. It relates to basic questions of identity and self-image which existed for a long time in Jewish history and which have a lot to do with the rise of Zionism. The rage expressed by Bialik after the Kishinev massacres had existed for generations. Writing later about Kishinev, which he considered the classic prototype of the pogrom, Chaim Weizmann described his similar feelings of humiliation and impotence. Most tormenting to Weizmann was the fact that Jews had allowed themselves to be slaughtered. These reactions suggest that Kishinev became a prognostication in miniature of bigger things to come. The shame of the Jews for not resisting their murderers was a prototype of the same reaction on a much larger scale after the Nazi Holocaust.

The Holocaust also became a collective experience of castration. In *Totem and Taboo* and later in *Moses and Monotheism*, Freud anchored the rudimentary beginnings of religions in the castration fears of the sons in relation to the jealous father who ruled the primal horde. Freud also traced the origins of religions to the guilt and remorse felt by the sons after they managed to gang up on the father and kill him. The father was elevated to a deity in the form of a totem animal that was prohibited for hunting or eating except once a year. Subsequently, he was elevated into a monotheistic God, a Father in Heaven, so to speak. We have already seen that Judaism is mostly a father religion. This remains true in spite of the fact that in various Jewish mystical traditions (Scholem) the feminine component within the deity as well as the good-evil breach within God were emphasized. Although the God of Israel can be merciful, He can frequently be vengeful and He has a long memory, as the Bible warns its readers. Overt tokens of submission on the part of the sons are therefore needed so as to pacify the angry father. Hence circumcision, which ritualizes the submission and which in Judaism fixes it so early in life that the merit of submission to the father in heaven is presented as a "given" from the very beginning rather than as a "choice" later in life. As we may recall, Abraham had to obey his father in heaven and be willing to sacrifice his son Isaac. Isaac, in turn, had to obey his father on earth and submit to the sacrifice by Abraham. Thus the Jewish people have a covenant with the Lord and their special relation with him is symbolized by the mark of circumcision.

Concerning circumcision, Freud said that it is the symbolic substitute for castration, and was the punishment that the primeval father inflicted on his sons. Whosoever accepted this symbol demonstrated that he was ready to submit to the father's will, even at the cost of a painful sacrifice. This notion was reiterated by the theoretician of psychoanalysis Herman Nunberg, who underscored the importance of obedience to the father in the act of circumcision. In support of this idea he quoted Deuteronomy 10:16: "Circumcise therefore the foreskin of your heart, and be no more stiffnecked." In return for this submission the Jews were to be protected from mass retaliation by a jealous and vengeful God.

Yet somehow, somewhere, something misfired. The aim of ritual sacrifices is to fend off real castration through a substitute symbolic castration. It was this rationale which led the noted psychoanalyst Bruno Bettelheim, who emphasized the close link in the minds of many people between castration and circumcision, to name one of his books *Symbolic Wounds*. Castration is supposed to remain symbolic. The Holocaust however, was far too real. Similarly, Israeli casualties in the Six Day and Yom Kippur wars are real and the prospects for repeated wars and bloodshed are real. Little wonder then that the young generation of Israelis begins to ask why they are forever forced into the sacrificial role. One young kibbutz member (See Tzur et al) protested that he was no longer willing to be an eternal Isaac who agrees to be sacrificed with no questions asked. Shlomit Teub reported after interviewing the Israeli poet Eli Alon his assertion that after facing death, after being like Isaac stepping out of the sacrificial alter, young Israelis would never again be naive and unquestioning. The Israeli journalist Shulamit Hareven expressed her conviction that it was no coincidence that the youth of the kibbutzim chose the sacrifice as their symbol of going toward death during the Six Day War. In her opinion, just as the meaning of the term "sacrifice" *(akedah)* is not clear, the reason for the best Israeli youth's having to be sacrificed is not clear to the young kibbutzniks.

Baruch Kurzweil discussed the recurrence of the topic of the sacrifice, or binding to the altar, in modern Hebrew literature and concluded that the loss of understanding of this notion was due to the advanced process of secularization that had taken place in Hebrew literature. Thus modern secular interpretations of this notion, such as that the few should sometimes sacrifice themselves for the many, are shallow and unsatisfying. For Kurzweil, the sacrifice is an act of faith stemming from the absurd, which he defines as the felt incongruity between the godly and the human dimensions. In his opinion, this incongruous and absurd situation calls for an act of faith, a voluntary submission to God which is the essence of sacrifice. He therefore condemned modern Hebrew writers for their disapproval of Jewish martyrdom and sacrifice over the years. To many Israelis, however, the meaning of going to the altar is not as clear as it was to Kurzweil, and feeding them traditional Jewish beliefs spiced with modern existential notions (for Kurzweil did refer to Kierkegaard) will not do the trick. The crisis of faith among all peoples has advanced during our century, and the trauma of the Holocaust has deepened it even more among Jews. It will take more than a generation or two to come to terms with the Jewish historical sacrificial role which culminated in the Holocaust. Kurzweil's admonitions were therefore premature.

The decimation and castration of the Holocaust left many Jews shaken with the realization that God had not kept his part of the covenant or accepted the substitution of a "symbolic wound" for the real thing. Of course, the idea that the wound of circumcision is symbolic of castration, while recognized by some, is not palatable to others. Thus Erich Isaac, a specialist in the geography of religion, in his article "The Enigma of Circumcision" did his best to avoid the castration hypothesis. He wondered why circumcision was observed by all Jews while the laws of eating kosher food were not. Besides the obvious reason that circumcision was a permanent unifying sign of all Bnei Yisrael (Sons of Israel), I venture the guess that Jews feared the wrath of their God more if they gave up token castration than if they gave up kosher food. Isaac even goes as far back historically as Hittite times to argue that circumcision was a cutting ceremony which symbolized the making of a treaty or a covenant. To strengthen his case, he referred to the fact that in biblical Hebrew the expression for covenant-making is "to cut a covenant." Yet, how or why the ceremony of cutting of covenants changed from the dividing of animals to the cutting of man's foreskin, he did not bother to explain.

Recently while discussing the role of the Jew "as sacrificial victim," the psychoanalyst Alfred Schick related Freud's hypothesis on the origin of religions to anti-Semitism. Assuming that the primitive origin of religions is parricide, i.e., the murder of the father, and granting that fathers have to be repeatedly placated for the actual or intended murderous acts on the part of sons, some form of appeasement of the father becomes necessary. An obvious one is human sacrifice. Indeed, Arthur Koestler thought that the ubiquitousness of this phenomenon in the history of humankind is so extensive as to suggest an evolutionary defect in the species of man. What Schick proposed was an equation between anti-Semitic murder and human sacrifice. From this viewpoint, it is easy to imagine the rage and fear of other tribes and peoples when all of a sudden the children of Israel disposed of human sacrifice, thus exposing all people to the anger, castration, murder, and every form of vengeance by the unappeased father in heaven. An intuitive remedy in this case would be to sacrifice the culprits themselves, the children of Israel, the chosen ones, the different ones, the ones who in the first place put everyone else in jeopardy. This could be the ancient and primitive root of anti-Semitism. So for generations to come the Jews were set up by other nations in the role of sacrificial victims, and for generations they complied or were forced to comply with this role. Finally, however, they are no longer willing to play Isaac's role in each generation. The Holocaust has sealed this growing unwillingness with a final stamp of "Never again!"

At this point one difference between Judaism and Christianity comes to mind. In an article on the Holy Communion, the American psychoanalyst Daniel Schuster brought to light two important notions. The first is that Christianity more than Judaism retained many facets of old pagan rituals which antedate the monotheistic religions. To Jews, this is no revelation. They have regarded Christianity all along not as pure monotheism but as the corruption of Judaism by pagan ideas and rituals so as to make it more palatable to the many peoples who comprised the Roman empire. Schuster's second notion is that Holy Communion represents a ritualistic fusion of father and sons, and allows one through dual identification with both to experience the revolt against the father as well as his forgiveness. It seems to me that as far as Christianity is concerned this matter is related to the emphasized role of the madonna, especially in Catholicism. This, however, is not the subject of our present discussion. What is interesting here is that Judaism does not have a similar safety valve, and allows less leeway for expression of the father-son conflict than does Christianity. To ensure the obedience of its rebellious sons, Judaism always insisted on submission (Nunberg) and on love of suffering, both of which are regarded nowadays by many Israelis as passive and as sick. After all, we must realize that sacrificial submission combined with acceptance of suffering can get out of hand and result in real emasculation. Thus by the time love of suffering became a deeply engrained Jewish trait, psychological castration was real rather than symbolic. The great Hebrew novelist Hayim Hazaz may have had something like this in mind when he described the "different" and "nightly" psychology of the people who love suffering.

Since the Holocaust, the merit of submitting to the God of Vengeance has been questioned. Rather than being sacrificed to Him, there is now a danger that the children of Israel will emulate some of his traits and become just as vengeful. Since the days of Abraham and Moses the children of Israel have been cutting their foreskins in a covenant with their father in heaven that implied that this is where the cutting would stop. They were never supposed to lose their penises, not to mention their lives. But the God of Israel reneged on his part of the bargain. Why? There is no simple answer. From the vantage point of Gentile action, some answers will be forthcoming in Chapter 14. From the Jewish point of view, vague feelings of guilt for infringing on the father's territory might provide a reason why God broke the treaty. These suggestions stem from a psychoanalytic outlook and are not based on faith; believers may find different answers. Punishment for generations of sin and loss of faith could be one. Another, which would discourage questioning, might consist of the protestation that the ways of the Lord are beyond human comprehension. Existentialists, for their part, can regard it as a manifest call for submission to the absurd. Other suggestions by both believers and nonbelievers are probably forthcoming. In this connection it will be particularly interesting to see if those younger sabras who retain their faith will turn their "cute and thorny" chutzpah on their God, in an attempt to change the rules of the game, the game this time being their historical religion.

12.

The Arab Problem

TALK ABOUT A PALESTINIAN EN-
TITY MAKES MY BLOOD BOIL! A
NEW MADNESS!

—Akiva Govrin,
*Chairman of the Knesset
Committee for Foreign
and Security Affairs, 1969*

IT IS EXTREMELY HARD FOR ONE
MAN TO UNDERSTAND THE NA-
TIONALISM OF ANOTHER.

—Amos Elon

The tenacity and persistence of the Arab-Israeli conflict stemmed from the tragic situation of two peoples claiming the same land. The conflict was even further aggravated by various psychological needs on both sides. The following is an attempt to unravel the psychological factors in operation on the Jewish side, from which the situation was traditionally viewed as "the Arab problem."

When I was growing up in Haifa in the 1930s and 1940s I used to hear such slogans as *avodah ivrit* (Jewish labor) and *totzeret ha'aretz* (Jewish products) without understanding what they meant. I knew very little of A.D. Gordon's "religion of labor" or the national significance of developing a new brand of Jew who engages in physical work. Similarly, I did not realize that by calling local Jewish products *totzeret ha'aretz* (literally, the product of the land) rather than *totzeret Yehudit* or *Ivrit* (Jewish or Hebrew products), the local Yishuv was staking a claim to the land of Israel through subtle language games. *Ha'aretz*— the land—could have alluded to local Arab as well as local Jewish production, since we were all on the land, but everyone knew better. Referring only to the Jewish product of the land made it clear to whom the land really belonged.

The ideological zeal that accompanied the fight for Jewish labor and Jewish products was ferocious. I remember that an ageless Arab, who could have been forty to seventy years old, came to our house once a week to sell eggs to my mother. He was an institution: we expected him every Friday and called him *ha'aravi* (the Arab). Somewhere in the early 1940s the campaign to buy only *totzeret ha'aretz* intensified, and it was made clear to the rank and file that this time complete compliance was a must. For a week, Mother ran back and forth in the house like a chicken in a coop muttering "What shall I tell the Arab when he comes?" When he came at last, my mother was hysterical. She bought dozens and dozens of eggs from him, more than she had ever bought at one

time before, and then told him not to come again. He did not
seem surprised. Mother had to stand with her tribe or people or
whatever you call your own kind; there was nothing personal here.
To him it was probably *"min Allah"* (from God). He left and we
never saw him again. Mother kept walking around explaining, "I
had to do it, I had to do it." She was caught between two conflicting moral codes: her personal moral code, which told her it was all
right to buy from a man of integrity who had treated her fairly for
years, and the group ideology, which demanded *totzeret ha'aretz*. It
was not surprising that the ideology won. Zionist beliefs had made
her leave Poland at the age of sixteen against her parents' prohibitions and become a pioneer in Israel. Personal considerations had to
yield to the cause.

As I grew up, I took the Arabs for granted. They were usually
called Esma, which is a distortion of the Arab Isma, meaning "Hear!".
There was something derogatory about this custom. People do not like
to be called "Hear! Hear!" but this practice did not even come close
to anything like calling a Jew a Kike or a Black a Nigger. In the late
forties the term Arabush (plural Arabushim) became more popular. A
more demeaning term, it connotes the scorn that the efficient and
strong feel toward the weak and inept. It still does not convey the
pervasive sense of disgust and exclusion expressed in "kike" or "nigger." Although I did not love the Arabs I did not hate them either.
They seemed like competitors. My people and the Arab people were
drawing their bargaining positions, and I expected it to end in a compromise in which both sides would abandon their initial stand. I expected a prolonged bargaining ritual such as those which take place so
frequently in any Arab market, but my powers of prediction as to the
outcome left much to be desired.

The eye-capturing news headlines of several Arab-Israeli wars
since 1948 may obscure for the general public the fact that this conflict
is not new. Many of the perplexing dilemmas have been in existence
for about eighty years. The problems the early Jewish settlers at Rehovot had in dealing with their Arab neighbors have been described by
Jakov Roi. One such problem was the Jewish conviction that the Arabs
understand only the language of force, a bias that persisted for many
years and became especially pronounced after the Holocaust. In draw-

ing a profile of the native-born Israelis, Russcol and Banai emphasized the fact that the Holocaust and the failure of the European Jews to fight changed the sabra's conception of power and force, causing it to lose its evil nature. This development was conducive to the perpetuation of the notion that the only language Arabs understand is force.

Nor is this illusion the result of the experience with Arabs alone. As the Israeli Journalist Boaz Evron stated in an article entitled "Force Which Is Weakness," the Jewish heritage of being the victim of physical force has convinced Israelis that physical force is the only tangible political reality which carries weight and is significant in the affairs of nations. In Evron's opinion, the perpetual Jewish condition of physical inferiority and helplessness, which reached its culmination in the Holocaust, resulted in an overreaction, because of which a proper understanding of subtle political maneuvers has been lost and current Israeli political vision is mostly conceptualized in terms of tanks and jets, i.e., force.

Another problem of the early settlers was the derogatory attitude toward the Arabs. Roi quoted the remarks of some of the early Jewish settlers who were aware of this problem. They were critical of the naive Zionist perception of the land of Israel as being a virgin land, and of those insensitive Zionists who contemplated all sorts of methods for cultivating the land but none for cultivating the people who were already settled on it. These same critics also deplored the lack of Jewish motivation and conscious efforts to teach to Jews the language of the Arabs. It is not hard to understand that the early settlers, trying to effect a Jewish rejuvenation and a Hebrew revival, could not take care of the Arab language too. But it seems that they did not even want to. Attitudes established in those times were passed on to the next generation. I know I was not the only pupil in my high school in Haifa who resented the fact that we were not offered a choice of study of a second foreign language. The first foreign language under the British Mandate was, of course, English. But we were forced to "waste our time" on Arabic as a second language, while the pupils in another school were offered the chance to study French. We felt that this was unfair. What could Arabic offer us? Most of us learned it halfheartedly and forgot the little we learned soon after graduation.

The early settlers also naively believed that the Arab peasants welcomed the new Jewish settlers. True, they did not seem to, but this was believed to be only because their corrupt masters, who saw in the Jews dangerous economic and social competitors, had cultivated hostility. This may have been part of the truth, but it was not the whole truth. Revolutionary as well as national movements frequently arise first among the nobility and the intelligentsia. The Arab landlords rejected the growing foreign national culture around them, and the Jews, who were compulsively preoccupied in realizing their own national aspirations, were not able to see the revival of similar aspirations among their neighbors. On the whole, Roi's descriptions indicate how early tragedy was building up and how remarkably similar the psychology of the Arab-Israeli conflict remained for the ensuing eighty years.

From the very beginning of the Zionist endeavor most Zionists displayed a blind spot in their view of the Arabs, a blind spot that started as a total lack of vision and later became distorted vision. The absence of the Arabs from the Jewish visual field was sometimes total. Elon described how, during times of bloody clashes with Arabs at Sejera in 1903, Jews continued to discuss recondite issues of social ideology in political meetings and ignored the more tangible issue of Arab resistance. The blindness on the part of otherwise humane persons was appalling. In reviewing Elon's book *The Israelis* in the newspaper *Ha'aretz*, Robert Weltsch recalled how during the 1920s he had felt compelled to contradict the comments of an admired and beloved person, the eminent Zionist leader and writer Nahum Sokolow, who had said: "What is all this talk about an Arab problem? There is no such problem."

When defenses act to create a blind spot in perception, the results can at times be remarkable. Thus in his autobiography, Chaim Weizmann describes a visit he and his wife made to South Africa in the early thirties. Under the heading "A Strange National Home," he pays tribute to the physical beauty of the country, and especially to a game reserve which he toured for three days. Weizmann's reflections about the animals in this beautiful home ". . . with trees, water, grass, food, going about unmolested, as free citizens . . ." bear a remarkable similarity to Sholom Aleichem's portrayal of the only corner of Jewish freedom in the small shtetl, the only piece of land with trees and grass

where Jews can breathe freely—the Jewish graveyard. Sholom Aleichem's story "The Town of the Little People" suggests that a corner
of freedom must include more than a tiny graveyard or freedom
becomes a mirage and a divided self becomes a reality. Perhaps Weizmann was thinking along the same lines, although he does not say. Did
it occur to him that he and other Zionists were trying to build a game
reserve for his people, a stretch of land for the Jews where they could
be protected from massacres and environmental dangers? Weizmann
did point out that this home for the animals was only slightly smaller
than Palestine, and that it had no Arab problem. He concluded that
it was better to be an animal in a South African Game reserve than
a Jew in Warsaw or even in London. Deep fears were surfacing in these
reflections of Weizmann, which evoke the association of the Jews as
hunted animals with their numbers decreasing and with the extinction
of the species as a distinct danger, unless a game reserve is established
soon.

However, these reflections may reveal other feelings too. Would
it not be wonderful if Palestine, the game reserve for the Jews, were
free of an Arab problem the way the game reserve for animals in South
Africa is? The underlying feeling tone seems to be for the Arabs to
go away, for the Arab question to disappear. One must build a protective shelter around one's ardent beliefs, for if one were to listen to the
Arab problem and all the other problems, one might give up the whole
project. Thus it is better to ignore certain unpleasant facts. Maybe they
will go away, as one continues to realize one's dreams. Incidentally, it
is odd that Weizmann could reflect in this manner in South Africa and
ignore the fact that the South Africans had an even worse "Arab
problem," with the substitution of the word "native" for "Arab."
Indeed, it is ironic that of all countries in the world, Weizmann had
to choose South Africa as the place in which he could momentarily
escape the Arab question. Doubly ironic, in view of the fact that as a
participant in the Sixth Zionist Congress in 1903, Weizmann vehemently opposed the offer of a kind of African game reserve for the Jews
—the East Africa scheme.

Weizmann comes across here as a tired leader who has experienced political setbacks within the Zionist movement and is over-

whelmed with the realization of how badly his people need to have
their own home. The Zionist solution meant being fit to survive, and
Weizmann devoted his life to this goal with an ominous sense of
urgency. It is no surprise, therefore, that he had a desperate need not
to question the basic assumptions of Zionism and certainly not to call
off the whole Zionist project. Thus strong defenses of repression and
denial set in, causing a great, humane leader to walk around with
blinders on, even though his field of vision was still larger than that of
many other militant Zionists. It could not be helped. The Jews never
came to Palestine to kick the Arabs out. They came to Eretz Yisrael
to build it and be built by it, to rejuvenate themselves and to insure
their own survival. Their hearts were enflamed and their eyes focused
on their own destiny. In this frame of mind, only after repeated tragic
clashes could they take note of the Arabs and *their* national dreams.

The moral problem facing the Jews transcended the fate of individual Arabs and involved a clash between Zionism and the Arab
national aspiration for the establishment of an independent Arab nation in the whole of Palestine. An honest approach would have been
to acknowledge fairly and squarely the existence of this conflict of
aspirations and interests and to state it to the adversary. On many
occasions, however, honesty did not prevail. Too frequently, the Jewish
perception of Arabs was like that of Israel Cohen, who stated in one
of his books on Zionism that the Jews had always hoped that the Arabs
would in due time become reconciled to the Balfour Declaration as
they learned to appreciate the benefits that Jewish development of
Palestine had conferred upon them. This frequently voiced slogan is at
best naive. It was the wishful thinking of many Zionists that offering
the Arabs better medical care as well as other economic and social
benefits would distract the Arabs from voicing their national aspirations. Other Zionists adopted a more honest line and were willing to
confront the Arabs with the basic issue. They were willing to ask the
Arabs either to give up a part of the country for the sake of peace, or
to stick to their demand for the whole of Palestine at the risk of a
violent confrontation with the Yishuv. Intellectual honesty, however,
did not always imply a willingness to compromise. On the whole, both
David Ben Gurion and Vladimir Jabotinsky were honest in stating their

positions toward the Arabs. However, while Ben Gurion was willing to compromise, Jabotinsky was not.

In 1937, Vladimir Jabotinsky, the leader of the militant Revisionist Party, submitted testimony to the Palestine Royal Commission in which he demanded that the Jews be allowed to grow into a majority in Palestine (Laqueur). Although he, too, resorted to the rationalization of how the activity of the Jews improved the economic position of the Arabs in Palestine, Jabotinsky addressed himself mainly to the heart of the matter. He did not expect the Palestinian Arabs to like their transformation into a minority. However, he compared the conflicting Arab and Jewish claims to "the claims of appetite versus the claims of starvation." When the need of Palestine Arabs to live in an Arab State Number 5 or Number 6 is weighed against the need of the Jews to live in the only state of their own, he argued, "the decisive terrible balance of need" is clear. Jabotinsky's presentation was not characterized by empathy with the Arabs. His attitude toward them was: "I have the profoundest feelings for the Arab case, insofar as that Arab case is not exaggerated." Nevertheless, in comparison to the broken record of how economically and medically the Palestinian Arabs benefited from the Jews, of how they should feel lucky and would have felt so were it not for the instigation of malicious Arab leaders who wanted to retain the Arab masses in bondage, Jabotinsky's remarks indicated a fair amount of intellectual honesty. Certainly he could not be accused of being wishy-washy or engaging in self-delusion. However, in the name of survival or the priority of starvation over appetite, he wanted to override the Arab claim rather than compromise with it. So he clung to the land on both sides of the Jordan River, saying, to put it in talmudic language, *"Kulah sheli"* ("It is all mine").

It was a different story with Ben Gurion. He was as militant, as adamant, and as determined as Jabotinsky. In a speech in 1943, while the Second World War was still raging, Ben Gurion looked forward to the postwar period and promised to persist in and accomplish the Zionist build-up even against Arab armed resistance. He also promised to overcome Arab obstruction even if it were backed by British bayonets. Actually, he was following in the footsteps of his mentor, Berl Katznelson. At the beginning of 1941, Katznelson had stated:

We have known that you cannot cheat history. We have
also known that we would not lie to the Arabs and we do not
wish to lie to ourselves either. We have known that should
an agreement between us and the Arabs materialize, it would
not be founded on the decimation of Zionism but rather on
the implementation of Zionism. We should say to the Arab
peoples: In us, Jews, you see an obstacle in your way toward
independence and unification. We do not deny it. As long
as you negate Zionism and plan to suffocate us, as long as you
pile obstacles on our way—we cannot view with favor your
increasing power. We shall certainly do our best to stop you.

In following this line, Ben Gurion was like an irresistible force. Nevertheless, militant as he was, he repeatedly agreed to partition offers
which would give the Jews a large enough part of the country to
establish a viable state. He remained loyal to this partition notion even
after the Six Day War and for this reason was duly credited by Elon
for his commendable rejection of expansionistic aspirations.

I doubt that Ben Gurion cared less for the Zionist endeavor or the
fate of the Jews than Jabotinsky did. He was, however, able to tailor
his aspirations to the demands of both realpolitik and morality. From
a sheer political standpoint, there were more chances for the Jews to
realize their dream and hassle it out with the British and the Arabs if
they did not lay claim to the whole of Eretz Yisrael, which also included
Jordan. The principle of partition was an ethical one. The Talmud
teaches that if two persons grab hold of a *tallit* (a prayer shawl) and
each one says, "It is all mine," then "they shall divide." Obviously
dividing is not an ideal solution, but mundane justice is hardly ever
ideal. Ben Gurion adopted the attitude of "they shall divide." Jabotinsky, and now his followers, keep reiterating "It is all mine." Native-
born Israelis are notorious for being both "cute and thorny." However,
when it comes to the "it is all mine" attitude of some Israelis, one
cannot blame the Arabs if from their vantage point this kind of thorny
chutzpah is not at all "cute."

It is regrettable that the Israeli attitude toward the Arabs has been
characterized over the years by arrogance that stood in the way of

empathy. It is hard to step into the Arab's shoes if the Arabs are looked down upon and named Arabushim. Part of this lack of empathy stemmed from ignorance of Arab tradition, with which the Jewish Eastern European immigrants to Palestine were unfamiliar. Another part was a result of the great need to ignore any other claimants to the ancestral Jewish land. However, to a certain degree this lack of empathy was a matter of conscious choice. In the eyes of many Israelis, it was no tragedy for Jews to push Gentiles around for a change, and for non-Jews to find out what the Jews have had to put up with for generations. From this attitude sprang the myth that the Arabs understand only the language of force.

The Israeli lack of empathy for the Arab predicament manifested itself in cocky fashion in a popular song during the late 1940s. It was sung in Hebrew with a deliberate Arab accent and with vocal imitations of the sounds of ouds or mandolins, so as to make it clear that it was being sung by defeated Arabs. The first verse of the song went as follows:

> For thousands of years we ate Arabic bread and
>   drank from *finjans* (coffee cups),
> Before the arrival of the Ben Gurions and
>   Shertoks and Weizmanns.
> By the life of the *Mufti* (Islamic judge) may
>   he live long,
> That Filastin to us will belong!

The mocking derogation of the Arabs received a clear expression in this song. The Sinai campaign of 1956 did not result in a meaningful change of attitude; even then this song was still sung by Israeli soldiers.

The scornful attitude toward the Arabs, which prevailed for many years, found an interesting expression in 1965. In an article entitled "The Israeli Who Seems Pretty to Himself," the journalist Hadassah Mor reported on an interview with Kalman Benyamini, a member of the Psychology Department of the Hebrew University in Jerusalem who was conducting research on the way Israelis, Americans, Germans, and Arabs look to Israeli youth. The results shocked him so that he decided not to publish them. Benyamini had discovered that the image of the Arab in the eyes of Israeli youth was very distorted and negative. After the Six Day War, he repeated his study and found that Israeli youth viewed the Arab as even sicker, drunker, and uglier. At the same time he found an overestimation of self on the part of the Israelis, which in his opinion could be interpreted as a natural result of a victory in a fast war. Of particular interest was Benyamini's report that when he presented officers of the Israel Army with these results they were perturbed. The officers not only regarded the negative images of the Arab as gross distortions, but also as an unwarranted underestimation of the enemy. In the interview, Benyamini expressed the hope that young Israelis would change their perceptions as new social and political developments took place.

But the contempt persisted. Indeed, the biased attitudes found their culmination right after the Six Day War when Israelis were still intoxicated by the great victory, and before the deeper self-examination began. At that time one could hear such boasts as: *"Oolai ain brera ela lehakiz la'arabushim dam kol kamah shanim"* (Perhaps there is no choice but to bleed the Arabushim every few years). The victory was so astounding that it seemed that this time even the Arabushim might draw a lesson from it. But if not, then there was no question about the Israeli ability to bleed them whenever they got smart or got the wrong ideas, until they learned better. For a brief moment it seemed as if all problems were over. The Arabs would either sign peace now or sign it later. The whole world now knew that they could be clobbered again and again and sooner or later this realization must penetrate even the thick skulls of the Arabs. So the Israelis waited for the "phone call" from the Arab side, a call which never came. Since then, Dayan and other Israelis have acknowledged that this expectation was a mistake. In spite of the fact that Israel had just taught the people who "understand only the language of force" a momentous lesson in the art of warfare, the Arabs still failed to "understand" and to initiate submissive phone calls. Of this period, the Israeli political scientist Shlomo Avineri said that most Israelis believed, with a mixture of naiveté and arrogance, that the Six Day War had finally opened the door to peace.

History was repeating itself. According to an expert on the making of Israel's foreign policy, Michael Brecher, as early as 1957—one year after the Sinai Campaign—the former Israeli Prime Minister Moshe Sharett delivered a lecture in which he characterized the Israeli hope that the campaign would lead to peace as an illusion and an absurdity. He also regarded it as a failure to realize how things look from the Arab side. Similarly, the maverick politician Uri Avneri lamented the fact that Israel did not initiate a decisive peace offer right after the war. This major opportunity for peace was lost for a variety of reasons. The immediate and large-scale military aid provided to the Arabs by Russia helped to foster in them an uncompromising attitude. So did the Israeli stance of waiting for the Arabs to finally "learn their lesson."

Now it was the Israelis who learned better. The Arabs remained adamant, their humiliation only driving them to the extremes of seeking ways to regain their pride. The Arab guerilla movement, which never posed a serious security threat to Israel, was instrumental in injecting the Arabs with pride. One Jewish friend told me that "it wouldn't hurt the Israelis to find out that Arabs too are willing to die for a cause they believe in." This has become clear to many of the younger generation. Young Israelis are much more sensitive nowadays to the Arab plight. A cocky Israeli song mocking the Arab people's traditional way of life is unimaginable at present. Israelis may not know what to do about the Arab tragedy, but they no longer think that it is funny. Nevertheless, mental blocks still exist, especially among the members of the older generation. It is hard for them to relate to the heart of the problem—the existence of another claimant to the land, a claimant who was already settled there. Today the yardstick with which to measure the degree to which Israelis overcame the blind spot concerning the Arab problem is their willingness or lack of willingness to acknowledge the national aspirations of the Palestinian Arabs, which came to be known as the Palestinian entity *(yeshut Palestina'it)*.

Recognizing the Palestinian entity is not a theoretical issue devoid of practical implications. It involves the realization that the rival national movement and its people also have a moral and political right to independence and statehood in a part of Palestine. Don Peretz, the American scholar and Middle East specialist, shed light not only on the tangible development of a Palestinian national movement but also on the similarity of its emotional content with that of Zionism prior to the establishment of the State of Israel. He termed this feeling "Arab Zionism" and asserted that because of its emotional intensity it would be a mistake to dismiss it as a transient phenomenon. There is no doubt concerning the emotional intensity of "Arab Zionism." Elon drew attention to the power of the living memory of the lost homeland among Arab refugees as well as to the distress of Israeli soldiers who met up with these refugees and encountered this intense form of Zionism in reverse. These memories and emotions, deeply rooted among Palestinians, are the stuff of which national identity is made. It would be a mistake to expect this kind of Palestinian consciousness to disappear in the face of political setbacks. King Hussein's Jordanian army can crush Palestinian guerila units but not the Palestinian identity. The Israeli hope that Hussein will rid them of the Palestinian problem represents a stubborn refusal on the part of the ardent nationalists to recognize in their adversaries the very same elements which they cherished in themselves.

Peretz was correct in his assertion that the Palestinian entity is with us to stay. He was therefore critical of Prime Minister Golda Meir's statement on June 15, 1969, that there were no such things as Palestinians. Meir's statement is perhaps the most notorious case of refusal to behold the Palestinians, but not the only one. The labor leader Yitzhak Tabenkin stated in 1970 that the Palestinian entity exists nowhere except in the imagination of its Jewish promoters. And in a newspaper article the same year the Israeli reporter Eliyahu Amikam voiced his opinion that the only content of a Palestinian identity is the wish to obliterate Israel. By narrowing the content of the Palestinian entity to nothing more than a wish to take revenge on Israel, Amikam deprived it of any positive characteristics which would define it as a nation. It is tantamount to saying that the Palestinians exist only because of the Israelis. In the past, Jews resented the definition of Jews as whoever Gentiles identify as a Jew. Nor did Jews appreciate other people telling them that they are a religion but not a nation or that they have no future as Jews. Jews did not solicit other people to advise them as to their identity. Now, however, they volunteer definitions to another people without awareness of the fact that in the process they do unto Arabs as the Gentiles did unto Jews.

Fortunately, this attitude is not shared by all Israelis. For instance, the Israeli Arabist Menahem Milson has criticized Israeli leaders and writers for arguing in pseudohistorical and pseudosociological fashion that the Palestinians are not a nation. He blames this practice for inducing false notions concerning Arab feelings, and compares it to the similar degrading practice of Fatah members who try through "historical" research to prove that the Jews are not a nation. Finally, he deplores the Israeli pseudohistorical arguments for their educational impact on the Israeli public, which have encouraged the development of despair, cynicism, and nihilism. Indeed, the educational outcome *is* tragic. Amos Kenan, a journalist who is frequently critical of the Israeli government, has also deplored this situation. In wartime, he points out, the Israeli is courageous, optimistic, confident, and dynamic. When it comes to the issue of peace, however, he loses these admirable qualities and becomes pessimistic, apathetic, static, and despairing. The Israeli ineptness concerning peace might change, however. One way it could come about is as a result of a more empathic image of the Arabs which recognizes the psychological reality of an entrenched sense among some of them of Palestinian nationalism.

Another impediment to Israeli peace efforts is a historical conditioning which prompts Israelis to assume a peculiar attitude toward the Arab leadership. Hannah Arendt has suggested that generations of political impotence and of being the target of persecutions and cruel assaults by Gentile masses fostered in Jews an orientation of turning toward the Gentile leadership and away from the masses. This remoteness from Gentile popular sentiments resulted at times in Jewish blindness toward the political dangers of rising anti-Semitism. While Jews aligned themselves with the nobilities and authorities, they felt a deeprooted distrust of the masses, who more frequently indulged in violent anti-Jewish outbursts. These historical developments led to the establishment of the court Jew, the shtadlan or pleading Jewish leader who interceded with the authorities on behalf of the Jewish community. It also led to a traditional Jewish overestimation of how much can be achieved by agreement with the leaders of a people. It was this tradition which led Weizmann to put too much hope in the outcome of his discussions with Amir Feisal. Similar overestimations characterized

Golda Meir's talks with King Abdullah and the more recent secret negotiations between Yigal Allon and King Hussein.

There is nothing wrong in itself in bargaining with Arab leaders. It represents false hopes, however, when done as part of a deliberate attempt to bypass the Arab masses. Talking with Hussein is no substitute for talking with the Palestinians. Deciding matters over their heads would only make them feel as if it were another Balfour Declaration all over again. They would hate it with venom just as Gamal Abdel Nasser did. In his book *The Philosophy of the Revolution,* Nasser mentioned his reading Weizmann's autobiography and his ensuing reflections on the Balfour Declaration. Nasser came to view Zionism as a hateful imperialism which by means of the Balfour Declaration furthered its cause at the expense of all the Arab peoples. To him and many Arabs, this declaration represented a dirty deal cooked up by Zionists and imperialists behind the back of the Arab masses. Any Israeli move that would look to the Arabs like a repeat performance of this insult, even if the deal were concluded this time with Arab leaders (who may nevertheless not represent popular opinion), is doomed to worsen an already very bad situation.

On the other hand, a public recognition of the Palestinian right to self-determination could eventually lead to Arab support of a future agreement. This kind of support could never be delivered by the leaders alone. It is a mistake to hinge all hopes on Arab leaders and at the same time regard the Arab masses as completely subservient to their leaders' will. As a rule, it works the other way around: Arab leaders have frequently yielded to strong popular Arab sentiments. Objectively speaking, Zionists perceive Arab nationalism in strange ways. In the beginning, Arab nationalism was regarded as not genuine and as instigated by the Arab leaders, who were the real culprits. At present, Arab nationalism is tacitly acknowledged, but it is regarded as impossible to deal with except perhaps through the medium of Arab leaders, who now represent the last hope. In reality, however, there is no substitute for Israeli people dealing with Palestinian people. Arab leaders cannot deliver what their people do not accept.

It is hard for those who dream of a Greater Israel to recognize the Palestinian entity. I suppose most Jews would have liked to inhabit their ancestral land on both sides of the Jordan River. Yet they realized that they would have to be content with less than that because of the other claimant to the land. Giving "a land without people for a people without a land" à la Israel Zangwill would have been ideal from a Jewish viewpoint, but reality did not present them with a country without people. The question therefore arose as to what should the borders of the new Jewish state be? What would be ethical at least in the sense of minimizing injustice to both sides? As a rule, the Jews did not define the borders of their claim, either through unwillingness to give away bargaining cards prematurely or through an unwillingness to give up any parts of the old historical claim to the whole of Eretz Yisrael. This lack of definition served to arouse Arab fears of "Zionist expansion." Many Israelis regarded this supposed Arab fear as a figment of Arab propaganda. They sincerely believed that all that Israel wanted was peace and that it could not care less about expansion. They did not credit the intensity of the Arab fears, just as the Arabs failed to credit the intensity of Jewish fears of genocide before the Six Day War. Even an Arab scholar like Hisham Sharabi in discussing this period uttered the nonsense that Israel could not have entertained serious fears about its security. He based his judgment on Israel's dominant military position. In other words, his vision was focused on Israeli might, not on Israelis, on flesh-and-blood people who were gripped with dread. Thus on both sides the problem of squaring the circle was set. The fighting Israelis, proud of their present deeds but still burdened by their origins as passive shtetl Jews, feared "genocide," and the desert warriors, the Arabs, feared "Zionist expansion."

Not all Israelis are aware of the connection between Arab fear of Zionist expansion and the traditional Jewish vagueness concerning territorial claims. The lack of definition of what the borders of the new Israeli state are, or should be, is not something new. When I was a schoolboy in Haifa at the age of ten, before the State of Israel was established, I was taught geography. The textbook as well as my teacher were drawing the distinction between present borders and borders of destiny *(gvulot ye'ud)*. The *gvulot ye'ud* included Transjordan and reached Mesopotamia. The textbook, the teacher, and the students were all glossing it over somewhat mechanically. It was the kind of distinction students memorize because it may come up in an examination, not something which one puts his heart into and tries to figure out. Thus, I cannot recall anyone's touching upon the delicate issues involved in this distinction. Destiny borders by virtue of what destiny, religious or national? What about the Arabs? What means, peaceful or not, will be used to achieve borders of destiny? Such questions were never discussed. Indeed, the way this geography was taught inculcated in the pupils, including myself, an insensitive, defensive attitude toward the Arab question which had characterized the Zionist movement from the start. This teaching also served as an inconspicuous staking of a claim. Its mentality went something like this: The practicalities of reaching the borders of destiny will be handled more concretely when the time is ripe. For the time being, let us not forget the borders of destiny, but let us not talk too much about it either.

By now the talk has intensified. The core of former Revisionists who in loyalty to their old credos support the Greater Israel Movement is joined by more than one johnny-come-lately. In addition to the traditional right-wingers, the Greater Israel Movement is supported by persons who belong to the political left, to the religious parties, or even to the secular Canaanites. Some people from the left support it because it is a direct expansion of the old virtues of settlement and pioneering. That was enough to make Tabenkin talk about the occupied territories as "liberated" territories. For the left-winger Zvi Shiloah, a graduate of Gordonia and an admirer of A. D. Gordon's "religion of labor," the danger of becoming more like an ethnic community than a modern and highly developed Jewish state was enough to make him an advocate of the Greater Israel Movement. He regarded his present support of this movement as consistent with the traditional notions of Zionism. Supposedly a basic concept of Zionism was "the doctrine of cruel Zionism," which, Shiloah explained, is anchored in the central conviction that no compromise is possible in the conflict between Zionism and Arab nationalism. Therefore, in loyalty to what he considered to be authentic and well-established Zionist convictions, he voiced the aspiration for the establishment of a southern federation of the land of Kedem or the Fertile Crescent which would be dominated by Israel. All this will come about in the future when "the peace is signed in Bagdad." It is cruel Zionism indeed.

Some religious persons support the Greater Israel Movement because, they say, the God of Israel promised the whole country to the sons of Israel. In the name of a divine title deed (the Jews are the only people in the world to whom the Torah bequeathed the land of Israel), they claim possession of the newly acquired territories. This is the prevailing rationale in a special 1971 issue of *Matat*, an Israeli monthly for Jewish studies, which was dedicated to the Israeli-Arab conflict. As for the Canaanites such as A. G. Horon, they also cherish big dreams. Greater Israel is merely a first stage leading to the larger Canaan alliance and Middle Eastern (Kedem) alliance respectively. (The mythological rationale for this big dream is too complicated to discuss here.) For a variety of reasons, some Israelis regard the occupied territories not as a defense line to be given back when peace prevails, but as a liberated country to which they have a natural or divine right. Thus, in comparison to the times of the "state on the way" prior to 1948, many more persons talk nowadays about their claim to Greater Israel. The post-Six Day War era saw right and left, religious and secular Israelis raising their voices in support of Greater Israel, which is in effect a partial fulfillment of the old dream for borders of destiny. Unlike the early 1940s it is now more practical to stake the claim and justify it on historical religious moral and legal grounds.

It is unfortunate that as a result of the Six Day War some Israelis began to feel not only more secure but also more powerful than ever before. Their initial sense of relief following a great victory was transformed into a corrupt version of a sense of power—the feeling that might makes right. It was this development which prompted the historian Jacob Talmon to publish his article "Could Force Be the Answer to Everything?" His response, after viewing both Jewish and non-Jewish history, was in the negative. His scholarly article, however, cannot successfully combat popular sentiments of a segment of the Israeli population which is becoming more and more militant. The increased militancy has found its expression in controversies over the true meaning of Zionist history.

In the early 1970s the Israeli newspapers began to discuss more frequently the sensitive question of whether Jewish acquisition of and settling on the land *(hitnahalut)* was necessarily associated with the intentional dispossession of Arabs from the land *(nishul)*. The discussions did not center on single incidents but on the very meaning of Zionism. Those who upheld the willful dispossession of Arabs as a historically valid tenet of Zionism were characterized by two important traits. First, they focused their attention not on what the Jews merely said but on what they actually did. For instance, Yeshayahu Ben-Porat stated in *Yediot Aharonot* of August 11, 1972: "I am talking about the meaning of Zionist implementation and not Zionist theory as written in collections of speeches and in festive brochures." Thus, some of today's militant Israelis ignore not only Gentile but even Zionist small talk. Second, those who sought *nishul* in the history of Zionism cared more about the future than the past. For them, the issue at stake was not really how much dispossession of Arabs has already taken place but rather how much will still be needed to bring the implementation of Zionism to completion. They focused their gaze on the occupied territories and sought to legitimize future acts of *nishul* as within the mainstream of Zionism.

The new militant and chauvinistic mood was given full expression during 1972 in two articles which became a subject of controversy in the Israeli newspapers. In the first, "Without Complexes," the former commander of the Israeli Air Force Ezer Weizman flatly stated that Israel's raison d'être is not security, but national goals. Therefore, the Israeli stand concerning Israel's new borders should be determined not by security considerations alone but also by long-term national and historical interests. The second article, by Ben-Porat, was called "The Mistake, Naïveté, and Hypocrisy"—all of which referred to different ways of denying what Ben-Porat considered to be important Zionist truths. The most crucial of these truths, he insisted, "is that there is no Zionism, and there is no settlement, and there is no Jewish state without evacuation of Arabs and without expropriation and fencing of lands." Using strong language, Ben-Porat issued an open challenge to all Israelis to realize what has been the true meaning of Zionism both in the beginning of the century and in 1972. It is to the credit of the open Israeli society that such challenges do not go unanswered. But the frequency of such debates indicates a change of political climate in comparison to the pre-Six Day War days. The growing momentum is on the side of the aggressive nationalists. Cruel Zionism is on the ascendancy.

The new look at the history and meaning of Zionism led to new conceptualizations concerning the Six Day War. All of a sudden, voices were heard which questioned the assumption that the war was a war of survival. Such questions did not arise among the Israeli people during the tense days prior to the war, not because people suppressed their doubts in deference to the national interest, but because there was no doubt in people's minds as to what they were facing. Later, as politicking resumed its habitual prominence, it became a fad to argue over the meaning of war. Those who tried to impose a new meaning on the event were largely oriented toward the future rather than the past. By characterizing the past war as a calculated decision to further national goals, they hoped to legitimize future political decisions. First and foremost among these could be a decision to keep the new territories as part of Greater Israel. In reference to all these debates and political commotion, the former Minister of Transportation Moshe Carmel said: "All those people are using the privilege of hindsight in order to justify their present political stand" (Segal). He was right but the damage was already done. These pronouncements made it possible for Egyptian President Anwar el-Sadat to claim that even the Israelis themselves admit that in 1967 they did not face a threat of extermination. Therefore, from his viewpoint, the myth that Israel was exposed to the danger of extermination was now being dissipated by those who had created it in the first place.

The debated long-term national goals that are presumably no less important than security refer, of course, to territorial claims. Small Israel ought to become Great Israel. Once more the question arises as to what are the territorial aspirations of Zionism. In 1898, while on a train to Constantinople, Herzl inserted the following remark in his diary (Patai): "Discussed with Bodenheimer the demands we will make. Area: from the Brook of Egypt to the Euphrates." This is precisely the land promised to Abraham's seed in a covenant between him and God (Genesis 15: 18). These are the borders of destiny in regard to which even Greater Israel is only an intermediary goal. Nowdays, the advocates of Greater Israel wish to retain the occupied territories so as to create room for mass Jewish emigration from the Soviet Union. The end goal to which this kind of logic leads is not hard to envision. The Greater Israel Movement is known in Hebrew as "The Movement for the Complete Land of Israel." For now, the "complete" land refers to the territories which are being held by the Israeli army. For the long run, the "complete" land is by no means the land that is chopped in the middle by the Jordan river. It is the land referred to in a famous political slogan: "The Jordan has two banks." Indeed, the land promised by God to Abraham's descendants includes both banks of the Jordan and more. In this connection, the Israeli historian J. L. Talmon sometimes complains that he cannot really be expected to face sophisticated colleagues abroad and tell them that the Jews have a divine title deed to the land and that this title deed preempts all other legal claims. But a divine claim is good enough for many Israelis. For them, the history of the State of Israel and its wars proceeds with its own logic and momentum. A look at this logic suggests a fascinating train of thought.

The underlying rationale of *hagshamah* or implementation of Zionism revolves around the concepts of *aliyah* (immigration), *hitnahalut* (settling the land), and *gvulot* (borders). The specific logic behind each concept leaves room for growth and expansion. The logic of *aliyah* or Jewish immigration refers to all Jewry and does not stop with ingathering from Russia. Similarly, the logic of *hitnahalut* or settling on the land of Israel does not stop with the West Bank. The concept of borders also carries with it its own momentum. "Security borders" is one thing and "historical borders" another. The first should serve as a springboard for the second if one is to approach this issue as Ezer Weizman recommends, i.e., "without complexes." The final fixation of borders is dependent on the Zionist implementation in toto, for which events will have to progress in a certain sequence. First, the West Bank will be retained and settled by Russian Jews with the help of heavy financial support from American Jewry. Then, Arab intoxication with their own war cries will once again lead them to a miscalculated war in which Greater Israel will be extended from security borders to the historical borders, i.e., the biblical "borders of destiny." Then, and only then, Israel will become "the complete Land of Israel." After that, Rabbi Meir Kahane's prophecy of an impending racial and anti-Semitic explosion in America will come true. As the imminent holocaustal threat to American Jews begins to materialize, the final massive effort in the Zionist saga will be enacted. Millions of American Jews—the fat cats who were reluctant to immigrate until their physical existence was threatened—will go to Israel in a final great aliyah. Once more, the *mitzvah* of ingathering will be coupled with the *mitzvah* of settling the ancestral land, this time up to the Euphrates. The logics of *aliyah, hitnahalut,* and *gvulot* will have run its full course to bring about the full completion of *hagshamah* or Zionist implementation.

At present this is just a vision on the part of those who advocate Great Zionism as opposed to Small Zionism, and is usually spelled out in full only in relation to the presently occupied territories. But the vision of the "complete" land is there and has acquired momentum ever since the Six Day War. The Arab folly of tenaciously clinging to a perpetual state of belligerency unless Israel de-Zionizes fans the flames of Jewish chauvinism. From this chauvinistic outlook, matters are quite clear. Victors deserve some spoils and defenders certainly deserve security. If victory is won by those who fight for defense and security and the fruits of victory include land which is within the borders of destiny, then both justice and logic combine into a compelling argument that wherever Zionist implementation takes place the new status quo becomes sacred.

A sad example of someone who was swayed by this logic is David Ben Gurion. In August 1972, the Israeli newspapers took note of the fact that his attitude had shifted closer to Dayan's and even to Ezer Weizman's hawkish stance. Ben Gurion was well known for his conviction that "peace is more important than real estate" and for his opposition to annexation plans concerning the Sinai. New developments, however, changed his mind. The Israeli Government proceeded with settling Jews in the Sinai up to the town of El Arish. The river of El Arish is commonly identified as the biblical river of Egypt, which was promised in Genesis 15:18 as the southern border of the land that will belong to the descendants of Abraham. There is an uncanny similarity between the biblical border and a well-known Israeli plan to withdraw to a line extending from El Arish to Sharm el Sheikh in the event of a political settlement (See Harris). Thus, the new Israeli settlements were confined to the biblical borders of destiny. Within these borders, Zionist implementation once it is effected is sacred and should never be reversed. This is true even if it was carried out as a *harig* incident, meaning an exceptional act that was allegedly done without the knowledge and approval of the government. After holding out for five years, Ben Gurion finally yielded to this sacred status of *hagshamah* or Zionist implementation. *The Jerusalem Post Weekly* quoted the statement he made to a *Davar* correspondent: "Something has changed in the territories in the past five years. It is one thing to return desert and another to return areas settled by Jews." Thus, a policy of creating facts, which in turn are supported by biblical accounts, becomes irresistible to many Israelis. The expansionist potential of this policy has a limit that was set in the Bible: "Unto thy seed have I given this land, from the river of Egypt unto the great river, the river Euphrates" (Genesis 15:18). Perhaps the Arabs should bless their luck that "the river of Egypt" is not taken to mean the Nile.

The mythos-driven craving for the ancestral land is tied to deep unconscious layers in the Jewish psyche. Hints of the origins of this craving surface every so often in writings on the subject of Jewish renascence. In 1944, Ernst Frankenstein, an expert on international law, put forward moral and legal claims for the establishment of a Jewish state in Palestine. He described Jews as "a ghostlike, homeless people." (The morbid implications of "a ghostlike" existence will be discussed in Chapter 14.) Frankenstein contrasted this sort of existence with "a miraculous transformation" which came over the country and the people, "a modern version of the giant who renewed his strength by touching the motherly soil." The reference is of course to the Greek legend of the giant Antaeus, the son of Poseidon who ruled the sea and of Gaea, goddess of the earth. Since renewed contact with earth his mother always renewed his strength, no one was able to beat Antaeus, who always killed his opponents. Finally, the hero Heracles killed him by lifting him off the ground long enough to make him lose his strength. Frankenstein's free association is more determined than meets the eye. This legend did not surface into his consciousness for no reason as he just happened to think about a miraculous transformation of both the reunited people and country. As he put it, the "humiliated Jews suddenly became happy, strong, and self-reliant people, and life and beauty returned to the devastated land." In the light of our previous discussion of the timeless love for Zion, we would put it somewhat differently. The banished and weak sons returned to their motherland to beget and be reborn. They touched the devastated motherly soil and gave it life and beauty. As a result of this loving intercourse they became happy, strong, and self-reliant. They became giants of men, the strongest on earth as long as they retain their renewed touch with their motherly soil. Therefore, whenever and wherever Jews regain possession of a piece of the motherland, they should cling to it for their lives and never, never let it go. There will be no modern Heracles to dislodge them. All the lands within the borders of the historical Eretz Yisrael are sacred and their Zionist reclamation is irreversible.

It is an irony of history that an Arab willingness to reach a political compromise could have long ago put a final stop to the process of Jewish expansion. Time and again, both before and after 1948, the Arabs rejected plans which could effectively have blocked the development they so greatly feared. Thus, their response of belligerency was not adaptive. What alarmed them, however, was not altogether a figment of the well-known Arab predilection to embrace fantasy. They sensed the great potential for Jewish expansion and they suspected that this tendency was not confined to only fringe Jewish groups. As a Palestininian colleague, Dr. George Awad, told me:

> I think that there is a genuine fear among all the Arabs that Israel wants to expand and that expansion is not the idea of an extremist group or a minority of the Israelis. . . . [but] the official policy of Israel. . . . I am one of those and I feel that Israel has done nothing to dispel that fear. In fact, everything the Israelis have mentioned or everything they have done since the war and since before the war has been expansionist.

In this emotional utterance, "everything" is obviously an exaggeration. Nevertheless, the deep fears are there and the history of Zionism so far suggests that they have some bases in reality. It would be futile for Israelis to try to conveniently brush aside the Arab fears of "Zionist expansion" as based on nothing but misleading propaganda.

The recent growth of Israeli chauvinism manifests itself in more than one way. In discussing the impact of "cruel Zionism" on Israeli life, Avneri noted that the Hebrew language was now being affected. Special meanings have come to be attached to certain charged terms, such as *harig* (a deviation from official policy presumably without governmental knowledge or approval), "to move inhabitants" and "precedent." Indeed, in many instances these terms were used whenever dispossession of Arabs took place for alleged security reasons. Avneri thought that the new emotionally laden meanings attached to these Hebrew terms signify an Israeli shift toward a colonial mentality. In seeking the impact of political orientations on the use of language Avneri was, of course, following a well-known idea which was illustrated by George Orwell in his famous book *1984*. Just as "freedom" could mean "slavery" in the totalitarian regime of 1984, so *harig* or deviation may come more and more to mean the norm or the established policy in a society which shifts toward a colonial mentality. Similarly, just as in the war in Vietnam "protective reactions" really meant self-initiated bombing raids, so in Israel "not setting a precedent" could mean setting a precedent, while "to move inhabitants" became a gentle euphemism for the confiscation of lands and the explusion of Arab villagers from their homes.

The colonial mentality alluded to by Avneri is of a peculiar kind. Israelis do not seek colonies and do not wish to subjugate other peoples either politically or economically. The underpinning of Israeli chauvinism is a myth-enforced craving for the ancestral land. The national thirst is for land, not for subjugated inhabitants who, from this particular vantage point, may well just pack up and disappear. To foster this disappearance, Rabbi Kahane offers Arabs money for the purpose of emigration. In the process he stumbles and includes in his offers the Druze communities, which in fact prefer the present arrangement. Dayan is much cleverer than Kahane. Every so often the Israeli papers allude to his unofficial plan to turn the occupied lands into Israeli territory and the Arab occupants into Jordanian citizens. The alleged rationale behind this plan of the pragmatic Dayan is the conviction that territories stay while people may go. The lands will not emigrate to Jordan but the people, who knows, they may. And just in case they don't, they do not have political rights in Israel, which reduces the demographic risk. This is indeed a peculiar sort of colonial mentality: clever, pragmatic, and very un-Jewish.

The conscious and unconscious urges to reinhabit the whole of the ancestral land bred an insensitivity to the plight of those Arabs who were displaced from the land in 1948. The Jewish insensitivity was probably enhanced by the fact that the war started with the invasion of Israel by the armies of five Arab countries. Since that time a major area in which Israelis manifested lack of empathy for Arabs is the issue of Arab refugees. Some Israelis may have felt that a fair trade took place and that the issue should therefore be closed. Israel absorbed Jewish refugees from Arab countries and the Arab countries received though not always absorbed Arab refugees. The Israeli myopic vision centered on the topic of why the refugees fled. They probably fled for many reasons, not the least of which is that people flee away from wherever the bullets are flying. Nadav Safran, an authority on the Arab-Israeli conflict, has analyzed how at first it was in the interest of the Arabs to evacuate potential battle grounds. Later on, as the tide of the war turned in favor of the Israelis, the Israeli interest lay in driving Arabs out of newly acquired territories. Even if some Arabs fled because their leaders urged them to, they did not forfeit their right to return after the dust settled down. If, however, they were denied reentry to Israel because of security reasons, this should have been stated openly rather than being obfuscated by moral arguments of questionable validity. On the whole, the original reasons for the flight were no justification for denying most of the refugees the right to return to their homes. As for security considerations, they militated against taking back the majority of the refugees. But no valiant efforts were made to offer them direct and indirect help and the Israeli public preferred to not identify with their plight. The refugees of Israel did not care to be preoccupied with the refugees of Palestine.

It is true that Jewish insensitivity toward the Arab refugees is more than matched by the Arab governments' disregard for their fate. As on many other issues that have been touched upon in this chapter, there is ample room for an even harsher criticism of Arab than of Jewish attitudes. Arab mistakes and follies in handling Zionism have been well enumerated by Safran and Elon. Our focus, however, is the Jews, not

the Arabs. The Jews chose to center their attention on Arab maltreat-
ment of their own refugees in comparison to Jewish rehabilitation and
absorption of Jewish refugees. It is a valid point but too narrow in focus.
For instance, Feigenberg-Eamri in making this point accused the Arabs
of trading on the suffering of the refugees in the marketplaces of the
world. Such a scolding bears an uncanny similarity to Bialik's admoni-
tion of his own people trading with their own misery. Israelis are quite
familiar with the lines of his poem "In the City of the Slaughter" in
which he called his people beggars and urged them to go to the
graveyard and dig out the bones of their ancestors as well as their
brothers, fill their bags with this merchandise and go out on the road.
With great disdain the furious poet told them that they shall use this
merchandise for schnorring in all the market places. It is as if Israeli
criticism of Arab behavior has transformed them into angry Bialiks,
while their own previous role of being chastised for trading on misery
is now fulfilled by Arabs. It is the Arabs who are now the *schnorrers*.
Among the psychological mechanisms which produced this transformation, one could be the defense mechanism of identification with the
aggressor. By becoming like the Goyim who laughed at the begging
Jews, the Jews in turn could now do the laughing, and in the process
could acquire the envied Gentile sense of mastery and security.

We know that when identification with the aggressor is exercised
by children at a very early age, the emulated model is frequently one
of the parents. Similarly, the Jews may have identified with their own
parental figure—the prophetic poet who lashed at them and derided
them for their begging role. Bialik may have been incorporated into the
Jewish superego the way aggressive parents become part of their children's superego. However, more than one defensive process could be
involved. The classical defense of reaction formation may be in operation. In this case, the focus is not on an external aggressor but on the
self. The essence of this defense is the adoption in consciousness of
feelings and ideas that are the opposite of strong unconscious urges.
With the help of this defense, the self-image of Israelis can shift from
schnorring beggars into people of dignity. When this particular defense
is supplemented with the mechanisms of projection and displacement,
the focus shifts to the Arabs. In this case, schorring is projected on

them and self-anger is displaced outward against them also. Whatever the mechanisms involved, the outcome is a rigid moralistic stance coupled with a smug sense of superiority. What is more, the narrow focus is not conducive to honest inquiries as to how many Arab refugees wish to return to their previous homes and what part Israel should play in rectifying their situation.

It is obvious that for many Jews there existed a cruel psychological dilemma: whether to engage in a sole quest for "justice for my people" or to allow Judaic morality to confront directly the issue of injustice to another people. Such an encounter could at best result in a compromise with the other claimants to the land. It could also result in scrapping the Zionist project in order to avoid even minor injustices to others. Most Zionists spared themselves this cruel dilemma. They gazed at Arabs as if with X-ray eyes, thus depriving Arabs of a flesh and blood quality and seeing through their transparent bodies the real object of their dreams, the glory of the ancestral land of Zion. This bizarre way of fixating on the tangible land behind the intangible people led Avineri to assert in an interview (Ben Ezer) that the Jews viewed the Arab problem through the glasses of defense mechanisms. Even now there are Israelis who fixate their gaze on the "territories" and conveniently ignore the "people" who inhabit them.

Indeed, most Zionists, including leaders and the rank and file, needed tunnel vision to protect them from seeing the Arabs. At most they could see an Arab problem which meant an inexplicable obstinacy of a backward people, a blind obstructionism fostered by ignorance and by malicious and corrupt leaders, as well as procrastination that so maddeningly stood in the way of progress for both peoples. This accursed Arab stubbornness could in no way be perceived as a rise of genuine Arab national aspirations. With Arab nationalism out of sight, there was no perception of a tragic ethical dilemma, which implied all along a giving of a share of Palestine to the Palestinian Arabs. The more dovish among the Israeli leaders believe that even practical reasons dictate this course. Otherwise, absorbing a million Arabs in the Jewish state, with or without political rights, will have its inevitable effect on the character of the state, which will no longer be a Jewish state. This problem is usually known as "the demographic problem."

Former Finance Minister Pinhas Sapir, a leading dove, was known to be very perturbed over the demographic problem. In contrast, Shimon Peres, formerly Transportation Minister and now Defense Minister, is hawkish. In criticizing Sapir's stand, Peres stated that "the Zionist movement never had a statistical advantage" (*The New York Times*, November 10, 1972). The statement is in the best Zionist tradition of winning against overwhelming odds by tenacity, vision, and chutzpah, yet it does not mean that statistical advantage is not important. What it does mean is something like, "Today a minority in the administered territories, tomorrow a majority." How today's demographic problem is going to vanish tomorrow is not quite explicated. A massive Jewish aliyah in the future is one benign answer. Mass Arab emigration from Israel for a variety of push and pull reasons is another and less benign one.

Perhaps the most penetrating criticism of the Israeli aspiration to retain the bulk of the occupied territories was published by the Israeli historian Yehoshua Arieli in *The New York Review of Books*. He was subsequently attacked for his views as well as for his publishing in America. In fact, he has been publishing these views in Israel all along. Starting with the assumption that Israel could retain the territories by force, Arieli went on to analyze the social, political, economic, cultural, and ethical consequences of such a policy. His conclusion was that such a policy of enlightened and intelligent colonialism would inevitably result in a complete change of structure, purpose, and mentality of Israeli society.

There is no lack of Israelis who frown upon people like Yehoshua Arieli or Arieh Eliav, who in their writings and their speeches advocate peace through compromise. These people, the Israeli version of the American intellectual "peaceniks," must seem like the modern reincarnation of Ahad Ha'am the cultural moralist. At best they look like people of good intentions tossed into a ruthless world of realpolitik that they fail to understand. At worst they look like the new *melamed* and *luftmensch* types of teachers of whom even Weizmann tired in .his time. "Pretty souls" is the new derogatory nickname in Israel for such persons who care about moral issues, the rights of the Palestinians, the demographic problem, and the effect of prolonged occupation of the territories on Israeli society. In contrast to their presumed feebleness, the alternative being offered is uncomplicated toughness. In settling scores with the "pretty souls," the reporter Aharon Shamir stated in *Yediot Aharonot* of August 18, 1972: "The nation of Israel decided to return to her (the land of Israel), and if it decided to return to her— once again she shall be his, and only his." This is another reiteration of the militant "It is all mine" sentiment. Concerning the worrisome demographic problem, Shamir indicated that should the Arabs become a majority in the Jewish state they would still not be given equal representation. "Whoever is unwilling to put up with it—let him emigrate from here." This statement is presumably directed at Arabs who want political rights, or at Jewish "pretty souls," or both. It is quite apparent that the Zionist sentiment of return to the source has flowered into Jewish chauvinism. The Judaic tradition includes both ruthless nationalistic urges and universalistic aspirations. The former can lead to narrow chauvinism; the latter, to rootlessness and helplessness. But there are other options between the two. The "pretty souls" seem determined to remind Israelis that these other choices exist.

Can peace come to the Middle East? The literature on international relations and conflict resolution in the fields of psychology and political science is staggering, yet it yields few concrete or plausible suggestions. The American psychologist Charles Osgood underscored the value of GRIT (Graduated and Reciprocal Initiatives in Tension-reduction) policy. The policy consists of unilateral gestures and countergestures which by small steps and with only minimal risks for loss of face gradually lead to meaningful changes. Indeed, the famous Ping-Pong diplomacy between the United States and The Peoples' Republic of China was the public phase of a prolonged private GRIT play on the part of both sides. Osgood maintained that with the proper use of both the carrot and the stick to signal good intentions as well as firmness, a GRIT policy constitutes the application to international relations of the famous psychological laws of operant conditioning and of shaping behaviors. Chances are that the pragmatic approach of GRIT can reduce the level of belligerency in the Middle East just as the reverse approach of calculated unilateral and reciprocated escalation moves can increase the level of violent incidents. The GRIT approach, however, can serve only as the first series of steps. It cannot bring about peace. Gestures and countergestures can only work up to a point. To bring about peace, basic decisions have to be made by both sides concerning what they are willing to give up. These decisions in effect determine how far each side could go with reciprocated gestures. The basic decisions concern what the social psychologist Ralph White termed "overlapping and conflict of territorial self-images." This concept can best be explained through examples.

Israelis have a few territorial self-images of their country. There is Small Israel prior to the Six Day War, today's Great Israel including the occupied territories, tomorrow's Complete Land of Israel which would extend over Transjordan to reach the Euphrates or whatever the fuzzy borders of destiny *(gvulot ye'ud)* are, and other grandiose territorial self-images that include various chunks of the Fertile Crescent based on different federation schemes. The Arabs too have various territorial self-images which include de-Zionized and Arab Palestine, a variety of unification schemes such as the Greater Syria or Greater Iraq, and the pan-Arab dream of a great and unified Arab nation whose territorial extension over major chunks of Asia and Africa would match the renascent grandeur of its awakened people. Obviously there is an overlap and conflict between the Israeli and Arab territorial self-images. The conflict could only be resolved when both sides clarify the borders of their territorial self-images in mutual agreement. That means a lot of "give" even when the opponent compromises too. There is more to it than geography. In giving up territory, both sides would also give up some pride, live with some shame, and be subject to psychological doubts concerning the meaning of their decisions. They may not be sure whether they have let wisdom triumph or whether they have been "had," whether what they went through represents castration or self-assertion, whether they have secured basic rights for themselves or instead, by giving in some, have signaled to the opponent that in the future they could give in much more. To achieve the Talmud's prescription of "They shall divide," both sides will have to cope with issues not only of territory but of self-images such as emasculation and self-assertion. It is difficult to be a therapist of individuals who face such issues; for nations that suffer similarly there may be no thereapist.

Perhaps only cruel reality can bring about what the application of psychological and diplomatic techniques fails to accomplish. The Arabs could find a loss less intolerable if a solution were handed down by mighty world powers with no right to appeal. In a way they have indicated this themselves in the past when they attempted to present their losses in 1956 and 1967 as defeats not by the hand of Israel but by world powers. The Israelis may find territorial and other forms of self-assertion less rewarding when accompanied by incessant bleeding. People, after all, empathize first of all with themselves, and the small Israeli nation is extremely sensitive to Israeli casualties and not nearly as much to Arab loss of lives or Arab territorial and psychological setbacks.

The basic weakness of tension-reduction models is that they neglect the reality aspects of conflicts and focus instead on communication problems. In reviewing some of this literature, Fred Sondermann drew attention to this flaw. Removing misunderstandings and fears could improve the prospects for conflict resolution but would not be enough. There would still remain real differences of interests and goals. It is primarily for this reason that this very cursory look at a sample of the literature on international conflict resolution results in disappointment. Some of the major stumbling blocks to peace are psychological, yet the field of psychology views the situation helplessly. The piles of literature on "attitude change" do not deal with the kinds of attitudes that operate in this real-life Middle East conflict. Two peoples grab hold of a country, each saying "It is all mine." To get them to say something different would require much more than standard "communication and persuasion" techniques, such as the famous "two-sided" communication as an efficient approach to persuasion. The Arab-Israeli conflict defies traditional remedies of academic psychology and political science.

Things are changing, however, and as a result of the Yom Kippur War both sides are growing in psychological sophistication. At first, the surprise Arab attack on this holiest of Jewish days seemed to turn most Israelis into hard-liners. But after the initial shock wore off, it was becoming evident that a spirit of accommodation was gaining the upper hand. The war gave the Arabs a much needed sense of pride and consequently a psychological ability to engage with the Israelis in face-to-face negotiations. It was in the midst of grieving for the dead that Israelis gained awareness of this new opportunity for a negotiated settlement. To the Israelis, the war gave a sudden jolt that fostered a healthy sense of skepticism as opposed to their traditional cocky self-assuredness. Most Israelis no longer believe that the Arabs can be effectively dealt with by the magic formula of giving them one big *zbeng* (whack) and the job is done. The coordinated Yom Kippur attack made it clear that the Arabs had been gravely underestimated, and for the Israelis this was a rude awakening. They are still trying to absorb the trauma of new war in which the Arabs fought bravely while the Israeli Government issued misleading reports concerning the battlefield situation. What is more, the Arabs displayed great skill in wielding the oil weapon, thereby teaching the Israelis a momentous lesson in the art of weaving together political and military action. Thus, after six years of enjoying what Israeli newspapers usually refer to as "the intoxication with power," the shocked Israelis discovered that their practice of mingling myth with realpolitik was very unfortunate. While they were embracing myth the Arabs had become talented masters of power politics.

All this was not completely unexpected. After the stunning Israeli victory in the Six Day War, Talmon warned that "Israel may be able to win and win and go on winning till its last breath, win itself to death." Now the terrible price in blood of this latest war brought home what the full cost of future Israeli "victories" could be. At last the man in the street feels what most historians have felt for a long time. It is unfortunate that nations do not learn from history as quickly as good historians do, and that the national price for a belated lesson is so dear. It is especially dear to the numerically small Israelis. One Hebrew word for casualties is "sacrifices." It signifies the heightened Israeli sensitivity to the loss of life and to the tragic Jewish history of going to the altar as innocent victims of man's cruelty to man. It is this sensitivity which could give Israelis an incentive to become as good in waging peace as they have been at waging war.

All in all, the Yom Kippur War and its political aftermath demonstrate that the doctrine of cruel Zionism is unrealistic. If it is now difficult to hold on to occupied territories, it would be doubly hard if further expansion were implemented. It is no longer easy to cling to illusions such as that the present territorial and military status quo equals a de facto peace no matter how much the Arabs grind their teeth in rage. The psychological transformation taking place among Israelis seems to have all the hallmarks of an end of an era.

This feeling was reinforced by the death of David Ben Gurion soon after the war. His death was symbolic of past lost opportunities and the present dearth of an adequate leadership. It is a tragedy that following the Six Day War Israel was not led by a leader of Ben Gurion's stature. In 1947 and 1948 the "old man" had a strong intuition that this was the time to establish the Jewish State. Consequently, he did not shrink from striking alliances with politicians from other parties, against opposition in his own party, in order to be able to act on his feeling. After the Six Day War he was again gripped with a feeling that a historic moment of action had arrived. The time was ripe for peace and he entreated his people to take decisive steps to bring it about. Peace is more important than real estate, he kept saying, and even a bad peace would be better than a good war. By and large, his remarks were not welcomed. He was expected after all to sit quietly in retirement as DeGaulle did and hopefully live long enough to finish his memoirs. He was not supposed to meddle in current affairs and to become a political embarrassment as the aging German Chancellor Adenauer once did. So the old seer stayed in kibbutz Sde Boker writing his personal history and waiting for the inevitable next "good war."

It is clear that the Middle East is heading toward a moment of decision. Both sides are more heavily armed than they have ever been. Both view with alarm their growing dependence on the big powers and the increasing intervention of the two superpowers in regional affairs. And each party to the conflict is more able to moderate its demands and to understand the situation of the other party. Israelis are less hopeful that King Hussein will rid them of the Palestinian problem, and understand that they must accommodate the national yearnings of the Palestinians. In like fashion, most Palestinians, including the moderate wings of the guerilla movement, have given up on the unrealistic demand to replace Israel by a new Palestine. Both sides will have to continue to reconcile themselves to reality if peace is to come. On the part of the Israelis this means a basic psychological switch from the clever chauvinism of Dayan to the decent nationalism of Ben Gurion. Then a military strong and morally right Israeli nation could confidently look forward not to the next "good war" but to the forthcoming "bad peace." Who knows, it might even be a good one!

13.

Samson and Masada Psychologies

NEITHER A MASADA NOR
A VICHY!

IF DIFFICULT AND GRAVE
DAYS OF STRUGGLE LIE AHEAD,
LET US KEEP REMEMBERING
THAT WE ARE NOT PREPARING
FOR A LAST FIGHT AND OUR SOUL
DOES NOT WISH TO DIE WITH THE
PHILISTINES, AND THAT WE DO
NOT STAND ON THE THRESHOLD
OF DESPAIR AND SUICIDE.

—David Ben Gurion

The Jewish people have a long history of being besieged by formidable enemies. On many occasions the sieges led to desperate suicidal fights to the finish. These events form the basis for potent myths which have had a lasting impact on Jewish history. Today, because of Israel's besiegement as well as the horrid tragedies which befell the Jews in this century, the heroic behavior of Jews who went down fighting in deliberate acts of individual or mass suicide is even more influential.

Israel Drapkin, in his brief historical survey of individual and mass suicide among Jews, enumerated some of the more famous biblical and postbiblical cases. Two of the most notable instances of individual suicides were those of Samson and King Saul. The latter threw himself upon his sword to avoid capture and humiliation by the Philistines (I Samuel 31:4–5). In an earlier period, when Israel was ruled by judges rather than kings, the legendary Samson was not as lucky and did not escape capture by the Philistines. His eyes were torn out and he was displayed before the Philistines for public entertainment. Finally he avenged himself in Dagon's temple by demolishing two of its central pillars, thus bringing down the temple not only upon himself but also on his Philistine enemies.

Samson's story has many psychological meanings. One of the issues it raises is the control of huge force. The ancient Israelites had a problem in controlling Samson; the more he avenged himself on the Philistines, the more danger there was that the latter would retaliate against the Israelites. At one point the Israelites even pleaded with Samson and persuaded him to submit to voluntary arrest so as to be delivered to the Philistines. Samson was a threat not only to his enemies but also to his own people. Even his last suicidal act bears the quality of a final eruption, of an explosion into eternity. There is something open-ended about it, as if he were applying force to the limit, in effect, pushing as far as it would go. One may speculate that by being endowed with such immense force, which verges on the realm of the uncontrolled, Samson was sooner or later bound to be destroyed just like the famous Golem of Prague in Jewish folklore.

To many non-Jews, the most popular notions concerning Samson's life and death relate to his entrapment and emasculation by Delilah. The prevailing moral of the story is that men should be aware of deceitful women and that females are dangerous. However, for the Jews, another dimension of this story took prominence and assumed its place in the collection of lore which exercised mythical powers upon Jewish readers. When the helpless Samson was led to the temple of Dagon in Gaza for the amusement of his Philistine masters, he stood between two pillars of the temple, prayed to God to give him back his strength for the last time, and said: "Let my soul die with the Philistines." The temple came crumbling down, and in his death he avenged himself upon the Philistines and took many of his enemies with him. This "let my soul die with the Philistines" psychology relates to the frame of mind of the cornered and entrapped. It refers to the end phase of the game when no hope is left except an honorable end, a symbolic freedom, and a last desperate vengeance.

This sentiment was not forgotten. In 1724 the famous Jewish Italian scholar and poet, Moshe Hayim Luzzato, wrote the play *Ma'aseh Shimshon (Samson's Tale)*. The last stanza of the play demonstrates the vitality of this living sentiment:

> My heartbreaks I shall overcome,
> I shall dress myself with heroism and kill my soul,
> I shall die a hero's death and then be peaceful,
> I shall live in my death and put an end to my pain,
> I shall die, I do not fear death, I loathe fear—
> Let my soul die together with the Philistines!

One reason why this sentiment has not been forgotten is that there were many "Philistines" in Jewish history, ranging from Assyrians to cossacks, from Syrians to Spaniards, and, of course, from Romans to Germans. It is no secret that those who are currently foremost on the list are the Arabs and Russians. Thus, the Samsonian psychology of meting out death to the enemy, when self death seems imminent, might have modern implications. The implications of this psychological reality for present-day Israelis become clearer when discussed in conjunction with the "Masada complex."

In 73 A.D., Masada, the last stronghold of the great Jewish revolt against the Romans, fell. Just before its fall, the leader of the Zealots, Eleazar ben Ya'ir, allegedly made a resounding speech in which he convinced his warriors to slay first their families and then themselves. All in all, about 960 defenders committed suicide rather than be captured by the Romans. The victorious Romans discovered unburned caches of food which the defenders deliberately left intact so as to make it clear that their deaths, at that particular time, were of their own choosing. Eleazar's speech to his men was reported by Flavius Josephus in *The Jewish War.* It added a powerful example to the Jewish lore.

Eleazar succeeded in persuading his men. But while the mass suicide was being executed, two women and five children hid in a cavern and survived to tell the tale. One of the two women was described by Josephus as "related to Eleazar, in intelligence and education superior to most women." Josephus has probably reconstructed Eleazar's speeches, but the original exhortations must have been very persuasive, judging from the results. Thus the legend lived on. We also learn from Josephus that Masada, the last stronghold, was not the only place where Jews perferred self-inflicted death to Roman capture. Earlier in the struggle, about 5,000 defenders of Gamala in the Golan Heights did the same. If the whole of Judea had preferred liberty in death à la Masada, there might not have been a Jewish people—at least as we know them today. Nevertheless, the legend and example of Masada were admired by Jews for centuries; the admiration was further enhanced in this generation by the Nazi Holocaust. With people who decided "Let us die unenslaved by our enemies," one need not ask such questions as "Why didn't the Jews fight?"

Eleazar's speech was one of the "liberty or death" types which were sounded on many occasions in human history during moments of great hope or great despair. Many meanings are imbedded in "liberty or death" calls. Sometimes such calls stand for superficial patriotism in the form of flag-waving and the sounding of slogans. The simpleminded devotees who can be counted on to answer these calls are known in

Jewish culture as *hassidim shotim* (foolish followers). Such calls can touch primitive layers of individual psyches and produce rousing group emotions and goose pimples. They can also evoke noble sentiments of a desire for freedom and equality for all.

Some implications of the "give me liberty or give me death" stand were pointed out by the psychiatrist Jerome Frank. In discussing various psychological aspects of war and peace, he unraveled the fallacious belief held by those who are willing to fight to the finish that the enemy, in contrast to themselves, can be punished into submission. This is one of the glaring instances of enemies having a mirror image of one another. It is usual for opponents to attribute the same virtues to themselves and the same vices to others; indeed, with a "liberty or death" stand each warring nation believes in its own readiness to fight to the finish and in the enemy's propensity to yield after being punished sufficiently. Frank regarded the persistence of this fallacious belief in cases of holy wars as an unresolved mystery of human behavior. Yet it may not be such a mystery after all. Should the opponents attribute the same virtue, such as willingness to fight to the death, to each other, a big question mark would be placed on the chances for victory as well as the rightness of the cause. In addition to that, what was passing as worship of heroics would now be interpreted as a worship of death. That, after all, is what a mutual fight to the death implies. Thus, without the use of projection to attribute one's own vices to the enemy, many nagging doubts would arise. The motivating force behind this projection defense is one's own naricssism—a pervasive and soothing feeling of "no one is as noble as I am." How it all evolves will be explained later in this chapter.

In spite of its many connotations, the "liberty or death" call is very simple in structure; it is sharply polarized and forces an either-or or black-or-white thinking. This structural rigidity of style also forces a simplified choice between slavery and freedom. It does not allow other considerations such as the relative merits of life and death to complicate this choice. One could hope for liberty, prepare for death, but consider nothing in between. However, life and history include other options for action that lie somewhere in between and are not so neatly polarized. Israelis keep saying "This is not Czechoslovakia." Indeed

Israel is in a better position to resist the Russians than Czechoslovakia was. The Czechs were wise, however, in their avoidance of a "liberty or death" approach to the Russian-led invasion of their country. The tendency to polarize choices in the form of liberty or death usually happens in the beginning when hope reigns supreme and freedom seems within grasp, or at the end, when the bitter truth dawns and it becomes obvious that only death is within certain grasp. Eleazar's speech was delivered when the end was in sight.

In his speech, Eleazar ben Ya'ir underscored the ideas of freedom, honor, and justice. He regarded the forthcoming death of the defenders as justice, and urged his men to execute this justice with their own hands. His speech was the kind of emotional appeal which leaves only one honorable choice; all other options become narcissistically intolerable. Making use of these options is like being a "bad boy" and feeling unloved. That is what "bad boys" are usually threatened with—the withdrawal of love by important adults as well as by their own superegos. On a less primitive and regressive level, and on a more developed and conceptual one, what happens to alternate options of behavior is that they are regarded as too shameful to live with, i.e., they are relegated to the realm of the negative ego-ideal and become utterly unacceptable. Instead of tomorrow's slavery, Eleazar offered his warriors today's chance to die as free men. With dialectical reasoning in which death becomes eternal life and defeat an act of self-assertion, he urged them to make a final use of their freedom by jabbing their swords into themselves for purposes of preserving their liberty.

At this point it is important to take note of Freud's assertion in *Thoughts for the Times on War and Death* that "Our own death is indeed unimaginable, and whenever we make the attempt to imagine it we can perceive that we really survive as spectators." The basic reason for this, according to Freud, is that "in the unconscious every one of us is convinced of his own immortality." Similarly, the British psychiatrist and psychoanalyst Erwin Stengel maintained that in psychoanalytic thinking it has been speculated that suicide is sometimes motivated primarily by a wish for self-perpetuation and self-assertion rather than by a wish for self-extinction. In a paradoxical way, the suicidal individual denies that there is a barrier that separates life from death, and achieves in fantasy an immortality whereby life continues after death and one can enjoy the consequences of the self-assertion displayed by the suicide. Indeed, Eleazar's speech touched upon the contradiction of achieving freedom through death, and presented suicide as an act of self-assertion and a means to immortality. To those who choose self-inflicted death, Eleazar promised the immortal though invisible existence of their souls. Death was thus presented as the gate to immortality.

The psychologist David Bakan recently proposed the somewhat similar idea that in some instances of suicide, individuals grope for immortality through the deliberate action of putting death under the control of the will. The suicidal act is the living proof that death is under control, and also suggests that so is life and so is immortality if a person wills it strongly enough. This brings us back to Stengel's interesting idea that persons who commit suicide have the fantasy that they will remain immortal and live to see the consequences of their self-assertion. The defenders of Masada may have fantasied themselves watching the astounded Roman legionnaires looking at the corpses and at the intact food stores, and realizing with dismay that Jewish rather than Roman will was asserted. Similar visions may impel present-day Israelis to the extremes of self-destruction in moments of great despair. In such a case, the fantasies would include contemporary Arabic- and Russian-speaking "Romans" who view with disbelief and admiration the inexplicable triumph of Israeli will.

Like the story of Samson, the Masada tale has also inspired poetic creation, in this case by Yitzhak Lamdan, who gave repeated expression to the pioneering spirit of the Third Aliyah. His 1927 poem "Masada" is usually regarded as the peak of his creativity. One of its lines, "Masada shall not fall again," became famous. It could be seen painted on city walls, the work of ardent Zionists who wished to share with the general public their determination that this time Jewish nationalism will win. To this day, Masada is a source of a mysterious fascination for both adults and children. Moshe Pearlman's English book *The Zealots of Masada*, written for young people, links the ancient suspense story of the heroic death of the defenders of Masada to a modern suspense story that took place in 1963–1965 when former general and now archeology professor Yigael Yadin, with the help of volunteers from many countries, was excavating Masada. The diggers have the suicide story in mind and wonder whether they will discover the remains of some of the warriors who killed themselves centuries ago. This children's book has a happy ending: Under the direction of the general turned archeologist, the diggers succeed, to the delight and excitement of many Israelis and Jews abroad.

Similarly, the Hebrew children's book *The Glory of Masada* (Gafni) glorifies the Jewish will to continue a war in which all hopes for victory were lost. This particular trait was termed "the marvelous virtue of our nation, the virtue which insured its survival to the present day." Presumably the young readers would not think of the question of how many Jews would have survived at all if indeed every Jew followed the Masada example. The book describes how, between battles, both adults and children study scrolls of the Scriptures. It is a historical fact that the sect of the Essenes put an emphasis on the study of the Scriptures. It is also more palatable for most young sabras to think of the Masada warriors as students of the Bible rather than of the Talmud. Besides, the studying of scrolls alludes to the subsequent discovery of the Dead Sea Scrolls. The book continues to describe how right after Masada's fall Jewish rejuvenation began as soon as Jews heard the Masada tale which reminded them that Jews "are the sons of the people of the Bible" (once more the Talmud is omitted). Naturally, the book ends with the excavation work of "one of the most glorious commanders who led our army during the War of Independence," General Yigael Yadin who was "both a pre-eminent military leader and an outstanding archeologist." His discovery of the remains of the heroic Zealots constitutes a renewal of a covenant—"our covenant with Masada."

Children's stories prepare children for serious adult games. The original adult version of these parallel suspense stories of the first and twentieth centuries appeared in the Yadin book on the Masada dig, but the story did not end there. The latest scenario, which found its way into the Israeli papers and *The New York Times*, involves the Israeli army. This development was later retold in George Brauer's book *Judaea Weeping*. After describing events from the year 73 A.D., the author reported that on July 7, 1969, the remains of twenty-seven warriors, who were discovered in the Masada dig, were given a military funeral by the State of Israel; they were buried as religious martyrs near the ramp of the besieging Roman camps commanded by Silva. Thus, warriors who died in the first century were buried in the twentieth. There is quite a jump here; it symbolizes the tendency among many Israelis to want to drop nearly nineteen centuries of exile from their vision of Jewish history.

We shall not discuss here the meanings of this episode in regard to the Israeli obsession with archeology, the mythical return to the remote Jewish past, and the connection between military leaders and archeology. For the moment, it is important to ask why a military hero burial by the Israeli army? What is so great about the immortal example of mass suicide? Here we obviously face an obsession which values pride more than life. In Jewish history, putting up with death was almost the Jewish daily bread, but being intoxicated with warrior's pride was a rare luxury. This long psychological starvation receives expression in the form of the "Masada complex."

A clear explanation of the meaning of the Masada complex was provided by the left-wing Israeli leader Mordecai Bentov. According to him, "Masada" means a preference for going down fighting rather than surrendering. However, an obsession with this choice, when in fact it is not the only available choice, is irrational. The fear of destruction may be understandable, and can be exploited by demagogues on both sides, but the obsession with this one and only choice is nevertheless unrealistic. In Bentov's opinion, the absurd thing about the Masada complex is that right now neither side in the Middle East faces such an inevitable choice between destruction and surrender. For the foreseeable future the Arabs cannot overcome Israel. He therefore called upon Israelis to free themselves, as well as the Arabs, from the "Masada complex" by focusing their attention not on the choice between fight to the death and destruction, but rather on more realistic choices. This is easier said than done; unfortunately the Masada complex is deeply ingrained. In the August 3, 1971, issue of *The Jerusalem Post Weekly*, an unsigned article appeared under the heading "Sisco and the Masada Complex," in which the U.S. Assistant Secretary of State for Near

Eastern Affairs, Joseph E. Sisco, was described as trying to cure Golda Meir of her "Masada complex." The article made it clear that Prime Minister Meir does not suffer from a personal affliction but rather shares in a "national neurosis." Furthermore, the article suggested that Sisco's "therapy," in the form of a political settlement along the Suez Canal, could achieve the opposite of the intended results and aggravate Israel's Masada complex even more. Thus, the basic message of the article to those who would like to rid Israel of its Masada complex is: Who can tell what is neurosis and what is reality? Subsequently it was reported in *Ha'aretz* that in October 1971, during the private discussions within the Israeli government concerning the American initiative, Golda Meir used strong language and mentioned the fortress of Masada as a symbol of the kind of resoluteness that Israel will display if it finds itself isolated. It therefore seems that Sisco's therapy did not work and that the Masada complex was not cured.

Not long afterward, the journalist Boaz Evron published an article in *Yediot Aharonot* under the title "We Are Not Being Annihilated," in which he said: "We must liberate ourselves once and for all from the psychotic nightmare that the military-political game we are involved in is a question of our continued existence, that we always are in Masada." Thus, in spite of the pervasive obsession with the notion of Masada, not all Israelis adhere to Masada psychology. On July 7, 1969, at the funeral for the remains of the Masada warriors, some speakers expressed reservations. As reported in *The New York Times*, Yadin stated: "We will not judge the way you chose to preserve the honor and freedom of Israel." Menahem Begin, the former Revisionist and Irgun leader, was more explicit. After stating "Never another Masada," he advocated the achievement of honor through victory, life, and freedom rather then by an honorable death. Objections were voiced from other quarters too. In the Israeli periodical *Ha'olam Hazeh* a short time later there appeared a call by "The Movement for Peace and Security," under the title "The 'Impossible'—Is Possible!" "Let us free ourselves from digging in for a hundred year war," it said, "Let us remove from within us the myth of Masada." It is heartening to note that in Israel there is an awareness of the dangers inherent in such a psychological mood as a Masada complex.

The Masada psychology of liberty in death, in combination with the Samsonian psychology of dying with the Philistines, is a potent reality among Israelis. It would be a grave mistake on the part of the world powers to fail to take note of the suicidal and homicidal potential of these psychologies or to dismiss their contemporary impact on Israelis. The emotions of vengeance and liberty in death infiltrate into complex political considerations to form an intricate mixture of primitive impulses with seemingly rational and delicate calculations of realpolitik. Sometimes one can sense beneath the thin veneer of rational calculations the power of raw emotions. It is difficult, though, to sort out and separate the primitive and less differentiated ingredients which enter into this admixture from the more developed and differentiated ones. The task is complicated by the interpersonal meanings of suicide. Many acts or gestures of suicide also stand for psychological murder; a suicide is also frequently a homicide and stems from the need to murder or punish someone (Stengel). A further complication is the well-established tradition of using the threat of self-inflicted death as a political tool. Gandhi's hunger strikes are classic examples of the use of suicidal threats to achieve political gains (Stengel). Israelis have reason to hope that America could not view it with indifference if Israel went down fighting. Such an American inaction would unquestionably negate many accepted principles of the American identity and would no doubt constitute a severe psychological blow. Should America remain passive, it would have to live with a perhaps unbearable shame. Therefore, an Israeli act of suicide could turn into an act of psychological homicide against the American identity. Nevertheless, the American identity is extremely complex and has room for contradictions, although not without strain and difficulties. America could abandon Israel to its fate and learn to live with the trauma involved in the desertion of democracies and friends. The book *If Israel Lost the War*, by Chesnoff et al., represents this potential reality, as good fiction sometimes does. America could conceivably stand aside if and when Israel is destroyed by superior forces.

In mid-1970, people in Israel were talking about the Russian buildup of missiles and the flights of Russian-manned airplanes in Egypt as a danger with which Israel could cope. One could hear such talk as "Let them come, we'll show them," or "I bet what the Russians fear in this area is not the American Sixth Fleet but the Israeli Air Force," or "We've got the best air force in the whole world and if the Russian pilots come, our pilots will handle them." True, this kind of talk is not characteristic of the Israeli leadership; it is more typical of the common folk. Nevertheless, Israeli leaders also talk like this on occasion. *Ha'aretz* on May 1, 1970, reported the views of Arieh Dulchin, a member of the government, on the possibility of battles between Israeli and Russian pilots over Egyptian skies. If the Russians were aiming for such a confrontation, he said, Israel could withstand it. However, he also expressed Israel's hopes that the United States and other countries would finally realize that war in the Middle East would involve not only Israel and the Arab countries, but the whole world. It seems that Dulchin wished the American government to regard this possibility as a certainty. However, it is not certain; and the Americans in effect have more options than Dulchin would like them to have. This is one example of how myth can mingle with realpolitik to the detriment of the latter.

Aggressive popular pronouncements during a period in which Israel does not have to make a last-ditch defense seems like so much boisterous chest-beating. However, let the Israelis be convinced that the Russians and Egyptians are moving in on them with a new "final solution" version of the 1970s, that they are embarking on an attempt to obliterate the State of Israel, and many of them will immediately fall back on the psychologies of "Masada" and "Let my soul die with the Philistines." In that case, popular emotions would either engulf or overrule the decision-makers. The predominant sentiment on the part of a good many Israelis would be to fight to the finish no matter what, even if it meant "Give me liberty or give me death," and in the process take as many of the "Philistines" as possible with them.

Although the Samson and Masada psychologies are masked by cunningly intricate calculations, the outer layer of complex political considerations and logical deductions cannot always cover the underlying erupting impulses. Beneath the rational surface lurks the urge to abandon caution and reason, and feel free to seek liberty and vengeance unabashedly even at the price of death. The temptation is to become immersed in the fulfilling practice of fighting both Arabs and Russians until victory or death. It is obviously contrary to reason, but since when is everything Jewish reasonable? Wasn't Zionism itself considered at the time to be against the odds and unreasonable? It is more fulfilling to protect the newly won Jewish pride, which was resurrected by the blood of Jewish warriors, than to be reasonable. The Jews want to be emotional not only in Israel but also in the United States. The tendency seems to be to let the Gentile do-gooders, who care so much about reason, lean on the Arabs for a change and pressure them to be reasonable. For example, the Jewish Defense League seems to be driven by similar strong emotions, but its members do not have an independent state to make or break in the process. As for the Israelis, their Samson and Masada psychologies drive them toward a suicidal course of action but also keep up the hope that they will get away with it; there is always hope that a Masada stand will prevent a Masada. An unflinching resolve to fight the Russians in Masada style, if need be, may serve as a deterrent which would make another Masada unnecessary. If that does not work, then a Masada in progress could induce the big powers to stop it before things get out of control and become a Masada for everybody. If, however, the big powers allow an Israeli Masada to run its course, then "Let my soul die with the Philistines" is the consolation prize. And there is always the mystical hope, after all, that *Sar ha'umah* (the Minister of the nation) will take care that *am Yisrael hai* (the nation of Israel lives), Masada or no Masada. He did it many times before with Amaleks, Hamans, and Hitlers, and He can do it again.

What can be sensed in the Masada obsession is the intricate work of history. Centuries of dialectic history with its ups and downs and its full share of spiritual glory and shame, political triumph and defeat, have contributed to this peculiar juxtaposition of the primitive with the sophisticated and of the undifferentiated with the very cunning and complex.

The results of this complexity are politico-military considerations which are induced by basic emotional needs. For instance, in 1970 Tabenkin argued that it would not be so simple for the Soviet Union to transfer sufficient military power to the Middle East in order to vanquish the Israeli Army in battle. He concluded that it was up to the

Israelis to make the Russian threats result in a loss of face to their initiators rather than a loss of the "liberated" territories to Israel. The trouble is that throughout his book, Tabenkin alerted Israelis to the danger of slipping back to the old and degraded habit of "passivity." These repeated warnings make the apparent levelheadedness of his political calculations highly suspect. It seems that the history of persecution by Gentiles and murderous rage toward them dictate "never again" passivity, and that the scorching shame of past historical humiliations pushes toward unyielding defense of both the soil and the soul, of both the homeland and the newly acquired positive identity. Should the Israelis engage in a head-on collision with the Russians as a result of a *seemingly reasonable* calculated risk, the outcome could be another Masada in which the Israelis would protect their liberty and honor through death. In that case, they would not go down the drain cheaply. They would attempt to go down like a Samson who, by shaking the two pillars of the "Philistine" globe—the Soviet Union and the United States—would bring the entire globe tumbling down.

All this may seem like a farfetched fantasy, but myths have the power to mobilize primitive emotions so as to infiltrate and corrupt the supposed cool and levelheaded logic of realpolitik. Realpoliticking is an ego function and aims at striking a balance between external conditions and internal needs of a nation. However, when an internal need for the worship of Jewish heroics deteriorates into a death wish and assumes the obsessive qualities of the Israeli preoccupation with a Masada stand, the function of realpolitik is "corrupted." The mechanisms involved in such a process of corruption can be gleaned from the psychoanalytic literature. The literature on ego and superego corruption by primitive and aggressive id impulses can enhance our understanding of current psychopolitical happenings in Israel.

In developing his psychoanalytic theories, Sigmund Freud came to recognize that side by side with libidinal drives go hostile impulses which also play a predominant role in the ongoing intrapsychic play of forces. As a result of this increased awareness, he viewed death wishes and aggressive drives as potent and chronic characteristics of human nature. However, his postulation of a death instinct remained controversial. While Franz Alexander made use of it in his clinical speculations, others such as Otto Fenichel rejected it. More recently, Norman Brown condemned neo-Freudianism for its rejection of the death instinct, which he regarded as the major impetus for such distinct human developments as separation and differentiation into individual uniqueness. These disagreements relate to intricate metatheoretical issues. One such issue is the need to postulate two qualitatively different primary psychic energies. Another concerns the alternate possibilities that either form of energy can be traced to the other or that both were derived and differentiated from an underlying and unified form of energy. This controversy has not been settled, but most experts agree that at the pragmatic level, clinicians keep encountering pervasive manifestations of not only sexual but also aggressive impulses. Regardless of their ultimate origin, murderous impulses toward others and the self are almost omnipresent. The intrapsychic battle against these impulses rages on, but usually only with indefinite results, some partial victories, and most often impermanent compromises. One result is sometimes a corruption of the superego, or, worse, of the ego.

In *The Ego and the Id*, Freud underscored the idea that the superego is in close touch with the id, and serves as its representative toward the ego. This closeness stems from the fact that during the early period of superego development, id impulses served as the original building blocks of the forming superego. The primitive hostility of the id, which was evoked by the frustration of instinctual gratifications, was originally directed against the prohibitors of gratification—the powerful parental or adult authorities. However, to be spared these frustrations as well as the fears of retaliation by hostile adults, an internal inhibitor of instincts replaced the external prohibitors. The newly formed internal regulator is the superego. To block the id from instinctual discharges, the superego uses the id's own murderous rage to threaten it with destruction if compliance is not forthcoming. Thus, the archaic superego, which is in close touch with the primitive id, has mastery over raw impulses, both sexual and aggressive.

The superego is therefore a potent and sadistic psychic structure. Under the banner of morality, it seeks to legitimize the expression of primitive hostile id impulses. Clearly these hostile impulses cannot simply be discharged as "hostile impulses" without disguise. On the contrary, under the banner of morality and legality they assume the form of just retribution. Punishing the guilty is not being mean; teaching offenders a momentous lesson is not being cruel, but rather educational and for their own good. In general, dishing out generous punishments which more than fit the crimes is not considered to be sadistic, but a means of upholding morality and protecting the highest human ideals. In this steadfast willingness to engage in severe acts of punishment which are formally correct, the superego betrays the fact that it represents the id and its primitive impulses, which are not only of love but also of hate. Thus, this guardian of morality, this sadistic upholder of conscience, welcomes instinctual gratifications and is by no means incorruptible; it adheres to a formal code of morality, and as long as formal propriety is upheld, it is open to bribes.

Franz Alexander drew attention to this "corruptibility" of the conscience and described its frequent occurrence in neurotic people. It comes about by means of a clever game, initiated by the ego and designed to secure from the superego a license for the gratification of forbidden id impulses. The game is as old as man, and goes as follows: The voice of the superego, the primitive conscience, forbids many instinctual gratifications. For the transgressions of many "don'ts," the superego inflicts punishment in the form of anxiety, suffering, and tormenting guilt. Punishment was therefore originally meant to serve as inhibitor of aggressive libidinal impulses. However, through weird quirks of development, self-punishment and suffering became in effect a license to express hitherto forbidden impulses.

The individual learns first that punishment follows sin; later on he learns that sin which follows punishment does not result in further punishment. This learning is guided by more than laws of conditioning. It is fostered by the superego, which, containing so much id, prefers to collaborate with the id and unofficially encourage impulse gratification. The major reason for the transformation in significance of the suffering is the corruptibility of the superego, which, being only human, can be bribed. If one pays the punishment of suffering in advance, one can then tend to the id without fear of the bribed superego, which, caring for formal propriety, will not punish twice for the same offense. In this game, suffering becomes the local currency while freedom from

anxiety and guilt becomes the gold or international monetary standard
in the intra-psychic economic juggling of a person. The desired commodity is instinctual indulgence. With enough suffering, a person can
exchange it for a certain freedom from anxiety which in turn allows
gratification of primitive or forbidden impulses. When freedom from
anxiety finally runs out, more suffering is needed before new acquisi-
tions of id gratifications become possible.

In the case of the neurotic, the local currency of suffering is
devalued and that of gold, or freedom from anxiety, is upgraded. As a
result, the neurotic person needs much more suffering to acquire gold,
i.e., a license for guiltless instinctual gratification. Even more important, in the neurotic there are hardly any trade restrictions; as long as
he can drum up sufferings in large enough quantities, he can convert
them into gold. The superego is willing to relax trade restrictions in
return for all sorts of local currencies. Human imagination is quite
inventive and there are many ways to pay a penalty or serve a sentence;
the superego is keenly aware of, and interested in, all of them. It is
interested in suffering because its original purpose—to prevent or block
transgressions—involved the infliction of suffering as a punishment and
deterrent for past and future transgressions. Nevertheless, the superego
is also interested in freeing the trade of gold even though this trade
provides tickets for licentious expressions.

As for the ego of a neurotic person, when it plays this bribery game
with the superego it sacrifices considerations of external reality. Even
when objective conditions militate against impulsive behavior, the ego
goes ahead with an attempt to bribe the superego to withdraw its
objection. The corrupted ego commits this sacrifice of realistic considerations because it cares more about removing internal superego objections than it does about objective conditions of external reality. The
corrupt ego has not "learned" (i.e., not profited from maturational
experiences) that punishment by the sadistic superego is to be feared
less than real danger from the outside. In fact, it has not "learned" to
differentiate the one from the other.

The neurotic bribery game has its high price. Both ego and superego become corrupted, external reality is misperceived, internal regulation of instincts is mismanaged, and suffering becomes a style of life.

Therefore, neurotic people are not happy people. For one thing, the misperception of external reality makes it even more difficult to secure gratification from the environment. For another, the mismanagement of internal regulation of impulses can result in too much aggression turned inward. A person's own self then becomes the target of the murderous drives, at which times death wishes become apparent.

Although it can be corrupted by bribery, the superego is the carrier of the banner of morality. Even when it accepts bribes it still has to adhere to formal codes of ethics. Hostile murderous impulses cannot be licensed unless they fall under the category of just retribution and conform to the primitive moral code of an eye for an eye. Therefore, nasty aggressive urges are very conveniently attributed not to one's own self but rather to malicious others. The person then feels free to carry out his own impulses either for the sake of survival (kill before you get killed) or for the sake of justice (an eye for an eye, a tooth for a tooth). That is why the neurotic person resorts to the defense mechanism of projection while carrying out the bribery game for the sake of guiltless indulgence in hostile acts.

It was the psychoanalyst Sandor Rado who drew attention to the importance of projection in these neurotic developments. Through the extensive resort to this mechanism, the ego transforms the internal perception of forbidden impulses into an external perception. In the process, the important ego functions of reality testing and critical judgment become distorted. The ego's reward for this falsification of external reality is narcissistic gratification. Since the bad impulses are disowned and attributed to the outside, the ego is supposedly a "good" and "nice boy," and receives from the superego love, reassurance, and narcissistic gratification. The superego—the internal representative of the once external and all powerful parental authorities—can give this gratification. It can punish severely, but it can also give love and make a person feel secure. The price of being gratified like a little child by a towering superego is loss of critical judgment. As Rado put it: "An ego which stays on the level of narcissistic gratification will allow its critical reality function to be paralyzed."

This brings us back to the particular neurosis of the Israelis—the obsession with Masada. In these Israeli ruminations, where does the ego function of realpoliticking end and indulgence in aggressive id impulses begin? The old Masada myth carries with it the emotional satisfaction of wreaking havoc on the Gentiles and proving to them, even in death, the Jewish superiority in fighting and spirit. It is a myth which when mingled with realpolitik can only be to the detriment of the latter. In spite of the lessons of the Holocaust and the unwavering intransigence of the Arabs, present-day reality is that the Arabs, who wish to destroy Israel, cannot, and the Russians, who can, do not wish to. External reality looks pretty grim even when political analysis is not clouded by myth. However, a dispassionate vision of the arena of global power politics is free of doomsday forecasts. In this arena, Masada is not what Israel has to face, as was pointed out so clearly by Bentov. When Israelis nevertheless brace themselves obsessively for a Masada-style last stand against the modern, Russian-speaking "Romans," they are projecting their own impulses in the way that was described by Rado.

It is no surprise that after all that happened to them, Jews have a bottled-up murderous rage toward Gentiles. Nor is it a surprise that, after the great boost in self-esteem that Zionism has provided, Jews can now turn more of their rage outward rather than inward. Further, it is no wonder that in accordance with the high ethical codes of Jewish superegos, the obsession with Masada is rationalized, probably along the primitive emotional lines of "Kill before you get killed," and "It's high time for Jews to give Gentiles tit for tat." Unfortunately, these two rationales of survival and just retribution distort the true reality of the military and political plays of the world powers. The narcissistic gratification of being "good boys" who can once again engage in active fighting of the fatherly Lord's battles damages the critical ego function of realpoliticking.

The corruption of realpolitik by myth, as part of a superego and ego corruption by the impulse to gratify primitive urges, is amply illustrated in the ideas advocated by Israel Eldad. This former member of the underground Fighters for Israel's Freedom during the days of the British Mandate is presently a writer and staunch supporter of The Greater Israel Movement. In his book *The Jewish Revolution* he outlined the logistic difficulties that the Russians will encounter if they try to initiate a mass military intervention against Israel. Like the left-wing leader Yitzhak Tabenkin, Eldad too expected a Russian blackmail attempt, and was willing to call the Russians' bluff. And like the right-wing leader Ezer Weizman (See Oren), he trusted the Russians to shy away from a world war over the Middle East. However, in contemplating the possibility of Russia's blackmailing Israel with another world war, he concluded that if carried out, this would be a catastrophe for the world, but first and foremost for Israel. Nevertheless, Israelis had made up their minds that *"we are here to stay"* (italics by Eldad). This seems like a cool political and military analysis coupled with commendable emotional resolve.

However, in a newspaper article at about the same period we learn that the political calculations are not so cool and that the emotional resolve promotes an unrealistic vision of future developments. When both of Eldad's writings are taken in conjunction it becomes clear that the resolve to face Russia unflinchingly is coupled with a sweet foretaste of the outcome of an Israeli "liberty or death" stand. The taste is sweet because, according to Eldad, if Israelis follow the call of Russian Jewry to assume the stance of "liberty or death," they will be victorious. His article in *Yediot Aharonot* of January 22, 1971, was titled "An Open Letter to Rabbi Meir Kahane." In it, he expressed his conviction that Kahane's slogan "never again" not only applies to Auschwitz, but also means "never again Warsaw Ghetto revolt, never again Masada, and never again 'Let my soul die with the Philistines'."

In discussing contemporary Jewish battles on a variety of fronts, Eldad vehemently objected to any Jewish withdrawal on any front, whether Russia, United States, or Suez. By so urging, he put his trust in the fact that "the nation of Israel is in a period of its increasing power and honor." For him this was a sufficient reassurance that in case of outright confrontations with other nations, Israel will live and the Philistines will die. As he put it: "Our present war is a war for our lives without Philistines."

Such mystical trust in Israel's ultimate survival is usually anchored in concepts like *netzah Yisrael* (the eternity of Israel), *sar ha'umah* (the minister of the nation), *sar ha'historia* (the minister of history), *tzur Yisrael* (rock of Israel), and other ill-defined notions that carry with them religious connotations. Indeed, the State of Israel Proclamation of Independence includes the sentence "With trust in the rock of

Israel, we set our hand to this declaration. . . ." Religious Jews take this
to mean God—the rock on which Israel can lean forever. On the other
hand, secular Jews could see Israel itself as the eternal rock of strength.
Similar dual interpretations are possible in regard to *netzah Yisrael*.
Evidently people can read into these notions their own emotional
needs, be they religion or secular nationalism.

The power of myths and mystical beliefs cannot be discounted.
Certainly the fervent Jewish historical belief that *Am Yisrael hai* (The
nation of Israel lives) represents reality. It is in effect a powerful force
to be reckoned with, but there are other realities too. Eldad's notions
imply a convenient formula which ignores other realities. As I understand his call, it can be summed up as follows: Never again Masada and
never again "Let my soul die with the Philistines," plus outright confrontations on all fronts, equals liberty for the Jews and death to the
Philistines. The Jews will get the "liberty" and the Philistine Gentiles
the "death"; it is not a nice dream, and it certainly is not reality.

What it *is* is the outcome of an intrapsychic corruption. The id
ached for action and got its due—a license for aggressive discharges.
The superego, which had been bought off by prolonged sufferings,
including the added anxieties engendered by obsession with impending
Masadas, approved this urge as a just retribution in the form of "our
lives without Philistines," i.e., death to the Philistines. Finally, the
corrupt and damaged ego acquiesced, and in support of the proposed
action, provided an analysis of external reality which falsely predicted
almost insurmountable difficulties for the Russians. The "realistic"
prediction this time is not that of a "catastrophe," first and foremost
for Israel, but of death to the Philistines and an Israeli victory on all
fronts—including the Russian. In this instance, the taxed and corrupted ego shuts one, or even both, eyes to factual external information,
and sanctions both impulse discharge and narcissistic gratification.

An added irony to the tragic obsession with Masada is the fact that
"give me liberty or give me death" no longer makes sense in the nuclear
era. In drawing attention to this loss of meaning, Frank stated that,
unlike previous times, "a person could not die for his ideals in a nuclear
holocaust without taking millions of innocent bystanders with him."
What is more, the sacrifice would not contribute to the realization of
the ideals for which it was offered, because the mass destruction would

eradicate the social fabric on which these ideals are based. Thus, "liberty or death" could make sense to Patrick Henry, but in the era of modern weapons the only promise it can deliver is a mass execution à la "Let my soul die with the Philistines."

In this connection, it is revealing to notice that Evron, in his article "We Are Not Being Annihiliated," alluded not only to "we always are in Masada" but also to the Israeli awareness of their nuclear potential. He pointed out that with a "sly wink" the Israeli newspapers quote the foreign press on the topic of Israel's "sophisticated" weaponry. The wink serves as a hint that "sophisticated" is something more than "advanced," and relates to that kind of "special advanced weapon capable of wiping out every living soul, including cats and cockroaches, from the mountains of Kurdistan to Timbuktu, seven and twenty and one hundred provinces." Evron's sardonic description indicates that he too is well aware of the senselessness of a "liberty or death" stand in a nuclear era. That is why he included even the innocent cats and cockroaches among the victims of the mass destruction, and why he referred to the biblical book of Esther in the expression "seven and twenty and one hundred provinces," which describes the extension of Ahasuerus's kingdom. To this day Jews celebrate in the festival of Purim the fall of Haman, who urged Ahasuerus to destroy all the Jews. The reference also suggests that Evron was keenly aware of what a thin line separates aggression turned inward from aggression turned outward. The need to perceive oneself on the verge of extermination is also a license to destroy others.

One should bear in mind Evron's article when reading a news item in the March 16–17, 1972, issue of the airmail edition of *Yediot Aharonot*, which cites the *London Daily Express*'s contention that Israel has become a nuclear power. There the Israelis are depicted as regarding their nuclear capabilities only as a deterrent. Nevertheless, the Arabs are warned to take note of the notorious, sometimes unconscious and at other times conscious, Israeli "Masada spirit." Such news items make one wonder whether the Masada stand will avert another Holocaust or help to bring it about. The tragic history of the Jews left them starved for Jewish heroics. Unfortunately, it also made them amenable to the deterioration of the worship of heroics into the worship of death.

Being aware of such emotional temptations and dangers among Israelis, the Israeli entertainer and writer Dan Ben Amotz discussed them in his regular column in *Ha'olam Hazeh* of March 24, 1971. He pointed out that if common sense prevails in the Israeli government, it would have to bow to American pressure. Unless the government is obsessed with "madness" and intends to threaten both superpowers with putting this madness into effect, it will have to yield. Ben Amotz asks with sarcasm whether Israel's President Shazar during his recent visit to the United States gave President Nixon a gift of a Bible in which the phrase "Let my soul die with the Philistines" was underlined with a thick line. About a month later, Avneri declared, also in *Ha'olam Hazeh*, that should America pressure Israel by signaling its refusal to neutralize the Russians if a new war breaks out, Israel should follow American diplomatic solutions and not head toward a second Masada —the romantic dream of Begin and his hawkish followers. Thus, in essence, Avneri's public stand concerning the Masada complex and the issue raised by Ben Amotz is that "madness" will not prevail. So far, the events which follow the Yom Kippur War seem to bear him out.

Yet the psychological makeup of the Israeli nation includes the obsessive Masada complex and the potential for mass suicide in the form of a heroic last stand. This potential can be counteracted from both within and without. From within by the voices of such people as Evron, Bentov, Ben Amotz, and Avneri, who by rendering the suicidal and aggressive feelings more conscious and by placing them in the context of Jewish history, help to loosen up the unconscious control that these feelings have on the Israeli public. The more there are open discussions of the Masada complex the less is the propensity to act out a Masada. From without, the Masada potential can be counteracted if the big powers, especially Russia, which backs the Arabs, make it perfectly clear that no "imposed solution" would even remotely resemble a "final solution." The Arabs would destroy Israel if they could. If Russia manifests its determination not to back the Arabs in this case, but to oppose them, then it would reduce the probability of a new Israeli Masada. The chances increase that the big powers will include these emotional factors in their political considerations as Israelis continue to bring their Masada obsession into public consciousness.

14.

The Psychology of Anti-Semitism

THE JEWS WERE CLEVER, AND AT
THE SAME TIME APPEARED TO BE
CONNECTED WITH OLD PRIME-
VAL POWERS WITH WHICH THE
OTHERS HAD LOST TOUCH. WHEN
THE AUTHORITIES SAID THAT
THESE "UNCANNY" PEOPLE
WERE EVIL, THE OTHERS READILY
BELIEVED THE AUTHORITIES BE-
CAUSE OF THEIR OWN OBVIOUS
MISERY.

—Otto Fenichel

No description of the intricate relationships between Jews and non-Jews would be complete without a discussion of the nature of anti-Semitism and its impact on Zionism. Anti-Semitism, the irrational hatred of Jews, is frequently an unyielding, rigid, and totalistic attitude. Jean-Paul Sartre once described the anti-Semite as so absorbed in his mission as "holy destroyer" of evil for the sake of an ultimate good, and therefore so confronted by many tasks, that he has no time to think about the nature of the "good." With this frame of mind a person is not very amenable to change. Indeed, anti-Semitism resists change and does not depend for its perpetuation on the variety of ideological dressings which coat it at different times and places. To fair-minded persons it seems like something sick and distorted which persists without reasonable explanations—in other words, a symptom.

In *A General Introduction to Psychoanalysis*, Freud conceptualized symptoms as compromise formations designed to deliver substitute gratification. The compromise is between conflicting tendencies. One tendency is to act upon a strong impulse charged with energy. A conflicting tendency is to censor the impulse because of an inhibition from within by a person's own conscience and anxieties, or a prohibition from without by powerful authorities. The result of this opposition between force and counterforce is a compromise formation. The nature of the compromise is such that it gives rise to behaviors which are deeply ingrained and institutionalized, that is, chronic and rigid behaviors. The essence of the compromise is, on the one hand, to forbid direct and full expression of an impulse but, on the other hand, to give it partial expression indirectly by means of symbolic representation. It is this open avenue for partial expression which depletes the impulse of some of its energy and allows the censoring forces to "keep the lid on" what is left of the impulse. A person with a symptom is in a way a person who chose what he regarded as the least of three evils: full expression of an impulse, full censorship, or a compromise. Of course, full expression could have been possible if we lived in a magical world where all our wishes are immediately granted without unpleasant consequences. In reality, however, we do not, and uninhibited discharges of impulses might result in deprivations and even be a threat to survival. Therefore, none of the three options mentioned above is fully satisfying but compromise seems to be the least troublesome of all three. It is this fear of adverse consequences that prompts people to fixate on their symptoms with an attitude of "let sleeping dogs lie," which gives the symptoms an "untouchable" status and turns them into a chronic malaise. When a balance of power between opposing forces is achieved in this manner, the person worships the status quo for fear of unpredictable turbulence. The compromise behavior therefore becomes rigid and chronic but the loss of flexibility is compensated by the guarantee against unpleasant sudden jolts.

Although a symptom allows the censored impulse to be given partial gratification, this still has to be done by means of indirect substitutes. One way is for the object of the impulse to change. For instance, the craving for little girls as sexual objects may be changed by an adult man into a somewhat more socially acceptable desire for girls in their teens with budding sexual features. Another way is for the impulse itself to be slightly modified. A sadistic impulse to torture helpless victims can turn a person into a cruel military commander who under the guise of turning boys into men abuses the soldiers under his command. A third way is for the final expression of an impulse to take the indirect form of symbolic gratification. For example, the wish to publicly display the genitals can receive an indirect symbolic expression by wearing the wrong clothes at the wrong time and in the wrong places. In all these symptomatic manifestations the persons most often do not know the true meaning of their behavior. The dirty old man would be aware of his fascination with youthful teenagers but not with little children, the harsh officer would be aware of his joy in being a tough leader of men but not of his delight in unnecessarily torturing them, and the woman who was the only one to come to a party on a hot sunny day wearing a heavy raincoat would know that she wants to attract attention but not that she has a more specific wish to display her genitals to the public the way she did as a little girl. Similarly, in spite of his arsenal of logical rationales for his Jew-hatred, the anti-Semite does not know the true meaning of his symptomatic behavior.

If anti-Semitism is indeed a symptom, an analytic approach should detect the conflicting tendencies which formed it. This was brilliantly done by the psychoanalyst Otto Fenichel. In viewing anti-Semitism, Fenichel detected compromises between opposing tendencies on both an overt and a covert level. On a more manifest level, anti-Semitism gave the masses a way of satisfying simultaneously two contradictory tendencies, those of respecting the authorities and of rebelling against them. The rebellion could be expressed by harming the defenseless Jews; the respect, by obeying the commands of the ruling powers to go and punish Jews. On a more latent level, anti-Semitism served as a compromise between two more basic tendencies, the tendency to unleash all the primitive aggressive and sexual urges of the uncivilized id and also the opposing tendency to censor unbridled instinctual urges, to put a halt to the rampant id and to impose the constraints of civilization. The first tendency involves giving expression to one's own repressed unconscious, including all the archaic, aggressive, bestial, and sexual impulses which people frequently wish to believe they do not possess. All this is therefore repressed and becomes "foreign." "Foreign" is that which people fear and do not wish to know. As Fenichel put it, one's own unconscious is foreign. So were the Jews in their host countries—foreign. This resulted in the symbolic equation of the foreign Jews with one's own foreign unconscious, and in the projection onto the Jews of all the ugly, raw impulses of the anti-Semites themselves. Jews were therefore feared and hated because they came to symbolize to non-Jews all the fearful tendencies that existed within themselves.

The prevailing image of Jews as a foreign people is a historical fact and existed for many generations. Anti-Semites, of course, tended to emphasize this very image. For instance, Adolf Hitler wrote in *Mein Kampf:* "At the time of Frederick the Great it still entered no one's head to regard the Jew as anything else but a 'foreign' people. . . ." Anti-Semites had a stake in perpetuating this image because the symbolically "foreign" Jews provided an opportunity to give vent to two conflicting tendencies. The tendency to give expression to all that fearful id material manifested itself in obsessive preoccupation with the alleged demonic and bestial practices of the Jews. The opposing tendency, to censor direct gratification of id impulses, to stamp out urges for voluptuous sex and urges to murder fathers and brothers, also received expression through intense hatred of Jews and all that they supposedly stood for. Thus, incensed with fantasies of the murder of children and revolting sexual practices, "good" Christians were able in the midst of pogroms to grab the alleged offenders, those uncanny Jews, and molest and murder them. Again and again the superegos of anti-Semites were sufficiently bribed to obtain the condonement of these merciless "just retributions." This happened countless times and there was not always a Bialik among the afflicted Jews to record the horrid events with piercing poetry.

The opposing tendencies that find expression in anti-Semitism stand for a very old conflict in the history of humankind, which was conceptualized at different times with varying degrees of sophistication. Examples include the conflict between Ahriman and Ormuzed, Christ and Antichrist (or sometimes Christ and Judas as might have been the case with Hitler [Slochower]), God and the Devil, Greeks and Barbarians, and finally Jews and anti-Semites. Recently, Dimont conceptualized this conflict as "culture man" against "jungle man" and maintained that anti-Semitism is a "counterrevolution to annul the march of civilization." It was the misfortune of the Jews to be hated for being a civilizing force. Their alleged uncivilized, satanic activities, including murders and perverted sexual practices, existed only in the imaginative projections of their enemies. A prime example is that of Hitler's projecting his own incestuous wishes onto the Jews (Bromberg). The history of anti-Semitism is a living testimony to the correctness of Freud's delineation of the high price of neurosis or discontent that civilization entails. Civilized living is based on compromise formations and partial gratifications that fall far short of the magical promise of uncomplicated full indulgence. It seems that in the case of anti-Semites this discontent led to the exacting of a high price from the Jews —the "strange" people who in the eyes of many became the simultaneous symbol of all that is base and all that is civilized in humanity.

At this point we should reiterate Schick's notion of the Jews as sacrificial victims, as discussed in Chapter 11. Schick equated anti-Semitic murders with human sacrifices. In the pre-Christian era, as the Jews became more civilized they were able to renounce first human sacrifice and later all forms of sacrifice, using prayer instead to appease the angry father in heaven. Other peoples with more primitive moral codes were alarmed by this renunciation and feared vengeance from gods or men—the same kind of vengeance they themselves felt capable of. They therefore offered the more civilized Jews as human sacrifices to their gods. As paganism was replaced by Christianity the same sentiments persisted. And why not? Were not the Jews the people who committed deicide, who killed Christ? Therefore, with an "eye for an eye" sense of justice, every so often those who had killed God were themselves sacrificed. Logic and historical authenticity had nothing to do with it. The persecution centered not on Italians, the descendants of the Romans who crucified Jesus, but on the Jews who delivered him to the Romans. There is not much logic there. What is more, it is historically incorrect. It was pointed out by the British Zionist leader Norman Bentwitch that the famous passage from Book 18 of Josephus's *Antiquities of the Jews*, which ascribes Pontius Pilate's action as having been prompted by the suggestion of Jews, was quoted by Eusebius in the fourth century A.D. but was unknown to Origen in the third century. This discrepancy between the two Church fathers, Origen and Eusebius, strongly suggested that the role assigned to the Jews by Josephus was a later Christian addition to the original text for self-serving reasons. Nevertheless the author Paul Winter, who also suspected Christian interpolations, suggested that the original text by Josephus did include some references to the death of Jesus. This now seems correct. Recent evidence indicates (See Grose) that an Arabic translation of that same passage, unlike the Greek translation which in all probability was tampered with by tendentious Christian hands, attributes no role whatsoever to the Jews in the description of Jesus' death.

Unfortunately, the lack of historical authenticity of the accusation of Jews as killers of Jesus did not matter much. In facing the sophisticated Hellenistic world during the first three centuries A.D. the Church could not hope to win new converts by admitting that it shared many of its Scriptures with the Jews. In the opinion of the Church of England clergyman James Parkes, this reluctance to admit the Jewish origin of the Scriptures and of the Messiah led the Church to take a stand which fostered anti-Semitism for generations to come. The unfortunate stand was the blaming of Jews not for anything contemporary, but for a figment of the imagination. The famous French researcher of anti-Semitism Léon Poliakov traced in detail the development in the Church of this theme of the Jews as killers of the saviour and as cursed people. This theological anti-Semitism finally crystallized in the third century in the writings of Origen and set the stage for countless Christian retaliations against the "murderers of the Lord." Time and again these "murderers" were murdered. The victims, the cursed Jews, were highly civilized people who clung to, God forbid, the parent religion from which Christianity had sprung. This combination was enough to create a hostility that fostered the perception of Jews as strange people and ideal sacrificial humans.

Fenichel's conceptualizations are complemented by the astute historical observations of the German Jewish sociologist Adolf Leschnitzer. In discussing the magical background of modern anti-Semitism in Germany, Leschnitzer drew attention to its connection with the witch hunt frenzy from 1575 to 1700. Both before and after this period, when there were only a few Jews in Germany, flare-ups of anti-Semitism occurred. Leschnitzer suggests that when Germans did not have Jews to hunt, they went after witches, only to resume their Jew-hunting frenzy when Jews once more became available. Thus, in the nineteenth and twentieth centuries the persecution of Jews replaced the persecution of witches. We have already mentioned that Jews were persecuted because of the strange feelings evoked by "foreign" people. Similarly, the prosecution of witches was mostly a persecution of the female sex because, as Leschnitzer put it, "people were filled with a queer feeling of the strangeness of the female sex." He also suggested that the persecutions of Jews and of witches served the same instincts and anxieties. Both were used to divert the attention of the masses and to intimidate political enemies.

The notion of a shift in scapegoat was also advanced by the American historian Erik Midelfort as an attractive speculation which nevertheless cannot yet be documented. In this connection, he reported a significant event that took place in December 1643, when Bavarian troops led by Colonel Von Sporck occupied the city of Schwäbisch Hall northeast of Stuttgart. Since many of the soldiers' wives were suspected of witchcraft, the Colonel decided to subject them to the old test of immersion in water. First, however, he offered a reward of twelve thalers to any volunteer who was willing to take the test and demonstrate that innocent persons do indeed remain afloat. Only one person, a Jew named Löb, dared to volunteer. He floated three times and collected his reward. This incident suggests that in this region the public was so obsessed with witches that a Jew, rather than being a potential scapegoat, could serve as a criterion of innocence.

In discussing the European witch craze beginning in the 1560s the British historian H. R. Trevor-Roper has emphasized that the major etiological factor for its revival was the bitter strife between Catholicism and Protestantism. Both camps regarded themselves as two forms of society that were incompatible with each other and both resorted to the dualism of God and the Devil as an explanation. The bitter struggle within Christianity seems to be a more plausible cause for the revived witch craze than Leschnitzer's suggestion that the dwindling number of Jews in Western Europe prompted a search for new scapegoats. However, even if a causal relationship between Jew hunt and witch hunt is at best indirect, a similarity of function does exist. Trevor-Roper indicated that both witches and Jews served as a stereotype of the incurable nonconformist, and that both were used as scapegoats. He also asserted that both anti-Semites and the Hammerers of Witches built up a systematic mythology out of disparate pieces of scandal, or of mental rubbish of peasant credibility. "Rubbish" it was indeed if all that material concerning the Devil and his fifth column on earth was supposed to represent objective reality. As a *subjective* reality, however, it was no rubbish at all, but an obsessive externalization of evil potentialities that people sensed within themselves. The Jews were a visible target which could readily serve as a focus for such a process of externalization.

It was particularly in Germany that Jews seemed like an uncanny blend of the foreign with the familiar because of their use of the

Yiddish language. Yiddish is mostly a blend of old Hebrew and Germanic dialects from around 1000 A.D. To Germans it sounded both comical and archaic (Leschnitzer) and made its speakers seem like ghosts from another era who speak a language which in some ways is homely and familiar to listeners but in others is foreign and strange. It was therefore easier for Germans than for other people to perceive Jews as eternal ghosts of the past.

The ghostly Jews who wandered into the present from the past speaking their archaic dialect acquired the image of "the wandering Jew." Leschnitzer drew attention to the fact that the original German idiom *"der ewige Jude"* means not the wandering Jew but rather the eternal or everlasting Jew. This meaningful conceptualization casts the Jew in a similar role to that of the Flying Dutchman: cursed, wandering, and everlasting. The eternal Jew is a ghostly Jew; his immortality is due to a pact with the Devil, to an evil and frightening mode of existence. Thus, Jews were seen as living corpses suffering under the curse of cheating death forever (Leschnitzer). This image persisted, so that in the twentieth century the famous British historian Arnold Toynbee characterized the Jews as fossils of history. To him, Jews were spoilsports. They cheated death and continued to exist like living corpses after their Syriac civilization died, until in the twentieth century they became an exception to Toynbee's theories about the history of civilizations. Toynbee, who made no bones about his sympathy with the Arab side in the tragic Middle East conflict, may have fossilized the Jews because of his love for the Arabs. He may have been further angered by the Jews because in their mere existence they provided facts that could confuse his theories. However, it is not inconceivable that Toynbee's conception of the Jews as fossils of history is also a reaffirmation of an old anti-Semitic image, the image of eternal and weird people who cheat on death and have no business being alive.

Eternal creatures who have cheated on death, whether Jews or witches, are usually supposed to engage in unusual and evil practices of both murderous and sexual nature. For instance, the Witches' Sabbath was popularly believed to be sort of a convention of evildoers, including demons and witches, who would gather together and after paying homage to the goat-shaped Devil by kissing him on his behind, would engage in cannibalism, group orgies, and bestial practices. The British historian Pennethorne Hughes attempted to separate what actually happened in these Sabbaths from what popular imagination made of them. What was actually going on was a cross between ritual proclamations of a secret society, an institute picnic, a drunken orgy, and a carnival including group dancing as well as marching with phosphorous torches. What was made of it in the imagination of the frightened or enticed populace was a series of vile but also powerful magical acts. Witches allegedly flew from place to place, instead of hallucinating under the influence of wine and toxic substances. The Devil was routinely kissed on his rear end and not on a mask of a second Janus face which covered his bottom. Witches were often charged with cannibalism and the eating of unbaptized children. In reality, however, this fall back upon "the Old Ways" took place only on rare occasions. In this regard, Hughes drew attention to the fact that similar charges were made against the Jews.

Besides their great effects on popular imagination, the Sabbaths were influential on the judicial system and on the spread of prosecution as well as panic. Erik Midelfort focused attention on the important fact that the Sabbaths were frequently regarded as the only place of contact for witches. These unique gatherings enabled people in one town to testify against Sabbath attendants from other towns, thus providing a link from one accusation to the next. The result was not only a geographic spread of witch trials but also large local trials. As large trials started to decimate communities, panic spread and social, political, as well as judicial traditions began to break down. All in all, the Sabbaths exercised two important functions. They provided a vehicle for the focusing of blown-up popular fantasies, and served as a crucial link for the spread of accusation and panic. Because of the Sabbaths it was possible for evil to pop up everywhere to engulf all.

The consequences of the Sabbaths for Jews were most unfortunate. Popular notions concerning Jewish practices and way of life did not need to start from nowhere. The wealth of ideas concerning witches and their congregations could simply be transferred to the Jews and become Jewish practices. Ritual murders, voluptuous sexuality, and living under a pact with the Antichrist were all attributed to the Jews.

Thus, both Jews and witches merited the term "foreign," and "deserved" to be hunted.

In the mind of some Christians, a link was even established between Jews and vampires. The British novelist and journalist Anthony Masters reported that in Rumania, Serbia, and Bulgaria, the "Children of Judas" were feared. These were specific kinds of red-haired vampires, presumably the descendants of the red-haired Judas Iscariot who sold Christ for thirty pieces of silver. One bite from a "child of Judas" would suffice to drain all the victim's blood. On the bloodless flesh the Devil's stigmata will be left in the form of three scars shaped like three X's, the Latin number thirty. Such folklore obviously did not endear the Jews to the local populace. Jews are, of course, aware of the image they have among some Christians. This is why the novelist Abraham Rothberg alluded to "Jewish vampires" in his fiction *The Sword of the Golem.*

The perception of "eternal" creatures involves both fear and envy. The fear is of revenge if these everlasting beings are identified as deceased people against whom a person sinned either in reality or in fantasy. It also involves the notion that eternal youth is gained at the expense of other people's life-spans, including one's own. The envy relates to the acquisition of mastery over magical techniques and their application to the securing of eternal life for oneself. This was particularly evident in Nazism. As Leschnitzer pointed out, the Nazis developed paranoid notions concerning the Jews. Out of their fear of destruction and their pseudohistorical concept of "eternal Jewry," they developed a wish to destroy the eternal enemy and thus gain eternity for themselves. This relates to a primitive psychology of oral incorporation in which the victor is able to acquire the envied qualities of the dead enemy. Thus, the Nazi fear of doom to which they reacted with a cry for a thousand-year Reich led to an attempted implementation of the Nazi eternity by destroying the eternal Jews. The result was the Holocaust, which Leschnitzer characterized as "a descent into fiendish bestiality." Fiendish bestiality was supposed to be found among participants of the Witches' Sabbath or the Jewish Passover ceremony. It seems that the hunters of fiendish creatures were willing to search anywhere for the abominable beasts except within their own selves.

Ghostlike creatures, whether Jewish or not, who lead eternal lives are perceived as a mortal danger to the living. As any horror-movie fan knows, vampires need to suck blood in order to perpetuate their weird existence. That is where murder enters into the picture. Like vipers, Jewish money lenders who were worse than Shakespeare's Shylock allegedly sucked the blood and the life out of their Christian victims. More literally, Jews supposedly would kill innocent Christian children to drink their blood in a magic Passover ceremony. In fact, of course, Jewish ritual does not provide an opportunity for even a symbolic drinking of blood and eating of flesh. What mattered, though, were not facts but the projected image of Jews that was created in the minds of those who hated them in order to satisfy internal needs.

It is not a matter of chance that Jews were usually accused of killing and eating children rather than older victims. In this instance Jews were perceived as being like witches who kill and eat infants or like the Devil who is especially eager to do harm to young and uncorrupt maidens. The authors of the fifteenth-century work *Malleus Maleficarum (The Witch Hammer)* (See Summers) took note of this preference for youth and innocence. The Devil is more eager to seduce "saintly virgins" because in them there is more good to be corrupted and because he is more interested in those he does not possess than in those he already possesses. (It is therefore no surprise to find the authors stating that above all the Devil hates the "Blessed Virgin"). This preference for youth weathered the passage of generations so that at the end of the nineteenth century we find the famous literary figure of the evil Dracula practicing vampirism on beautiful young women. His choice of beautiful and virginal women was interpreted by the literary critic C. F. Bentley as an exercise in a perverted droit du seigneur. Thus, a comparison of vampires with the seigneurs of old reveals a similar predilection, i.e., the desire to spill both blood and semen by violating virginal young girls.

Latter-day vampires of the movies also cherish youthful victims from whose blood they can derive a longer new lease on life and who are more attractive as sexual objects. The preference of Transylvanian vampires can be witnessed time and again on television late shows. The ghostlike creatures prefer young, pretty, innocent-looking women.

Murderous and sexual impulses are well fused in each person's id and therefore also in the actions of vampires. Evil or instinct power is a very potent power. It is not for naught that people fear the tremendously alluring temptation of instinctual discharge. The temptation can work like magic. In the classic book *Dracula*, by Bram Stoker, a remarkable heightening of sexuality occurs in the former virginal woman turned vampire (Bentley). In Dracula movies the metamorphosis is even more astounding. With a flicker of a bite that leaves two tiny red marks on a young woman's neck (an erogenous zone), a virginal maiden acquires a joyous but evil smile and is transformed into a satanic creature with voluptuous desires, capable of turning other innocent beings into evil creatures with the same ungodly speed. If this alarming process is not checked, it can multiply geometrically and speedily corrupt the whole world. Therefore, good people everywhere should beware of living corpses who never die and who feast on human flesh, drink toasts in human blood, indulge in bestial sexuality, and adore everything about Satan from bottom to top, in that order. All good people should beware of such eternal evil creatures, be they witches or Jews.

The old and popular notions of the danger and power of evil are clearly illustrated by these repeated scenes of the pure maiden turned into evil vampire. Such instantaneous and total transformation suggests that magic is expected to be successful because of qualities which are inherent in the victims. The fearful maiden is quick to betray signs of joy. The reason this metamorphosis is so easily accomplished is that it is not that much of a change after all. It represents a switch from one side of the same coin to the other. It is only a thin line that separates purity and goodness from the knowledge of evil which, once tasted, erupts uncontrollably into unabashed indulgence in all that is base and animalistic in humankind.

I once viewed an unusual movie scene of the opposite transformation. The loving maiden kissed her former loved one, now turned vampire, and with this act of love turned him back into a normal man. This scene is like one in a fairy tale, where the lovely maiden kisses the enchanted frog and he turns back into a prince. Magic in fairy tales is accepted as make-believe and is not frightening. On the other hand, in the Witches' Sabbath a witch rather than a maiden kisses a huge toad on the lips, thus paying him homage. He is the Devil rather than a transformed prince, and the scene is taken for real. Whatever happens in the Witches' Sabbath is frightening because it is not supposed to be an agreed-upon and shared fiction. Similarly, the sublimation and humanization of a vampire in fairy-tale style does not evoke anxiety, while the opposite—the monsterizing of humans for real—evokes dread. Nevertheless, people are frequently preoccupied with and fascinated by that which is fear-arousing. The vague anxieties or even focused fears are the defenses we construct to block the fulfillment of forbidden and inhibited wishes. These hidden wishes are the sources of our mysterious fascination with things we dread.

But that which we overtly dread yet secretly wish for is to return to the primary age of narcissism, before the pressures for socialization and the establishment of our conscience repressed certain acts and relegated them to the realm of the taboo. That is why human beings are forever deeply attracted by "uncanny" events in which they encounter that which was once familiar but must be concealed, that which they once explicitly were and still latently are. That is why in the history of literature we find a long preoccupation with metamorphoses. This is especially evident in the *Malleus Maleficarum*. There we come upon the idea of vampirism or of the living dead and the related idea of werewolves and of men changed into beasts. The *Malleus* explains that among other names the Devil is called "Behemoth, that is, Beast, because he makes men bestial." In the *Malleus* we can also find the idea that "the devils disturb a man's fancy according to certain phases of the moon, when the brain is ripe for such influences." Indeed, the full moon is traditionally associated with the metamorphosis from man to wolf. The works of the Devil found in the *Malleus* include both changing men into beasts and the use of bodies that remain incorrupt in the grave for schemes to harm mankind. The common theme of all these variations of vampire or werewolf is that of an evil metamorphosis.

In explaining the nature of such malevolent transformations, the authors of the *Malleus*, Heinrich Kramer and James Spranger, followed the guidelines laid down by Saint Augustine in *The City of God*. After discussing tales of metamorphosis by Homer, Apuleius, and others,

Augustine advanced the notion that such changes are the work of demons. What is more, the changes do not involve the substance of things but only their appearance. Similarly, Kramer and Spranger concluded that those who look at a person and see a beast form are deluded by a "glamour." Glamour is a kind of devilish trickery by which the sense of vision is prevented from apprehending the true substance of things. Among the alarming deceptive changes it can create is that a person has lost his penis. In effect there is no loss but the penis is hidden from view by glamour. In spite of the obsession with Satan's trickery and his ingenious deceptions of men (with God's permission), the real focus is the malevolent transformation itself. Both Saint Augustine and the authors of the Malleus described it as psychologically real for the victims even though there is truly no change of substance. The ease with which people can be deluded about such changes alludes to an inherent psychological readiness for change from good to evil or from man to beast. It is as if people react with fear to sensing an evil potential within them, and all that is left for the Devil to do is to play clever games with such fears.

The history of ideas and literature reveals an ongoing fascination with metamorphoses. Nevertheless, the fascination does not dispel the dread. Uncanny encounters with the unfamiliar but once familiar lead to fear and hate of those who happen to foster these encounters, such as "foreign" and "eternal" Jews. The perception of the Jewish people as "foreign" (Fenichel) and as "eternal" (Leschnitzer) adds up to what Freud termed an "uncanny" experience. As expressed in his article "The 'Uncanny'," Freud's ideas can be presented in simplified form as follows.

The earliest stage of psychic development for all infants is that of primary narcissism. During this time the little infant does not recognize any differences between himself and others. He and the whole external world are one, or to put it even more narcissistically, the whole world is he. The age of narcissism is also the age of omnipotence. As far as the infant is concerned, his wishes are materialized and accomplished not by his mother and by others but by himself. His wishing per se is what brings about his wish fulfillment. He thus lives in a world which is characterized by the omnipotence of thought. What the baby imagines is also what happens; no distinction is drawn between inner psychic reality and external material reality. This blissful existence cannot last forever, as the baby soon discovers to his great chagrin. This wonderful existence, though, is exactly what the little baby wants. He wants immediate gratification to go on forever. In other words, he wants to live forever. Later, as an adult, after learning that this is impossible, he will be gripped by "uncanny" feelings whenever he encounters what he believes to be eternal creatures such as living corpses, roaming ghosts, and sometimes, we may add, "eternal" Jews.

Already during the first few months after birth the infant learns that his body and his mother's body are not the same. He also finds out to his great dismay that his feelings and wishes do not always coincide with his mother's actions. What is more, he learns of the existence of other independent objects in the environment although he attributes to them the same psychic reality that is true for him. He is therefore in the midst of the age of animism where a soul, or a feeling and willing agency, is attributed to all things, even to inanimate objects. This early period in life is also the era of magic. Since wishes and their fulfillments, or thoughts and their accompanying actions, are all being equated, reality can supposedly be radically and materially changed by the sheer act of imagining or of willing. However, serious cracks soon develop in the unified and narcissistic perception of the self and world as a result of painful experiences, which are of two basic kinds. The first is the frequent failure of the omnipotence of thoughts. Whenever the baby's wishes do not lead to wish fulfillment, the fallibility of the early narcissistic omnipotence is exposed.

The second kind of painful experience consists of infantile complexes involving early rivalries within the family. In time, a baby boy learns that someone else, the father, also has a mighty claim on the mother. In his rage the little boy sometimes wishes to destroy the father because of this narcissistic wound of having to give up sole possession of the mother. This may sound extreme, but for the unconscious it is not extreme at all. "Indeed, our unconscious will murder even for trifles" said Freud in *Thoughts for the Times on War and Death,* and his terse statement depicts a sad truth about the human condition. We all have murderous thoughts and as small children we only have greater reasons to fear retaliation. When an infant wishes his father dead, wishing even once would be enough in a world where wish and action were the same. Therefore, in omnipotent and magical thinking a wish is as liable to be punished as an act. That is why toward the end of the narcissistic period dangerous actions as well as dangerous wishes are equally forbidden because of fears of retaliation by mighty adults. In fact, an internal inhibiting force is formed—the superego. It is a long and painful process and involves massive repressions of uncivilized impulses. As the infant represses these urges, and as he "surmounts" magical thinking, he abandons the way of life of primary narcissism. His unconscious, however, neither forgets magic nor forgives affronts. And since in the unconscious nothing is ever lost and everything is potentially retrievable, it makes possible future uncanny encounters of the adult with the little child as long as life lasts.

Thus throughout their lives people encounter occasional incidents which retrigger the narcissistic experience of the pre-superego era. Such encounters are characterized by weird feelings of being gripped by dread of something unknown yet for some reason familiar. Freud asserted that many people experience this uncanny feeling most intensely in relation to dead bodies, the return of the dead, and the appearance of spirits or ghosts. Two factors may contribute to the eerie feeling of anxiety a person experiences as he runs into something which should be impossible and is nevertheless familiar—and would better remain hidden. In the context of our discussion of the psychology of anti-Semitism, we could name the two as the "eternal" and the "foreign" elements involved in the encounter. By "eternal" we refer to that factor which Freud regarded as the reemergence of the magical and animistic ways of thinking that were supposedly surmounted and replaced by more realistic thinking modes. By "foreign" we mean Freud's assertion that the reappearance of repressed infantile complexes of both sexual and murderous nature is a major cause of uncanny feelings.

The uncanny encounter with archaic modes of thinking and with primitive impulses can hit a person like a ton of bricks. This old stuff was supposed to be forgotten long ago or at least surmounted, and cannot appear in reality *as* reality without shaking our basic perceptions of what reality is. If a person believes for even a moment that in truth, here and now, he is encountering a living corpse, it throws him back to the early age of omnipotence that he overcame so painfully. Creatures who live eternally are, after all, the living manifestation of the validity of omnipotent and magical thinking. The fulfillment of the impossible wish for "eternal" life (don't forget that in the unconscious nothing is impossible) means that we do have or at least could have the ability to turn our wishes into material reality with no limits imposed. Once again thoughts are omnipotent and with the help of magic, wanting is having.

The omnipotent thinking of the small baby was hopelessly entangled in infantile complexes that were supposed to be repressed for good. For the adult person, even a dim sensation of the old conflicts and the cosmic rage that accompanied them is enough to create dread. At the pre-superego time in which the infantile complexes were raging, the omnipotent thinking of the baby promised him magical, sweeping solutions including the sexual (pregenital) possession of all that is loved and the murder and extermination of all competitors and obstacles. Thus, reliving this era entails great joys but also evokes anxieties; it involves the reliving of the terrible fears of retaliation that finally brought an end to primary narcissism. Therefore, in uncanny encounters one never fully relives the experiences of primary narcissism. There is too much anxiety, related to the facts that this is what the adult person once was, still unconsciously is, and is never quite ready to reencounter. Coming into renewed contact with the original infantile experiences of pre-superego times is too threatening for people and is only partly possible because of the many repressions that took place. Running into these magical and cannibalistic experiences as "reality" is enough to produce uncanny feelings.

The uncanny is primary narcissism revisited. It contradicts the repressions, socializations, and sublimations of the adult person; it casts away the constraints of logic and instead of realistic delays of gratification it promises immediate indulgence forever in all impulses, including some very nasty ones. There is something extremely alluring about this. The whole world becomes one big womb where our needs will be lovingly taken care of forever. Our wishes become king and our rivals are obliterated by our sheer grunt of annoyance, not to mention a raging desire for them to evaporate. It is this tremendous allure which in popular folklore enables vampires to execute such a quick metamorphosis in their victims. The victims half want it and, if allowed to regress to primary narcissism, will fully want it. What is frightening is the great drawing power of that which has been repressed. It is not a discovery we make with equanimity that we prefer to live an "eternal" life without an ego, i.e., without logic and without delays of gratification. Nor do we greet calmly the feeling that deep underneath we prefer to live a different or "foreign" style of life without a superego —that is, with no restrictions at all on any sexual loving relations and on any murder or torture of our rivals to our heart's content. Anything that can foster such an encounter in us we regard as uncanny, and may come to fear it and hate it, be it psychoanalysis or Jews.

Civilization is not about to spare its members from uncanny encounters. It cannot rest on primary narcissism, and has to force its members to repress their infantile complexes and to surmount their omnipotent thinking. This necessity to instill a conscience in human beings and to impose the reality principle on their conduct produces a permanent state of discontent which flares up again and again whenever occasional lapses toward primary narcissism take place. It is *la condition humaine* and cannot be eliminated, only coped with. The Jews are stuck in a symbolic role that always throws them into the midst of the vortex created by the tugging and pulling between the socializing forces of sublimation and the isolating forces of narcissistic, instinctual discharges. Can the Jews extricate themselves from their dual symbolic roles of the people who paid the price of civilization in full to become the great standard-bearers of culture, as well as the people who outsmarted the conscience and cheated on the reality principle so as to enjoy eternal licentious pleasures? They are bound to come under fire again if they continue to remain a symbol of civilization. Nevertheless, it is doubtful that Jews would care to change their civilized image even though it makes them an obvious target whenever non-Jews become intensely discontent with the restrictive price of civilization. Jews are also likely to come under fire if they remain a symbol of magical accomplishment, that is, if they appear as people who succeeded in acting on their discontent with civilization's as well as reality's constraints. In this case, they would look like people who through magical and mysterious ways acquired extra special powers that secure for them everlasting survival. This image may possibly change in a few generations as Israel continues its existence as a nation state like all the nation states. This more recent kind of Jewish existence does not call upon magic for explanation the way the scattered and stateless Jewish existence in the Diaspora did. Should this happen, it could reduce somewhat the prevalence and magnitude of anti-Semitism. However, historical images which acquired the power of shared symbolism to trigger unconscious impulses are not likely to change quickly. And when it comes to anti-Semitism, it would be foolhardy to count even on a slow change.

15.

Anti-Semitism and Zionism

TO THEM (JEWS WHO OPPOSED ZIONISM) ANTI-SEMITISM SEEMED TO TRIUMPH IN ZIONISM, WHICH RECOGNIZED THE LEGITIMACY AND THE VALIDITY OF THE OLD CRY: 'JEWS, GET OUT!' THE ZIONISTS WERE AGREEING TO 'GET OUT'.

—Isaac Deutscher

As soon as Jews learned, sometimes the hard way, that anti-Semitism was a chronic malaise, they began to doubt their future in the host countries. As the pervasive and unyielding nature of anti-Semitism was increasingly sensed by Jews during the nineteenth century, hopes for liberation through assimilation and emancipation were dashed. Hannah Arendt characterized the freedom that emancipation offered Jews as ambiguous and the equality it offered them as treacherous. Under the impact of anti-Semitism it became impossible for many Jews to escape these conclusions. The ill-understood nature of anti-Semitism may have fostered Jewish denials and prolonged the agony. Eventually, however, it was difficult to persist in denying that dreams of freedom were tarnished and hopes for full acceptance in European societies had now to be cast aside. Therefore, more and more Jews began to conceive of the idea, which was emphasized later on by Arendt, that a political solution was the only remedy for this malaise. By indicating that Jews will never be fully accepted in non-Jewish environments, anti-Semitism implied that the solution would be for the Jews to create their own politically independent environment.

This implication of anti-Semitism—the need for a Jewish political remedy—was picked up by Zionism. In his book on the history of the movement, the Zionist leader Nahum Sokolow reiterated Pinsker's conviction that anti-Semitism is a psychic disease which seems incurable. To Sokolow, Pinsker's main importance lay not in his search for the causes of anti-Semitism but in his formulation of a program of self-emancipation as the only logical Jewish response to this persistent problem. Sokolow also quoted Ahad Ha'am, who in evaluating Pinsker's ideas agreed with the premise of the perpetuity of anti-Semitism. What is more, Ahad Ha'am believed that the people of Israel appeared to other nations as a disembodied spirit, a ghost nation, and that this appearance evoked the reactions of terror and hatred. This is like saying that the Jews seemed uncanny or looked like eternal and foreign people.

The "foreign" quality of Jews, which was an impetus to their expulsion from many countries by anti-Semites, was also felt by the Zionists. It was as if both anti-Semites and Zionists were saying, "Why don't you foreigners go back where you came from!" However, while anti-Semites confined themselves to the negative aspect of this message, Zionists were mostly interested in its additional, positive implication, of going to the land of Israel to build it and be rebuilt by it.

In this connection it is interesting to note Jean-Paul Sartre's comment that the Zionist idea adds fuel to the fire of anti-Semitism. By insisting on nationhood in Israel, he charged, the Zionists lend credence to the anti-Semitic claim that in each host country the Jews constitute a people of a foreign country. Indeed it was this common perception of the Jews as a foreign people which fostered one of Theodore Herzl's hopes. Herzl hoped that he could reach an agreement on Zionist activities in Russia and Turkey with W.K. von Plehve, the notoriously anti-Semitic Russian Minister of the Interior. Herzl therefore met von Plehve and also corresponded with him in 1903. The results were nil and Herzl was subsequently criticized for associating with an anti-Semite. Herzl's rationale was nevertheless not groundless. To this day, Israeli hopes for increased Jewish immigration from the Soviet Union are based on this assumption of a shared mutual sentiment of "good riddance" to "foreign" Jews. This, however, does not warrant the occasional cynical attacks which characterize Zionism itself as anti-Semitic. An anti-Semitic expulsion of Jews is not the same as a Zionist ingathering or aliyah, and Zionists did not instigate the former in order to foster the latter.

The impact of anti-Semitism was sometimes slow. Herzl's own disillusionment with assimilation and his conversion to Zionism was allegedly sudden and dramatic. However, it did not occur as precipitously as it is sometimes popularly believed, and the Dreyfus Affair, which caused his change of heart, was merely the last straw. When he was only twenty-four years old Herzl still regarded anti-Semitism as a transitory phenomenon (See Patai). A year later, however, he withdrew from the Albia fraternity because its members participated in anti-Jewish demonstrations. Albia in turn insisted that Herzl did not withdraw but was disbarred. In discussing Herzl's conversion to Zionism,

Henry Cohn made it clear that Herzl's concern over anti-Semitism preceded the Dreyfus Affair. Prior to the Dreyfus trial he was already disturbed by the writings of the anti-Semitic journalist Edward Drumont and by personal experiences. Eventually he was to be shaken up by the Dreyfus Affair. However, it was in his daily life in Vienna long before he went to Paris that he experienced the totality and adamancy of anti-Semitic attitudes. These experiences of Herzl became the cradle from which modern political Zionism sprang.

Still, Herzl's disillusionment with assimilation as a result of anti-Semitism took place relatively quickly. Sometimes the bitter disappointment needed much more time to assert itself. This was especially so in cases where the initial hopes for successful assimilation were highest. Hopes were high indeed among those Jews who became inflamed with revolutionary socialistic ideals. True egalitarian socialism seemed to offer liberation for all, including Jews. Therefore, many idealistic and devoted Jewish revolutionaries in Russia joined the Jewish socialist movement, the Bund, rather than the Zionist movement. The historian of the Russian Revolution and its leaders, Isaac Deutscher, asserted in the article "The Russian Revolution and the Jewish Problem" that in effect the majority of Eastern European Jews remained opposed to Zionism until the Second World War. The most ferocious opposition came from members of the Bund who saw in Zionism a despicable surrender to anti-Semitism. It was as if anti-Semitism triumphed in Zionism when Zionists agreed with the anti-Semitic cry of "Jews, get out!" These socialist Jews, like the Bolsheviks and others, underrated what Deutscher termed "the depth of anti-Semitic instincts in Christian folklore." They underestimated the power of religion as well as the strength of nationalism and ardently believed that once capitalist oppression was thrown off, everybody, including the Jews, would achieve equality and freedom. This intoxication with social revolution cost Zionism many devoted pioneers who instead sacrificed themselves for the liberation of other peoples. For some of these socialist Jews, the process of detoxification from internationalism and socialism as a solution to the problem of the Jews was slow and painful. One of the most telling cases was that of Leon Trotsky.

In his three-volume work on Trotsky, Deutscher unraveled the interesting progression of Trotsky's attitudes regarding the Jewish problem. As a young man, Trotsky believed that the Jews had no future as a separated community in any territory, including Israel, and that their salvation lay in the various countries of the Diaspora. During this time, Trotsky was unwilling to acknowledge the tragic truth contained in the Jewish traditional distrust of the Gentile environment. Thus in 1903 he wrote in the Marxist newsletter *Iskra (The Spark)* an attack on Zionism, in which he described Herzl as a shameless adventurer and the Zionist endeavor as the hysterical sobbings of the romanticists of Zion. But as the years went by, the changing situation resulted in a change of attitude. In 1918 the Russian White Guards created much ado about Trotsky's Jewishness. What is more, in order to discredit Lenin, they accused him too of being Jewish.

What was especially tragic for Trotsky was the fact that with the passage of time, attacks on him with strong anti-Semitic overtones were not confined to antirevolutionary forces alone. As anti-Semitism from the reactionary right was joined by anti-Semitism from the revolutionary left, Trotsky could no longer escape certain conclusions. In an interview in 1937 with an American Jewish newsman, Trotsky finally admitted that after encountering the anti-Semitism of the Third Reich as well as of the USSR, he had given up his hopes for a successful assimilation of the Jews and had decided that even under socialism the Jewish question requires a territorial solution. He did not believe, however, that this territory necessarily had to be Palestine. This represents a remarkable change of heart for one of the major architects of the Bolshevik Revolution, a leading Communist ideologist and the first commander-in-chief of the Red Army. A frequent change of heart was also the fate of Trotsky's brilliant biographer, Deutscher. His collection of articles in *The Non-Jewish Jew* illustrates how until the day he died he was torn between acknowledgment of the historical necessity for Zionism and hatred of the movement. To him, Zionism frequently looked like a reactionary, regressive nationalism that put a spoke in the wheels of world progress toward international socialism.

We have seen that during the first half of the twentieth century the winds of social revolution again filled the sagging sails of assimilationism and rekindled Jewish hopes for equality and for acceptance in

European countries taken over by social revolution. Because of these developments Zionism lost many spirited souls to the international brotherhood of socialism. These Jews believed in a general solution to the Jewish problem in the form of an egalitarian and classless society. Other Jews, however, heeded the warning of their own feeling hearts, did not dismiss their traditional distrust of the Gentile environment, and looked for a specific Jewish political solution in the form of a national Jewish state in Eretz Yisrael. They recognized the pervasiveness and perseverance of anti-Semitism, and this recognition dealt a body blow to assimilationism, even assimilation under utopian socialism.

Nevertheless, discarding the false hopes for assimilation did not mean writing off socialism as well. Many Zionists hoped that in Eretz Yisrael, where Jews would be freed from anti-Semitism, they could still cultivate socialism. There, free from Gentile oppression, a true marriage of Zionism and socialism could take place and give birth to an exemplary society which other nations would want to emulate. The old biblical ideas of Israel's being a chosen nation and a light to other nations may have contributed to this ardent wish on the part of secular Jews to set up a socialistic example. Thus one occasionally hears a reference in an eloquent speech about the Israeli kibbutzim or about courses at the Afro-Asian Institute of the Histadrut labor union as fulfillment of the biblical prophesy: "I will also give thee for a light of the nations" (Isaiah 49:6).

Most Jews who sought their future in socialism in many countries and who were therefore lost to Zionism underestimated the tenacity of anti-Semitism. Even some of those who did cast their lot with Zionism were still blind to the impact of anti-Semitism because of their ideological commitment to socialism. Socialism, after all, was not supposed to be anti-Semitic. These socialist Zionists hoped that the marriage of Zionism and socialism would create marvelous and enviable results—that the two would complement rather than contradict each other. Whether this was truly so remained to be seen. It was A.D. Gordon, the prophet of the religion of labor, who with the eyes of a seer envisioned the future of Zionism as tied to Jewish nationalism but not to socialism. In preference to the imported general socialism of the

Gentiles he advocated the unique nationalism of the Jews. His advice was not accepted by the socialist left, which courted Communism like an ardent lover. I can recall my personal frustration and rage at the repeated display of servility and blindness toward "the world of the revolution" by leaders and rank-and-file members of Hashomer Hatza'ir (the Young Guard) and later on Mapam (United Workers Party). Although it was obvious that under Stalin, Communism became a ruthless dictatorship and blatantly anti-Semitic, it nevertheless still represented to the Israeli left "the world of tomorrow"—the future hope for humanity, including Israelis.

In this "world of the revolution" or "world of tomorrow" or "peace camp," however, notorious and farcical public trials followed each other. They were a travesty of justice filled with "confessions" by the accused to long lists of hideous crimes stretching over most of their lives. In 1949, Rajk confessed in Hungary and Kostov in Bulgaria, and from that time for three years show trials proliferated all over Eastern Europe. The Israeli left, however, regarded these cruel mockeries of due process of law as socialist justice. By November 1952, lifetime Czechoslovak Communist leaders such as Slansky and Clementis were prosecuted for a long list of heinous crimes, including that of being Zionist American spies. Members of the Israeli left still continued to believe in socialist justice. Finally one of their own men, Mordecai Oren, was arrested in Czechoslovakia in 1952 as a Zionist spy and saboteur, and duly "confessed." At the time of his trial, members of Mapam talked about it as a "false accusation" and a "tragic mistake." Presumably, similar confessions constituted "justice" but this particular one by a member of Mapam could not but be a mistake. It was in relation to this presumption that Ben Gurion asked in the Knesset session of November 24, 1952: "If Oren's 'confessions' are false, why are those of Slansky and his colleagues valid?"

The willingness of the Israeli socialist left to look the other way when it comes to antidemocratic, anti-Jewish, and anti-Israeli acts by the world of "socialism in our time" was eventually challenged even more fiercely by Ben Gurion. In a series of articles in the newspaper *Davar*, which later appeared under separate cover (See Yariv), he called on the Israeli left to explicitly state with whom it sides in the growing antagonism between Israel and the Communist bloc. In effect, he raised the painful issue of "conflicted" or of "dual loyalties." Ben Gurion's challenge received great publicity. It was published under the name S.S. Yariv, an achronym for Saba Shel Yariv, meaning Yariv's grandfather. This was the best-planned unkept secret in Israel, for nearly everyone knew that Ben Gurion's grandson was named Yariv. I can recall the glee with which my family read these articles. For myself, I admired Ben Gurion's stand and felt that it was high time for a respected leader to add his authoritative voice to what many a man in the street was thinking. Israel was the fruit of the Zionist endeavor to effect a Jewish national revival, not to implement a self-effacing imitation of Marxism degenerated into a dictatorship. Ben Gurion's challenge was a reaffirmation of the earlier position taken by Gordon during the time of the Second Aliyah. If in the beginning of the century Gordon had been able to sway most Zionists his way, decades of blindness by the zealous adherents of socialistic Zionism to the anti-Semitism of the Communist movements could have been spared.

History is full of ironies. As the historian and political scientist Walter Laqueur points out in his comprehensive and updated history of Zionism, European Zionists had criticized the assimilationists for their inability to analyze anti-Semitism objectively, yet these same Zionists were unable to understand Arab nationalism in a realistic, unemotional way. To this one may add that the Israeli left, the offshoot of European socialistic assimilationism, was also blind to anti-Semitism. Yet, more than other Zionists, the left-wingers were able to recognize the Arab national aspirations, so that for many years they advocated the establishment of a binational state. Indeed, no side was free from a blind spot.

The thesis that socialistic Zionism was basically a carryover from assimilationism relates to a particular Jewish angle which was operating all along. From the Jewish point of view, choices had to be made in relation to an old dialectic conflict in the life of the Jews, that between being a chosen people or just a nation like all other nations. This choice between being unique or being like most others had acquired additional connotations. It came to mean being orthodox or secular, abnormal or normal, scattered and stateless or concentrated in the homeland. Per-

haps the most crippling emotionally was the added connotation of
being rejected or accepted by society at large. It is in relation to this
last dimension that history played its worst dialectic jokes.

The assimilationists opted for acceptance, a choice that made
them blind to anti-Semitism. Their chronic enchantment with the
socialist "peace camp" represented the lingering effects of the historical assimilationist aspirations for acceptance. Acceptance, however,
could not easily be secured. Jews could well remain the target of
anti-Semitism even after the establishment of a Jewish state. If not on
an individual basis, then at least on a national basis anti-Semitic feelings
toward Israel could be expressed by other nations through their foreign
policies. From this point of view, which may have motivated many
sincere souls in the Israeli extreme left, only the establishment of a
Jewish socialist nation among other socialist nations could ensure true
acceptance of Jews on this earth. Thus, the old aspiration for the
assimilation of Jewish individuals in host societies was reincarnated into
a new aspiration for the assimilation of the Jewish state with other
states.

In Palestine, socialistic Zionists and latent assimilationists were
protected from anti-Semitism and could dedicate themselves to socialism—the key to future acceptance by other "progressive" nations.
However, in typical dialectic fashion they could also tend to the opposite pole of acceptance or of being like all others—the idea of a chosen
nation. Now it was possible to cultivate the old idea of a chosen nation
in the new form of model socialism. The kibbutzim could represent the
best communal settlements the world over. Devotion to the local brand
of socialism, which would follow the Russian pattern but would outdo
it, was like killing two birds with one stone. It carried with it the dual
promise of Jewish uniqueness and Gentile acceptance in the socialistic
camp. Basically, the choice of socialism was a choice for acceptance
now and uniqueness later. Presumably with the passage of time and the
progress of revolution, uniqueness or model socialism would no longer
carry with it the danger of rejection.

Those Zionists who clearly placed Zionism above socialism and all
other "isms" made a different choice which was also fraught with
dialectics. They opted for a unique national endeavor that made the

Jews the only people who were able to rebuild a national home after close to 2,000 years of exile. The object was normalization—to be like all the nations—yet the means that preceded the ends were quite unprecedented. Thus, Zionism was literally contributing to the unique aura of the Jews while it sought normalization, or risking ridicule and rejection now for the sake of acceptance later.

In retrospect, it seems that Zionism did not bring about the desired acceptance. Among some European, African, and Asian states Israel is ostracized more than many other nations. As for socialism, it did not fare better. Israel did not become a place of model socialism and a bastion of uniqueness. In spite of the romanticism surrounding the kibbutzim, most Israelis admit that socialism is declining fast while nationalism is on the ascendancy.

We have seen that Jewish socialism in Palestine and later Israel was polarized into acceptance in the present and uniqueness in the future. We have also seen that because of that, Jewish left-wingers had to expend great energy in order not to see the anti-Semitism of the Communist world. Yet the most taxing conflict of all was the inherent contradiction between socialism and Zionism. In the Communist jargon, socialism implied, at least in theory, internationalism. In practice, it meant subjugation to the national interest of the USSR. In contrast, Zionism meant first and foremost Jewish nationalism. As the twentieth century progressed with its decline of ideologies and triumph of nationalism, the inherent conflict became more apparent. The term "socialistic Zionism" could still be glibly uttered as a single concept, but the qualifying of Zionism became less and less appreciated and the dual message in the concept became exposed.

One need not have been a scholar or an ideologue to be aware of the dual message which was imbedded in socialistic Zionism. This fact, however, eluded me when I was still young. As a small boy in Haifa, I used to accompany my father to May Day parades. Like many other children, I walked by my father's side in a group representing the Solel Boneh, the Histadrut's construction company. I could have joined my mother to walk with the Working Women's Organization, but that would have labeled me a sissy. This was especially true because my older brother wore a shiny white uniform and marched in an orderly, military

manner with the Marine Youth Movement. Each year his group was
one of the major attractions of the parade. These were the late thirties
and early forties, the time of "the state on the way," when the sight
of Jewish boys in uniform created a surge of national pride in the
spectators.

I could not don a white marine uniform. All I could do was to put
on the blue shirt with the red ties, thus demonstrating, with many
others young and old who also wore it, that I belonged to the international brotherhood of the rising world of socialism. As we marched and
paraded, children and adults, as we assembled and listened to speeches
reverberating through unsynchronized loudspeakers, we could lift our
eyes to the hills around us and see a sea of flags everywhere—blue and
white flags for Jewish nationalism, red flags for socialism.

Before dispersing, we all stood up and sang. We sang "Hatikvah"
(The Hope) or "Tehezaknah" (Let Their Hands Be Strengthened) or
both as the national anthem. We also sang "Ha'internatzional"—the
international socialist anthem. Thus, with singing hearts we affirmed
the union of Zionism and socialism. We all got the message, adults and
children alike, and each year on May first we celebrated once again the
union of national and socialistic goals within Zionism. Little did I
suspect that the message I was getting was a double message, and bore
the seeds of tragic conflicts.

Today, most Israelis no longer celebrate May Day, no longer wear
blue shirts with red ties, no longer wave red flags, and no longer extol
the virtues of the socialist camp in resounding speeches. However, this
did not happen overnight. The relief from local anti-Semitic pressure
within the Jewish population in Palestine and later Israel enabled the
remnants of assimilationism to take longer to die out. The death blows
to these remnants had to come from hostile manifestations by Gentiles.
Just as in the exile before so in Israel now the coup de grace to
assimilationism was dealt by anti-Semitism. The implacable hostility of
Gentile nations, especially from the Communist camp, could finally
convince the Israeli left that even socialistic anti-Semitism is tenacious
and unyielding. This meant a verdict of no acceptance.

One of the dire effects of anti-Semitism was the internalization
by Jews of anti-Semitic notions. The tragic result has been Jewish

self-hate. In reference to this hate, Avineri stated in an interview (See Ben Ezer) that by hating the image of the Diaspora Jew, the Israeli sabra shares in the psychology of the Gentile anti-Semite. To this bitter realization Avineri added, however, a consolation. He suggested that for generations anti-Semites hated Jews not only because Jews were weak and easy targets but also because Jews were a successful intellectual elite. Hate was therefore a result not only of Jewish vulnerability but also of envy. The implication of this suggestion is that some Israelis who hate Diaspora Jews are similarly motivated by envy of cultivated intellectuals on the part of men of action.

Jewish self-hatred and acceptance of anti-Semitic judgments is a notorious phenomenon. I remember how as a boy in Israel I used to hear children make remarks about modes of prayer. Synagogues were "phooey" and consisted of *yehudim mitztofefim vetzorhim* (overcrowded Jews shouting). The blurted-out Jewish praying in crowded synagogues was unfavorably compared with the unhurried Christian singing in roomy churches where one could feel *hashra'ah* (inspiration).

The negative image that anti-Semitism imparted to Jews found its way into Jewish folklore as well. A good example of one such image can be found both in the writing of an anti-Semite and in a Jewish joke. This is the image of the greedy Jew for whom money is the only yardstick with which to measure all things. The biographer and novelist Hector Bolitho, a British anti-Semite who at least felt guilty about being one, described one Palestinian Jew as follows: "I asked him then about commerce, because, when you are with the Jews, you are bustled and moved so that you do not pause for a moment to look at anything so unimportant as a temple or a tomb. His eyes sparkled at my question. I had touched his Jewish heart. 'Ah, business! It is very good now.' " The same image appears in a Jewish joke, recounted by Sela and Har-Gil, in which two Jews, by a miracle, find time to pause and reflect in front of a holy site, the Wailing Wall, or the western wall of the Second Temple. One of them notices that the other is weeping profusely over the destruction of the Second Temple. "Why are you crying so much?" he says. "True, the Temple has been destroyed, but the lot is still worth something!"

Among the Jews of the Diaspora, self-hate often reached the

proportions of self-negation. The psychoanalyst Nathan Ackerman and the social scientist Marie Jahoda, who studied "Jewish anti-Semitism" among Diaspora Jews, made a very interesting observation. Jews with extreme and pathological anti-Semitic attitudes differed from Gentile anti-Semites. For one thing, Jews could not become anti-Semitic by conforming to their own ethnic group, as Gentiles could. For another, Jews could not resort so readily to the use of projection onto Jews, not unless they established the pretense that they stood outside the Jewish group. The maintenance of such a pretense required continuous expenditure of energy. These conditions resulted in two other differences between Jewish and Gentile anti-Semitism. The first is that in the projections of Jewish anti-Semites there is a total absence of good qualities. Jewish anti-Semites could not even afford an attitude of tokenism and grant Jews a good point here or there, something that Gentile anti-Semites were able to do. The second is that the hatred by Jewish anti-Semites was exclusively directed against Jews, while Gentile anti-Semites could afford a variety of prejudices. Ackerman and Jahoda speculated that unresolved oedipal conflicts had something to do with this singleminded prejudice. Other possible analytic speculations include "identification with the aggressor" and "negative identity." The etiology of the pathology of Jewish anti-Semitism leaves room for argument but the end result does not: self-hate becomes self-negation.

Unlike Diaspora Jews, Israeli Jews could adopt anti-Semitic notions with the illusion that it did not involve self-hate. The hate is allegedly directed only toward Diaspora Jews who seem to be rotting in a stultifying state of affairs which Israeli Jews have successfully rid themselves of. A study of Israeli students between the ages of fifteen and twenty-two was conducted by Tamarin and Ben-Zwi. Using a story completion method, they discovered in the literary productions of the students stereotyped descriptions of Diaspora Jews. The flaws depicted in the personality and appearance of these people seemed to these researchers to mirror "a caricaturic conception of East-European Ghetto-Jew of the turn of the century," and they concluded that these stereotypes had been transmitted to the Israeli youth by their parents. They also suggested that in this transmission the process of unconscious identification with the anti-Semitic aggressor played an important role.

The effects of anti-Jewish notions on Jewish political activity was discussed by the great Israeli biblical scholar Yehezkel Kaufman in his article on anti-Semitic stereotypes in Zionism. In the article he underscored the fact that manifestations of the "disease of Jewish anti-Semitism" can be found in both the Haskalah (Enlightenment) literature and in the Jewish national movement. In Hebrew literature, Jews were portrayed as possessing undesirable character traits and as ridiculous in dress and appearance. And he quoted a headline from the Histadrut (Labor Federation) newspaper *Davar* which read: "National Renaissance, the Regeneration of a Parasitic Nation." Kaufman was alarmed over this borrowing by Zionism of anti-Semitic notions and over the failure to realize that what was being made to look obnoxious was not just the Galut (Exile) but the Jewish people itself. In other words, he was alarmed over manifestations of not merely self-hatred but self-negation. Another who expressed a similar opinion was Kurzweil, who in an article entitled "The Roots of Jewish Self-Hatred," viewed this symptom as a result of the crisis of faith. On another occasion he expressed his disdain for the teaching in Israel of too much of the anti-religious Haskalah Hebrew literature, which contains many self-derogatory and anti-Semitic concepts.

My own understanding of the phenomenon of Jewish self-hate is that in past generations it was largely nourished by the psychological mechanism of identification with the aggressor. Jews who felt victimized could identify with the aggressing Goyim and in the process incorporate into their own psychological makeup a badly needed sense of mastery. Zionism served as an effective antidote to this traditional self-hate on the part of Diaspora Jews. The basic remedy of Zionism was the psychological switch from passivity to activity and the founding of the Jewish state. Currently, those Jews who are being oppressed by Gentiles (as are many Russian Jews) need not turn to Gentiles as they seek an example of mastery, statehood, self-reliance, and staunch nationalism. Now there is Israel with which to identify. As for American Jews, they are not subject to crude oppression or to the typical stress that Diaspora Jews were subjected to for generations. Identification with the aggressor is a defense that is being called into operation to meet a felt stress. If there is no stress—that is, if there is no aggression

along the old historical patterns of pogroms and legal restrictions—
then there is no need for this defense. Things are therefore different
for American Jewry. On the one hand, the current Gentiles are signifi-
cantly less oppressive. On the other hand, a new Jewish model of
mastery and security is now available for Jews who search for security
and mastery. The "push" for the search may still be provided by
aggressive Gentiles but the "pull" is exercised by the new Jewish model
of competence. This newly available model made a big difference. By
emulating Israelis rather than Gentiles, Jews have succeeded in reducing substantially the hitherto stiff price of Jewish self-hate.

The current manifestations of self-hate in Israel are mostly of a
different order. They are not a result of identification with others which
boomerangs and inflicts wounds of self-hate. Rather, they are the
results of identification with one's own ego-ideal. The background for
this development is the deep crisis of historical continuity. The sharp
break from centuries of "the Jewish way" produced intrapsychic conflicts and fluctuations of self-esteem. This fluidity reflects ongoing
changes in the balance of forces among alternate identities such as the
negative ego-ideal, the positive ego-ideal, and negative identity. Thus,
the current Israeli manifestations of self-hate are but an overt symptom
of negative identity or of the self-negation which comes about as a
consequence of a sharp break with history. A description of this crisis
of historical continuity will be found in the next chapter.

Recently, the Israeli journalist Shlomo Tanai drew a major distinction between Jewish self-hate in the past and in present-day Israel. In
the past, self-hate and the resultant self-destruction were largely an
individual matter, leading to assimilation or suicide. In today's Israel,
self-hate is directed against the collective Jewish existence as such. In
the past, the Diaspora Jew could not blame the collective existence of
Jews. There was no Jewish collective holding the reins of power and
bearing sole responsibility for its way of life. But now there is one, and
sometimes it can serve as a target for hate. Therefore, we now witness
a new form of self-hate which, oddly enough, has become possible only
because of the establishment of the Jewish state. Thus one can hear
such talk as: "Everywhere in the world the Jews are the most successful
businessmen, but not in Israel; everywhere else they are financial wiz-

ards, but not in Israel. You want to know why? Because here in Israel they can deal only with other Jews." The implication of such talk is that Jews might work magic as individuals, but once they function as a collective they falter.

Ill feelings concerning the new mode of Jewish national life are expressed with regard to other undertakings, such as the production of creative films. The main complaint heard is that for some reason the Jews are the imaginative leaders in this field almost everywhere except Israel, and guess why. The real "why," the truly stinging insinuation, is that in Israel there are too many Jews who have to deal with each other. Such needling remarks express an inheritance from anti-Semitism. On the whole, incorporation of anti-Semitic notions is not the major force behind Israeli self-hate, but it is there. After all, allusion to the idea of "too many Jews" is an old practice of anti-Semites, among them some whom Weizmann in his autobiography named "the tender-hearted variety." He referred to those anti-Semites who were telling the Jews "You are the salt of the earth," or who regarded the Jews as "leaven." These were left-handed compliments since, as Weizmann pointed out, too much salt or leaven spoils food. Indeed, such compliments clearly allude to the notion that Jews in small numbers may be nice and spicy for society but Jews in large numbers would spoil everything they touch. Thus, manifestations of Israeli self-hate that have their roots in anti-Semitic notions reflect the lingering effects of the traditional defense of identification with the aggressor. Yet in today's Israel the major driving power for expressions of self-hate is not this defense, but something different, which relates to issues of ego-ideals, negative identity, and the enigmatic crisis of historical continuity.

It is an intriguing phenomenon that both Zionism and anti-Semitism, in directing their magnifying glass at the Jewish people, tended to focus their attention on the same issues, yet differed in their respective judgments of what they had seen. Again the accounts of the anti-Semitic Englishman Hector Bolitho can serve as an illustration. Sensing his anti-Semitism and misjudging its tenacity, he tried to reach a fairer outlook toward Jews by visiting Palestine and seeing things for himself. His biased look resulted in gross misconceptions of the nature of the Zionist activities. For instance, he believed that the Jews were overconcentrating in cities and surmised that without adequate foundations in the countryside they would not be able to withstand the assault of Arab hordes which in time was bound to come. He thus foresaw an impending armed clash between Arabs and Jews which would serve as the final sink-or-swim test for the birth of the Jewish state. His biased appraisal of what he saw led him to make false predictions concerning the outcome of the Zionist endeavor in general and the outcome of the bloody initiation rite to Jewish nationhood in particular. He believed that he was witnessing a pitiful people who had no idea how to go about the business of building a nation. "The hideous nightmare in Zionism," he wrote, "comes with the recollection that they are *buying* (italics by Bolitho) their land instead of fighting for it. And no great nation has ever bought its earth. . . . Zionism has enlisted too many scholars and too few farmers and soldiers." In other words, the traditional Jewish skills in conducting monetary transactions would prove worthless when the true test of nationhood, the test of blood, came about.

This notion of the true test of nationhood is something that both anti-Semites and Zionists adhered to. A bloody test was the notion behind the motto "In blood and fire Judah fell in blood and fire Judah shall rise again." This slogan was first adopted by Hashomer (Guard), a Jewish defense organization that was established in 1909 and provided armed guards to protect Jewish property. Not all members of the Yishuv adhered to this slogan. On one occasion in 1917, A.D. Gordon and some of his followers left an assembly in protest when members of Hashomer were waving a flag on which this slogan was inscribed (Kushnir). Later on, the same slogan was adopted by the underground military organization Irgun Zvai Leumi (National Military Organization) and served as the natural complement of its other famous motto, *"Rak kakh"* (Only this way). This latter slogan was printed on posters depicting a hand holding a gun over a map of Eretz Yisrael on both sides of the Jordan River. The envisioned test of blood did come and not only in 1948 during the War of Independence. Russcol and Banai characterized the entire decade preceding the establishment of the State of Israel as a "bloody trial," the kind of trial which determines whether a people become a nation or die.

We witness here an interesting phenomenon. Bolitho was an anti-Semite. His book is filled with blatantly biased anti-Jewish remarks which clearly attest to his prejudice. Nevertheless, he was able to focus on crucial issues: Are the Jews cowards? Can they fight? Can they be not only city dwellers but also farmers? His answers consistently underestimated the Jewish abilities, and many Arabs and Englishmen shared his opinions. History had a surprise in store for them. The Zionists too regarded these as important questions, but they differed from Bolitho in their answers. They founded agricultural settlements such as kibbutzim and moshavim and cultivated the land. They also built cities. They fostered education and produced scholars, but in the meantime also provided military training in underground military organizations. These organizations and training activities formed the nucleus of what was to become a superb army. Throughout this period, however, Zionists were distressed by the image of the Jews as cowards.

There is nothing new about this image. On March 14, 1896, Herzl wrote in his diary that the Aryan duelling associations at the University of Vienna had decided to deny duels to Jews because "all Jews are without honor and are cowards" (Lowenthal). It was therefore with pride that Weizmann recounted a story that he had heard from Major Orde Wingate, the British commander of the special Jewish defense squads. During one nightly raid with Jewish fighters, Wingate heard the Arabs calling to each other to run away because they were facing not Englishmen but Jews. The image of the cowardly Jews began to fade with the passage of time but not sufficiently so. This led in 1947 and 1948 to gross misjudgment by many people concerning the ability and willingness of the Jews to fend for themselves and protect their new state.

Anti-Semitism and Zionism have influenced one another in the past and will continue to do so in the future. At the end of the last century, anti-Semitism played an important role in pushing the Jews to do something to convert their old messianic tradition and their longings for redemption into a viable political movement. In turn, the First Zionist Congress in Basel impressed anti-Semites as an important gain in the Jewish effort to achieve world domination. This congress probably inspired at least the title of that infamous document *The*

Protocols of the Elders of Zion (See Norman Cohn). Regarding this malicious fabrication of the tsarist police, Adolf Hitler later said that once this book became the common property of a people, the Jewish menace would be broken. Hitler averred that at first "sentiment" urged him to be tolerant toward Jews, but that eventually his "reason" emerged victorious. What finally dispelled whatever doubts he still had with regard to Jews was the claim to Jewish nationalism put forward by "the *Zionists*" (italics by Hitler). Hitler's *Mein Kampf* is full of obsessive fears of Jewish world domination, world conquest, world dictatorship, and world bolshevization. He was not a unique nut. Many anti-Semites shared his fears. To many of those who feared such a total and omnipotent Jewish power grabbing for world domination, a total remedy in the form of mass extermination seemed only logical. This fantastic cognition was translated into nightmarish action about half a century after the publication of the Protocols. A third of the Jewish people was executed by the Nazis, for whom the infamous plan for "the final solution of the Jewish question" seemed by their own account to be "fantastic" but also "thoroughly feasible" (See Hilberg's documents). The final solution was short of final only because the Nazis were defeated in the Second World War.

This trauma provided Zionism with an added impetus to make a desperate and successful "now or never" pitch for a Jewish state. The rise of the State of Israel and its victories in several wars left an added impact on anti-Semitism and anti-Semites. One tragic consequence of these events, the rise of an Arab species of anti-Semitism, was underscored by Elon. Nowadays, anti-Semites are no longer mostly Christians; their ranks have been swelled by Muslims. To Elon, this is one of the great prices paid for the Zionist revolution. On the other hand, the British historian of the Middle East Bernard Lewis regards Zionism as only one of three factors which account for the recent increase in Arab anti-Semitism. The other two are the importation of Christian European anti-Semitic literature into the Arab world and the general decline of tolerance toward minorities in the entire Middle East. There is truth in Lewis's assertion that Arab anti-Semitism, unlike Christian anti-Semitism, does not rely on a theology of guilt, scriptural condemnation, and racism. Nevertheless, the wide circulation of the imported

Christian anti-Semitic literature has its effects. The frequent accusation by the Palestinian guerillas that Israel is a "racist state" is largely a projection of the accusers themselves, who are frequently exposed to this racist literature.

Another consequence of Zionism is that anti-Semitism no longer confines itself to the hatred of Diaspora Jews. After several victories, Israel no longer looks like an underdog and is therefore a "legitimate" target for overt hatred. To anti-Semites, the tough and determined, though numerically small, Israelis may seem as the latest reincarnation of the old power-hungry Jews still dreaming of world domination. Thus, present-day anti-Semitism may proclaim itself to be anti-Zionist and anti-Israel, but not anti-Jew. However, as Poliakov's book clearly illustrates, an old and familiar impulse of Jew hatred hides behind the recent critical approach toward the Jewish state and its sympathizers in Eastern Europe. Sometimes the cat gets out of the bag. Maurice Friedberg, an American expert on East European languages and politics, documented some of the evidence of the belated attempts by the Polish authorities during July 1968 to undermine the equation of anti-Zionism with anti-Semitism. This equation became popular as a result of intensive anti-Zionist campaigns by the Polish government. Finally, Wladyslaw Gomulka had to caution his people over a radio broadcast not to assume this stance. He himself, however, was one of the major leaders who all along played on traditional Polish anti-Semitic attitudes under the guise of "anti-Zionism." As was said at the beginning of the previous chapter, anti-Semitism does not really depend for its perpetuation on the variety of ideological dressings which coat it at different times and places. Anti-Zionism is the latest ideology of anti-Semitism. There certainly are many fair-minded people who criticize Israel and who are not anti-Semites. However, there are many anti-Semites who have just switched labels and who are now never anti-Jewish, only ferociously anti-Israel. To Jews it matters not under which label the threat manifests itself. A rose by any other name . . .

Zionism and anti-Semitism will continue to have an impact on each other and to be intensely concerned with the image of the Jews. Zionists will continue their work to rid the Jews of a negative self-image. Anti-Semites will continue their efforts to perpetuate their projection of a negative other-image and to use the "foreign" Jews for the purification of their own self-image. Zionists and anti-Semites will also continue to perceive with alarm each other's power and intention. The First and Second Zionades, from Egypt and Babylon, were remarkable historical developments. It is a sad irony that the Third Zionade, the ingathering of scattered Jews and the establishment of the State of Israel after more than eighteen centuries of exile, serves not only as an answer to anti-Semitism but also as an impetus for it. This Third Zionade is such an unusual historical event that it fosters the notion of a "world conspiracy" as an explanation, and militates against the eradication of the perception of Jews as unique, peculiar, and, even worse, foreign. The many Christian eyes that look with disdain at the "foreign" people among them are now joined by millions of Arab eyes watching with rage the introduction of a foreign body or "cancer" in the Middle East. As usual, Jews are once more caught in tragic historical situations and resign to it with the traditional Jewish sigh of *Oi vay* or the more modern Israeli version of *Yihyeh tov* (Things will turn out O.K.). Perhaps a few generations of a normal existence of the Jewish state in peacetime conditions will make Jewish existence seem less bizarre and more normal. In the meantime, neither anti-Semitism nor Zionism is approaching the end of the road. Both have a long way to go, and they will keep an eye on each other.

16.

The Crisis of Historical Continuity

AN INNOVATIVE AND CREATIVE
GENERATION DOES NOT THROW
ITS HISTORICAL HERITAGE ONTO
THE GARBAGE HEAP.

—Berl Katznelson

It is clear that many Zionists experienced adverse emotional reactions to the course of Jewish history. They viewed Jewish life over the centuries as too passive and too masochistic, and thought that Jews had developed a warped attitude to life characterized by the love of suffering. Many Zionists also wondered whether Jews had made history at all in the last eighteen centuries or whether history had been done to them. A literary work that is famous for giving expression to these feelings is the short story "The Sermon" by Hayim Hazaz. It is the story of Yudkah, a silent kibbutz member, who one day feels a compelling need to deliver a sermon during a committee meeting. Like an overflowing dam the quiet Yudkah delivers a lengthy treatise on how history was done to Jews by Gentiles. Looking at a seemingly endless chain of persecutions, he concludes that it is no wonder that Israeli children dislike Jewish history and prefer to read Gentile historical novels where heroes act and adventures happen. Feeling the children's agony, Yudkah suggests that when the time comes to study Jewish history, they should be told that ever since the Roman exile Jews had no history, and the children should go out and use the time for playing soccer.

Yudkah's sermon includes a few provocative ideas. It accuses Diaspora Jews of clinging to messianic hopes precisely because these hopes seemed futile. Jews, with all their supposed longing for redemption, did not really want to be redeemed. They had developed a love for suffering, and began to coat it with an attire of heroism. It is as if things had turned upside down in a world of darkness. Sorrow became preferable to joy, pain to happiness, destroying to building, slavery to liberation, dreams to reality. Hope replaced the actual future while faith replaced common sense. The terrible result of such contradictions had been the creation of a sort of "nightly psychology." The essence of this complaint is that the unbounded ability to tolerate suffering is nothing but a distorted sense of heroism. Obviously Hazaz rejected this notion of heroism just as some Jews rejected the notion of the schlemiel as a hero, as was discussed in Chapter 2.

Hazaz also puts in Yudkah's mouth statements that relate to all Zionists, the gist being that Judaism and Zionism are two contradictory things. When a man can no longer be a Jew he becomes a Zionist. Zionism starts where Judaism was destroyed, at the place where the strength of the nation was sapped. Therefore, Zionism is not a continuation of or a remedy for Judaism. It is an uprooting and a destruction or, as Yudkah puts it, "not new and not renewed but different." There are those who refer to this something "different" as Judaism. Language games, however, cannot mask the basic fact that this "Judaism" is not the Judaism of the last two thousand years. Calling different things by the same name does not make them the same. Judaism is dead and Zionism has risen from its ashes. In Israeli culture this basic perception is known as "the crisis of continuity." The driving power behind this crisis is a deep sense of historical discontinuity.

Similar feelings were captured by James Michener in *The Source*, in which he described an argument between the old Rebbe Itzik and the young sabra woman Ilana. The time is the Israeli War of Independence and the question is as to what is being defended by blood—old Judaism or new Zionism. Ilana ends by telling the old man that she and her contemporaries are building in Israel a new state and not a pale copy of the pitiful Jewish existence in Poland or Lithuania. She therefore demands the creation of new laws and customs and insists that new life in Israel be based on Jewish life as it was in ancient times. Only a small step separates the literary pronouncements of Hazaz or Michener from the more extreme ideology of the Canaanites, which will be discussed in the next chapter.

The core of the crisis of historical continuity is negation of the past. This feeling has appeared to be escalating in recent times. Not too long ago the American Zionist leader Ludwig Lewisohn, who was also a professor of comparative literature, worried that negation of the emancipation movement with its resultant assimilation was leading to a wholesale rejection of the Diaspora (See Glatzer). Yet the critic Baruch Kurzweil was already worried about the next step—that negation of exile was leading to negation of Judaism. He warned that for Jews to take the dangerous step from negation of exile to negation of religious Judaism amounts to what can be termed "historicide." Kurzweil, therefore, could never condone the abandonment of the belief in a personal God of Israel and the related belief in the transcendental or extrahistorical uniqueness of the Jews.

Kurzweil believed that he detected such a negation on the part of those who dedicated their lives to the scientific study of Judaism. He particularly resented the view that there has been a basic discontent with Judaism throughout, and that Zionism is only its most recent manifestation. Obviously, if the Zionist aspiration to overthrow religious law is very old while only the Zionist political methods are new, then something oppressing and unhealthy was imbedded in Judaism not only during the last two hundred years but throughout the last two thousand. Kurzweil regarded this as an untenable position which betrays the nihilistic and even demonological impulses of some contemporary Israeli scientists. The main culprits in his eyes were the modern researchers of Jewish mysticism led by the "demonological" figure of Gershom Scholem. Kurzweil took issue mainly with two of Scholem's most renowned works, a two-volume work on the false Messiah Sabbatai Zevi and an article which in the original Hebrew publication was titled "A Mitzvah Which Comes Through a Transgression." This old mystical concept that Scholem explicated involved the basic notion that good can be promoted by a descent into the domain of evil. Holy sparks are imprisoned by evil forces and can sometimes be freed only by venturing into the evil domain. The necessary acts of transgression will, paradoxically enough, aid God in the cosmic struggle to separate good from evil. Thus, transgressions committed by mystically enlightened people who know why they are doing them can be the greatest mitzvah of all—a shared work with God toward redemption. Kurzweil was alarmed by the new popularity of dialectical mysticism. Such paradoxical thinking carried with it the seeds of nihilism. Its antinomistic nature was too dangerous. The outcome could be the implementation of only the first half of this brazen doctrine. The descent into evil could be accomplished but the subsequent good, which ought to more than compensate for the initial transgression, would remain unrealized.

The major danger, in Kurzweil's eyes, was the drawing of analogies between old mystical concepts and modern Zionist notions. After all, if the Jewish mysticists of old could believe that the cancellation of

Torah equals its preservation, then why should not modern Zionist mysticists believe that the cancellation of Judaism is the best means for its preservation? The toying with ideas such as that Torah is being upheld by being transgressed was potentially destructive. Such nihilistic notions could lend a false sense of comfort to secular Israelis and lull them into unawareness of the break in historical continuity. They could simply decide in good conscience to uphold the Jewish tradition by transgressing it. In time, however, just as with Sabbatai Zevi who converted to Islam, so with the modern secular heretics—the bitter truth will finally become clear for all to see. Judaism will be successfully transgressed but not upheld in the least. Kurzweil was therefore alarmed by Scholem's conclusion that there is a clear dialectic development which leads from the belief in the Messiah Sabbatai Zevi to the religious nihilism of the Messiah Jacob Frank, and later on to the negation of religion in the Jewish Enlightenment which, in turn, formed the background for the contemporary crisis in Judaism. This conclusion by Scholem implied that an underlying current of nihilism was inherent in Judaism all along.

What Kurzweil cared for was a living faith, yet what he saw in the scientific study of Judaism was a new scientism which was slowly killing such a faith. He also believed that the demonological and anarchistic orientation that was promoted by some scientists could consume not only Judaism but Zionism as well. Nihilism knows no restraints and is not going to dissolve Judaism but absolve Zionism. He did, however, concede some ground to his cultural opponents. He acknowledged that Jewish mystical movements did adopt paradoxical lines of thinking. Yet he thought that Scholem exaggerated the prevalence of these ways of thinking and that he was mistaken about their link to modern Zionism. What is more, most of the secular Zionist rebels were not familiar with kabbalistic or other mystical notions.

It seems that Kurzweil did not wish to know that the growing interest in Jewish mystical traditions had deeper psychological roots than the alleged demonological charm of Gershom Scholem. The new and growing fascination stemmed from the perception that the mystical movements represent a Jewish tradition of active engagement in changing fate. The mystics within their religious framework rebelled, and strained the traditional system to the limits. Instead of waiting passively for God to do the job by himself, they joined God in his active struggle to purify himself from evil and to bring about an early redemption. Like future Zionists they played an active role in trying to implement a radical change of conditions. In order to do this, they developed whole lines of paradoxical thinking which enabled them to violate traditional rules and to take bold jumps into the domain of evil. They did not succeed in bringing about redemption, but they certainly did not wait around passively for it. It was no longer up to God alone to decide when he deems it fit to uplift instantly and by a miracle all the captured holy sparks from the domain of evil. Man's active cooperation in this task had a lot to do with the timing of redemption. So these devoted messianic Jews embarked upon their bold excursions and nearly got lost in the process. Some, like the followers of Jacob Frank, were actually lost to Judaism. But these mystical Jews were "gutsy"; this is why contemporary Jews show a growing interest in them. It is reassuring to feel that some among the past generations of Diaspora Jews chose an active course of taking fate into their own hands.

To put it differently, there was a touch of Zionism in the old Jewish mystics. They were not willing to let the Lord be. They opted for sharp reversal in the rules of fate. They were in a position similar to that which Zionists found themselves in relation to Orthodox Jewry. What the Orthodox Jews regarded as a transgression, the mystics and later the Zionists regarded as a mitzvah. In a way one could regard the State of Israel itself as "a mitzvah which comes through a transgression." The rabbis kept shouting "sin" but the Zionists went on with their transgressions until the results of a renascent Jewish state looked more like a good deed ordained by God.

Kurzweil was deeply suspicious of the application of modern science to Judaism. He saw in it literally a demonological act of burial. On one occasion he referred to Scholem and his colleagues who resort to Jungian depth psychology as "the archeologists of the soul" (*Ha'aretz*, June 30, 1967). On another occasion he warned against any illusion that the break in historical continuity has been bridged, and renewed his attack on "the archeologists and the undertakers of Judaism." With sardonic rage he asked: "What is Judaism today? Perhaps it is a corpse used for archeological, historical, ethnological, and ecological post-mortem operations" (*Ha'aretz*, September 30, 1970). His standpoint was clear. If Judaism is no longer a personal living faith, no amount of digging by the archeologists of the soul or of the soil is going to rectify the situation. That the issuing of a death certificate for Judaism was being carried out scientifically was small consolation for him. He therefore kept repeating his challenges, which generated a cultural debate in Israel about the nature and legitimacy of scientific enquiry as well as about the crisis of historical continuity.

We ought to take note of the fact that Kurzweil directed his attacks against "the archeologists of the soul" whom he identified as "the priests of depth psychology." Such an expression by a very perceptive person is born of poetic sensitivity and therefore reverberates with meanings. The analogy between the archeology of the soul and of the soil is not new and was a favorite of Freud. One of the better known examples appeared in *Civilization and Its Discontents*, in which Freud asked the readers to try and imagine Rome not as a human habitation but as a psychic entity which, like the real Rome, has a rich past. Indeed, in both archeology and depth psychology one can become occupied with surface signs, with different layers of existence as well as with exploration and discovery. While noting Freud's "many analogies between the mind's layers and archeological research," Erik Erikson made an important observation. Freud's concern with the past that is entombed in the human mind led him to great discoveries and to a feeling of mastery over the past. If this mood of mastery over the past resembles somewhat "the ritual reenactment of beginnings (creation, spring, birth), then it would seem plausible that psychoanalysis appealed above all to people who had lost their origins in soil, ritual, and tradition."

Erikson's observation in his "Autobiographic Notes on the Identity Crisis" suggests something interesting about Jewish history. Since the Jews *were* people who had lost their origins in soil, ritual, and tradition, they could be expected to seek a sense of mastery of the past through psychoanalysis. The best example of a person who lost many of his Jewish origins yet found a new sense of mastery in psychoanalysis is no other than Sigmund Freud himself. There were others too. But as the Zionist search for lost origins centered more and more on the ancestral soil, the alternate and somewhat analogous archeological route toward mastery of the past began to predominate. As Erikson pointed out, the original analogy opens two pathways for recovering a sense of mastery and for a return to the lost origins—psychoanalysis and archeology. To this we can add the observation that the Jewish use of these pathways differed in various times and places. Away from the ancestral soil, Jews fell mostly upon psychoanalytic explorations as a means of creation and birth. Once reunited with the old-new land, they gravitated more and more to a different kind of digging. Archeological excavations of the soil could then provide the budding nation with the mood of spring and rebirth.

What it adds up to is that both psychoanalysis and archeology can provide a sense of mastery over the past and are therefore alluring to people like the Jews. Outside Israel, Jews excelled in psychoanalysis much more than in archeology. In contrast, on the soil of Israel their archeological breakthroughs by far surpassed their achievements in psychoanalysis. While Israel could not produce a local Bruno Bettelheim, Diaspora Jewry could not offer the equivalent of a Yigael Yadin. The growing popularity of archeology among Israelis is difficult to exaggerate. Indeed, Israelis are all getting to be archeology addicts and excavating the past is becoming their national pastime. Kurzweil sensed the hopes for rebirth through both archeology and psychology but discarded them with disdain. These new obsessions—the gregarious indulgence in archeology and the application of depth psychology to Jewish mysticism—offered no rejuvenation, in his view. Instead of healing the crisis of discontinuity in Judaism, the archeologists of the soul as well as of the soil served as "undertakers."

"Undertakers" is a term that Kurzweil kept reiterating in his writings. It was his way of counteracting the fantasies of birth and of a new spring which were entertained by secular Zionists. With a sense of tragedy he warned that Judaism had been in effect laid to rest in the midst of the big clamor over the Zionist renascence. The admired archeologists and priests of depth psychology were certifying not birth but death. No other Israeli public figure was as obsessed as was Kurzweil with the crisis of historical continuity and with the false illusions about its being overcome. As a prominent literary critic he was also keenly aware of the symbolic meanings of acts and events. One may therefore wonder whether his reportedly taking his own life was not, among other things, a symbolic act. Though the reasons for this act are unclear, he might have intended it to serve as a final verdict, or at least as a last-minute warning, that the undertakers had won. Judaism had collapsed, as Yudkah claimed in his sermon, and the historicide of the Jewish religion and culture was nearing completion. It was an agonizing thing to watch but nevertheless he could not let Jewish history out of his sight and go instead to play soccer as Yudkah advised. He had to look at it and see discontinuity and death. And what he saw in his people he enacted on himself.

Echos of the famous Kurzweil vs. Scholem cultural dispute were reported by the American rabbi Herbert Weiner under the heading of "Tourism in Place of Worship." It is an appropriate title. Kurzweil wanted a living Jewish faith but witnessed merely tourism—temporary visits to sites of historical Jewish significance. One of his worries was that the researchers of Jewish mysticism would engage in what can be termed "futurism." From the scientific analysis of Jewish mysticism they would derive predictions and even recommendations for the future of Judaism and Zionism. Weiner found that personal contact with Scholem could not dispel such fears. Scholem underscored his relentless efforts to maintain distance from immediate historical events. But he did make some comments that had a tint of recommendation to them. He maintained that just as the expulsion of Jews from Spain at the end of the fifteenth century resulted in a delayed mystical reaction in the form of Sabbatianism in the seventeenth, so the catastrophic Holocaust may yet result in a delayed mystical reaction. It is difficult to sort out what is prediction and what recommendation in Scholem's forecast of a surge of some form of secular mysticism that is yet to come in reaction to the Holocaust. Either way it does not serve as a reaffirmation of traditional classical Jewish faith. This grieved Kurzweil, who regarded it as malevolent nihilism.

Kurzweil's lamentations over the loss of a living Jewish faith and the divorce from the Jewish past received a poignant reaction by the book reviewer Moshe Gil. While acknowledging that as a subject for scientific enquiry the Jewish religion is not a living faith, he nevertheless objected to Kurzweil's distress over modern Hebrew literature's representing a revolution rather than continuity. Modern Israel was built mainly by people who were not religious, and there is no point in blaming them for not having religious faith and thereby giving up historical continuity. He further said that the complex difficulties encountered by secular and national Judaism do not imply that a return to old-fashioned religious belief is feasible. What is more, even if such a return were possible for most Israelis it would create bigger problems than it would solve. There were historical reasons for the mass desertion from traditional Jewish faith both before and during the Zionist era. This fact suggests that it is time to create new solutions rather than recreate the original problem. These and similar cultural arguments hinge on individual perceptions of modern Hebrew literature. It is possible to see in it continuity and/or revolution and to arrive at optimistic or pessimistic conclusions. Whatever the conclusions, most people seem to feel that literature is the arena where the battle for the soul of the Jewish people is being waged. This feeling is not a novelty, and was a major preoccupation of *the* poet of Jewish national revival —Hayim Nahman Bialik.

What could be done to ensure a sense of continuity between past and future generations of Jews is a question which was prominent in Bialik's mind. As an answer to this perplexity he promoted the notion of the Kinus, which means the collection for safekeeping of the treasures of the past. In the thirteenth century Moses Maimonides tried something like this in relation to the talmudic laws. He collected, summarized, and classified them in his monumental work *Second Torah*. Now Bialik attempted to do something similar with the talmudic stories and fables. He engaged in gathering Agadah (talmudic folkfore) just as Maimonides once engaged in gathering Halakhah (talmudic law). He even advocated the somewhat dubious notion that both Agadah and Halakhah are two faces of the same being. In some respects this is true, since both are interwoven into the Talmud. Yet the many Israeli schoolchildren who enjoy studying the former but not the latter testify to their marked difference. Bialik himself was aware of such feelings, and in one article argued against the impression that studying the Mishnah (the oldest layer of the talmudic law) is "dry."

The idea of a Kinus or collection has it problems but also holds a promise. It could mean the gathering of precious items for safekeeping as in a museum. The public would then come to see some of these works on rare special occasions. What is more, people would view this special selection but not the original works in their full breadth. This practice could degenerate into an institutionalized form of "tourism" in the sense in which it was discussed by Weiner. Fleeting visits to observe sparkling chunks of Judaism would signal the end of Judaism as a living credo. It would become incarcerated as a gathering of collector's items in the halls of the museum-like Kinus.

However, a dynamic interpretation of Bialik's suggestion illuminates its potential for healing the historical crisis of continuity. This interpretation, which was recently reiterated by the Israeli scholar on Jewish mystical and ethical literature Yeshayahu Tishbi, seems close to the original meaning and hopes that were inherent in Bialik's initial suggestion. Tishbi underscored Bialik's innovative notion of anchoring the continuity of Judaic values on the continuity of literature. Past religious literature as well as present and future secular literature all combine to form a continuous national literature. A new and national Kinus or collection of the best of Hebrew literature of all times is a dynamic concept. It implies that old writings will be reread, or even read for the first time, by modern eyes. Consequently, they will be interpreted by modern tastes and outlook. In some ways, the old will remain old and will still belong to its past time. But in other ways, it will look different and will acquire a new light. This entire array of literature which is saturated with old and new meanings will be the continuous and national literature. If Tishbi's interpretation of Bialik's intention is accepted and followed, the Kinus will turn into a daily coping with individual and national life. It will not be incarcerated in a museum-like, untouchable display. Tishbi reported that efforts were made to follow this orientation in the teaching of Hebrew literature at the Hebrew University. Such efforts hold a promise. If a feeling of continuity of Hebrew literature is achieved, a sense of a continuity of identity is likely to follow.

17.

The Canaanite Movement

A MUCH WORSE SECT IS, THERE-
FORE, THE ONE WHICH AIMS TO
BRING SALVATION BY A FUTURE
WHICH IS DEVOID OF THE PAST; A
SECT WHICH BELIEVES THAT,
AFTER A HISTORY EXTENDING
OVER THOUSANDS OF YEARS, A
PEOPLE CAN ONCE AGAIN HAVE A
FRESH START LIKE A NEWBORN
CHILD: MAKE FOR ITSELF A NEW
NATIONAL LAND WITH NEW NA-
TIONAL LIFE AND GOALS.

—Ahad Ha'am

We have seen that Zionism is a movement fraught with dialectics. It sought a return to the past while calling for a sharp break from it. It craved to recapture the creative source of the Jewish people, yet experienced the pangs of historical discontinuity. Out of this fertile ground of paradoxes, some people were bound to shape for themselves a more puristic and less contradictory ideology. All that was needed was to select ideas from only one side of the Zionist spectrum and carry them to their logical conclusion. Inevitably the outcome was an extreme but simplistic ideology that could better satisfy a minority of people who sought ideational purity. Armed with the new strength of ideological conviction, these people were willing to embrace a most radical cure for the national malady of the people of Israel.

The movement which took these radical steps is the Canaanite movement, whose small but ideologically minded members represent one of the more interesting offshoots of Zionism. The movement illustrates what happens when certain central Zionist ideas, such as starting afresh, shaking loose from a sick past, or striving for normalization are carried to their logical extreme. The result was what Ahad Ha'am dreaded: the formation of a "negative sect." While members of this sect were ready to open their ranks to Jews who wanted to be cured, they wanted nothing to do with those who chose to stay with the old "sect"—traditional Jewry.

An informative description of the history of the various Canaanite groups and ideologies, mostly in Israel and France, was provided by Avneri, who for many years was interested in the movement and had personal contacts with its leaders. His report reveals an astounding ideology. In simple terms, this ideology claimed that there has never been a Jewish nation, but that there is and has always been a Hebrew nation. This notion of a Hebrew nationality was considered by Avneri the most innovative idea of the Canaanites. In the past the Hebrew nation, as conceived by the Canaanites, comprised the Hebrew-speaking people of what is today Israel, Jordan, Lebanon, Syria, and Iraq. The Canaanites consider it most unfortunate that this Hebrew nation was beset during the period of the Babylonian Exile by the disease of Judaism, from which it still suffers. The essence of this "malady" is the misconception that a nation can be bound together not by a common land and language but by a religion. Zionism espoused the healthy course of bringing the Hebrew people back to their land. However, it betrayed this goal and retrogressed to sickness by coexisting and compromising with the Jewish religion. In Canaanite ideology, Judaism is such an all-permeating disease that it can afflict even those who, like the Zionists, fought it at first. In bringing the Hebrew people back to their ancestral land so as to substitute country for religion as the basis for a national identity, Zionism tried to provide an antidote to the disease of Judaism. Yet in the midst of this rebellion against Judaism and the efforts to restore the original state of health, Zionism itself was plagued by this awful sickness. As a result, Zionism too suffers from a total misconception of the true meaning of nationality. In order for the Hebrew people to cure themselves of Judaism and reestablish their *authentic* national identity, radical changes have to take place. Religion, history, tradition, literature, the entire culture, must be reexamined and radically changed, for only radical changes can lead to a revival of the old culture of the Hebrews.

The Canaanites actually called themselves "Young Hebrews." The term "Canaanites" came into being after they allegedly reenacted ancient rituals that seemed more Canaanite than Hebrew. There were rumors concerning ritual dancing at night around a fire, and a naked woman who represented the goddess Ashtoret (Avneri indicates that in one rumor the "goddess" was the daughter of Prime Minister-to-be Levi Eshkol). It all sounds like one of those happenings in which the participants would have kept warm even without a fire but which is not expected to leave an impact on the history of a people. Yet this one did. The widely circulating rumors about this Canaanite ritual prompted the Israeli poet Abraham Shlonsky to react with derision and to name the Young Hebrews "Canaanites." The name stuck. The quick acceptance of the new term by the Israeli public suggests that the message of the Young Hebrews, "We don't want Jews," was being answered, "We don't want Canaanites."

The Canaanite movement always remained a small minority and by the late 1950s it had almost completely disappeared. However, it has never been a question of numbers but of ideology as such. Many Israelis were shaken by the fact that both in Israel and abroad a movement, even though a small one, could arise which advocated the abolition of both Zionism and Judaism. What added to the shock was the fact that young intellectuals of high caliber were among the active members of the movement. They were poets, artists, and cultured persons who were interested in archeology, history, philosophy, and sociology. Kurzweil's impression was that the high intellectual level of their periodical *Aleph* testified to the fact that the spokesmen for the movement belonged to the ranks of academic youth.

Avneri raised the important question of the origins of the Canaanite ideology and also suggested some answers. One origin was the general malaise in Europe between the two world wars. At that time, Europe experienced waves of resurgent nationalism which involved mythical and romantic preoccupations with the past and which finally developed into rigid chauvinism, especially in Germany. During this period Palestine was not isolated from European ideologies, including romantic nationalism, which looked back eagerly at the remote but glorious past.

Another origin was the renewed interest in archeology which according to Avneri had not yet deteriorated into an official fad boosted by the state. Biblical as well as prebiblical history was being explored in archeological diggings which led to the potentially explosive realization that both the Bible and the land of Israel are but a small part of a wider, older culture as well as a wider ancestral land. This old land and culture ought to be termed Semitic or Hebrew, not merely Israeli, and certainly not Jewish.

Still another source of influence, according to Avneri, were the biblical studies of the famed German scholar Julius Wellhausen. The central thesis of Wellhausen's theories would seem to be the sharp distinction between preexilic Israel and postexilic Judaism. What mostly distinguishes postexilic Judaism from ancient Israel is the written Torah. As long as oral tradition prevailed, conditions were optimal for creative spurts by the Prophets. The codification of some of the law during the Assyrian period signaled the beginning of the end of this period of freedom for those great promulgators of monotheism. It was the postexilic Prophet Ezekiel who provided the connecting link between the Prophets and the new "artificial product, the sacred constitution of Judaism." His writings are therefore sometimes lively and some other times quite deadening. Canonization put an end to the forces of spontaneity which characterized preexilic Israel. The results were the rise of a theocracy in the form of a constitution and the metamorphosis of a great idea into an institution.

All in all, what Wellhausen was saying was that the glory of ancient Israel did not start as early as some people wished to believe and that it was short-lived. With the postexilic reforms a process of degeneration started from which the Jews never recuperated. The new Judaism "left no free scope for the individual." The supremacy of the cultus and formal laws formalized and killed the natural way of living. For instance, festivals lost their connection to seasonal changes, that is, to nature. Most other things that the cultus covered lost their "natural significance" also. Unlike the old days of an oral tradition, the written cultus was no longer tied to sensuality. It became "nobler" but "nature had been killed in it." This deadening cultus was the means employed to preserve "a religious community even after all bonds of nationality had fallen away." It worked, but whether it was a real blessing to the Jews and the world "may very well be disputed." Perhaps it was easy for the Christian Wellhausen to adopt these convictions without paying the price of self-hate. We could not expect the same from the Canaanites.

The spread of Wellhausen's ideas led to a distortion of the image of the reforms in the Judaic tradition which are known to have started in the Babylonian Exile and to have continued in Israel after the return to Zion. Two major reforms that were given prominence in the Babylonian Exile were underscored by Dimont. These are the substitution of the synagogue for the Temple and of prayer for sacrifices. In making these changes, the reformers were not killing prophecy, but only trying to preserve its heritage. What is more, the reforms were of the Jewish religion and were not antinationalistic. Subsequently these same reformed synagogue-goers returned to Judah hoping to rebuild a nation. It was a religious task, but it was also a major nationalistic effort. Yet it was this spiritualization of the Jewish religion which the Canaanites came to regard as a disease. What they saw was a sick metamorphosis from Hebrew nationalism to a diseased Jewish religion. Viewing the postexilic reforms through Wellhausen's binoculars, it was easy to conclude that the disease of Judaism had afflicted the Hebrew nationality and killed everything vibrant and breathing in the short-lived glory of ancient Israel.

The Canaanites were aware of the problem posed for their doctrine by the fact that the postexilic Jews had implemented a nationalist revival. This, after all, should be impossible for people who identified with religious and community life but who completely disengaged themselves from a political identity or national aspirations. The Canaanite leader A. G. Horon solved this Canaanite dilemma by rewriting history here and there. He contended that the independence that was eventually secured during the period of the Second Temple was achieved not by reformed Jews in the Babylonian tradition, but by assimilationists of the time who had come under the influence of Greek culture. Only Bar Kokhba's rebellion against the Romans, which received the blessing of the religious leader Rabbi Akiba, was an exception. But this unique exception only reaffirms the general rule. In Horon's opinion, classical rabbinic Judaism ever since the Babylonian Exile was engaged in consistent efforts to make the Jews forget their times of liberty. It is hard to imagine how jubilant rabbis who tell and retell throughout Passover night the miracles and joys of independence fit into this description. It is a fair assumption that the Canaanites have passed a certain point in their ideological commitment beyond which consistency counts more than verity.

A fourth major source of influence on the Canaanite ideology, according to Avneri, were views of the German metahistorian Oswald Spengler as expressed in his famous book *The Decline of the West.* There he developed his own notions concerning the enfeeblement of the Jewish people ever since the Babylonian Exile. His ideas resemble those of Wellhausen. In comparison to the Persian doctrine of Zoroastrianism, the Judaic prophecy of Amos and Isaiah paled or deteriorated into apocalyptic visions. "The *little world of Judaism lived a spiritually separate life*" (italics by Spengler) while the Jewish people as a whole adapted to living in dispersion. The subsequent national revival in Israel was merely a short-lived illusion by a minority of this people in exile. The Roman war against Judea, which was directed by Vespasian, put an end to this illusionary Jewish claim to a land and to nationhood. Ever since the Babylonian Exile the Jews adhered to Magian notions of nonterritorial and geographically unlimited existence, so that they were in danger of disappearing, unlike other peoples who adopted Faustian notions of fatherland and mother tongue.

Spengler developed other notions which left an impact on the Canaanites. He proposed that history works in cycles in which civilizations rise and fall, and that all civilizations are doomed to death or winter after going through the periods of spring, summer, and autumn —that is, youth, the prime of life, and the eventual decline. He predicted that the old civilization of the West was dying and was about to be replaced by a Sinic or Slavic civilization. Under the impression of his ideas, the Canaanites drew an analogy between the declining civilization of the West, about to be superseded by Sinic or Slavic civilization, and the declining civilization of the Jews, which could be superseded by a Hebrew civilization if, and only if, the Jews would be willing to make the mythical jump back to the ancient Semitic, Hebrew culture that had been the cradle of their civilization.

As the Canaanites forged a rigid ideology out of disparate Jewish and Gentile sources, they reached the overwhelming conclusion that radical measures were needed to rid the Hebrew nation of the disease of Judaism. Such a conclusion carried with it the price of self-hate. In talking of the Canaanites, one should perhaps use the term "Hebrew," rather than Jewish, anti-Semitism. Avneri was incensed by the anti-Semitic way in which the Canaanite poet Yonaton Ratosh depicted certain Israeli Jews. Ratosh claimed that in Israel, the old familiar Jew changed his clothes, cut his *payes* (earlocks), and learned to talk eloquently in Hebrew about country and nation. Yet closer inspection reveals that this new Jew is the same old Jew, the eternal Diaspora Jew, who in France pretends to be a Frenchman, in Germany impersonates Germans, and in Israel plays the same old game but this time in Hebrew. No less offensive to Avneri was Ratosh's notion that the "Elders of Zion" are not legend. At least in regard to the Hebrew nation and the land of the Hebrews, there *is* a complex international organization of world Jewry which tries to dominate this land and nation. Another contention of Ratosh's which infuriated Avneri was that as long as the land of the Hebrews is not cleared of Zionism and the hearts of the Hebrews of Judaism, all efforts will be in vain and all sacrifices wasted.

Avneri was not the only one to be incensed by Canaanite anti-Semitic pronouncements. Georges Friedmann recalled a shocking statement made to him by a young Canaanite intellectual, to the effect that the Jewish Agency would do better to help Jews to remain in the Diaspora rather than leave it. This particular Canaanite must have felt something like "Who wants Jews?" On reading such statements one comes to the bitter realization that it is now the turn of young Hebrews to fear contamination by Jews the way Gentile anti-Semites do. It makes one wonder sometimes whether Jean-Paul Sartre should not write a new *Anti-Semite and Jew,* this time referring to a single person who is both.

The phenomenon of the Canaanite movement attracted the attention of the Israeli literary and cultural critic Baruch Kurzweil. In the article "The Nature and Origins of 'The Young Hebrews' Movement," he found the Canaanite negation of the Jewish past more determined and final than any previous act of assimilation in Jewish history. For Kurzweil, the divorce of the Jewish people from religious content represented new Israeli singing of old Diaspora tunes, coupled at times with the illusion that such tunes are really innovative. It was clear to him that the cultural ideologies of the Diaspora, which found strong expression in the Haskalah Hebrew literature and in Zionist pronouncements in favor of normalization, fostered a situation in which sooner or later the chickens were bound to come home to roost. To him, Canaanism was one inevitable outcome of that major brand of Zionism which promoted modern and secular nationalism at all costs. Now, as some Old Guard Zionists were viewing with alarm this fruit of the modern normal secular nationalism they had promoted, Kurzweil could only ask sardonically what these gentlemen had expected all along.

It is interesting to reflect upon the fact that both the Canaanites and the supermilitant Zionists had large territorial dreams. Avneri was aware of this similarity between the Young Hebrews and the supporters of the Greater Israel Movement. He was intrigued by the fact that opposite ideologies, Canaanite and Revisionist, yielded similar orientations. In all likelihood this is a result of falling back upon myths. There are no Arabs to contend with when time is rolled back by ancient mythologies. Avneri reported the claim by the poet Ratosh that there are no Arab nations, only Arabic tribes. Similar ideas were expressed by Horon, who under the name Gourevitch was one of the original leaders of the early Canaanite group in Paris. He spoke not of the Arab world but of the Arabic world. Arabs in Hebrew is Aravim. But if one wishes to imply that there are no Arab nations, only disparate and mixed subnational units, then one uses the term Arviyim.

These are not meaningless language games. The distinction expresses skepticism concerning the viability of Arab nationalities, not to mention pan-Arabism. Turning the Arab nations into subnational units enabled the Canaanites to aspire to a large land of Kedem (Near East) populated by Hebrew peoples. All "Hebrews" would of course be equal in such a Semitic renascence, but somehow one is left with the impression that it would be the Israeli Hebrews who would call the tune. At any rate, one could search in vain for "Arabic peoples" who aspire to a healthy revival of their "Hebrew" peoplehood. The Canaanites were simply justifying their territorial dreams by a mythical denationalizing of the Arabs. On the other hand, the by far more numerous adherents of the Greater Israel Movement acknowledge the Arabs as Arabs, yet they want all the Arab land that is claimed by Jewish lore. In their view, the Jewish claims should predominate because the Arabs have so many other lands while the Jews have no other. Even though this approach refrains from the insult of calling the Arabs "Arabic" or *Arviyim*, it still is a militant orientation which tells Arab inhabitants that their land is Jewish.

The basic Canaanite distinction between Hebraism and Judaism is not really an innovation. Like many other ideas, it has fathers and grandfathers. In this case, the grandfather is perhaps the founder of the modern scientific study of Judaism, Leopold Zunz. Nathan Rotenstreich drew attention to the fact that Zunz divided Jewish literature between the biblical period of Hebraism and the postbiblical period of Judaism. Although Rotenstreich emphasized that in Zunz's view the transition from the former to the latter was smooth, other interpretations of this division are also possible. Wellhausen had already drawn the dividing line during the late biblical period and contrasted degenerate Judaism with a healthy "ancient Israel." The Canaanites swung back to the division of Judaism and Hebraism. In this they followed the general trend of the Yishuv in Palestine. For the Yishuv, the most important ventures were "Hebrew," not "Jewish." The Yishuv strove to establish Hebrew labor, Hebrew education, and a strong labor union of Hebrew workers. What is most important, the Yishuv itself was referred to as the Hebrew Yishuv, not the Jewish Yishuv, and the primary goal of those days of "the state on the way" was to establish a Hebrew state, not a Jewish state. As a child I frequently joined other children in demanding a "Hebrew" state. We used to shout the popular slogan: "Free aliyah, a Hebrew state, boo to the White Paper." A "Hebrew" state, not a "Jewish" state, is what we shouted. We knew that there was a wide world in which there were Jews and Judaism. But in our Eretz Yisrael under British control what we had was a Hebrew Histadrut (labor union), a Hebrew Yishuv, and, one day yet to come, a Hebrew state.

Ben Gurion may have sensed that things had swung too far in the direction of Hebrew identification. This could have been a reason for his declaring on May 14, 1948, the establishment of a "Jewish" state. The State of Israel Proclamation of Independence talks about a Jewish state, not a Hebrew state. By the 1960s, after the Canaanites achieved notoriety and after it became evident that Jewish identification among young Israelis leaves much to be desired, a remedy was concocted. In 1963 the Minister of Education and Culture, Zalman Aranne, initiated a program for teaching "Jewish consciousness" to the young. It was one of those episodes in human affairs where the real suspense lies not in waiting for the outcome, which is no mystery at all, but in figuring out the lines of thinking that made people in authority believe their venture would succeed. In this fiasco, the story lies in the ways of thinking of Old Guard Zionists. I can only speculate about the underlying rationale. The schools were where young people were educated to become new Hebrews. Therefore, the schools were also where the young could be reeducated to absorb some old Jewishness. What this line of thinking ignored was that it was not just the schools which estranged young persons from Jewishness, it was the entire culture. What is more, to the degree that some of the battles had to be waged in school, they could be better fought by modifying the teaching of history, literature, and the Bible rather than by adding specific hours for "Jewish consciousness." Needless to say, this formal program did not heal the identity split.

As time went on the new reality of the State of Israel had begun to affect the language. A basic psychological cleavage remained, but the split began to be conceived more as between Judaism and Israelism. This point was made by the Israeli scientist-philosopher and publicist Yeshayahu Leibowitz. He was perturbed by the strength of anti-Jewish Zionism and regarded the Canaanites as the caricature expression of this basic trend in Zionism. He acknowledged that the Canaanites remained a marginal minority but claimed that their ideology left an imprint on the entire settlement effort in the Land of Israel. The result was that the old Zionists cultivated a new young generation which is so national and so secular that it no longer needs to even demonstrate its objection to traditional Judaism. For this new generation it is simply an axiom that "Israelism" is an antithesis of "Judaism." In other words, the small number of Canaanites is no consolation. Not when instead of only a few Young Hebrews there are many young Israelis who could not care less about Judaism. The implications of Leibowitz's contention are not encouraging to the advocates of Judaism. Once again we face a variation of the Wellhausen split between Israelis and Jews. But unlike the fanatic Canaanite fighters for Hebraism, the new generation which espouses Israelism does not even feel the need for militancy against Judaism. To them, one could not even say that they protest too much.

Obviously we face a basic identity split that runs within Zionism. The roots of the split are in the Diaspora and the past. Its most glaring manifestation has been the Canaanite movement and its current expression is crystallizing along the dichotomy of Israeli versus Jewish. It is no surprise that this development causes distress to many persons.

Yet what the distress leads to can also be distressing. In the 1960s, at the same time that Aranne was concocting his ill-fated cure for this malaise, a different curiosity was also being put together. This was a research project which suggested either that the cure had largely worked or that there was not that much of a problem to begin with. The results were published by the Israeli psychologist Simon N. Herman under the astonishing title of *Israelis and Jews: The Continuity of an Identity*. This tendentious conclusion is based on the results of questionnaires and interviews administered in 1964 and 1965 to junior-year students. The questionnaire included such items as: "Does the fact that you are Jewish play an important part in your life?" "If you were born all over again, would you wish to be born a Jew?" and "Do you feel your fate is bound up with the fate of the Jewish people?"

It is an open question as to what degree survey and questionnaire methods can tap the intricacy of identity issues which reverberate throughout the years and illusively pop up and disappear, only to pop up again. It is illuminating that one subject in the study indicated during an interview that he usually does not give serious thought to such matters. Yet in spite of this lack of reflection he was able to flatly state that "Jewishness had little importance to him, while Israeliness possessed great importance." This fits Leibowitz's conception of the new generation of young Israelis who espoused Israelism and no longer need to obsess over Judaism or assume a militant stance against it. At any rate, Herman's joy over "the continuity of an identity" was not shared by most critics. A review in *Commentary* (January 1972) stated that "Almost every page of *Israelis and Jews* offers evidence of a rejection of Jewishness." Other reviews in *The Jerusalem Post Weekly* (January 19, 1971), *Contemporary Psychology* (February 1972), and *The American Zionist* (May 1972) expressed similar reservations. It is hard to avoid the conclusion that the same alarm which gave birth to the "Jewish consciousness" teaching program also created American-style research to support the comforting notion that after all these years of undue worry it turns out that people were making a mountain out of a molehill.

The Jewish-Hebrew split is keenly felt both by those who would like to accentuate it and by those who would like to suppress it. Because of these conflicting motivations, funny games are sometimes played in Israel around the term "Hebrew." In a newspaper article entitled "A Persecuted Name and a Persecuted Citizen" the reporter Shlomo Shamgar protested the high-handed bureaucratic treatment of a private citizen. As it turns out, the persecuted name is "Hebrew" and the persecuted citizen is none other than the Canaanite Ratosh. Shamgar indicated that he had no sympathy for Ratosh the ideologist who offers Israel a Canaanite dictatorship in lieu of the historical link between Israel and Diaspora Jews. Nevertheless, he could not condone the practice of the Ministry of the Interior that made it impossible for thirteen years for Ratosh to replace his lost identification card in which he was originally listed as "Hebrew."

Ratosh finally resorted to court action and won the right for a replacement with the original "Hebrew" designation. Shamgar's main contention was that the terms "Jew" and "Hebrew" were both used historically and in effect do not contradict one another, unless a ministry lacking in wisdom refuses one of these terms. Nevertheless it took time for the Ministry of the Interior to wise up. In *Ha'aretz* of March 29, 1972, it was reported that the Ministry of the Interior was advised by the Attorney General, Meir Shamgar, that children of the Jewish religion could be registered as "Hebrew" if their parents so desired. The reasoning was that the terms "Hebrew" and "Jewish" are identical. The motivation behind this advice by the Attorney General was to avoid unpleasant court fights that would otherwise ensue.

It is evident that the Canaanite ideology is a rigid belief system which aims to resolve an acute identity crisis. We therefore need to reiterate some of the things we previously said about the sense of identity. Identity denotes the overall integration as well as the consistent internal organization of a person's attitudes, identifications, and learned roles. It secures a sense of sameness and continuity over time, provides a sense of belonging to a group as well as a sense of individual uniqueness, and, last but not least, yields a sense of self-esteem. If self-esteem is lacking, a temptation to break away from the past is bound to arise. Persons in such a predicament would be tempted to disrupt the sense of sameness over time so as to refrain from identifying themselves with the despicable beings they think they have been in the past.

In relation to the Uganda Affair, we saw how in times of upheaval, when the sense of self-esteem and that of sameness and continuity seem incompatible, people can be caught in a bind. The positive ego-ideal, consisting of the recommended personal and cultural standards, is unattainable. On the other hand, the negative ego-ideal, of cultural standards which mortify people with shame, is close to realization and causes great humiliation. Persons with a sound holistic integration of identity can impose organization and discipline on such a diversity of feelings which is so riddled with tensions. Such persons are therefore able to persist in their quest for the hitherto unattainable positive ego-ideal. Blows to self-esteem which they suffer by getting too close for comfort to the standards of the negative ego-ideal are not misinterpreted as a verdict of total failure. However, not everyone is capable of this. Such a tolerance for diversity of views and for a mixture of both positive and negative feelings necessitates a basic sense of self-trust even in the midst of anxiety, doubts, and shame. An inner security which remains relatively unruffled by adversity rests on a sophisticated integration of disparate and even conflicting identifications. The hallmark of such a high-level organization of an identity is tolerance for diversity and ability to withstand inner tensions. Those not endowed with this tolerance might prefer shortcuts to pride and to consistency. The shortcuts, however, are based on more primitive modes of organizing a sense of identity. People who are frustrated by the unattainability of the positive ego-ideal, and humiliated by reaching the despicable standards of the negative ego-ideal, can take flight into the more primitively organized negative identity.

We have emphasized, following Erikson, that negative identity is perversely based on identifications, attitudes, and learned roles, which were presented to a person as most undesirable but also as most real. These are the ways of conduct that authority figures abhorred yet acknowledged the potency of. We also underscored Whitman and Kaplan's notion that negative identity can be a way out of a predicament of an utterly unattainable positive ego-ideal and an utterly unacceptable negative ego-ideal. As a solution it is far from ideal, but at least it is real. During the stormy days of the Uganda Affair most Zionists rejected this quick way out. They stuck to the arduous ordeal of striving toward the positive ego-ideal of Zion in spite of severe burns by the

negative ego-ideal of exile. The negative identity solution in the form
of an intentional Diaspora, a state like all other states, in Uganda or
anywhere else on earth but Zion, was rejected.

In contrast, the Canaanites embraced negative identity. With the
links to tradition further lessened and shame further heightened because of Jews who stay in exile even in the Zionist era, some people
became prone to this embrace. The Canaanites were caught in a bind.
To be a talmudic or other form of religious Jew was out of the question.
This way of life represented the old negative ego-ideal of no country,
no common language, no initiative, only lots of religious mumbo jumbo
to create the sickening illusion that this is how it should be. These old
ways had become an utterly unacceptable insult. On the other hand,
to be a healthy Jewish nation-state in a Jewish Israel into which *all* the
exiled Jews had gathered was an impossible positive ego-ideal. The
obstructions to this dream were not only external ones in the form of
restrictions on Jewish immigration. There were internal blocks as well.
Many Jews either liked it where they were or wished to concentrate
their efforts on improving conditions in their present habitats. Given
these circumstances, how could Israel ever become a normal and
healthy nation if major chunks of its people were to live in exile and
even like it there? Israel, therefore, could be both very real and very
healthy only if it were not Jewish. Then it would no longer suffer from
the abnormal situation of having its "Jewish" citizens scattered all over
the globe.

It adds up to a consistent emotional conception. Let the dispersed
Jews practice their precious religion wherever they are, but let the State
of Israel cleanse itself of this religious disease of Judaism. Then all those
dispersed Jews would not be regarded as sick citizens of the Hebrew
state and could not cast aspersions on it by their abnormal existence.
In other words, if sick, denationalized religious or talmudic Jews are
unacceptable while healthy, nationalistic Jews with no more Jews in
exile is an impossibility, then an anti-Jewish Hebrew nation is a real and
potent alternative. At least the Hebrew nation will have a future un-
shackled by diseases of the past. Thus the Canaanites embraced a
negative identity solution to the crisis of historical continuity and clung
to the ardent wish to skip centuries of postexilic Jewish history as if they

were a nullity. This potent desire represents no less than a repetition of a primitive split between the sense of self and not-self. This agonizing split is usually experienced more than once in a normal life-cycle. In order to clarify this matter, we need to take a look at some additional implications of the formation of a negative identity.

The psychological toll exerted by a negative identity is a heavy one. For one thing, it is hard to maintain a sense of identity in the face of a society which suppresses rather than condones the norms upheld by the negative identity. This leads persons with negative identities to develop rigid ideologies so as to be able to sustain their sense of negative identity even in the face of stiff opposition. Unfortunately, the clinging to ideologies carries with it the danger of totalistic thinking which is typical of many ideologies. It is in their nature to engage in total inclusion of persons and ideas that are "in" and complete exclusion of all those that are "out." Although being "in" is a source of strength, especially for individuals who find themselves in a condemned minority and need desperately the stamina that comes with ideological conviction, the excluded "out" may frequently include authentic features of the individual himself. It is easy to regard ideologies as totalistic and ultimate explanations since, as Erikson has pointed out, it is in their nature to demand uncompromising commitment to an absolute hierarchy of values and to rigid principles of behavior. This commitment is what ideologies demand and frequently get from their adherents, especially in the case of people who desperately need ideologies to support their already established negative identity and their resistance to social, cultural, or political opposition. Such persons may find it easy to make a full commitment and to endow their ideologies with totalistic —that is, all-inclusive and all-exclusive—dimensions.

Erikson has also discussed the more general relation between the development of identity and of ideologies. Both share the common denominator of linking common identifications, which are the specific roles, beliefs, attitudes, and esteemed examples to be followed, although not the overall integration of the sense of self as identity is. This common denominator means that the formation of either an overall identity or ideology provides integration and coherence to a person's disparate learned roles. Thus, ideology is one way of providing integration, and if a sense of identity does not accomplish it adequately then resorting to an ideology is tempting. There is a catch, however. Erikson underscored the fact that in ideologies, totality, or the polarization and rigid delineation of absolutely inclusive and exclusive boundaries, is achieved at the expense of wholeness. Wholeness, unlike totality, refers to internal, organic, logical, and consistent integration of the many values and beliefs that form the particular ideology or identity. Wholeness is neither all-inclusive nor all-exclusive; it does not dictate either-or choices and does not violate its many parts. Thus, wholeness does justice to all, while totality overvalues as well as overnegates.

If we bear in mind that those persons with negative identity who resort to a rigid ideology achieve totality at the expense of wholeness, we can see that negative identity can be considered a malaise in two senses (See Gonen). First, the strong rebellion against established norms and their almost automatic rejection inevitably involves some self-negation. The totalistic rejection of the norms instilled in a person during his growth is bound to include some norms which have already been well internalized and well accepted by him. The subsequent negation of these already internalized norms is self-destructive and involves self-hate. Second, the tendency to cling to a totalistic ideology, rather than to a holistic set of beliefs, results in "conformity in reverse" and in a generally rigid style that fits everything into the procrustean bed of a totalistic ideology instead of treating each thing individually so as to fit the varied needs of the self. In sum, negative identity is two malaises in one: it is a tragic double coercion of individuality by subordinating it to self-negation as well as to a totalistic belief system.

To take up the first of the two malaises first, self-negation is the rejection of norms which once were part of the self. The result is hate. At first glance the hate may seem to be directed at others who still cling to the rejected norms. For instance, adolescents in turmoil may seem to hate their "square" parents but to love themselves for "doing their own thing." They are understandably proud of being spontaneous even though their "doing their own thing" may strike an outside observer as being depressively uniform. But the hate for "square" others and the vehemence of this rejection signals more than a negative interest in others. It betrays self-hate. The adolescents themselves are the former "squares" who now loathe what they were and, alas, what they may even still be. Therefore, with great tenacity they declare their revulsion at dear and close persons who have "sold out to the system." The delicate therapeutic task in some of these cases is to help the young person learn the lesson of "thou doth protest too much" without further aggravating the identity crisis.

The story of the Canaanites is somewhat similar. Their vehement rejection of Jewish values is not merely a hatred of others. The Jew-hating Hebrews are truly Jew-hating Jews. None of them was born Hebrew or Canaanite. Jews is what they once were and pretend to no longer be. Yet people who were once one thing and have successfully become another do not need to lash with venom at what they no longer are. But the poisonous anti-Jewish declarations of the Young Hebrews, which so incensed Avneri and others, clearly indicate that the Canaanites do have such a need. So while the Young Hebrews go on protesting that they are not old Jews, their self-hate and unresolved identity crisis do not remain hidden from the public. It is a fair speculation that had the general public not been able to sense this malaise of self-hatred and self-negation, the Canaanites would have had greater following.

It is important to reiterate the crucial role that the crisis of historical continuity plays in this self-hatred. A Young Hebrew does not necessarily begin life as an Orthodox Jew and later rebel against his historical disease of Judaism. The analogy between Canaanites and adolescents can go only that far. A Young Hebrew is simply born into a culture which teaches a split. It teaches the glory of the present-day great Jewish renascence which, at least by implication, replaced the chronic Jewish disease which prevailed before. It also teaches the glories of the remote past and the praiseworthy organization for self-help and for collective passive resistance on the part of Jewish communities in the Diaspora. Taken together, these teachings could easily add up to a rejection of that which one also loves. The confusing cultural heritage calls for a clear-cut primitive ordering of this mess along the lines of negative identity, unless a person has the ego resources for an identity organization that can tolerate much diversity and even outright contradictions. The conclusion to be drawn from all this is that

Jewish self-hate in Israel is only in part the old phenomenon of an identification with the Gentile aggressor. Mostly it is a newer phenomenon. It is that self-hatred which results from a primitive organization of a complex culture into one simple split. This brings us to the second malaise in negative identity, the totalitarianism that can result from the repetitive experience of the early and ominous split between self and not-self.

Totalistic ideologies are a frequent outcome of that primitive mode of organizing identifications which we termed negative identity. The Canaanites, with their anti-Jewish negative identity, are no exception. Their sharp-edged division between the Hebrew nationality that is "in" and the disease of Judaism that is "out" is in the best tradition of totalism. It may therefore be enlightening to mention briefly what Erikson said of those who tilt toward the totalistic rather than the holistic side of integrating experiences. Clinging to totality is a primitive maneuver that can recur in the developmental history of persons. Its essence is a sudden and total realignment of outlooks with great conviction but with gross simplification. The simplification lies in the tendency to witness a basic split in the psychological field between two basic sides. The earliest split in the course of development is between self and not-self. As the baby discovers that he and mother are two different beings, he can learn to live in a heterogenous world with trust, if his parents are understanding and tolerant. But under adverse conditions he may form a total realignment of outlook in which he assumes a basic stance of mistrust. If he mistrusts himself, then his parents are good. If he mistrusts them, then they are bad while he is good. Other variations of the split are also possible. In adult life these early primitive splits may crystallize into "black-white" thinking with an "us" vs. "them" perception of the world. This is totalitarianism at its worst. Similar splits can recur around the age of five during the formation of the superego as well as during adolescence when all identifications are again in a fluid state. The upheaved adolescent can fluidly organize and reorganize his attitudes and beliefs as he searches for a stable identity. Total realignment of convictions is then the rule rather than the exception.

It can happen, though, at any age. The resurgent old insecurities of childhood because of issues of trust and mistrust might always be handled by sweeping realignments of roles along a primitive, dichotomous organization of the world. Infantile rage is a strong component of such totalitarian revisions of attitudes and is easy to detect. In any sharp division of people into "us" and "them," the "them" are going to get it. When the "us" are Young Hebrews and the "them" Jews, then the Jews get it. That much is not very disputable. Whether the rage is of infantile origin and forms a primitive reenactment of previous totalistic realignment of attitudes toward a split world is, of course debatable, but if, as I suspect, it is the case, then surely there is an infantile streak in the Canaanites.

18.

Zionism in Perspective

AND ONE SAID TO THE MAN
CLOTHED IN LINEN, WHO WAS
ABOVE THE WATERS OF THE
RIVER: HOW LONG SHALL IT BE TO
THE END OF THE WONDERS? AND
. . . HE LIFTED UP HIS RIGHT
HAND AND HIS LEFT HAND UNTO
HEAVEN, AND SWORE BY HIM
THAT LIVETH FOREVER THAT IT
SHALL BE FOR A TIME, TIMES,
AND A HALF; AND WHEN THEY
HAVE MADE AN END OF BREAKING
IN PIECES THE POWER OF THE
HOLY PEOPLE, ... ALL THESE
THINGS SHALL BE FINISHED. AND
I HEARD, BUT I UNDERSTOOD
NOT; THEN SAID I: O MY LORD,
WHAT SHALL BE THE LATTER END
OF THESE THINGS? AND HE SAID:
GO THY WAY, DANIEL; FOR THE
WORDS ARE SHUT UP AND SEALED
TILL THE TIME OF THE END.

—Daniel 12: 6–9.

Jewish legend has it that in the sixteenth century the Kabbalist Rabbi Judah Löw ben Bezalel of Prague created a Golem. The Golem was a humanoid made out of clay which could be animated by the insertion in his mouth of a slip of paper on which one of the secret Divine Names of God was inscribed. Before each Sabbath, Rabbi Löw removed the Name from the Golem's mouth and put it back in only after the Sabbath was over. Therefore, the animated Golem served his creator during the weekdays but rested, inanimate, during the Sabbath. Thus, Rabbi Löw treated his creation as the Creator treated men. Unlike God, however, the rabbi was not omnipotent, and the Golem was alleged to possess superhuman strength and extraordinary powers that could be an ominous threat to his own creator. This Jewish version of the Frankenstein's monster story yields an expected outcome. One Friday afternoon Rabbi Löw forgot to remove the Divine Name from the Golem's mouth. As the Sabbath drew closer, the Golem became more and more agitated. When he threatened to destroy everything in his path, people were gripped with panic. No one had the kind of force which would match the Golem's and there was no stopping him from an insane rampage. Rabbi Löw was summoned from the Altneuschul (Old-New Synagogue) and in the eleventh hour managed to extricate the Divine Name of God from the Golem's mouth. The Golem fell lifeless to the ground and the rabbi never again revived that mass of clay. The obvious moral of the story is that imperfect man should not tinker with powerful forces that he can summon but not control.

The theme of the Golem stirs the imagination. It led Abraham Rothberg to write a fascinating fiction called *The Sword of the Golem*. In this book, the Golem is named Yossel and is taunted as "dumb Yossel" by other Jews. Rothberg humanized this humanoid by giving him the power to speak and the ability to feel something akin to love as well as agitation over his sexual sterility. As the Golem in Rothberg's tale becomes more and more human it remains for Rabbi Löw to assume the unpleasant task of reminding him that he is a special creature created for a particular purpose—to use his superior strength in defense of Jews against Gentile carnage.

How interesting it is to watch the reverberation of this "beauty and the beast" theme in Jewish history. Once it was Samson's job to protect the Jews from the Philistines and he became an uncontrollable force for his fellow tribesmen. Now it was the Golem's job to protect Jews from anti-Semitic enemies. He was less able than the human Samson to distinguish between friend and foe. In the Jewish legend he was about to hurt Jews, and in Rothberg's fiction he actually did but repented before his death and fought to spare Jewish life while destroying known enemies of the Jews. His conduct suggests that the beastly Golem had a soft spot in his heart for the Judaic beauty.

As we move from the legendary events of the sixteenth century to actual events in the nineteenth century, we witness the rise of Zionism. This new political force, this new Golem, if you will, offered similar protection. Zionism had an answer to anti-Semitism and was going to rescue Jews from its claws. Once again help was offered in the eleventh hour. It came not from the Old-New Synagogue but from the author of *Old-New Land*. What Theodor Herzl offered—the Zionist credo—could have looked to Orthodox Jews like another Golem. He was stirring up a strong force, secular nationalism, which could easily get out of control. Again, it was that old tinkering with powers that imperfect man ought to leave to the Lord.

One can imagine the dread of many Orthodox Jews as they contemplated this modern rescue offer. They perhaps felt something like a trembling beauty in the grip of a King Kong, needing protection from their protector and loving abductor. They were convinced that powers that belong to God had been expropriated by men who were too impatient to wait for God to use them. They feared that sooner or later these immense powers would be turned against their users and perhaps against all the Sons of Israel. God can surely handle it when man, his creation, turns against him. But what are men to do when uncontrolled forces that they have unleashed result in an onslaught against them? Putting it somewhat differently, would beauty be spared by the beast and would traditional Judaism survive? A gut-level reaction to such fearful questions was probably "Why take any chances?" It seemed safer for the trembling Judaic beauty not to fall into the clutches of the new Zionist beast to begin with. Judaism could probably survive without the Golem of Zionism, while the Lord could take care of anti-Semitism as he in his infinite wisdom deemed best.

In Rothberg's fantasy, the similarity between the need for a Golem and the need for Zionism is manifest. For instance, Rabbi Löw was compelled to engage in a public debate with Brother Thaddeus. It is indeed a historical fact that throughout the centuries many Jewish rabbis were forced to engage in public theological debates, in which it was prudent for the rabbi to lose while making a creditable stand. Winning would spell trouble from the dominant Christian majority, while losing overwhelmingly could be too demoralizing for the Jews. In this particular fictional debate, Rothberg put these words in Rabbi Löw's mouth: ". . . you offered us only three bleak choices: annihilation, expulsion, or conversion." These "choices" are familiar and were discussed by Hilberg (1967) in his monumental work on the Nazi Holocaust. He asserted that since the fourth century there have been three major anti-Jewish policies: conversion, expulsion, and annihilation. The implication is clear. Holocaustal threats have been with the Jews for a long time. Such dangers induced Rabbi Löw to create the Golem, but this solution went awry. More recently these same threats prompted Jews to pin their hopes on Zionism. This new political power proved more forceful than the Golem, and unlike the Golem, this modern force was not controlled by rabbis. What is more, in the age of "never again a holocaust," Zionism must succeed and must not share the fate of the Golem.

But what happens when people who are vulnerable to human error control immense power? Jews were sensitized to such threats because the release of enormous powers usually hurt them, whether it was occasioned by Gentiles or Jews. In the seventeenth century the Jews were traumatized physically by the cossack hordes of Chmielnicki and emotionally by the aborted mass messianism of Sabbatai Zevi. But the dread of the release of uncontrolled powers is not merely a Jewish but a general human concern. Norbert Wiener, the American mathematician and father of cybernetics, was preoccupied with this issue. In *God and Golem, Inc.*, he reflected on the enormous implications of recent technological developments. He discussed machines which learn and which can reproduce themselves, and searched for the proper relationship between such sophisticated machines and man. His reflections led him to conclude that the machine "is the modern counterpart of the Golem of the Rabbi of Prague." He thus identified the question of control as a central issue. Nor is this surprising, when God, man, and machine all have the ability to create in their own image.

Wiener's idea of the machine's being the Golem was picked up by Gershom Scholem. After Israeli scientists designed and built the first Israeli computer in the Weizmann Institute at Rehovot, Scholem proposed that it be named Golem Aleph. His suggestion was accepted on the condition that he deliver the dedication speech. He agreed and on June 17, 1965, he dedicated the computer with a speech titled "The Golem of Prague and the Golem of Rehovot." In it, he reminded his listeners that Kabbalistic writings warn against making a Golem and link the death of God to the realization of the idea of the Golem. The implication is that if man does what God did, then man replaces God. But can he? Can he really control his creation or is he bound to serve that which he created to serve him? Scholem did not presume to have all the answers. He finished his speech with a humorous, yet serious, note: "So I resign myself and say to the Golem and its creator: develop peacefully and don't destroy the world. *Shalom* (Peace)."

The theme of world destruction also occupied the psychoanalyst Harry Slochower, who warned against the danger of a new type of fascism—"the computerized Goiem"—which could result in a new "final solution" for the human race. These particular symbols of world destruction are imbedded in Jewish history and folklore so as to have special meaning for Jews. In spite of the yearly celebration of Passover, Jews suspect that whenever uncontrolled forces are unleashed, the destruction will not "pass over" them. Surely the havoc of the Second World War, which included the Holocaust, testifies to the fact that the miracle of Passover is not a recurrent phenomenon.

It was this fear of uncontrolled outbursts which prompted Jews to pin more of their hopes on Gentile leaders than on the Gentile masses, whom they distrusted most (Arendt). The distrust, however, was aimed at other Jews as well if the latter were to serve as the instrument for the breakout of gigantic forces. The religious messiahs were viewed with deep suspicion and so was the new breed of Zionist messiah, Theodor Herzl. Jewish history suggests that the modern fears of being destroyed by mechanical forces and/or impersonal political forces were foreshadowed by the Jewish dread of messianism, including Zionism. Zionism must have looked like an impending second deluge, God's punishment to sinful man. It seemed that Zionism could destroy that which it wanted to protect. It was too political, secular, imitative of Gentile ways, and plainly too mundane. Thus, it was too sinful and too enchanted with power to be the right salvation for Jewry. Even if it succeeded in gaining the political clout it sought, the results could be too impersonal and mechanical for the people who above all else served the Lord. Somehow Zionism's victory could spell defeat and its messianic fulfillment could mean the end of the Jewish people.

This tension between Zionism and the Orthodox Jewish way is still very much alive. From an Orthodox vantage point, Zionism is to Judaism as the Golem is to man. The former should serve the latter and never rebel. And when its service is over, there will come time for it to die. God willing, Zionism will serve as the instrument of God, as King Cyrus once did. But Zionists are already behaving like Golems who disregard their creator, when they clamor for separation of synagogue and State. They forget that Zionism came into being to serve Judaism, and that Judaism was not created in order to give birth to Zionism. If one loosely imagines this problem as a Jewish variation of the "beauty and the beast" theme, then what this viewpoint implies is that Judaic beauty ought to survive the inevitable death of the Zionist beast. One cannot let beasts run around loose, just as one cannot afford to let huge forces rage out of control. The computerized Golem—whether it stands for modern automation, impersonal political powers, or Jewish secular nationalism—must be deactivated.

It is because Zionism represented chiefly secular nationalism that it evoked such alarm in Orthodox quarters. Nationalism in itself, however, was well within the realm of the religious heritage. The one and only God of Israel set his eyes on the Chosen People and gave them the Promised Land. This is nationalism par excellence under the auspices of the mighty Lord. Under the umbrella of religion, nationalism could continue to remain a controlled force: the divine laws of the God of Israel had to be obeyed at all times, but a national salvation was destined for the future when God finally wills it so. National cravings therefore received religious sanction, but were also held in check.

Independent, secular nationalism, however, was another matter. It was not sanctioned and it was not successfully checked; therefore it was an unholy and dangerous eruption. As seen through Orthodox eyes, the modern crisis of faith produced hordes of rationalists and even skepticists who rode high on the waves of ungodly nationalism. The unrestrained secular multitudes could stir up the tides of godless nationalism to such heights that they would force all tempestuous human emotions to run their full course. Lacking fear of the Almighty, the secular multitudes were bound to let human frailty triumph and self-destruction succeed. After all, even within the bounds of religion the monster of nationalism was able to cause eruptive destructions in the form of false messianism. Outside religious boundaries, the monster was completely free to devour foolish men. Thus, the tragic crisis of faith has already bred its first poisonous fruit—secular nationalism. A crisis of faith, however, is not altogether a new phenomenon in Jewish history.

In the second half of the twelfth century, Moses Maimonides faced a contemporary crisis of faith which he dealt with by writing his book *The Guide of the Perplexed*. The similarities and differences between that crisis and the issues which perplex Zionism today are worth noting, and shed additional light on the difficult problem of the relationship of Judaism to Zionism. The "perplexed" for whom Maimonides wrote his book were a small minority of people who had both Jewish religious education and philosophical as well as scientific knowledge. They had learned enough to become doubtful and dissatisfied with traditional religion, but were not yet secure in their new knowledge on two major counts. The first was how to integrate the sciences and philosophy into a view of the universe that was not fraught with uncertainties. The second was how to conduct themselves in relation to "the multitudes" who remained within the bounds of naive faith. Thus the Guide was written to be the bearer of great secrets to the perplexed few, and

Maimonides took extensive precautions to ensure that the common people would not be exposed to the manuscript and would not be able to decipher it.

Maimonides took care of the first question mentioned above by providing an integrated philosophical view of the world, consisting mainly of basic Aristotelian doctrines sprinkled with later neo-Platonic notions. In spite of its touches of mysticism, it is basically a rational and largely pantheistic view which starts with the world as a given. Maimonides drew attention to the philosophical postulation of the eternity of the world and contrasted it with the alternate view of its creation in time. The second view needs God the creator while the first view does not. Maimonides made it clear that both views are acceptable although there are reasons to assume that the second or religious view is more plausible. Yet even his manifest statements constitute heresy since they admit the plausibility of that view which dispenses with the religious God of creation. Even more heretical was his implicit message, which was aimed at the minority of people who were educated in the sciences and philosophy. The gist of the message was that the philosophical view is the correct one while the alternate religious view is designed to fit the needs of the multitudes whose understanding is limited.

The second major question was dealt with by Maimonides on a pragmatic social level. His guideline was that since the multitudes cannot comprehend philosophy or live by it, they should not be exposed to it. They should never transcend religion because of its important social functions. Even pagan religions share these useful functions. It is religion which enables people to congregate in peace and to arrive at a limited understanding of divine matters. It therefore follows that the community is in a sense divided into many common people and a few learned philosophers. Most people "adhere to the law," meaning the Jewish religious law. In contrast, a small minority lives by "our opinion," that is, the opinion of the philosophers. The responsibility of the philosopher is to provide leadership and guidance to the multitudes on both religious and social matters. The few enlightened philosophers are not entitled to dwell only in the realms of philosophic truth, there to enjoy their secret and hard-won knowledge. Their wisdom dictates that they follow the example of dutiful leadership that was once set up in Plato's writings.

The philosopher in Plato's *Republic* returned from the sunlight back into the shadows of the cave. He had to teach the cave dwellers that the world of shadows was not the true world of reality. He also had to take care not to inflict pain by exposing the inhabitants to too much sunlight. In like fashion, Maimonides taught that all accomplished philosophers should assume the guidance of common people and take care to gauge this guidance to the limited potential of the masses. The aim was not to cause pain from too much "sunlight" but to strengthen social and religious laws as well as to help the community to thrive. The dissemination of philosophic knowledge was therefore to be curtailed. Speculative philosophy was to serve as the guide for the precious few, the philosopher-kings, so to speak. The latter could even enlighten the masses with crude explanations of certain speculative truths such as that all corporeal attributes of God should be negated. But on the whole, speculative philosophy was to be kept out of sight of the masses.

To fulfill his obligation to the multitudes, Maimonides wrote in Hebrew the *Second Torah*. By gathering and arranging the scattered talmudic law, he planned to guide the multitudes in living according to the religious law. Thus, he was fulfilling his duty as a philosopher just as his esteemed predecessor, Moses, once did. Moses had given Jews the first Torah and now Moses Maimonides gave them the second Torah. Eventually it was said of him that "from Moses to Moses there has not been anyone like Moses." While the *Second Torah* was written in Hebrew, the *Guide of the Perplexed* was deliberately written in Arabic. This insured its accessibility to philosophers but kept it out of reach for the multitudes. As a further safety precaution, Maimonides scrambled the book, making it difficult to pick up the continued discussion of each particular point. This confusing disorganization could have been attributed to an inability to integrate material rather than to deliberate obfuscation, if it were not for the fact that the Maimonides of the Guide is also the Maimonides of *Second Torah*. There he proved himself as a great systematizer and organizer of voluminous but scattered material. It stands to reason, therefore, that the ideas in the Guide were deliberately presented in a disorganized fashion.

On face value, the material in *The Guide of the Perplexed* is frightfully disorganized and could further confuse rather than guide the perplexed. But the book is not chaotic and those readers who were familiar with philosophical treatises were not doomed to confusion. It is full of guiding references to points which were discussed before. It also includes promises to pick up in the future matters which are dropped at present. What is more, to keep the readers motivated, the book frequently alerts them to the fact that certain points contain great secrets. The secrets are in effect the results of speculative philosophy. Maimonides' frequent allusions to them as secrets suggest that he regarded them as most valuable but dangerous conclusions which should remain the hidden possession of those few who were thoroughly educated in the sciences and philosophy.

One way of finding where Maimonides stood is to compare his treatment of the biblical texts with that of the Aristotelian texts. The biblical expressions are repeatedly allegorized, symbolized, and reinterpreted to denote Aristotelian notions, but not vice versa. In other words, the two sources of truth, that of religious revelation and philosophic speculation, were not treated the same. The former was deprived of its original meaning in order to suit the latter. From Maimonides' formal point of view, no misinterpretation was involved since both sources expressed the same truth, only in different languages. Therefore, demonstrating how the Bible alludes to the results of philosophic speculations is but an explanation of what is already there. Yet Maimonides never twisted and turned Aristotelian expressions in order to make them conform to biblical pronouncements.

The Guide evoked bitter controversy and was even banned and burned. Orthodox Jewry did not appreciate the elevation of a heretical philosophy to the status of "truth" or the identification of religions as the cement which binds members of each society in a peaceful, lawful, and somewhat enlightened state. The fact that to the "multitudes" religion was indispensable for social coexistence and for limited intellectual elevation was a poor consolation. While for the multitudes religion is God-sent, for the elite minority it represents merely crude approximations of more refined speculative truths. From this vantage point, both religion and philosophy were needed but the priceless jewel was philosophy, not religion. This message was not lost on Orthodox Jews. They rejected the recommendation of secular rationalism as the truth for the few and the prescription of religion as the socializer of the many.

Maimonides did not regard religion as the opiate of the masses, however. He saw in it an indispensable potent tool for the education of the multitudes within the limits of their comprehension and capability. It was therefore the rational duty of the philosopher to contribute his share to this process of social and intellectual public education. As for the crisis of faith that beset the philosophical few, it could be treated in secret. The enigmas and anxieties which accompanied philosophical education were not the problem of the masses and did not have to come into the open.

In contrast, Zionism arose to a significant degree because of a crisis of faith among the masses. It now faces the enigmatic task of securing Judaic continuity among multitudes who have lost faith in religion. The crisis cannot be settled by a secret prescription for the few. In this day and age there are multitudes of believers as well as multitudes of nonbelievers. The course of action that each group adopts cannot remain a secret. Modern guides for the perplexed, such as Bialik's advocacy of the Kinus, are bound to be in Hebrew and clearly elucidated for the masses. But the public search for new solutions is stalled. The situation is temporarily frozen with the famous political "status quo" in the Israeli government concerning the degree to which religious institutions serve as state institutions. This status quo secures the power gains of each camp and is presumed to serve as protection from a disastrous culture war. For the time being, this fear is used as a powerful rationalization which enables secular Zionism to bide its time and to try to complete without interruptions its initial overriding goal of full national renascence for the Jewish people.

The essence of the Zionist revolution was the reclaiming of the Jewish right to live as a nation. The accent was not on religious reawakening, or on ethnic renascence, but on national revival. That is why the notion of "ingathering of the exiles" was so important for Zionism. After all, just "religious" Jews can freely practice their religion in any democratic country outside Israel and are not compelled to regard aliyah as a religious must. This fact is not palatable to Israeli Zionists and they sometimes try to refute it. Ben Gurion fought American Jews in vain over this issue. In the 1950s he repeatedly claimed that only in Israel can a Jew live like a full Jew in the religious sense. But in spite of his quoting the Talmud to support this contention, he remained unconvincing. By and large, religion can be practiced anywhere while nationality must be tied to a territory. The Zionist call for ingathering in the ancestral land was first and foremost a call to correct a national, not religious, abnormality.

Yet a clear-cut Israeli emphasis on the national meaning of Zionism could be counterproductive. Such an emphasis could be effective in Russia but is not likely to succeed in the United States. In societies that persecute them, Jews are likely to feel that they belong to a separate national entity. For instance, many Russian Jews feel that their true nationality is Israeli, for in Israel they would be accepted, rather than Russian, for in Russia they learn in both crude and subtle ways that they do not belong. Therefore, if Russia were to lift all restrictions on emigration, an Israeli national appeal to Russian Jewry would result in mass aliyah.

This is not so in the United States. As a rule, American Jews feel and think of themselves as American. Their feelings of uncertainty relate not to their being American nationals but to the nature of their being Jewish. When implored by their "fellow nationals" to join them in Israel, the majority of American Jews reject the appeal. American Jews resent the chutzpah of Israelis who tell them how they ought to feel. They know what they feel and they are not under duress to change. They feel that they have special ties to Israel by virtue of religious and/or ethnic heritage. It is because of this feeling that Israeli emotional claims on American Jewry have to be based on a blend of religious, ethnic, and also national ingredients. Reliance on pure national appeal invites mass rejection. It could yield a small trickle of immigration but it would be tantamount to giving up on the dream of mass ingathering of the American exiles into Zion.

Hence, there is a strong intuitive reluctance in Israel to separate state from synagogue. Such an official separation would give American Jewry a final way out of the most central of all Zionist obligations—

an aliyah to Israel. If it is an officially acknowledged fact that Jewish nationality and Jewish religion are two separate entities, then most American Jews are likely to forego aliyah not only in practice but even in theory. They will declare themselves as Americans of Jewish persuasion and ask Israelis to kindly keep nationality out of their communications. But if the Israeli appeal is based on the special circumstances of a hopeless entanglement of national religious and ethnic Jewish identity, then the appeal cannot be rejected out of hand.

The result is cognitive inconsistency concerning the relation between religion and state. One yardstick is applied to other countries while the opposite is applied to Israel. In every country except Israel, Jews ardently support the separation of state and church. Without such a separation, the adopted state religion is not likely to be a Jewish "church," which could place the Jewish religion in a disadvantageous position. That is why in the name of freedom and democracy Jews insist on keeping state and church apart, except in Israel. There is no separation of synagogue and state in Israel, but there are plenty of apologies concerning the reasons why. Presumably, the special nature of Jewish nationality is that it is so inextricably interwoven with Jewish religion that separation of the two is either impossible or at least very destructive. The implication is that what is fair for other countries is not fair for Israel. But it is highly unlikely that the separation of state and synagogue would hinder Orthodox Jews from free practice of their religion. Nor is it likely that such a separation would dilute the national zeal of secular Israelis. Yet the opponents of separation advance the belief that unless the two are mixed, everything will fall apart. It is an illogical but nevertheless effective argument, because it touches on the dread of what could follow such a separation.

The threat of *kulturkampf* gives Israelis the shudders. It evokes historical associations of tragic bickering among rival Jewish factions which delivers them into the hands of their common non-Jewish enemies. These historical associations are not going to be dismissed lightly as long as a state of war exists between Israel and the surrounding Arab countries. They therefore strengthen the hand of those who want to avert a culture war at all costs. The threat is usually discussed in two basic terms The first is the estrangement of Diaspora Jewry from the

Israeli mainland, which is allegedly bound to result if synagogue is separated from state. The estrangement would be based on religious feelings and not on national sentiments. For instance, most Jews might find it hard to swallow the fact that civil marriages sanctify the union of Jewish couples and includes them in the body of Israel. In fact, however, most Russian and American Jews do not cling to the conviction that those who are not married by an Orthodox rabbi segregate themselves and their descendants from the congregation of Israel. An additonal argument concerning the effects on Diaspora Jewry is that the Israeli example of civil marriages would open the floodgates for mixed marriages in the Diaspora. American Jewish leaders are indeed worried about the increasing rate of mixed marriages. However, the dating patterns on American campuses do not seem to be a function of the presence or absence of an Israeli constitution which separates synagogue from state. So far there is a glaring absence of a written constitution because of the historical stiff opposition of the religious parties and the fear of *kulturkampf* on the part of the secular political parties (See Zucker). In conclusion, it seems that the argument of the danger of an estranged Jewish Diaspora is not valid and is used as an excuse by those Israelis who wish to protect the status quo of no separation.

The second context in which the threat of *kulturkampf* is discussed is the development of an unbridgeable schism within the Israeli society itself. Civil marriages will not be recognized by the religious law and will create whole families of people who are disqualified from marrying religious Jews. Therefore, two segregated communities will evolve and the national unity will be dealt a body blow. Yet the secular majority in the Israeli population could elect to let the religious segment worry about segregation. When a furor was created because Jewish congregations from Ethiopia and from India were disqualified from marrying Jews, the rabbis finally found ways to circumvent the issue. So there are ways in which the rabbinate could adapt to the demands of modern Israeli reality. Some rules can remain unenforced by simply refraining from inquiries which might reveal facts which violate them. Other rules can be reinterpreted or cancelled on the authority of contemporary rabbis who have to cope with modern circumstances. But thus far the secular majority has not elected to toss the issue of national unity back into the lap of Orthodox Jews. Ben Gurion explained his capitulation in the 1950s to the religious minority in terms of concern for the feelings of Oriental Jews who were immigrating en masse to Israel. They were largely religious and it would have been more difficult to integrate them into a society with only a secular law. This "explanation" is questionable even for the 1950s and is certainly not going to hold good for generations to come.

As mentioned above, one reason for the mass capitulation of the secular majority to the demands of the religious minority is the reluctance to give up a good claim for aliyah. If Diaspora Jews are given the opportunity to espouse Jewish religion but to disavow Jewish nationality, they may elect to stay where they are. An added reason for the capitulation is the desire to extend Israel's borders. The appetite for more territories can conveniently rest its claim on old religious promises. Of course, not all the ardent supporters of the Greater Israel Movement are deeply religious. However, since religion supports their aspiration, why should they grapple with religion exactly at this point of time?

This opportunism by secular Israelis used to incense Kurzweil, who over the years complained in articles published in *Ha'aretz* that the name of the God of Israel is being cynically misused by nonbelievers. But corruption of personal integrity which results in exploitation of the Divine Name is not confined to secular Jews. It has now spread to the religious authorities who are willing to lend God's name to the political schemes of the Israeli hawks. The result of this growing process is a stultified rabbinate which is becoming less able to respond to the enormous challenge of adapting Judaic laws to the needs of modern reality (See Zohar). There is a historical irony about this 180-degree turn which the rabbis took. They now willingly place the Divine Name under the tongue of modern and militant Israeli nationalism and endow its aspirations with God's blessing. In return, they receive their fair share of power. Both sides render favors to each other. One side supplies "in the name of God" certificates while the other side provides governmental IOU's. Presumably these paper documents are palatable when placed under the tongue. Yet, in this corruption game who is a Rabbi and who is a Golem?

The prophetic Weizmann, one of the wisest and most pragmatic of Zionist leaders, had a clear premonition of things to come. In his autobiography he made a few forecasts which still hold. Concerning the Israeli state, he said that ". . . it cannot put the clock back by making religion the cardinal principle in the conduct of the state." With regard to the rabbinate he stated: "It is the new, secularized type of rabbi, resembling somewhat a member of a clerical party in Germany, France, or Belgium, who is the menace, and who will make a heavy bid for power by parading his religious convictions." Lastly, he said: "There shall be a great struggle. I foresee something which will perhaps be reminiscent of the *kulturkampf* in Germany, but we must be firm if we are to survive." I tend to agree with Weizmann's premonitions.

It is apparent that the secular supernationalists in Israel benefit from the growing politicization of religion there. They are therefore in no rush to lock horns with the Israeli theocrats. Even though they do not appreciate the clericalization of the state they can afford to wait. Thus they respond to the widespread feeling that the task of national rebuilding which has always been the major Zionist goal, is not yet complete, and that it should therefore continue to come first. They want Jewish nationalism to thrive now and they feel that its purification from religious mumbo jumbo can come later. The strong sentiment that the Zionist national buildup still has a long way to go was intensified after the Six Day War. Yet the conviction that the establishment of the State of Israel did not finish the task of Zionism was there all along. This feeling relates to the dialectic gravitations toward political and spiritual orientations which seem to form the warp and weft of Jewish history.

That the task of Zionism was regarded as incomplete even after Israel came into being can be learned from the choice of a name for the new state. The name which stirred Jewish hearts all along was Eretz Yisrael, or the Land of Israel. It was an insult to Jews that during the days of the British Mandate the Hebrew inscription on coins was Palestinah while Eretz Yisrael was allowed to be inscribed only in parenthesis and in abbreviation. Yet in 1948 the term Eretz Yisrael did not become the name of the new country. Instead, the name "the State of Israel" was adopted. Obviously the State of Israel was not nearly as big as the original Land of Israel. The choice of name thus clearly drew a distinction between the actual achievement and the larger hope for complete ingathering of all the Jewish exiles in the entire Land of Israel. The distinction is made equally clear in the national anthem, which is called "The Hope." In it, Israelis still vow the following:

> Our hope is not lost,
> The two thousand year hope
> To be a free nation in our land,
> The land of Zion, Jerusalem.

"Hatikvah" was the anthem of "the state on the way," and it made eminent sense then. But at face value it is nonsensical for independent Israelis to sing with gusto that their hope to become a free nation in their land is not lost. It is possible to advance the notion that historical anthems become symbolic and sacred and should therefore not be replaced even if their wording is somewhat outdated. Yet after the creation of the Israeli state there was plenty of talk about changing the national anthem. So its traditional sacred status did not seem a sufficient reason for maintaining an outdated slogan. That it was retained in the poststate era is an indication that it was not outdated after all. "The hope" was only partly fulfilled; ever since 1949 there has been a keen awareness that much more immigration is needed, and ever since 1967 there has been a growing conviction that much more territory is also needed. The story of the Israeli national anthem betrays a persistent feeling that only when the entire nation of Israel resides in the complete Land of Israel will "the hope" be fulfilled. Then, and only then, it will be appropriate to replace the national anthem.

Thus, for reasons of national buildup, *kulturkampf* is to be avoided even at great costs. Because of this basic conviction, nagging issues of democracy remain unrectified and sufferings by innocent individuals are allowed to stand (See Aloni). It has been a repeated embarrassment that the giving of state power to the religious laws proved undemocratic. Yet the need to complete the national Zionist dream seems overriding and compels inaction in this matter. However, the paucity of political action does not mean that emotions in response to this situation are also at a standstill. It is not hard to detect a great deal of rage which is building up between those who want a secular state law and those who want the *halakhah* to be the state law. The issue is not out of sight and out of mind although a blend of unconscious repression and conscious suppression keeps the lid on the surging turmoil. The dreaded culture war is thus being avoided like a plague. Nevertheless, when it finally erupts, its effects rather than being sickening may prove to be cathartic. Be that as it may, the current smoldering rage is unlikely to stay indefinitely in a relatively stable state.

The postponement of a *kulturkampf* and the growing collaboration between religious fanatics and nationalist fanatics is an ominous fact for the Arabs. The obsession with the primary task of completing the national buildup dampens the feelings of empathy toward the Arab antagonists, because the buildup would have to be accomplished at the Arabs' expense. Any future Zionist drive to control the whole of Eretz Yisrael from Sinai to Mesopotamia would inevitably nullify Arab rights. Not only is such a course of action immoral, but also risky. The complex political and military reactions on the part of Arabs as well as non-Arabs could put Israel in a position of facing another Masada stand. Those Israelis who are motivated by old myths as well as by new territorial appetites are predisposed to gamble with death. What is so tragic about this surge of chauvinistic dreams is that even a "successful" outcome would be hollow. After all, if Israel ever extends "from the river of Egypt to the great river, the river Euphrates," the reaction of the Arabs would be equally biblical. They would say "The Lord will have war with Israel from generation to generation." Consequently, a "successful" outcome would be beset by chronic difficulties and cast the Israelis in a too "un-Jewish" role. It therefore seems likely that as Israel travels along that chauvinistic route it must at some point apply the brakes. Self-induced inhibition is likely to do it. Indeed, the explosion of a *kulturkampf* could signal the waning of Israeli chauvinism and the waxing of empathy and peaceful intents toward the Arabs.

The mere potential for a culture war indicates the existence of sharp differences in self-concept among Israelis, which carry far-reaching implications. The three basic conceptions that could shape the future orientation of Jewish identity are the religious, the national, and the ethnic. These definitions, in turn, differ in their basic assumptions, in their implications concerning the Diaspora, and in their vigor and vitality.

The cornerstone of Jewish religion is belief in the personal guid-

ance of the Lord of Hosts. The children of Israel believe that the Lord
chose them to be his people. Thus, the notion of distinct peoplehood
or even nationhood is imbedded in the Jewish religion. However, the
worship of God comes first. The Jews are a distinct people only because
they are God's Chosen People. Therefore, if religious worship is abandoned, Jewish distinctiveness goes with it. Contemporary secular Jews
no longer adhere to this Orthodox viewpoint. Yet the religious definition is the oldest of the three conceptions of identity and originally
encompassed all of them. Centuries ago, having a unique religion also
meant membership in a distinct cultural and political group. But after
the appearance of Christianity and, later, Islam, the situation of the
Jews became quite uncommon. Had there been many Jewish nations
warring with each other as Christian nations did, there might have
developed a sharper dividing line between various Jewish nationalities
and between them and the Jewish religion. Had there been just one
undemolished Jewish state in one land plus many Jewish communities
in other countries, the dividing line between religion and nationality
could have been clearly drawn. But Jewish history did not unfold that
way. For a stateless and scattered people, it was religion which preserved Jewish existence as a separate collective. The national elements
within the Jewish religion remained confined to a messianic mood and
yearning for redemption which includes both religious salvation and
national rectification. This confinement ended when the confinement
of Jews within ghetto walls ended. The national elements within the
Jewish religion finally acquired separate demarcation as a result of the
modern crisis of faith as well as rising waves of nationalism. Since then,
Jewish nationalism has become increasingly capable of battling Jewish
religion for dominance.

Thus, religion is not as powerful a force as it once was. But even
though it is on the decline it remains a vigorous factor in Judaism. It
not only has direct and conscious effects on its adherents but it also
retains an influence on nonpracticing Jews. This influence is exerted
through the indirect and largely unconscious impact of potent symbols
which sustain not only religion but also nationality. Their impact has
sometimes been paradoxical. For instance, the secular Zionist rebels
who in their youth espoused a tough antireligious line now evidence
regression to Orthodox Jewishness and to accommodation with the

rabbinate (Elon). The expected conservatism of old age may have something to do with it, but there is more to it than that. Symbols that were originally rooted in religion were the driving power behind the secular Zionist revolt. Therefore, the lifelong Zionists who in their youth rescued Zion or God's bride from desolation now manifest a persistent reluctance to give up on religion. Thus, religion shows admirable vigor though not refreshing vitality. For the time being it does not seem to offer creative solutions, but it by no means is about to expire. Its stamina should come as no surprise to those who accept the implication by Maimonides that religion will always be needed by the multitudes to make socialization possible.

Each of the three conceptualizations of Jewish identity has implications concerning the status of the Diaspora. From the religious point of view, the Diaspora is a legitimate phenomenon. The long Jewish history includes examples of the fruitful contiguous existence of one Jewish center in Eretz Yisrael and other dominant Jewish centers in Babylon or Egypt. It was the Babylonian Talmud which became so comprehensive that it overshadowed the Talmud of Jerusalem. There is therefore nothing new or alarming if today leading Jewish authorities on the religious law reside both in Israel and in America. Indeed, it is not seriously contested by religious Jews that the Lord of the universe can be served devoutly anywhere. From the religious vantage point, the existence of a Diaspora is an old and legitimate fact of life.

In contrast, the many ardent Zionists who are revolted by the Galut mentality of Diaspora Jews are driven by nationalism rather than religion. They think that the Zionist task of "negation of the Galut" ought to be completed and that the best way to get rid of this obnoxious mentality is simply to do away with the despicable Galut itself. For religious adherents, ending the Diaspora is an option but not a necessity; what is a necessity is for religious law to become full-fledged Israeli state law. This is not the case for proponents of nationality. For them, the Diaspora represents a remnant of past abnormality which should be remedied by aliyah. What is more, the law of the modern Israeli state should be secular, not religious. Religion and nationality are therefore bound to clash, but the final battle is being postponed. The secular nationalists want aliyah as well as a secular state law. However, in their order of priorities aliyah and negation of the Diaspora come first, and a certain amount of clericalism is tolerated for the time being. For now, pushing for a separation of powers looks like putting the cart before the horse. When it no longer looks that way, the day of reckoning will come. At that time a clear-cut national ascendancy over religion will be asserted, *kulturkampf* or no.

The reason for the different implications concerning Israel and the Diaspora is that religion and nationality stem from different basic assumptions. For religion, God comes first, while for nationality, the nation is an article of faith. Therefore, for religious persons, the secular state law is a passing fad as compared to the eternal validity of the Torah. But for secular persons the eternal yoke of the Torah is a burden which can be assumed voluntarily but cannot be imposed by the power of the state. In the meantime, the disparity between the accepted convictions of the public majority and the requirements of the law of the land is wide and confusing (See Roshwald). The end result is that respect for the arbitrary laws is diminishing, while concern for freedom and democracy becomes "politics" and is dealt with in terms of taking expedient measures to preserve a ruling coalition, and secular and religious law both suffer from the mingling of the two.

The third major conception of Jewish identity is the ethnic one. The vaguest of the three, it is usually referred to in terms of a broad cultural heritage and a set of moral values. Its meaning is not as clear as that of the national or religious definitions. For instance, Sigmund Freud was an ethnic Jew. He was not a religious Jew, not the person who discussed religion under the title "the future of an illusion." Neither was he a Jewish nationalist. He never espoused Zionism and he did not aspire to live in the Land of Israel. In his address to the Viennese society of B'nai B'rith on May 6, 1926, he said that what bound him to Jewry was neither faith nor national pride but many obscure emotional forces residing in the safe privacy of a common mental construction.

Obviously Freud discarded the notion of having either a religious or a national Jewish identity. What was left in his "safe privacy" cannot be asserted for certain. It probably included oedipal bonds to parents and to cultural images that accompanied him from the cradle. It probably also consisted of that ill-defined sense of group-belongingness which we loosely term "ethnic identity." What we witness in Freud's statement is the vagueness of what is roughly the ethnic definition. Even while being discarded, faith and nationality are briefly mentioned by him as concepts whose meanings are shared by people. But when it comes to that which is left over after religion and nationality are rejected, a quality of vagueness emerges. People who share this identity have "a common mental construction" but their identity consists of "many obscure emotional forces."

Since the ethnic definition is the vaguest of the three, it is the ethnic Jew who is liable to feel most frequently that he is a Jew because non-Jews identify him as such. A Jew who clings to nationality knows that he is an actual or potential member of the Israeli nation. He is different from others not because others keep reminding him of this, but because he has his own definition concerning his difference. Similarly, a religious Jew understands where he stands. He believes in the God of Israel. He too, therefore, knows very well how he differs from other people. But the Jew who adheres to neither of these two definitions is left with a vaguely defined sense of belonging to a group as well as a feeling of some inexplicable difference from non-Jews.

The lack of definiteness of the ethnic identity puts its vigor into question. Ethnic identity can linger on, but it always seems like an anemic leftover that is still available for those persons who shy away from the more forceful national and religious definitions of Jewish identity. Perforce, this "leftover" definition must rely on the more general, humanistic, and universal elements in Judaism. Otherwise, it could not accommodate the needs of those who can embrace only a broad cultural but also ill-defined feeling of Jewishness. Thus a decent American ethnic Jew knows that people should neither be discriminated against nor oppressed. He also knows that it has been the proud distinction of the Jewish people that they were ardent in their devotion to the humanistic ideal of freedom and equality for all. So he carries on this tradition. But it reaches a point where the commendable humanistic ideals are rooted mostly in the elements of universalism in Judaism. Sometimes the ideals may not even be specifically Jewish while the distinctive mark of Jewishness becomes the tradition of an unusual devotion to them.

When it reaches this point, we encounter Jews whose frame of reference transcends Judaism and who are exposed to more than one culture. This condition may result in an unusual strength or else, ironically, in weakness. Isaac Deutscher characterized Jews who transcend Judaism and live in more than one culture as "non-Jewish Jews." Their opportunity to view matters with more than one set of cultural glasses enables them to arrive at remarkable insights and to experience creative leaps. One of his prime examples was Freud. Many factors have undoubtedly contributed to Freud's genius, but a convincing case has been made to the effect that one of them was exposure to the Jewish mystical tradition (Bakan). Another "non-Jewish Jew" was Isaac Deutscher himself. He probably believed that his contributions to the understanding of the Russian Revolution and its leaders were largely due to the fact that he was not just Jewish or Polish, not living within the exclusive confines of any single tradition.

The vitality that characterizes Jews of multicultural exposure is frequently not invested in contributions to the enhancement of Jewish identity. The vigor that Freud derived from being exposed to Jewish and other cultures was used to create the psychoanalytic theory concerning the nature of humankind, not to enhance Jewishness. His Jewish ethnic identity endowed him with energies which he invested largely in non-Jewish contributions. However, regardless of the direction of its final use, the vitality that results from exposure to more than one culture is a well-known phenomenon.

Yet there is the other effect too, not of invigorating but of enfeebling. As we all know, Jewish ethnic identity can sometimes become wishy-washy indeed. Some Jews in the United States, for example, are pushed toward Jewishness because others identify them as Jewish, and are pulled toward it by questionable cultural and social customs. Their feeling of Jewishness is anchored in the consumption of lox and bagels, in the use of the health club of the Jewish center more than its synagogue, and in sending the children to a Jewish summer camp. When Prime Minister Golda Meir made official visits to the United States, these Jews sent requests for her recipe for chicken soup— requests that were deftly answered on her behalf by members of her staff. Thus, in a historically provocative moment two suggestive symbols meet—Golda Meir and chicken soup. The Prime Minister represents the vigor of Israeli nationalism. In contrast, the recipe stands for a deteriorated quality of ethnic identity. There is not much vigor in chicken-soup Judaism.

In a sense, what we witness among ethnic Jews is the old division between the knowledgeable few and the uninquisitive many that was once drawn by Maimonides. Those who think for themselves, and whose thinking does not turn them into national or religious Jews, become universal men (in Russia they would be called "rootless cosmopolitans"). These "non-Jewish Jews" find a field of endeavor where they can further the frontiers of knowledge. Noam Chomsky's use of his knowledge of Hebrew grammar to effect a revolution in linguistics serves as a prominent example of this. On the other hand, the multitudes need traditional prescriptions to live by as they did in Maimonides' time. These prescriptions are filled by a holiday here, an occasional Sabbath celebration there, Sunday school for the kids where they learn meager Hebrew that they will mostly forget, and Jewish cooking. For them a recipe for matzo balls serves as a recipe for how to be a Jew. The multitudes always seem to need prescriptions to live by. They can think for themselves to a certain point and no farther.

In the past, religion supplied most of the prescriptions. At present, many Jews need other prescriptions. In this respect they have different options, depending on whether they live in Israel or the Diaspora. In today's Israel a person can readily fall back on nationality if religion is not his bag. But a Diaspora Jew does not have this option unless he is willing to uproot his life, immigrate to Israel, and start afresh there. Not many American Jews are willing to take this step. Therefore, nonreligious Jews usually fall back on ethnic consciousness. It is not an impressive "inner identity" or "common mental construction," to use Freud's language. But it can linger on. People can stick with unimpressive notions if they can live with them. The more impressive and energizing concepts are the religious and the national. The major battle for Jewish souls is therefore being waged between nationality and religion, while most ethnic Jews are potential members of either, depending on historical developments.

We have seen that different conceptualizations of Jewish identity impart a different status to the Diaspora. The merit of the Diaspora is also tied, at least implicitly, to value judgments concerning the historical Jewish condition of marginality. Recently, American Jewish writers and Israeli writers carried on a symposium on the sources of Jewish creativity, and the debate focused on the role of the condition of marginality. It is fair to say that if marginality is viewed as a condition that fosters creativity and cultural productivity, an implication could be drawn that the Diaspora, which exposes Jews to more than one culture, should be upheld. This does not mean, however, that every person who sees merit in the Diaspora is also enthusiastic about the condition of marginality or about ethnic Jews whose creativity lies outside the realms of Judaism. In an apparent reference to Deutscher's list of "non-Jewish Jews," Rabbi Arthur Hertzberg said: "Spinoza, Freud, and Marx—men who saw their Jewish particularity as a kind of disease that had to be overcome if they were to realize themselves— have no Jewish children" (See Spiegel). In reflecting on Hertzberg's comment, it is important to take note of the fact that Spinoza was revered by Ben Gurion; that Marx became the idol of the Israeli left, which hoped to turn socialistic Zionism into a light to the nations; and that popularized Freudianism is now sprinkled in the weekend editions of Israeli papers. The impact of these "non-Jewish Jews" is therefore not lost on Jews. Hertzberg has a point, however. Neither the brainchildren nor the actual descendants of these great men were Jewish. Thus, the point he was really making is that Jewish existence in the Diaspora must put its hope in solid religion rather than on a weak solution of ethnicity which could easily dissolve in the surrounding sea of marginality.

As could be expected, members of the symposium on the sources of Jewish creativity were divided in their opinions. The role of marginal living or of the tension that results from exposure to two cultures was subject to disagreement (See Spiegel). The American novelist Herbert Gold thought that the tension which results from exposure to two cultures is the major source of Jewish creativity. On the other hand, the Israeli professor Ben Ami Sharfstein maintained that the specific needs and aspirations of a single society, such as the Jewish ghetto, are the basic origins. Both points of view have a claim on the truth, but it is important to point out that the argument can be interpreted as a debate on the desirability of a Diaspora. If marginality is an important source of creativity, then it would be helpful if the Diaspora coexisted with the State of Israel. If, however, marginality is not so much a source of creativity as of stress and even mental illness (as mentioned in Chapter 2 in relation to Weinberg's work), then the Diaspora which fosters it is harmful. These debates are not conducted in a vacuum. Obviously the participants bring with them value judgments that are determined by their sense of identity. Let us remember that for an ethnic Jew, the Diaspora is a necessity. For a religious Jew, it is acceptable as long as it is thoroughly Jewish. For a national Jew, it is an anachronistic malaise that should be cured. Bearing these value judgments in mind, it seems that Hertzberg, Gold, and Sharfstein explicated the standpoints of religion, ethnicity, and nationality respectively.

Value judgments seem to color individual perceptions of the Diaspora. Therefore, before I express my own opinion a personal note is in order. As a secular sabra who grew up in Israel, my choices were limited. I could be a national Jew or a universal man. Religion was not an option for me, since I had never embraced the Jewish faith, not even in childhood. When I came to the United States in my late twenties, I discovered that ethnicity was not an option for me either. Lox, bagels, and occasional broken Yiddish were not a solid base on which I could anchor my Jewish identity. Thus, only two "Jewish" options were available for me—being a national Jew or that kind of supersensitive universal man who is sometimes known as a "non-Jewish Jew." As I ultimately changed from Israeli to American citizenship, I have obviously become a "non-Jewish Jew." By now I know the meaning of the tension of two cultures, and I can no longer avoid it, no matter where I live.

My opinion concerning the future of the Diaspora is skeptical. I do not see much of a chance for a repeat performance of the fruitful interaction that once took place between the Jewish centers in Israel and in Babylon. I believe that a flourishing and generative Jewish life in the Diaspora would benefit Israel. It could serve as a check against Israeli chauvinism. In addition, it could accentuate the Jewish heritage of universalism and inject an awareness of cultural relativity which would broaden the horizons of both Israeli and Diaspora Jews. Yet I doubt that this is what the future holds in store. The generative powers of American Jewry are not all that impressive when it comes to the task of revitalizing Judaism. I recall how depressing it was for me to serve one year as a teacher in a Jewish Sunday School. I was advised to motivate the children by using baseball scores to award points for knowledge of biblical stories. These experiences with biblical "home runs" did not enhance my expectations of an impending spurt of Jewish creativity in America. My personal impression is therefore that as a general rule, creative Jewish life is likely to take place only in Israel. For the foreseeable future, nationality is the best hope for Jewish regeneration and Israel is the testing ground for the success or failure of this venture. Ideally speaking, it would be nice if a flourishing Israel and a creative Diaspora were to interact with each other. But the realistic prospects are for a vigorous Israel interacting with an anemic Diaspora. Most Jewish hopes, therefore, are pinned on the State of Israel.

Many Jews feel intuitively that Israel is the place where either a regeneration or a final collapse will take place. They view with relief the mounting signs that the historical verdict is that of revival rather than expiration. It was this basic intuitive feeling on the part of rank and file Jews which caused the Reform and other Jewish organizations to abandon their initial objection to the Zionist buildup in Israel. Yet as the new Israeli state became dearer and dearer to Jews all over, history played an ironic trick on them. It has become fashionable in New Left quarters to issue calls for the de-Zionization of Israel. It is done in the name of justice, at which time Zionism is called imperialistic. It is also done in the name of a bright new future, at which time Zionism is seen as an anachronism. It is easy for members of the New Left to brand Zionism as counterrevolutionary and to demand that Israelis give up their newly won nation-state to facilitate the coming of a progressive world order in which the nation-state would be outdated. Why this undoing of nation-states should begin with, of all states, not China or Syria but the Jewish state is not made clear. Presumably it is one of the most "reactionary" states there are, and possibly what it did and still does to the Palestinians is regarded as an unsurpassed atrocity.

There is something which is not quite "kosher" about these calls. This is not the place to debate whether we are indeed on the verge of the era in which the nation-state is passé. What is suspect is that these calls are directed to the Jews, who after centuries of dreaming about it are supposed to be the first to give up their state. Why the Jews first?

Why cannot they be somewhere in the middle of the line? Why should not they de-Zionize after the USSR de-Russifies and France de-Gallicizes? Apparently, it is because they seem to have a special destiny. To Michael Selzer, the commentator on Jewish affairs, this destiny consisted of the Jews' repeatedly offering themselves up as ready victims in order to help mankind "to recognize its own propensity for violence and evil." To him it seemed most unfortunate that this highly revolutionary tradition is now being cast off by the Zionist movement. To fair-minded people, though, it may not seem reactionary or odd that Jews do not wish to play the role of the self-sacrificing Jesus in each succeeding generation. It is not Zionist reactionism to cry out "Enough is enough!"

Another call which rallies the future for an attack on the State of Israel, and for a defense of Diaspora existence, was sounded by Arnold Toynbee. He contended that we are now passing from the old age of territorial national states to the new age of Diasporas. This will be the new age of civilization, characterized by a world-encompassing religious community. He also believed that the Jews can play a leading role in these new exciting developments if they fall back on their great expertise in Diaspora existence instead of clinging to the Zionist accent of old-fashioned nationalism. What is there to say regarding this stand? With some people the Jews just cannot win. First Spengler condemned them for their territorial detachment. Once that situation was rectified, Toynbee condemned them for their anachronistic clinging to the territorial national state. Presumably he had no axe to grind. All he did was to focus his futuristic gaze on the Jewish people and pass a dispassioned historical judgment, such as "I spy the wave of the future in the Jewish Diaspora." This kind of "support" from Toynbee can hardly be welcome by most Diaspora Jews who happen to care deeply about the welfare of the State of Israel.

To Israelis, the calls to dismantle their state seem hollow. Such calls reflect a glaring lack of empathy for a decimated people who are being asked to gamble with their survival chances. They also reflect a failure to understand that what is being asked is psychologically impossible. How irreversible is the new Israeli consciousness of statehood can be learned in many ways, including subtle developments in the evolution of the modern Hebrew language.

When Israel came into being and was joyfully perceived as Israel reborn rather than merely born, it was named "The State of Israel." Although in the old days of independence Israel was a kingdom, upon its rebirth it would have been inappropriate to name it "The Kingdom of Israel." From the start the idea was to establish a democracy. No one even toyed with the idea of a constitutional monarchy. After the establishment of "The State of Israel," it became important to emphasize a new consciousness of statehood. In this new mood, the welfare of the state was to assume priority over partisan politics and even class struggles. David Ben Gurion was one of the most persistent proponents of these new thinking habits. He became the great advocate of *mamlakhtiyut.* In a literal translation, *mamlakhtiyut* is "kingdomism." But it is being used in Israel to denote "statism," which is Elon's English translation of this word. At any rate, if "kingdomism" really means "statism," then why not use "statism" to begin with? What seems to have happened is that in response to the deep yearnings of the people for rebirth and not just birth, the Hebrew language evolved a new term which was constructed not from the word "state" (in which case the term would be *medinatiyut*) but from "kingdom." In preaching "kingdomism," David Ben Gurion was not trying to become a new King David. He was championing a slogan that denoted statism but also connoted historical continuity. "Kingdomism" far more than "statism" not only extolls the virtue of contemporary independence, but also links it to the independence of old.

Obviously the evolving Hebrew language accommodated the needs of the developing Israeli nation. The linguistic accommodations are as good a testimony as any to the depth and magnitude of the psychological needs which they serve. To approach a people who require the word "kingdomism" to denote "statism" and to request that they forego their cherished consciousness of statehood is sheer psychological myopia.

It is clear that after an era of great achievements and self-evident goals, Zionism is undergoing a crisis of values. In contrast to the earlier days of visionary faith and conviction in the rightness of the cause, it is no longer obvious what is right and what is wrong. Ever since the Six Day War it is difficult to tell where nationalism ends and chauvinism begins, where socialism terminates and capitalism starts, where

social equality gives way to class distinctions, and where Jewish uniqueness yields to self-effacing emulation of the Gentiles.

The history of Zionism is strung with paradoxes. A scattered,
stateless, seemingly helpless people, whom Ben Gurion once termed
"human dust," gathered like metal particles around the magnet of "the
land of Zion, Jerusalem." Zionism was conceived by Pinsker, Herzl,
and others as the only logical answer to *Christian* anti-Semitism; by the
second half of the twentieth century it was becoming evident that the
great price of Zionism has been the rise of *Arab* anti-Semitism. The
impressive revival of Hebrew was achieved by successfully battling the
influence of Yiddish; yet because of this success, some misgivings sur-
faced about the loss to Jewish culture resulting from the slow death of
Yiddish. In a bold secular revolt the Zionist children came to rescue
mother Zion from her desolation; they tossed the rabbis to the sidelines
and saved Zion against rabbinic prohibitions, only to deliver her into
the hands of the organized religious parties and the state rabbinate. In
the Diaspora the Jews reacted to Jewish adversity by trying to be like
Gentiles, but as they developed a new culture in Israel, they reacted
by trying to be unlike Jews. A persecuted people who vigilantly scanned
the world with a haunted vision of "the elephant and the Jewish
problem" psychology became an occupying force administering hostile
populations. A generation of schnorrers and luftmenschen raised chutz-
padikke sabras who sometimes looked more Goyish than Jewish.

The early Zionists followed Herzl's emphasis on the problem of
the Jews. Yet as they settled in the land of Zion, they encountered new
threats to their survival from the Arabs. They mostly rejected Ahad
Ha'am's emphasis on the problem of Judaism, but they now face a
spiritual crisis of historical continuity. They even gave birth to a
minority of Canaanites who told Judaism as well as Zionism to go jump
in the lake. They mated international socialism with Jewish nationalism, expecting the birth of a model form of existence that would serve
as a light to the nations. But socialism was undergoing prolonged
expiration even while the glorification of the kibbutzim was going on.
On the other hand, nationalism grew in potency and militancy. The
new Zionist offspring is therefore something different from what was
initially envisioned. If the major worry in the past was that its socialism
would tilt too much toward communism, the prevailing worry nowa-

days is that its nationalism will degenerate into chauvinism.

Since the First World War the reclamation of the ancestral land proceeded under the initial hope that Britain would play a key role in its realization. It was a shocking disappointment for Weizmann that eventually Israel won its independence in spite of, not because of, the tired lion of Albion. With the vulgarity of a Roman crowd in the arena, the world waited for the test of blood in which the desert warriors would make mincemeat out of the shtetl Jews. Instead, embittered post-Holocaust Jews with a "never again" determination proved their overwhelming superiority in both spirit and technology. Then, after a major victory in the Six Day War and recognition as a major military power in the Middle East, suicidal psychologies intensified and the Masada complex gripped the nation.

It is a history which is filled with astounding accomplishments but which is fraught with unpredictability. On the one hand, a fantasy became reality and the Zionist erection of the State of Israel finally made Jews stand up like men. Psychologically, Zionism is the Jewish reassertion of manhood. It restored potency after a seemingly endless and depressing impotence. On the other hand, a reality evolved into a fantastic nightmare. The sharp Arab reaction formed a morbid reality which the usually farsighted Zionists failed to expect. The history of Zionism is a testimony to the dialectical processes which propel a revolution. The specific psychohistory of this revolution is a living proof of the inexhaustibility of the timeless energizers of old myths and ancient lores. In perspective, Zionism seems to be saturated with irony. Exhilarating achievements fill the pages of the Third Zionade, but so do dismal failures. Key questions of the future remain unanswered. Will the rebelling Sons of Israel finally do away with "father God" for good? Will the Jewish Diaspora disappear? Will the State of Israel expand to become the Land of Israel? Will Israel go under in a Masada stand of its own making? Will the trauma of the Holocaust result in a chronic sense of inferiority? The story of Zionism is still unfolding and perhaps only the historian of a hundred years hence will have the answers. Yet it may not be unwarranted to assert even now that Jewry is far better off with Zionism and its problems than without them.

Bibliography

Ackerman, Nathan W., and Jahoda, Marie. *Anti-Semitism and Emotional Disorder: A Psychoanalytic Interpretation.* New York: Harper & Brothers, 1950.

Adler, Alfred. *Study of Organ Inferiority and Its Psychological Compensation.* New York: The Nervous and Mental Disease Publishing Company, 1917.

Adler, Joseph. *The Herzl Paradox: Political, Social and Economic Theories of a Realist.* New York: Hadrian Press and The Herzl Press, 1962.

Alexander, Franz. *The Psychoanalysis of the Total Personality: The Application of Freud's Theory of the Ego to the Neuroses.* New York and Washington: Nervous and Mental Disease, 1930.

Aloni, Schulamit. *Ha'hesder: Memdinat Hok Lemedinat Halakhah* (The Arrangement: From a State of Law to a State of *Halakhah*). Tel-Aviv: Otpaz, 1970.

Alter, Robert. "Confronting the Holocaust: Three Israeli Novels." *Commentary*, Vol. 41, No. 3 (1966), pp. 67–73.

――――― "Hebrew Between Two Worlds." *Commentary*, Vol. 45, No. 4 (1968), pp. 63–69.

――――― "The Israeli Novel." *Daedalus* (Fall 1966), pp. 972–985.

Amikam, Eliyahu. "Bitah Ha'horeget Shel Hatziyonut: Hirhurim Al Yeshut Palestina'it" (The Killing Daughter of Zionism: Reflections on Palestinian Entity). *Yediot Aharonot*, September 30, 1970.

Ansbacher, Heinz L., and Ansbacher, Rowena R. *The Individual Psychology of Alfred Adler.* New York: Basic Books, 1956.

_____ eds. *Superiority and Social Interest.* Evanston, Ill.: Northwestern University Press, 1964.

Arendt, Hannah. *Eichmann in Jerusalem: A Report on the Banality of Evil.* New York: Viking, 1965.

_____ "The Jew As Pariah: A Hidden Tradition." *Jewish Social Studies,* Vol. 6, No. 2 (1944), pp. 99–122.

_____ *The Origins of Totalitarianism.* Cleveland and New York: Meridian, 1958.

Arieli, Yehoshua. "The Price Israel Is Paying." *The New York Review of Books,* August 31, 1972.

Arlow, Jacob A. "The Consecration of the Prophet." *The Psychoanalytic Quarterly,* Vol. 20, No. 3 (1951), pp. 374–397.

Ausubel, Nathan ed. *A Treasury of Jewish Humor.* Garden City, N.Y.: Doubleday, 1951.

Avineri, Shlomo. "The Palestinians and Israel." *Commentary,* Vol. 49, No. 6 (1970), pp. 31–44.

Avneri, Uri. *"Halahatz Ha'hamishi"* (The Fifth Pressure). *Ha'olam Hazeh,* April 21, 1971.

_____ *Milhemet Ha'yom Hashvi'ee* (The Seventh Day War). Tel-Aviv: Daf Hadash, 1969.

_____ "The Third Year of the Six Day War." *The Muslim World,* Vol. 60, No. 1 (1970), pp. 59–73.

_____ "Tziyonut Akhazarit" (Cruel Zionism). *Ha'olam Hazeh,* September 6, 1972.

Bakan, David. *Sigmund Freud and the Jewish Mystical Tradition.* New York: Schocken, 1965.

_____ "Suicide and Immortality." In Edwin S. Shneidman ed., *On the Nature of Suicide.* San Francisco: Jossey-Bass Inc., 1969.

Baron, Nathan. "Hashtadlanim" (The Pleading Leaders). *Yediot Aharonot,* January 15, 1971.

Bateson, Mary Catherine. " 'A Riddle of Two Worlds': An Interpretation of the Poetry of H. N. Bialik." *Daedalus* (Summer 1966), pp. 740–762.

Bein, Alex. *Theodore Herzl: A Biography.* Philadelphia: The Jewish Publication Society of America, 1941.

Ben Amotz, Dan. "Sod Chutzpatah Shel Yisrael" (The Secret of Israel's Chutzpah). *Ha'olam Hazeh*, March 24, 1971.

Ben Ezer, Ehud. "Mehir Hatziyonut—Ehud Ben Ezer Mesohe'ah Im Doctor Shlomo Avineri: Shiabud Haemtza'im Letakhlit Hamedinah?" (The Price of Zionism—Ehud Ben Ezer Interviews Dr. Shlomo Avineri: The Subjugation of Means to the State's Ends?). *Moznayim*, Vol. 23, No. 2 (1966), pp. 118–124.

Ben-Gurion, David. *Bama'arakhah* (In the Struggle). Vol. 3. Tel-Aviv: Mapai, 1948.

———— *Israel: A Personal History.* New York: Funk & Wagnalls, 1971.

Ben-Gurion, David, and Pearlman, Moshe. *Ben Gurion Looks Back: In Talks with Moshe Pearlman.* New York: Schocken, 1970.

Ben-Porat, Yeshayahu. "Dr. Goldmann: Hamanhig Hatziyoni Hakofer Be'ikar" (Dr. Goldmann: The Heretical Zionist Leader). *Yediot Aharonot*, April 10, 1970.

———— "Dvarim Ishiyim Meod: Al 'Tziyonut Alimah' Ve'al Tziyonut Kepshutah" (A Very Personal Talk: On "Violent Zionism" and on Plain Zionism). *Yediot Aharonot*, August 11, 1972.

———— "Hata'oot, Hatmimoot Ve'hatzvi'oot" (The Mistake, Naiveté and Hypocrisy). *Yediot Aharonot*, July 14, 1972.

Bentley, O.F. "The Monster in the Bedroom: Sexual Symbolism in Bram Stoker's Dracula." *Literature and Psychology*, Vol. 22, No. 1 (1972), pp. 27–34.

Bentov, Mordecai." 'Tasbikh Metzadah' Shelanu—Veshel Ha'aravim" (Our "Masada Complex"—and the Arabs'), *Yediot Aharonot*, August 6, 1971.

Bentwitch, Norman. *Josephus.* Philadelphia: The Jewish Publication Society of America, 1914.

Bettelheim, Bruno. *Symbolic Wounds: Puberty Rites and the Envious Male.* New York: Collier Books, 1962.

Bialik, Hayim Nahman. *Divrai Sifrut* (Literary Matters). Tel-Aviv: Dvir, 1965.

———— *Kitvai H. N. Bialik: Sefer Rishon* (The Works of H. N. Bialik: Volume I). Tel-Aviv: Dvir, 1935.

Bolitho, Hector. *Beside Galilee: A Diary in Palestine.* New York: D. Appleton-Century Company, 1933.

Brauer, George C., Jr. *Judaea Weeping: The Jewish Struggle Against*

Rome from Pompey to Masada, 63 B.C. to A.D. 73. New York: Thomas Y. Crowell Company, 1970.

Brecher, Michael. "Ben Gurion and Sharett: Contrasting Israeli Images of 'the Arabs'." *New Middle East,* No. 18 (1970), pp. 28–33.

Bromberg, Norbert. "Hitler's Character and Its Development: Further Observations." *American Imago,* Vol. 28, No. 4 (1971), pp. 289–303.

Brown, Norman O. *Life Against Death: The Psychoanalytic Meaning of History.* Middletown, Connecticut: Wesleyan University Press, 1959.

Chesnoff, Richard Z., Klein, Edward, and Littell, Robert. *If Israel Lost the War.* New York: Coward-McCann, Inc., 1969.

Cohen, Adir ed. *Otzar Habdihah La'yeled* (The Treasury of Children's Jokes). Tel-Aviv: M. Mizrahi, 1967.

Cohen, Israel. *The Zionist Movement.* New York: Zionist Organization of America, 1946.

———— ed. *The Rebirth of Israel: A Memorial Tribute To Paul Goodman.* London: Edward Goldston & Son, 1952.

Cohn, Henry J. "Theodor Herzl's Conversion to Zionism." *Jewish Social Studies,* Vol. 32, No. 2 (1970), pp. 101–110.

Cohn, Norman. *Warrant for Genocide: The Myth of the Jewish World-Conspiracy and the Protocols of the Elders of Zion.* Harmondsworth, Middlesex, England: Penguin, 1970.

Deutscher, Isaac. *The Prophet Armed—Trotsky: 1879–1921, Vol. I.* New York: Vintage, 1954.

———— *The Prophet Outcast—Trotsky: 1929–1940, Vol. III.* New York: Vintage, 1963.

———— *The Prophet Unarmed—Trotsky: 1921–1929, Vol. II.* New York: Vintage, 1959.

———— "The Russian Revolution and the Jewish Problem." In Tamara Deutscher ed., *The Non-Jewish Jew: And Other Essays.* New York: Oxford University Press, 1968.

Dimont, Max I. *The Indestructible Jews: Is There a Manifest Destiny in Jewish History?* New York: The New American Library, 1971.

———— *Jews, God and History.* New York: Signet, 1962.

Drapkin, Israel S. "Aspects of Suicide in Israel." *The Israel Annals of*

Psychiatry and Related Disciplines, Vol. 3, No. 1 (1965), pp. 35–50.

Eban, Abba. *My People: The Story of the Jews.* New York: Random House, 1968.

Eldad, Israel. "Hail Ha'avir Neged Menachem-Mendel" (The Airforce Against Menachem-Mendel). *Yediot Aharonot,* February 27, 1970.

———— *The Jewish Revolution: Jewish Statehood.* New York: Shengold, 1971.

———— "Mikhtav Galui Larav Meir Kahana" (An Open Letter to Rabbi Meir Kahane). Yediot Aharonot, January 22, 1971.

Elon, Amos. *The Israelis: Founders and Sons.* New York: Holt, Rinehart and Winston, 1971.

Erikson, Erik H. "Autobiographic Notes on the Identity Crisis." *Daedalus* (Fall 1970), pp. 730–759.

———— *Childhood and Society.* New York: Norton, 1950.

———— *Identity and the Life Cycle.* New York: International Universities Press, 1959.

———— *Identity Youth and Crisis.* New York: Norton, 1968.

———— *Insight and Responsibility: Lectures on the Ethical Implications of Psychoanalytic Insight.* New York: Norton, 1964.

———— "Wholeness and Totality—A Psychiatric Contribution." In Carl J. Friedrich ed., *Totalitarianism: Proceedings of a Conference Held at the American Academy of Arts and Sciences March 1953.* Cambridge, Mass.: Harvard University Press, 1954.

Evron, Boaz. "Ko'ah She'hoo Hoolshah" (Force Which is Weakness). *Yediot Aharonot,* February 27, 1970.

———— "Lo Mashmidim Otanu" (We Are Not Being Annihilated). *Yediot Aharonot,* December 3, 1971.

Feigenberg-Eamri, Rachel. *Beshem Darai Mata* (For the Common People). Ramat-Gan: Massada, 1970.

Fenichel, Otto. "A Critique of the Death Instinct." In *The Collected Papers of Otto Fenichel First Series.* New York: Norton, 1953.

———— "Elements of a Psychoanalytic Theory of Anti-Semitism." In Hannah Fenichel and David Rapaport eds., *The Collected Papers of Otto Fenichel Second Series.* New York: Norton, 1954.

Frank, Jerome D. *Sanity and Survival: Psychological Aspects of War and Peace.* New York: Vintage, 1967.

Frankenstein, Ernst. *Justice for My People.* New York: Dial Press, 1944.

Freud, Anna. *The Ego and the Mechanisms of Defence.* New York: International Universities Press, 1946.

Freud, Sigmund. "Address to the Society of B'nai B'rith." In *The Standard Edition of the Complete Psychological Works of Sigmund Freud.* Vol. 20. London: The Hogarth Press, 1959.

_____ *Beyond the Pleasure Principle.* London: Hogarth Press, 1948.

_____ *Civilization and its Discontents.* New York: Norton, 1962.

_____ *Collected Papers.* Vol. 4. New York: Basic Books, 1959.

_____ *The Ego and the Id.* London: Hogarth Press, 1947.

_____ *A General Introduction to Psychoanalysis.* New York: Washington Square Press, 1965.

_____ *Group Psychology and the Analysis of the Ego.* New York: Bantam, 1960.

_____ "The Interpretation of Dreams." In A. A. Brill ed., *The Basic Writings of Sigmund Freud.* New York: Modern Library, 1938.

_____ *Jokes and Their Relation to the Unconscious.* New York: Norton, 1963.

_____ *Moses and Monotheism.* New York: Vintage, 1967.

_____ "Totem and Taboo." In A. A. Brill ed., *The Basic Writings of Sigmund Freud.* New York: Modern Library, 1938.

Friedberg, Maurice. "Anti-Semitism as a Policy Tool in the Soviet Bloc." *New Politics,* Vol. 9, No. 3 (1971), pp. 61–79.

Friedmann, Georges. *The End of the Jewish People?* Garden City, N.Y.: Doubleday, 1967.

Gad, A. ed. *Bdihot Hatzabarim Haktanim* (Jokes of the Little Sabras). Tel-Aviv: Joseph Sreberk, 1965.

Gafni, Shraga. *Tehilat Metzadah* (The Glory of Masada). Tel-Aviv: Amihai, 1970.

Gil, Moshe. "Sifrutenu Ha'hadashah Umashber Ha'yahadut" (Our Modern Literature and the Crisis in Judaism). *Davar,* December 18, 1959.

Glatzer, Nahum N. ed. *The Judaic Tradition.* Boston: Beacon Press, 1969.

Goldmann, Nahum. "The Future of Israel." *Foreign Affairs*, Vol. 48, No. 3 (1970), pp. 443–459.

Gonen, Jay Y. "Negative Identity in Homosexuals." *Psychoanalytic Review*, Vol. 58, No. 3 (1971), pp. 345–352.

Gottheil, Richard J. H. *Zionism.* Philadelphia: The Jewish Publication Society of America, 1914.

Greenstone, Julius H. *The Messiah Idea in Jewish History.* Philadelphia: The Jewish Publication Society of America, 1906.

Grose, Peter. "New Evidence on Jesus' Life Reported." *The New York Times*, February 13, 1972.

———— "Rogers Will See Shrine in Israel: He Is to Be Shown Memorial to Jews Slain by Nazis." *The New York Times*, May 6, 1971.

Ha'ezrahi, Yehudah, and Shim'oni, Yitzhak eds. *Shloshah Besirah Ahat: Haflagah Shlishit* (Three in One Boat: A Third Sailing). Jerusalem: Achiasaf, 1959.

Halkin, Simon. *Modern Hebrew Literature: From the Enlightenment to the Birth of the State of Israel—Trends and Values.* New York: Schocken, 1970.

Halpern, Ben. *The Idea of the Jewish State (second edition).* Cambridge, Mass.: Harvard University Press, 1969.

Handlin, Oscar. "Jewish Resistance to the Nazis." *Commentary*, Vol. 34, No. 5 (1962), pp. 398–405.

Hareven, Shulamit. "Ha'im Hakayam Matzdik Et Hara Shebo?" (Does the Present Status Quo Justify the Evil in It?), *Shdemot*, No. 37 (Spring 1970).

Harris, Mervyn. "From Nile to Euphrates: The Evolution of a Myth." *New Middle East*, Nos. 42 and 43 (1972), pp. 46–48.

Hausner, Gideon. *Justice in Jerusalem.* New York: Schocken, 1968.

Hazaz, Hayim. "Hadrashah" (The Sermon). *In Sipurim Nivharim* (Selected Stories). Tel-Aviv: Dvir, 1952.

Herman, Simon N. *Israelis and Jews: The Continuity of an Identity.* New York: Random House, 1970.

Hertzberg, Arthur ed. *The Zionist Idea: A Historical Analysis and Reader.* New York: Atheneum, 1969.

Herzl, Theodor. *The Jewish State: An Attempt at a Modern Solution of the Jewish Question.* New York: American Zionist Emergency Council, 1946.

Hilberg, Raul. *The Destruction of the European Jews.* Chicago: Quadrangle, 1967.

———— ed. *Documents of Destruction: Germany and Jewry 1933–1945.* Chicago: Quadrangle, 1971.

Hitler, Adolf. *Mein Kampf.* Boston: Houghton Mifflin, 1943.

Horney, Karen. *Neurosis and Human Growth: The Struggle Toward Self-Realization.* New York: Norton, 1950.

———— *Our Inner Conflicts: A Constructive Theory of Neurosis.* New York: Norton, 1945.

Horon, A. G. *Eretz Hakedem: Madrikh Histori Umedini Lamizrah Hakarov* (The Land of Kedem: A Historical and Political Guide to the Near East). Tel-Aviv: Hermon, 1970.

Hughes, Pennethorne. *Witchcraft.* Baltimore, Maryland: Penguin, 1965.

Isaac, Erich. "The Enigma of Circumcision." *Commentary,* Vol. 43, No. 1 (1967), pp. 51–55.

"Jewish Resistance During the Holocaust," *Proceedings of the Conference on Manifestations of Jewish Resistance: Jerusalem, April 7–11, 1968* (in Hebrew and Yiddish). Jerusalem: Yad Vashem, 1970.

Josephus. *The Jewish War.* Baltimore, Md.: Penguin, 1970.

Kaplan, Stanley M., and Whitman, Roy M. "The Negative Ego-Ideal." *The International Journal of Psycho-Analysis,* Vol. 46, Part 2 (1965), pp. 183–187.

Katznelson, Berl. *Ktavim* (Writings). Vol. 5. Tel-Aviv: Mapai, 1947.

Kaufman, Yehezkel. "Anti-Semitic Stereotypes in Zionism: The Nationalist Rejection of Diaspora Jewry." *Commentary,* Vol. 7, No. 3 (1949), pp. 239–245.

Kenan, Amos. "Ha'im Hashalom Kedai?" (Is Peace Worth While?). *Yediot Aharonot,* January 9, 1970.

Kirk, George E. *A Short History of the Middle East: From the Rise of Islam to Modern Times.* Seventh revised edition. New York: Praeger, 1964.

Koestler, Arthur. "Man—One of Evolution's Mistakes?" *The New York Times Magazine,* October 19, 1969.

———— *Thieves in the Night.* New York: Macmillan, 1967.

Korn, Yitzhak. *Dor Bemaavako: Hatnuah Hatziyonit Betkufat Hamedinah* (A Generation in Its Struggle: The Zionist Movement During the Period of the State). Tel-Aviv: Otpaz, 1970.

Kurzweil, Baruch. " 'Melekh Basar Vadam' Lemoshe Shamir" ("A King of Flesh and Blood" by Moshe Shamir). *Ha'aretz*, June 18, 1954.

———— "Noseh Ha'akedah Besifrutenu Ha'hadashah" (The Notion of the Sacrifice in Our Modern Literature). *Davar*, October 2, 1959.

———— "Pluralism Ha'anormaliyut—Keyesod Hakiyum Ha'yehudi" (The Pluralism of Anormality—As the Foundation of Jewish Existence). *Ha'aretz*, June 30, 1967.

———— "Shorshai Hasin'ah Ha'yehudit Haatzmit" (The Roots of Jewish Self-Hatred). *Ha'aretz*, June 4, 1957.

————*Sifrutenu Ha'hadashah—Hemshekh Oh Mahapekhah?* (Our Modern Literature—Continuity or Revolution?). Tel-Aviv: Schocken, 1959.

———— "Tatzpit Mihutz-Lat'hum Al Matzavenu" (An Observation From Outside the Domain on Our Situation). *Ha'aretz*, September 30, 1970.

Kushnir, Shimon. *Anshai Nevo: Pirkai Alilah Shel Anshai Ha'aliyah Hashniyah* (Men of Nebo: From the Story of the Second Aliyah). Tel-Aviv: Am Oved, 1968.

Laing, R. D. *The Divided Self: An Existential Study in Sanity and Madness.* Baltimore, Md.: Penguin, 1965.

Laqueur, Walter. *A History of Zionism.* New York: Holt, Rinehart and Winston, 1972.

————ed. *The Israel-Arab Reader: A Documentary History of the Middle East Conflict.* New York: Bantam, 1969.

Leibowitz, Yeshayahu. "Medinat Yisrael Me'Hanekhet Letmiah" (The State of Israel Educates for Assimilation). *Ha'aretz*, September 17, 1972.

Leschnitzer, Adolf. *The Magic Background of Modern Anti-Semitism: An Analysis of the German-Jewish Relationship.* New York: International Universities Press, 1969.

Levin, Nora. *The Holocaust: The Destruction of European Jewry 1933–1945.* New York: Thomas Y. Crowell, 1968.

Lewis, Bernard. "Semites and Anti-Semites." *Survey*, Vol. 17, No. 2 (1971), pp. 169–184.

Livneh, Eliezer. "Te'hushat Hagoral Ve'hayeud Ha'yisraeli" (The Israeli Feeling of Fate and Destiny). *Ha'aretz*, April 9, 1971.

_____ "The Test of Israel." In Philip Longworth ed., *Confrontations with Judaism.* London: Anthony Blond, 1967.

Lowenberg, Peter. "A Hidden Zionist Theme in Freud's 'My Son, The Myops . . .' Dream." *Journal of the History of Ideas*, Vol. 31, No. 1 (1970), pp. 129–132.

_____ "A Psychoanalytic Study in Charismatic Political Leadership." In Benjamin B. Wolman ed., *The Psychoanalytic Interpretation of History.* New York: Basic Books, 1971.

Lowenthal, Marvin ed. *The Diaries of Theodor Herzl.* New York: The Dial Press, 1956.

Luzzato, Moshe Hayim. *Ma'aseh Shimshon* (Samson's Tale). Jerusalem: Mosad Bialik, 1967.

Maimonides, Moses. *The Guide of the Perplexed.* Chicago and London: The University of Chicago Press, 1969.

Margalit, Dan. "Le'an Moshekh Moshe Dayan" (Where Is Moshe Dayan Heading). *Ha'aretz*, October 29, 1971.

Masters, Anthony. *The Natural History of the Vampire.* New York: G. P. Putnam's Sons, 1972.

"Matat" (M.T.T.). "Besikhsukh Yisrael-Arav" (Concerning the Israeli-Arab Conflict). *Metzion Tetzeh Torah: Bitaon Lehagut Yehudit*, Issue No. 8, (1971).

Meron, Stanley. "Hatziyonut Ketnuah Meshihit" (Zionism As a Messianic Movement). *Shdemot*, No. 37, (1970), pp. 54–61.

Michener, James A. *The Source.* New York: Random House, 1965.

Midelfort, Erik C. H. *Witch Hunting in Southwestern Germany 1562–1684: The Social and Intellectual Foundations.* Stanford, Calif.: Standford University Press, 1972.

Milson, Menahem. "Ha'emdah Ha'aravit Ve'yahasenu Eleha" (The Arab Position and Our Relation to It). *Shdemot*, No. 37 (1970), pp. 5–11.

Mor, Hadassah. "Ha'yisraeli Ha'yafeh Be'enai Atzmo" (The Israeli Who Seems Pretty to Himself). *Yediot Aharonot*, May 15, 1970.

Moreno, J. L., Zerka, and Jonathan. *The First Psychodramatic Family.* New York: Beacon House, 1964.

Morse, Arthur D. *While Six Million Died: A Chronicle of American Apathy.* New York: Random House, 1968.

Nasser, Gamal Abdel. *The Philosophy of the Revolution.* Buffalo, N.Y.: Smith, Keynes & Marshall, 1959.

Nunberg, Herman. "Problems of Bisexuality as Reflected in Circumcision." In *Practice and Theory of Psychoanalysis.* Vol. II. New York: International Universities Press, 1965.

Ohel, Mila. "Rak Bechutzpah" (Only by Chutzpah). *Yediot Aharonot,* March 13, 1970.

Oren, Uri. "Ezer Neged Dayan" (Ezer Against Dayan). *Shvuon Yediot Aharonot,* June 4, 1971.

Osgood, Charles E. *Perspective in Foreign Policy.* Palo Alto, Calif.: Pacific Books, 1966.

Pa'il, Méir. "The Moral Use of Arms." *New Outlook,* Vol. 16, No. 2 (1973), pp. 30–39.

Parkes, James. *Antisemitism.* Chicago: Quadrangle, 1969.

Patai, Josef. *Star Over Jordan: The Life of Theodore Herzl.* New York: Philosophical Library, 1946.

Patai, Raphael ed. *The Complete Diaries of Theodor Herzl.* Vol. II. New York and London: Herzl Press and Thomas Yoseloff, 1960.

Pearlman, Moshe. *The Zealots of Masada: Story of a Dig.* New York: Charles Scribner's Sons, 1967.

Peretz, Don. "The Palestine Arabs: A National Entity." In Michael Curtis ed., *People and Politics in the Middle East: Proceedings of the Annual Conference of the American Academic Association for Peace in the Middle East.* New Brunswick, N.J.: Transaction, 1971.

Podhoretz, Norman. "Hannah Arendt on Eichmann: A Study in the Perversity of Brilliance." *Commentary,* Vol. 36, No. 3 (1963), pp. 201–208.

Poliakov, Léon. *The History of Anti-Semitism Volume One: From the Time of Christ to the Court Jews.* New York: Vanguard, 1965.

———— *Me'antitziyonut Le'antishemiyut* (From Anti-Zionism to Anti-Semitism). Tel-Aviv: Sifriat Poalim, 1970.

Rabin, Chaim. "The Revival of Hebrew." In Israel Cohen ed., *The Rebirth of Israel: A Memorial Tribute to Paul Goodman.* London: Edward Goldston & Son, 1952.

Rabinowicz, Oskar K. "New Light on the East Africa Scheme." In Israel Cohen ed., *The Rebirth of Israel: A Memorial Tribute to Paul Goodman.* London: Edward Goldston & Son, 1952.

Rado, Sandor. "An Anxious Mother: A Contribution to the Analysis of the Ego." *The International Journal of Psycho-Analysis*, Vol. 9, Part 2 (1928), pp. 219–226.

Reik, Theodor. *Myth and Guilt: The Crime and Punishment of Mankind.* New York: The Universal Library, 1970.

Roi, Jakov. "Yahasai Rechovot Im Shkhenaiha Ha'aravim (1890–1914)" (The Relations Between Rehovot and Its Arab Neighbors 1890–1914). In Daniel Carpi ed., *Hatziyonut: Me'asef Letoldot Hatnuah Hatziyonit Ve'hayishuv Ha'yehudi Be'eretz Yisrael* (Zionism: Studies in the History of the Zionist Movement and of the Jews in Palestine). Tel-Aviv: Hakibbutz Hameuchad, 1970.

Rosenblum, H. " 'Richterwelt'." *Yediot Aharonot*, November 6, 1970.

Roshwald, Mordecai. "Who Is a Jew in Israel?" *The Jewish Journal of Sociology*, Vol. 12, No. 2 (1970), pp. 233–266.

Rotenstreich, Nathan. *Sugiyot Bephilosophia* (Problems in Philosophy). Tel-Aviv: Dvir, 1962.

_____ *Tradition and Reality: The Impact of History on Modern Jewish Thought.* New York: Random House, 1972.

Rothberg, Abraham. *The Sword of the Golem.* New York: The McCall Publishing Company, 1970.

Rubinstein, Amnon. "Anu Ve'hagoyim: Mikreh Shel Schizophrenia" (We and the Gentiles: A Case of Schizophrenia). *Ha'aretz*, April 15, 1971.

_____ "Why the Israelis Are Being Difficult." *The New York Times Magazine*, April 18, 1971.

Russcol, Herbert, and Banai, Margalit. *The First Million Sabras: A Portrait of the Native-born Israelis.* New York: Dodd, Mead & Company, 1970.

el-Sadat, Anwar. "Where Egypt Stands." *Foreign Affairs*, Vol. 51, No. 1 (1972), pp. 114–123.

Safran, Nadav. *From War to War: The Arab-Israeli Confrontation, 1948–1967.* New York: Pegasus, 1969.

Saint Augustine. *The City of God.* New York: The Modern Library, 1950.

Samuel, Maurice. *The World of Sholom Aleichem.* New York: Schocken, 1965.

Sartre, Jean-Paul. *Anti-Semite and Jew.* New York: Schocken, 1948.

Schick, Alfred. "The Jew as Sacrificial Victim." *The Psychoanalytic Review,* Vol. 58, No. 1 (1971), pp. 75–89.

Scholem, Gershom G. "The Golem of Prague and the Golem of Rehovoth." *Commentary,* Vol. 41, No. 1, (1966) 62–65.

———— "The Holiness of Sin." *Commentary,* Vol. 51, No. 1 (1971), pp. 41–70.

———— *Major Trends in Jewish Mysticism.* New York: Schocken, 1954.

———— *Shabtai Tzvi Vehatnuah Hashabta'it Bimai Hayav* (Sabbatai Zevi and the Sabbatian Movement During his Lifetime). Vols. 1–2. Tel-Aviv: Am Oved, 1957.

Schuster, Daniel B. "The Holy Communion: An Historical and Psychoanalytic Study." *The Bulletin of the Philadelphia Association for Psychoanalysis,* Vol. 20, No. 3 (1970), pp. 223–236.

Segal, Mark. "Matter of Survival." *The Jerusalem Post Weekly,* June 6, 1972.

Sela, Uri, and Har-Gil, Shraga. *Otzar Habdihah Hapolitit* (The Treasury of Political Jokes). Tel-Aviv: Otpaz, 1969.

Selzer, Michael. "Introduction." In Michael Selzer ed., *Zionism Reconsidered: The Rejection of Jewish Normalcy.* New York: Macmillan Publishing Co., Inc. 1970.

Shaked, Gershon. "Childhood Lost, Studies in the Holocaust Theme in Contemporary Israeli Fiction." *Literature East & West,* Vol. 14, No. 1 (1970), pp. 90–108.

Shamgar, Shlomo. "Shem Nirdaf Ve'ezrah Nirdaf" (A Persecuted Name and a Persecuted Citizen). *Yediot Aharonot,* September 4, 1970.

Shamir, Aharon. "Ain Shnai Soogai Tziyonut" (There Are Not Two Brands of Zionism). *Yediot Aharonot,* August 18, 1972.

Shapira, Avraham ed. *Si'ah Lohamim: Pirkai Hakshavah Vehitbonenut*

(Conversations of Warriors: Records of Things Heard and Seen). Tel-Aviv: Kvutzat Haverim Tze'irim Mehatnuah Hakibbutzit, 1967.

Sharabi, Hisham. *Palestine and Israel: The Lethal Dilemma.* New York: Western Publishing Company, Inc., 1969.

Shenker, Israel. "Israeli Historian Denies Jews Yielded to the Nazis 'Like Sheep'." *The New York Times,* May 6, 1970.

Shetzker, Hayim. "Megamot Betfisat Hasho'ah Ba'hevrah Ha'yisrae-lit" (Trends in the Israeli Society's Perception of the Holocaust). *Ha'aretz,* January 5, 1970.

Shiloah, Zvi. *Eretz Gdolah Le'am Gadol: Sipuro Shel Maamin* (A Big Country for a Big Nation: The Story of a Believer). Tel-Aviv: Otpaz, 1970.

Sholom Aleichem. *The Adventures of Menahem-Mendl.* New York: G. P. Putnam's Sons, 1969.

_____ *Collected Stories of Sholom Aleichem: The Old Country.* New York: Crown, 1946.

_____ *Collected Stories of Sholom Aleichem: Tevye's Daughters.* New York: Crown, 1949.

Simon, Leon ed. *Selected Essays by Ahad Ha'am.* Cleveland: Meridian, 1962.

Slochower, Harry. "Hitler's 'Elevation' of the Jew: Ego-Splitting and Ego-Function." *American Imago,* Vol. 28, No. 4 (1971), pp. 304–318.

Snir, Mordechai. "Im A. D. Gordon: Zikhronot Ureshamim" (With A. D. Gordon: Memories and Impressions). In D. Zakkai and Z. Shazar eds., *Tav Shin Yod Zayin: Shnaton Davar* (1956/57 Davar Yearly). Tel-Aviv: Davar, 1956.

Sokolow, Nahum. *History of Zionism: 1600–1918.* New York: Ktav Publishing House, 1969.

Sondermann, Fred A. "Peace Initiatives; the Literature of Possibilities: A Review." *The Journal of Conflict Resolution,* Vol. 7, No. 2 (1963), 141–149.

Spengler, Oswald. *The Decline of the West.* New York: The Modern Library, 1965.

Spiegel, Irving. "Fifty Artists Probe Jews' Creativity." *The New York Times,* August 5, 1973.

———— "Threat to the Jewish Heritage Is Sharply Debated in Israel." *The New York Times*, August 1, 1973.

Spiro, Melford E. *Children of the Kibbutz*. New York: Schocken, 1965.

St. John, Robert. *Ben-Gurion: The Biography of an Extraordinary Man*. Garden City, N.Y.: Doubleday, 1959.

Steiner, Jean-Francois. *Treblinka*. New York: Simon and Schuster, 1967.

Stengel, Erwin. *Suicide and Attempted Suicide*. Baltimore, Md.: Penguin, 1964.

Stern, Arthur. "The Genetic Tragedy of the Family of Theodor Herzl." *The Israel Annals of Psychiatry and Related Disciplines*, Vol. 3, No. 1 (1965), pp. 99–116.

Stonequist, Everett V. *The Marginal Man: A Study in Personality and Culture Conflict*. New York: Charles Scribner's Sons, 1937.

Summers, Montague ed. *The Malleus Maleficarum of Heinrich Kramer and James Spranger*. New York: Dover, 1971.

Tabenkin, Yitzhak. *Lekah Sheshet Ha'yamim: Yishuvah Shel Eretz Bilti-Me'huleket* (The Lesson of the Six Days: The Settlement of an Indivisible Country). Tel-Aviv: Hakibbutz Hameuchad, 1970.

Talmon, J. L. *Political Messianism: The Romantic Phase*. New York: Praeger, 1960.

Talmon, Jacob. "Hako'ah Yaaneh Et Hakol?" (Could Force Be the Answer to Everything?). *Ha'aretz*, September 8, 1972.

Tamarin, G. R., and Ben-Zwi, D. "Two Stereotypes of the National Mythology: The Sabra-Superman and the Inferior Diaspora Jew." *The Israel Annals of Psychiatry and Related Disciplines*, Vol. 3, No. 1 (1965), pp. 150–151.

Tanai, Shlomo. "Basin'ah Haatzmit Yesh Ktzat Hadash" (There Is Something a Bit New in Self-Hate). *Yediot Aharonot*, January 12, 1973.

Teub, Shlomit, interviewing Eli Alon. "Hitmodedut Im Havayat Hamavet Bamilhamah" (Coping with the Experience of Death in War). *Shdemot*, No. 37 (Spring 1970).

Tishbi, Yeshayahu. "Baayat Ha'retzifut Basifrut Ha'ivrit Be'haguto Shel Bialik Uveyamenu" (The Problem of Continuity in the Hebrew Literature, in Bialik's Thoughts and in Our Days). *Ha'aretz*, December 29, 1972.

Toynbee, Arnold J. *A Study of History. 8: Heroic Ages.* New York: Oxford University Press, 1963.

―――― "Zionism and Jewish Destiny." In Alan R. Taylor and Richard N. Tetlie eds., *Palestine: A Search for Truth—Approaches to the Arab-Israeli Conflict.* Washington, D.C.: Public Affairs Press, 1970.

Trevor-Roper, H. R. "The European Witch-Craze." In Max Marwick ed., *Witchcraft and Sorcery.* Baltimore, Md.: Penguin, 1970.

Tuchman, Barbara W. *Bible and Sword: England and Palestine from the Bronze Age to Balfour.* New York: Minerva Press, 1968.

Tzur, Muki, Ben-Aharon, Yariv, and Grosman, Avishai eds. *Bayn Tze'irim: Sihot Betzavta Batnuah Hakibbutzit* (Among Young People: Talks in the Kibbutz). Tel Aviv: Am Oved, 1969.

Weinberg, Abraham A. *Migration and Belonging: A Study of Mental Health and Personal Adjustment in Israel.* The Hague: Martinus Nijhoff, 1961.

―――― "On Comparative Mental Health Research of the Jewish People." *The Israel Annals of Psychiatry and Related Disciplines,* Vol. 2, No. 1, (1964) 27–40.

Weiner, Herbert. *9 ½ Mystics: The Kabbala Today.* New York: Collier Books, 1971.

Weisbord, Robert G. *African Zion: The Attempt to Establish a Jewish Colony in the East Africa Protectorate 1903–1905.* Philadelphia: The Jewish Publication Society of America, 1968.

―――― "Israel Zangwill's Jewish Territorial Organization and the East Africa Zion." *Jewish Social Studies,* Vol. 30, No. 2 (1968), pp. 89–108.

Weizman, Ezer. "Lelo Tasbikhim" (Without Complexes). *Ha'aretz,* March 29, 1972.

Weizmann, Chaim. *Trial and Error.* New York: Schocken, 1966.

Wellhausen, Julius. *Prolegomena to the History of Ancient Israel.* Cleveland and New York: Meridian Books, 1957.

Weltsch, Robert. "He'arot Ishiyot Lesifro Shel Amos Elon" (Personal Comments on Amos Elon's Book). *Ha'aretz,* August 20, 1971.

White, Ralph K. "Three Not-So-Obvious Contributions of Psychology to Peace." *The Journal of Social Issues,* Vol. 25, No. 4 (1969), pp. 23–39.

Whitman, Roy M., and Kaplan, Stanley M. "Clinical, Cultural and Literary Elaborations of the Negative Ego-Ideal." *Comprehensive Psychiatry*, Vol. 9, No. 4 (1968), pp. 358–371.

Wiener, Norbert. *God and Golem, Inc.: A Comment on Certain Points Where Cybernetics Impinges on Religion.* Cambridge, Mass.: The M.I.T. Press, 1964.

Wiesel, Elie. *A Beggar in Jerusalem.* New York: Random House, 1970.

Winter, Paul. "The Trial of Jesus." *Commentary*, Vol. 38, No. 3 (1964), pp. 35–41.

Wisse, Ruth R. *The Schlemiel As Modern Hero.* Chicago: The University of Chicago Press, 1971.

Yadin, Yigael. *Masada: Herod's Fortress and the Zealots' Last Stand.* London: Weidenfeld and Nicolson, 1966.

Yariv, S. S. *Al Hakomunism Ve'al Hatziyonut Shel Hashomer Hatza'ir* (On the Communism and Zionism of *Hashomer Hatza'ir*). Tel-Aviv: Mapai, 1953.

Zellermayer, Julius. "The Psychosocial Effect of the Eichmann Trial." In Gene Usdin ed., *The Psychiatric Forum.* New York: Brunner/Mazel, 1972.

Zohar, Danah. "The Corrupting Power of 'Dime Store Mysticism'." *New Middle East*, No. 57 (1973), pp. 33–34.

Zucker, Norman L. *The Coming Crisis in Israel: Private Faith and Public Policy.* Cambridge, Mass.: The MIT Press, 1973.

Index